15.99

Pragmatics

An Introduction

CA pp 195
214
217
230 repair
231 reference
232 marked/disputthered
242 adacency

𝔅

PRAGMATICS

An Introduction

Jacob L. Mey

The right of Jacob L. Mey to be identified as author of this work has been
asserted in accordance with the Copyright, Designs and Patents Act 1988.

First published 1993
Reprinted 1994
Reprinted with corrections 1994
Reprinted 1996, 1998, 1999, 2000

Blackwell Publishers Ltd
108 Cowley Road
Oxford OX4 1JF, UK

Blackwell Publishers Inc
350 Main Street
Malden, Massachusetts 02148, USA

British Library Cataloguing in Publication Data
A CIP catalogue record for this book is available from the British Library

Library of Congress Cataloging in Publication Data
Mey, Jacob.
Pragmatics: an introduction / Jacob L. Mey
p. cm.
Includes bibliographical references and index.
ISBN 0–631–18691–3 (pbk)
1. Pragmatics. I. Title.
P99.4.P72M487 1993 93–19925
306.4'4—dc20 CIP

Typeset in 10 on 13pt Sabon by Best-set Typesetter Ltd
Printed and bound in Great Britain
by Athenæum Press Ltd, Gateshead, Tyne & Wear

Contents

Preface

The present text arose out of an actual need: to teach a class in pragmatics to a group of first-year graduate students in an interdisciplinary program at Odense University, Denmark.

The students had very different backgrounds (some came from History, some from Philosophy, some from Economics, others again from various Modern Language Departments; in addition, there were people who had been out in the world for many years, and wanted to go back to school to pick up some more credits, or just to be in Academe again). The group was extremely motivated, and teaching them was pure pleasure, except that the available texts (mainly Geoffrey Leech's *Principles of Pragmatics* and Stephen C. Levinson's *Pragmatics*, both published in 1983) did not quite meet their needs and expectations. For one thing, the two books mentioned contain too much to be covered in a mere two-semester course for the students I described. Another problem was the somewhat uneven weighting of the various pragmatic topics throughout the two books (this, of course, is no criticism, and does not relate to Leech and Levinson alone; still, it may create difficulties for somebody else who is trying to put together a course on the subject).

In the end, I decided to produce a classroom compendium of the topics we were going to cover each week. The approach was mainly eclectic and followed very closely what was going on in class, so that (apart from a general outline) we were not bound to do exactly this or that in the next classroom period, but could extend or abbreviate our preliminary 'Syllabus' at will.

All of this happened in 1989. Since then, several things have changed.

I have taught the course several times now at my home university, and have received valuable feedback from the students. Also, I have been in touch with colleagues and friends in Japan, who had experienced the same kind of difficulties as I had, and who therefore were interested in some kind of collaboration. (A first, Japanese, version of my classroom notes was to appear in early 1993.) Another thing that happened was that my friend Peter Trudgill suggested that I send the text to Blackwell's, which I did. They were interested in producing an English version; however, they wanted some changes made, and it is mainly the process of revising the original manuscript that has delayed the appearance of the present version – in many respects, a wholly new text; it is about one-third longer, and a great many portions of the original text have been entirely rewritten. Also, a complete set of exercises and review questions for each of the chapters has been added.

As I said above, the mainstay of the first-time course were the books by Leech and Levinson. No wonder, then, that their presence looms large even in this text. Both authors may since have moved on to other topics of interest (I know that Geoff Leech has), and thus they may not like the idea of being 'canonized', so to speak, as the Grand Authorities on Pragmatics. Moreover, they may smile, or gnash their teeth, depending on a number of unknown factors, at the way I have allowed myself to handle their texts: mainly as repositories of ideas and examples, to be pilfered at will. I have had no qualms in quoting them directly and profusely, for the benefit of my students, on whatever I found of interest in their works; I hope they can live with this, and also with the criticisms I voice of some of their ideas. Since there is so much in this book that owes inspiration to Leech and Levinson's ground-breaking work, let my obvious indebtedness to these authors serve to express my appreciation for these texts, which still are the only ones that (together) give the most comprehensive picture of pragmatics as a field that is available, even a decade after their publication. (Another text that I came to find very helpful during the rewriting process, albeit on a more theoretical level, was Gerald Gazdar's *Pragmatics* from 1979: despite its age, this book contains some of the most thoughtful analyses of theoretical points in pragmatics, and still deserves to be mentioned and read.)

In a text such as this with a relatively limited purpose, I have not been able or willing to go into too much detail as regards controversies on more theoretical issues; thus, the book itself is intentionally not (too) controversial. An exception may be Part III, where I discuss issues of a broader character, such as 'metapragmatics', and the question of the 'societal' character of pragmatics which for a long time has been at the centre of my own attention. Here, the reader may find ample material for disagreement – especially since, in view of the very scant attention that these matters are receiving, I have permitted myself to reiterate some of the challenges that I threw out some years ago, when I published my book *Whose Language?* (1985).

I will end this introduction by thanking the people who have been helpful in all sorts of ways, by putting me to work, giving me the environment that I needed to work and encouraging me to keep it up, despite time and other pressures.

I'm thinking, first of all, of colleagues and students, both at Odense University and at Northwestern University; especially as to the latter, the helpfulness and support from faculty, staff and students that I have experienced at the Institute for the Learning Sciences have been quite unique. A special thanks to Roger Schank, my old student, who created and directs the Institute, and never fails to support me in whatever I do – with a piece of his mind thrown in for good measure. Thanks also to the Arthur Andersen Worldwide Organization, whose support made my several stays at Northwestern University possible.

I want to thank my friends in Japan, first of all Professor Harumi Sawada, then of Shizuoka University, now of Gakushuin University, Tokyo, who not only had earlier done me the favour of translating large portions of my 1985 book into Japanese, but whose suggestion it was that I start working towards a textbook proper. Professor Sawada also put me in touch with the other originator of the idea (who subsequently became my translator, along with Professor Sawada himself), Professor Masao Takaji, of Miyazaki City University, Kyushu, Japan. The collaboration with these two friends has been a great pleasure, as has been the encouragement I have received from my first publisher, Mr Isao Matsumoto of Hitsuji Co., Tokyo, a young publishing house that specializes in linguistic texts. (A note for punsters: the French equivalent of the Japanese word *hitsuji* is *mouton*.)

Philip Carpenter, of Blackwell's, Oxford, has been an unwavering support for the book throughout its second gestation. I would also like to extend my thanks to two of Blackwell's anonymous readers. Their comments and suggestions have been a pleasure to deal with, and they have been instrumental in bringing up the book to its present standards. Many of the good ideas that I now unabashedly (and also, unavoidably must) claim as my own have originated in remarks from these two hidden mentors, who didn't spare time or effort in order to improve my draft.

My friends Claudia Caffi, Hartmut Haberland, Alvaro G. Meseguer, Uwe Kjær Nissen and Deirdre Wilson have contributed with numerous and sometimes very specific comments, examples and ideas. During the final revision of the manuscript, Blackwell's desk editor, Jenny Tyler, was a great help. Her advice and critical comments proved invaluable on many occasions, not only in matters of editorial policy, but also with regard to substantial questions of style and content. I owe them all heartfelt thanks.

Also, I want to thank my home university for twice in two years providing me with an opportunity to work abroad, and my family for allowing me to be an intermittent factor in their existence for the duration, and for putting up with the inevitable pressures that writing over a long period of time generates and the resulting occasional explosions of the domestic pressure cooker.

A travel grant from the Scandinavia-Japan Sasakawa Foundation made it possible for me to sit down in the summer of 1991 with my two translators, in order to iron out the wrinkles in the Japanese version of the first draft, and discuss the many difficult problems involved in such a translation. This assistance is greatly appreciated, as is the support for travel and sojourn abroad that was offered me by the Odense University Faculty of Humanities on several occasions. Quotations from *Pragmatics* by Stephen C. Levinson are by kind permission of Cambridge University Press and the author, Stephen C. Levinson. Permission to quote from *Principles of Pragmatics* by Geoffrey N. Leech is gratefully acknowledged to Longman Group Publishers and the author, Geoffrey N. Leech.

I hope that using this text will be as much fun as writing (and not least, rewriting) it has been.

Evanston, Illinois
13 January, 1993

PART I

Basic Notions

1

Introduction

1.1 What is Pragmatics All About?

If you want to know what a particular human activity is all about, you may start out asking questions like: 'What are the rules of baseball?' or 'What is cricket like?'. But pretty soon you'll get to the point where you want to figure out what these sports enthusiasts actually are doing out there in the field. And, while it may be hard enough to explain a sport such as baseball or cricket to someone who doesn't know the first thing about ball games, certainly it will be impossible to explain, or understand, anything interesting about baseball or cricket without having access to watching people play.

Similarly, if you want to know what a particular religion is all about, you are of course entitled to ask what its beliefs are; but you will be more interested in, and enlightened by, the practices that are said to be characteristic of such a religion. The same goes for politics and politicians. 'Read my lips' may be a useful election slogan for somebody who promises lower taxes; but 'check my acts' is a better indicator of what that politician really stands for.

We could apply this line of thought to the 'young' science of pragmatics (I hope nobody will call it a religion – yet). Ask any pragmatician at a cocktail party what pragmatics is all about, and he or she will tell you that it is a science that has to do with language and its users, or some such thing. But if you want to know what pragmatics really stands for, you must try and find out how the game is played, what pragmaticians do for a living and how they are different from the people active in other, related branches of language studies, such as syntax or semantics. So, the question is: What could be called a typical pragmatic look at matters of language?

Here is an example of how pragmatics works. The Chicago alternative cultural weekly *Reader* had an advertisement in its 21 August, 1992 issue for a downtown cocktail lounge called 'Sweet Alice'. The ad carried the text

'I brought some sushi home and cooked it; it wasn't bad.'

Now what are we going to make of this?

Of course, this sentence is a joke: everybody knows that sushi is eaten raw, and that you're not supposed to cook it. Cooking sushi may strike one as funny, or stupid, or outrageous, depending on one's point of view. In an informal way, we could say that the above utterance makes no sense. And a linguist might want to add that, since everybody knows that sushi is defined as being eaten raw, a sentence such as the above is wrong, in the same way as are sentences of the type 'Colorless green ideas sleep furiously' (which made a certain American linguist famous in the early sixties: the example is from Chomsky 1957, and is by now one of the classics of the linguistic-example repertoire). When asked about the odd choice of wording in the advertisement quoted above, the linguist might go on to say that the sentence is semantically wrong: it doesn't make sense because the semantics of one of its parts (the sushi) contradict the semantics of another part (the cooking). So far, so good.

But, one could ask, why use such a silly sentence in an advertisement for a cocktail bar?

This is where pragmatics comes into the picture. Pragmatics tells us it's all right to use language in various, unconventional ways, as long as we know, as language users, what we're doing. So we can let ourselves be semantically shocked, if there is a reason for it, or if it is done for a purpose. Now, what could that reason or purpose be?

In this particular case, the joke has a euphoric effect, similar to that of a disarming smile; it invokes the silly state of mind that becomes our privilege after a couple of drinks. Which is precisely why this ad is effective as an invitation to join the crowd at Sweet Alice's, as I'll explain in a moment. (The invitation is in fact a 'pragmatic act'; see below.)

The big question, of course, is: Why do we call all this 'pragmatic'? Only because we cannot explain it using the 'normal' explanations of linguistics (here: the semantics of the language)? This reminds one of the saying that used to go the rounds among linguists, according to which 'pragmatics is the waste-basket of linguistics'; that is: whenever you cannot explain a phenomenon in language using regular, accepted linguistic theories, then you must have recourse to something else, something that is supposedly as undefined as it is tangible, namely, pragmatics.

However, there is another, more sophisticated way of looking at these things. Pragmatics is the science of language seen in relation to its users. That is to say, not the science of language in its own right, or the science of language as seen and studied by the linguists, or the science of language as the expression of our desire to play schoolmarm, but the science of language as it is used by real, live people, for their own purposes and within their limitations and affordances (to use a Gibsonian term; see Gibson 1979).

1.2 Pragmatic Acts

Pragmatics starts out from an active conception of language as being *used*. Pragmatics is where the action is; but what is the action? Clearly, the above ad is an attempt to 'sell' something: a cocktail bar, a particular ambiance, a particular clientele, a promise of good times, and so on. The ad invites us in, so to speak. But it doesn't do that by saying: 'Come into my parlour (or cocktail bar)' (such an invitation would be too blatant to be effective), and it doesn't invite us in by appealing to our baser instincts of greed, sex, violence, of getting plastered, or what have you. (Never mind that certain establishments do just that: they and their customers get what they are in the market for; so it can certainly be done.) No, 'Sweet Alice' uses a more roundabout technique. It talks to us in a voice that appeals to us as individual language users with a particular history, a living context: as such, we have been exposed to particular kinds of language that we have felt comfortable with, e.g. the footloose language that people like Goldie Hawn or Lily Tomlin ('Gracious Good Afternoon') have taught us to appreciate, and which is precisely the kind of talk which allows 'Sweet Alice' to invite us into the kind of company that such language emblematically represents. The parlour, or the cocktail bar, is sketched as a desirable place, and the invitation is by innuendo only: a *pragmatic act* of inviting, rather than a specific, codified language formula, such as a 'speech act' (on speech acts, see chapter 6; pragmatic acts will be dealt with in more detail in section 12.7).

Among the most common pragmatic acts are those of 'implicit denial'. Here's an example from the 1992 Republican National Convention, where a backer of George Bush's gave a speech praising the President's concern for people with AIDS. The speaker's credentials were beyond any doubt: not only was she a staunch Republican, a friend of Vice-President Quayle's, but she also was HIV-infected: she was introduced as 'having contracted the infection from her former husband'. The speech itself emphasized, among other things, the necessity of not being judgemental in matters of AIDS, in particular of not falling into the well-known moralistic (clap-)trap of regarding the disease as a punishment for people's sins; when a person has cancer, so the speaker said, we don't ask him or her how many packs of cigarettes he or she has smoked a day. In other words, we should treat the disease, not condemn the patient.

However, in her speech, the woman denied implicitly what she had just explicitly stated: that one should not worry too much about how one had contracted the infection. This could be seen from the fact that she had herself introduced as having contracted AIDS in a 'legal' way: she had been married; her husband had given her the disease; so she was not to blame. In addition, since she was now divorced, any links to immorality were further weakened, while the former husband and his way of life were being implicitly characterized as doubly bad, both for himself and for the virtuous, innocent victim.

All of these implicit assertions and judgements contradict the explicit message: 'Don't worry about where your AIDS came from: there is no reason to be ashamed.' As it turns out, the speaker herself was very much concerned about the origin of her disease, wanting clearly to establish that she contracted it practising a legal form of intercourse, involving permitted, non-adulterous 'normal' sexual activity.

The pragmatic act involved here is one of 'implicit denial'. Notice, first, that no explicit denial takes place, that is to say, no 'speech acts' of denying are found; and second, that solely the user's context (here: the speaker's background as a card-carrying Republican with AIDS) can explain her concern, as it was expressed in the language of the press-releases having to do with the origin of her disease. (In this connection, it is also worth noting that the reporters consistently used the unconditional affirmative: 'Mrs X had contracted the disease from her former husband', not: 'Mrs X who allegedly had contracted the disease . . .' or:

'Mrs X, who said/stated/maintained . . . that she had contracted the disease . . .'.)

1.3   WHY DO WE NEED PRAGMATICS?

A further question, of course, is what do we need pragmatics for? What does pragmatics have to offer that cannot be found in good old-fashioned linguistics? What do pragmatic methods give us in the way of greater understanding of how the human mind works, how humans communicate, how they manipulate one another, and in general, how they use language, in all the ways, and with all the means, and for all the ends they traditionally have done? All these questions will be dealt with at length in chapters 2 and 3; but let me offer an adumbration here.

The answer is: Pragmatics is needed if we want a fuller, deeper and generally more reasonable account of human language behaviour. Sometimes, even, a pragmatic account is the only possible one, as in the following example, borrowed from David Lodge's *Paradise News*:

> 'I just met the old Irishman and his son, coming out of the toilet.'
> 'I wouldn't have thought there was room for the two of them.'
> 'No silly, I mean *I* was coming out of the toilet. They were waiting.' (1992: 65)

How do we know what the first speaker meant? Linguists usually say that the first sentence is ambiguous, and they excel at producing such sentences as

> Flying planes can be dangerous

or

> The missionaries are ready to eat

in order to show what is meant by 'ambiguous': a word, phrase or sentence that can mean either one or the other of two (or even several) things.

For a pragmatician, this is, of course, glorious nonsense. In real life – that is, among real language users – there is no such thing as ambiguity, excepting certain, rather special occasions, on which one tries to deceive one's partner, or 'keep a door open'; the most famous example is the answer that the ancient oracle in Delphi gave the King of Epirus, Pyrrhus, when he asked what would happen if he attacked the Romans. The answer was that the king would destroy a great empire; whereupon he set out to win the battle, but lose the war, and thus indirectly destroy his own empire.[1]

In the dialogue from *Paradise News* cited above, the first speaker knows what she means; the misunderstanding is on the part of the hearer, but there is strictly speaking no ambiguity. The misunderstanding is, furthermore, cleared up in the next round; but notice that this can only happen in real dialogue: if we don't have a user to tell us what she or he means, we may speculate until the end of our days on the hidden meaning of utterances that are never brought to bear on a concrete situation, with real language users involved. Ambiguity exists only in the abstract.

Many linguists assert that it is the 'context' that we must invoke to determine what an ambiguous sentence means. This sounds OK, perhaps, if by 'context' we understand a rather undefined mass of factors that play a role in the production and consumption of utterances. But 'context' is a notoriously hard concept to deal with (I shall have more to say on this later; see sections 3.3 and 9.1); often, it is considered by linguists to be the sum and result of what has been said up to now, the 'prehistory' of a particular utterance, so to speak, including the prehistory of the people who utter sentences.

But no matter how we 'milk' the context, we will not automatically arrive at any pragmatic understanding of the phenomena involved. Whoever thinks so is at best a would-be pragmatician. It is as if such a person were saying: 'Give me all the information, and I'll predict what is going to happen, what this or that utterance is supposed to mean.' However, this kind of method will never work, because the concept of context that is invoked here is purely static; it bears a certain likeness to the thinking of classical physics, where the conditions preceding a particular state of affairs in the physical world are thought of as completely determining the next development: a bit like a controlled experiment in the physics classroom or in the laboratory. In such a conceptual framework, it is very hard to make sense of the following dialogue:

(Two linguists, call them Jacob and Mark, are coming out of a lecture hall at a university which is neither's home territory, but

where Jacob has been before; so he thinks he knows the campus, more or less)

Jacob: Do you know the way back to the dining hall? We can go in my car.

(Mark gets into the car; after the first turn, he starts giving directions, which greatly amazes Jacob, and irritates him a little – he was under the impression that he *needed to guide the other, not the other way round. After several more turns – which Jacob is taking at greater and greater speeds, so the other doesn't get a chance to interfere – Mark says:)*

Mark: Oh, I thought you *didn't* know the way to the campus.

(To which Jacob replies:)

Jacob: I thought *you* didn't know!

(whereupon they both start laughing).

In a case like this, the classical concept of 'context' as 'that which has been the case up to and including the present moment' makes no sense; it offers no way in which the original utterance 'Do you know the way back to the dining hall?' can be interpreted correctly. Clearly, Mark takes Jacob's utterance not as a 'real' question, but as a 'pre-request' (see section 11.5.1). Jacob, on the other hand, who really wanted to know if Mark was familiar with the campus, because otherwise he wanted to give him directions, or a ride, doesn't understand the other's reaction: giving directions makes no sense if you don't know where you're going.

The moment the situation is resolved, we can look back and understand what has happened: but the 'illocutionary force' of the first utterance was not a thing that could be 'predicted' on the basis of what had happened before.

Moreover, such a concept of 'context', if established independently of the ongoing interaction between the interlocutors, is completely useless: it is precisely the dynamic *development* of the conversation that gives us the clue to understanding. Such a development cannot be predicted, as it depends entirely on the individuals and their individual choices at every moment.

We are all familiar with these phenomena from our daily lives. Take the case of family fights and other arguments. As our mother used to say,

'One word takes the other, and you never know where you're ending up.' Afterwards, one looks back and is unable to understand how all this happened, and how things came to be said 'which are not easily forgotten' (Robert L. Stevenson, *Kidnapped*), with sometimes terrible consequences for one's relationships with other persons.

A context is *dynamic*, that is to say, it is an environment that is in steady development, prompted by the continuous interaction of the people engaged in language use, the users of the language. Context is the quintessential pragmatic concept; it is by definition *proactive*, just as people are. (To live in the 'here and now', the classical *hic et nunc*, is a philosophical abstraction.) By contrast, a purely linguistic description is retroactive and static: it takes a snapshot of what is the case at any particular moment, and tries to freeze that picture. Pure description has no dynamics; it can never capture the richness of the developments that take place between people using language.

1.4   WHAT USE IS PRAGMATICS?

This brings me to a further point: What is the declared aim of a pragmatic linguistics, as opposed to that of classical, descriptive linguistics, and what can it be used for?

In linguistics, it has long been an article of faith that the science of language has to be practised for its own sake. Linguists have talked about the 'immanence' of linguistic theory, by which they mean that linguistics is accountable only to itself as to its methods and objectives. Historically, this has been understandable in a young science such as linguistics: it needed to become independent of the surrounding sciences, and to carve out its own domain, so to speak. But for a developed science, the desire for 'immanence' is not a sign of maturity; on the contrary. The immanent approach to the study of language has tended to isolate its different aspects, and in many cases the practitioners of linguistics have not been able to talk to each other except in very general terms. When it comes to doing things for a purpose, such as describing languages, often thought of as the prime practical endeavour of linguists, the consensus remains largely theoretical. Here is an example.

In the course of the past decades, it has become increasingly clear that the descriptive endeavour of linguistics is in great danger of being irrevocably thwarted. The fact is that all description is a terminal process, that is, a process with a built-in *terminus ad quem*: when everything has been described that there is to describe, description has to come to an end.

Now, this never used to be a real concern for linguists in the past: there were always enough languages to describe. The times when every Ph. D. candidate could travel to the 'field' and pick him-/herself a language to work on are not so long past, after all.

However, with the increasing westernization and industrialization of the Third and Fourth Worlds, a number of the many languages of those worlds have begun to disappear, and have been doing so at an ever more rapid speed. According to well-founded projections, we are looking at a loss of languages in the order of several thousand in the next fifty years or so. These languages are in danger of disappearing; linguists speak of 'endangered languages', and vote on resolutions about what to do to 'save' those languages.

From a descriptive point of view, it is clearly a loss for the describer if the object or potential object of his or her description starts disappearing from the scene. And as long as the purpose of linguistics is seen as to go 'out there' and collect as many species as possible of the vanishing races of languages, it is clearly a catastrophe when species start disappearing on a grand scale, such as we are witnessing. The linguistic remedy for this evil is to save the languages by accelerating and perfecting the descriptive process, through better and more generous funding, through the training of native linguists, through providing teachers and other personnel that can help in 'alphabetizing' those mostly unwritten and unrecorded languages, so that we at least may have some documentation to show to our successors in the trade, and can parry the reproach of having squandered away the linguistic patrimony of generations to come by saying: 'Here's what we have done – it may not be perfect, but we did our best.'

However, the best in this case isn't good enough. Description, as the ultimate aim of linguistic science, digs its own grave, in the literal sense; and when all is said and done, describing the language that has disappeared has not done a thing for the people that went with it. The question 'Why do languages disappear, and what can we do about the causes of this linguistic decay?' is seldom raised. In other words, saving languages is thought of as a process of putting away, cataloguing, describing; not as a process that saves the *users* of languages, providing them with living conditions that allow them to continue using the languages they are speaking. In other words, a pragmatic look at the problems of endangered languages tells us not just to go out there and describe, but to fight

what some have called 'linguistic genocide'; for short: 'linguicide'
(Phillipson and Skutnabb-Kangas 1993).

1.5   A WASTE-BASKET?

Above, I alluded to the use of the term 'waste-basket' to characterize
pragmatics. Despite its negative connotations (a waste-basket is usually
for things that we don't want any longer), this way of speaking of things
pragmatic acquired a certain status among pragmaticians, especially in
the early years of pragmatics. Pragmatics is often called 'the waste-basket
of linguistics'. How did this come about, and how can this be reconciled
with the view on pragmatics I have been pleading for: as indispensable to
any sound linguistic treatment of people's ways with words?

The notion of waste-basket itself has not always been the same. It
started out with the Israeli logician-philosopher and linguist Yehoshua
Bar-Hillel (who died in 1978) calling semantics the waste-basket of
syntax (Bar-Hillel 1971). To see what he meant, consider the ambitions
of linguistics as a science in the late fifties and early sixties. The emphasis
was on formal reasoning and abstract symbolism; linguistics was thought
of as an algebra of language (the expression was first used by Hjelmslev
in 1943, but has been borrowed by many).

Now, what is it that usually happens when we try to apply formal,
mathematical methods to phenomena of daily life? We realize that life
cannot be exhaustively described by those methods; the abstractions of
mathematics, for example, are idealizations that strictly speaking do not
exist. A line is not a line in reality, but only a well-defined concept in
mathematics. The real line is but an approximation, one could say.

Similarly, when Chomsky started to develop his theory of language
that was to become famous under the name of 'generative-transformational grammar', he was aware that much of what the grammar pur-
ported to do could be said to hold only for a certain, limited subset of
real, 'natural language'. The fringes had to be cut off in order for the
system to account for what Chomsky considered to be the main components of the language. In his earliest attempts, he separated the syntax
from the semantics, the content, of the language, and postulated that a
sentence could be described perfectly well on the syntactic level without
having ever to have to 'mean' anything – just as algebraic formulas, taken

by themselves, don't mean anything until you assign values to the variables.

Consider again Chomsky's famous example (1957):

Colorless green ideas sleep furiously.

This sentence, Chomsky argues, is perfectly correct, from a syntactic point of view; however, it is nonsense from the point of view of content. It doesn't really say anything, since the entities that are being talked about cancel out one another (e.g. 'green', a colour, cancels out 'colourless', and so on). For syntacticians, those kinds of considerations were out of order, not to say useless; the syntacticians preferred for other people, such as semanticists, to worry about these useless things (that was how semantics came to be called the syntacticians' 'waste-basket').

Now, in the philosophy of the fifties, one didn't have to think about one's trash; it was not until much later that trash, and its disposal, got to be major worries in the world at large. And as the world changed, so did human science. Many philosophers and linguists began to be interested in what precisely went into the waste-basket and why. Even Chomsky himself came up with a solution for trash-disposal some years later: he tried to make explicit the fact that certain sentences didn't make sense, even though they seemingly were perfectly good constructions. The way he did this was by saying that you only could combine words into phrases if you took certain precautions in your selection process. Words could be assigned certain traits, called 'selection features', that would guide their possible coexistence with other words. The early transformational grammarians (along with Chomsky) thought of this selection process as something which went on under the guidance of the syntax, and hence could be formally explained by mathematical or quasi-mathematical rules. But even so, there were problems that could not easily be treated under such an assumption. Semantics remained an abstract, descriptive science; its favourite (and for a long time, unique) concern was the conditions under which a sentence was true or false.

But even under this interpretation, not everything could be captured that was of interest to the semanticist; I'm thinking here of the familiar problem of what came to be called 'presuppositions': How to explain that certain parts of a sentence remain true, regardless of whether the entire sentence is true or false? For example,

Fats regretted that he had to pay alimony to Bessie

presupposes that Fats indeed paid what he owed Bessie; but the negated sentence,

Fats did not regret that he had to pay alimony to Bessie,

presupposes likewise that Fats was not misbehaving, but actually paid his dues. (The technical reason for this is that the English verb *to regret* is a 'factive' verb, as we will see in the next chapter, section 2.6.)

These and other considerations led pragmaticians to the conviction that there was more going on between people using language than was dreamt of in the semantics of the logically-inspired philosophers. Thus, another waste-basket came into being, created to catch the overflow from the semantics basket, which itself had been filled to the brim. As time went by, and people dropped more and more of their unresolved problems with language into this basket, it became a not-too-tidy collection of sometimes rather heterogeneous problems, not all of which were considered by the linguists to be worthy of their attention.

The questions that kept bothering the linguists, or at least those among them that called themselves pragmaticians, were (among others): Why would people say a particular thing on a particular occasion? What are people trying to do with their language? How do people cooperate in conversation? More and more, it became apparent to these linguists that we cannot really say anything about the effects that language has, without going into some detail with regard to what motivates people to use language, and when they consider their language use to be successful, when not.

As to classical linguistic philosophy, pragmaticians found out rather quickly that the truth value of a sentence, taken in its abstract form, was of little interest to the users of language, who rarely would utter something in order to be proven true or false. Usually, it is much more interesting to try and find out *why* people say something than whether *what* they say is true or false; the latter consideration belongs in rather special surroundings, such as the philosophical debate or the courtroom. And the full meaning of an utterance may not even be clear to the utterer until she or he finds out what the sentence has done to the environment, in the broadest sense of the word. (This was the gist of the dialogue example given above between the two befuddled linguists, Mark and Jacob.)

Pragmatics rests on understanding, but even more on *cooperation* – to such a degree that one of the mainstays of pragmatic thinking is called, following the late philosopher H. Paul Grice, the 'Cooperative Principle' (see below, section 4.4.1). Far from being a receptacle for discardables, the pragmatic waste-basket is more like a can of worms: the problems that the basket contains will not only not go away, but they tend to spill over into all the domains of linguistic thinking. Instead of making linguistics neat and clean, in the best logical or mathematical style, the waste-basket imposes its unruly 'order' on our science. How it does this, to the extent that it does, will be explained in the following pages.

EXERCISES AND REVIEW QUESTIONS

1. The following three examples all contain a negation ('No') along with a noun. Usually, this kind of construction is not difficult to handle; it is often used in connection with some prohibition, injunction, etc. ('No Smoking', 'No Pets', etc.) Even so, all three examples exhibit some apparent irregularities. Explain these in terms respectively of syntax, semantics and pragmatics.

(a) 'No Parking Violators Will Be Towed Away' (sign in San Juan, Puerto Rico; example due to Bruce Fraser)

(b) 'No Shoes, No Shirt, No Service' (sign on door of the Bevo Shop on 'The Drag', the University area of Guadalupe Street in Austin, Texas)

(c) 'No Checks, No Exceptions' (hand-lettered notice on the cashier's counter in the cafeteria of the University of Chicago 59th Street campus).

2. Study the following sign, appearing at selected private parking sites throughout the Greater Chicago area:

ALL UNAUTHORIZED VEHICLES
WILL BE TOWED BY LINCOLN
TOWING SERVICE TO 4884 N. CLARK
FEE $80.00   CASH,
VISA & MASTER CHARGE ACCEPTED
PHONE 561-4433

Questions:

What does this sign tell you
   explicitly?
   implicitly?

Who do you think is the sender of the message:

   the owner of the parking lot?
   the owner of the phone number?
   the police?

(Argue your point of view)

Judging from the text of the message, would you say that illegal parking is a criminal act in Chicago?

(Justify your answer.)

3. Consider the following excerpt:

   'What are we going to do about Baba', she asked.
   'What do you mean?'
   'She can't remember anything.'
   'Did she ask you whether she was taking medicine?'
   'No.'
   'No she's not or no she didn't ask?'
   'She didn't ask.'
   'She was supposed to,' I said.
   'Well, she didn't.'
   (Don Delillo, *White Noise*. New York: Viking/Penguin, 1986, p. 61)

Questions:

What is ambiguous in this dialogue?

Where does the ambiguity originate, from a linguistic point of view?

How much context is minimally needed to clear up the ambiguity?

How do the participants resolve the ambiguity?

What is 'she was supposed to' (last turn but one) referring to?

How do you know?

Do you think the last reply is ambiguous?

How does this ambiguity compare to the first example in the text of section 1.3?

How much of it is syntactically, how much pragmatically based?

4. Consider the text below, appearing in a shop window on Aoyama-dori in Tokyo, close to the Aoyama Gakuin University underpass. The shop in question deals in high-class sporting goods, and is proud of having been in business for at least twenty-five years, witness its name, 'Sweat Studio 1978'. Their flagship sales articles are 'Authentic Color Sweat Shirts by IFCO Corporation', as a note in the window informs us. This note is flanked by a calligraphed text on a 12 by 18 in. laminated plaque, on prominent display among the goods, which reads as follows (original English text; store and brand names in original English):

> Here, healthy people who drain refreshing sweat gather.
> Here, people who know the pleasure of creation gather.
> Here, people who find the pleasure of designing one's life plentifully
>   gather.
> People with sound body and mind who will endeavour, will all win
>   eternal glory and utmost satisfaction.
> So, let's live the limited life utmost!
>
> January 1974

Questions:

What do you think is the meaning of this text, and what is its pragmatic function?

Are we looking at a pragmatic act? Which?

Who are the senders and the receivers of this message?

How would you evaluate its effectiveness, compared to the 'Sweet Alice' example in section 1.1?

2

Why Pragmatics?

2.1 INTRODUCTION: A LOOK AT HISTORY

The past twenty years have witnessed an ever-growing interest in pragmatics and pragmatic problems. There have been four international conferences (Viareggio, 1985, Antwerp, 1987, Barcelona, 1990, Kobe, Japan, 1993; a fifth conference will take place in Mexico City in 1996). The International Pragmatics Association, IPrA, has been in existence for more than ten years; an international journal (the *Journal of Pragmatics*) has recently increased its yearly volume from the original 400 published pages to 1,800 a year, and its frequency from quarterly to monthly issues, all in the course of barely twenty years; many other (official and unofficial) publications have seen the light (some of which have survived, some not). Add to this an unestablished number of working papers, theses, dissertations and books on pragmatic topics (among the latter, at least three major works), and the picture is complete. Pragmatics has come into its own, and it is here to stay.

But even allowing that this is a spectacular development, it still is the case that pragmatics didn't just 'happen' by itself, appearing out of nowhere. We must ask ourselves: How could pragmatics expand so fast and become such a popular trend in such a relatively short time?

The answer to this question is important, as it may give us a first approximation to a more profound understanding of what pragmatics is, and what it does. Our preliminary understanding will lead us to a tentative definition that necessarily has an 'intensional' flavour (it will tell us something about what pragmatics is supposed to be). It will have to be supplemented with an 'extensional' definition (even though it is notoriously difficult to limit the field in such a way that we can say where pragmatics stops, and the 'beyond' begins).[2]

The first, tentative efforts at establishing something like a pragmatic approach to linguistics date back to the late sixties and early seventies (as evidenced in work by Lakoff, Ross and others). What we see there is the collapse of earlier theories and hypotheses (in particular, of the 'pan-syntacticism' of Chomsky and his followers). Slowly and with intermittent success, a new model emerged: pragmatics was in the making, even though initially its practitioners were not aware of this themselves. Some would even say that we are looking at a 'paradigm shift' in the sense defined by Kuhn (1964). Levinson has described this shift from a more technical-linguistic point of view:

> ... as knowledge of the syntax, phonology and semantics of various languages has increased, it has become clear that there are specific phenomena that can only naturally be described by recourse to contextual concepts. On the one hand, various syntactic rules seem to be properly constrained only if one refers to pragmatic conditions; and similarly for matters of stress and intonation. It is possible, in response to these apparent counter-examples to a context-independent notion of linguistic competence, simply to retreat: the rules can be left unconstrained and allowed to generate unacceptable sentences, and a performance theory of pragmatics assigned the job of filtering out the acceptable sentences. Such a move is less than entirely satisfactory because the relationship between the theory of competence and the data on which it is based (ultimately intuitions about acceptability) becomes abstract to a point where counter-examples to the theory may be explained away on an *ad hoc* basis, *unless* a systematic pragmatics has already been developed. (1983: 36; emphasis in original)

Naturally, such a development of a 'systematic pragmatics' can only be seen as a contemporary need with the help of hindsight: from the vantage point of history, we may observe how the old paradigm came under attack, and how the contours of a new one gradually took shape. But at the time when all this happened, in the early seventies, all one could see was a growing number of unexplained (and, in fact, unexplainable) observations, along with certain theoretical paradoxes. Many of these were first noticed not by linguists, but by philosophers working in

the grey zone where philosophy and linguistics share a border. Others
came to the attention of linguists trying to overstep the narrow boundaries of syntax and, later, of semantics.

To name but a few of these phenomena: there was the troubled
relationship of language with logic, as originally evidenced in the realm
of syntax, but subsequently also in that of semantics; these problems will
be dealt with in sections 2.3 and 2.4. Then there were the closely related
linguistic problems that arose from the prestigious, but forever hidden,
tenet that a linguistic description had to be syntax-based or at least
syntax-oriented to be valid. It turned out that extra-syntactic, indeed
extralinguistic factors played a major role in what were called the 'rules
of the language'; these problems will be dealt with in section 2.5. Furthermore, there were difficulties of how to interpret and treat those assumptions that somehow guided our understanding of language, yet could not
be easily formulated in any of the available frameworks: presuppositions (these are discussed in section 2.6). And finally, the whole gamut
of problems having to do with users turned out to be crucial for the
meaning of what is being uttered at any given time, at any given place.
These problems will be the topic of section 2.7, where the notion of
'context' will loom large.

The 'pragmatic turn' in linguistics can thus be described as a paradigm
shift, by which a number of observations are brought to the same
practical denominator. Basically, the shift is from the paradigm of
theoretical grammar (in particular, syntax) to the paradigm of the language user. The latter notion will be of particular importance for defining
pragmatics, as we will see.

To obtain a better understanding of what the problems are all about,
I will now discuss in more detail some of the issues mentioned above.

2.2   Linguists on the (Plymouth) Rocks

The British pragmatician Geoffrey Leech has compared the development
of modern pragmatics to a process of colonization, by which some brave
settlers tried to expand their horizons by venturing into hitherto un-
charted (or so they thought) foreign territory:

> [this] colonization was only the last stage of a wave-by-wave ex-
> pansion of linguistics from a narrow discipline dealing with the

physical data of speech, to a broad discipline taking in form, meaning and context. (1983: 2)

The notion of 'colonization' as invoked here by Leech comprises two elements: first, there must have been some conflicts back home that forced the settlers into exile (just as the Founding Fathers left their native England because of its oppressive religious policies); furthermore, there is the question of the natives, the people who were there before them, and to whom, in the historical parallel, not much respect was paid.

As to the conflicts themselves, let me quote the eminent British linguist, Sir John Lyons, who argues that there was no real conflict between what he calls the 'abstract' and the 'practical' approaches:

[there is] no conflict between the peculiarly abstract approach to the study of language which is characteristic of modern, 'structural' linguistics[,] and more 'practical approaches'. (1968: 50–1)

While Lyons does not mention pragmatics in this connection, he does indicate the existence of certain 'practical' and 'realistic' tendencies which, however, are not opposed (in his opinion) to 'real' linguistics, except in the minds of people who (for whatever reason) insist on creating such an opposition. To quote Lyons once more:

However abstract, or formal, modern linguistic theory might be, it has been developed to account for the way people actually use language. (1968: 50–1)

Hence there should be no conflict, according to Lyons. But, whatever the case may have been for Lyons in 1968, with the benefit of hindsight we may wonder why a number of people apparently (and, as it turned out later, not without reason) thought there was.

Another conflict, a more 'internal' one, so to speak, arose as a reaction to the 'syntacticism' of the Chomskyan school of linguistics, whereby all of linguistic science (including phonology and semantics) was supposed to fit into the syntactic framework. Linguists such as George Lakoff and John Robert ('Haj') Ross were the first to protest against this syntactic straitjacket (cf. the numerous alternative 'frameworks' proposed in the late sixties, such as Lakoff's 'generative semantics'). But it was not until the publication of John Searle's landmark work *Speech Acts* (1969) that the first inroads were made by Chomsky's rebellious students into what later became known as pragmatic territory; to their great surprise, these Lord Marchers of the Language Realm found the region they invaded already populated:

> [w]hen linguistic pioneers such as Ross and Lakoff staked a claim in pragmatics in the late 1960s, they encountered there an indigenous breed of philosophers of language who had been quietly cultivating the territory for some time. In fact, the more lasting influences on modern pragmatics have been those of philosophers; notably, in recent years, Austin (1962), Searle (1969), and Grice (1975). (Leech 1983: 2)

What these philosophers cultivated had essentially been semantic virgin land; and the visions that struck the early colonizers there must have been quite refreshing after the emphasis on structure and syntax that they had been subjected to in the old country. What is especially interesting in this connection is the fact that it was not the linguists who were the first to discover the 'terra incognita' of pragmatics, but the philosophers. Their reflections on the phenomenon of language have thus had a significant and lasting impact on the development of modern linguistics, especially pragmatics. But what had these philosophers been doing?

2.3   LOGICIANS, LANGUAGE AND THE (WO)MAN IN THE STREET

Initially, the philosophers busying themselves with problems of language had concentrated on the relationships between logically defined expressions and sentences in natural languages. This is, of course, not any newfangled pastime; it goes back all the way to the ancient philosophers such as Plato (e.g. in his dialogue *Cratylus*); among modern philosophers, we have names such as Bertrand Russell, Ludwig Wittgenstein, Rudolf Carnap, and the school usually referred to as the 'ordinary language philosophers', whose most famous protagonist, John L. Austin, was mentioned above.

Such an interest in logic and its relations to language, however, is by no means restricted to practitioners of philosophy. One of the most inveterate and hard-to-change ideas that goes the rounds among ordinary people when they discuss language is the notion that language is a matter of logic. This is taken to mean that a correct use of language presupposes the use of logic, and that any use of language which is not in accordance with the laws of logic is simply bad. Logic thus is prior to language; and it is maintained that our everyday language is a bastardized and illegitimate variant of the pure language of logic, as it materializes in mathematics, formal logic and maybe even abstract music. To express oneself in illogical terms is the same as to speak badly; logic may be the handmaid of philosophy, but language certainly is the handmaid of logic.

In the following, I will say something about the way logic and language tie in with each other (or rather, perhaps, about how people think they tie in with each other – which is not the same).

2.4 ORDINARY LANGUAGE AND LOGIC

Perhaps one of the most effective incitements for the development of modern pragmatics has been the growing irritation, felt especially by many of the younger, 'non-aligned' linguistic practitioners, with the lack of interest that is the rule among most established linguists and logicians in what really goes on in language; in what people actually 'do with words'. Among the few exceptions to this rule was John L. Austin, the author of one of the classical works in the early pragmatic tradition, *How to Do Things with Words* (1962), a work which has had an enormous influence on the development of pragmatics. The title of Austin's book contains an implicit question, the answer to which is not, of course, that people should form correct sentences or compose logically valid utterances, but that they communicate with each other (and themselves) by means of language.

Many of the early discussions on the foundation of pragmatics have been about the possibility and desirability of letting pragmatic conditions govern the correct use of logical propositions, when disguised as 'ordinary language' utterances. As the facts would have it, however, logic and language are strange fellow-travellers: the amount of ground they cover between them is not very encouraging, at any rate for the logician. Let us consider a well-known case.

According to a familiar rule of logic, when conjoining two propositions (let us call them p and q, and symbolize their conjunction by the formula p & q), it is not important in which order the two constituents of the formula appear: p & q is logically equivalent to q & p.

Now consider the following example, due to Levinson (1983: 35). Somebody utters the sentence:

Getting married and having a child is better than having a child and getting married.

Supposing that we can identify our everyday language conjunction *and* with the logical conjunction '&', we would be looking at a logical proposition of the form p ('getting married') & q ('having a child'), expressed in everyday language by means of a sentence like the above. Such an utterance should then, by the laws of logic, be equivalent to the proposition q ('having a child') & p ('getting married'). Hence, the above utterance would be logically equivalent to the one below:

Having a child and getting married is better than getting married and having a child.

But although these two sentences have the same 'truth conditions' (which is the same as saying that they are logically equivalent), the two sentences clearly do not have the same meaning, in everyday life as in everyday language use; far from it. Which of the two is 'true' in the actual case of uttering can perhaps be inferred from the general observation that people usually let the order of their words follow the order of their actions (this observation is due to another logician and philosopher, H. Paul Grice, who assigns it to a more general principle, that of 'order-liness'; Grice 1981: 186). However, as Bruce Fraser has remarked (in personal communication), this is not even always the case, as seen from the following example, in which *and* does not necessarily imply an ordering:

I both crashed my car and got drunk.

A further, even more profound difficulty lies in the fact that there is no *a priori* guarantee that any logical symbols (such as *and*, ∧ or its logical 'sister' *or*, ∨) can be faithfully represented by the words of a natural language (such as *and*, *or* in English). Likewise, the words of the language do not each uniquely correspond to one particular logical entity: for instance, the conjunction *but* is very different from *and* in daily use, yet it normally does not have a separate logical symbol (such as, e.g., V for *or*). For instance, compare the following two sentences:

Mary is a nice girl *and* she takes swimming lessons

Mary is a nice girl *but* she is poor at tennis.

Here, many logicians would argue, both *and* and *but* have to be rendered by the same logical conjunction *and* (symbolized, e.g., by the symbol '&'); the difference is that *but* carries what is called a 'conventional implicature' (Grice 1978: 117) of 'adversativity' (more on conventional implicatures below, section 5.2.4)

Thus, a natural language conjunction of two sentences cannot be said to simply and always represent a logical conjunction of two propositions. Logic is in essence an abstraction from language; it should never be made into its dominant perspective. In the following section, I will discuss some other problems in language that cannot be dealt with using the logic-like rules that were devised by Chomsky and his school for describing syntax.

2.5   A PROBLEM IN SYNTAX

According to Leech (1983: 2), the 1968 article by G. Lakoff, 'On Generative Semantics' (reprinted as Lakoff 1971a), documents the earliest outbreak of the anti-syntax rebellion. However, rather than the somewhat programmatic article mentioned by Leech, it seems more appropriate to consider another article by Lakoff as evidence here: the one entitled 'Presupposition and relative well-formedness' (Lakoff 1971b, printed in the same volume). It is in this article that Lakoff for the first time, publicly and in writing, opposes the well-known Chomskyan criterion of 'well-formedness' as the ultimate standard by which to judge a linguistic production.

In the Chomskyan linguistic tradition, syntactic well-formedness plays the role of the decision-maker in questions of linguistic 'belonging': a language consists of a set of well-formed sentences, and it is these that 'belong' in the language; no others do. This is the definition that – assumed implicitly, or explicitly invoked – has been the pillar of the Chomskyan system for more than thirty years; it is also the definition that, from the earliest times, has most often come under attack from the quarters of so-called 'Ordinary Working Linguists' (often called 'OWLs'), and the one that makes least sense if we for a moment consider what it is that people *really* say, and how they judge their own language's 'well-formedness' or 'correctness'.

As Lakoff points out in his article, this latter notion is a highly relativistic one; it has to do (and a lot to do) with what the speakers know about themselves, about their conversational partners (often called 'interlocutors'), about the topic of their conversation, about its 'progress' (or what is felt as such) versus 'not getting anywhere'.[3] In the following, I will discuss this problem on the basis of a concrete example.

In grammar, correctness, as prescribed by the grammarians, often collides with what *we* perceive as correct. Classical examples include the *constructio ad sensum*, by which a noun in the singular denoting a collective body takes a plural verb form, since we perceive the plurality of the 'sense' as more important than the command of the grammar to use the singular (e.g. 'The Board of Directors have decided not to pay dividends this year' and similar constructions); the following example is another case in point.

There is a rule of English grammar that tells us to use the relative pronoun *who* when we are dealing with a noun which is human (and animate, of course), whereas we use *which* for a non-animate (and usually also for a non-human) referent.

Here are some examples:

The man who kissed my daughter ran away (*who* for a human subject)

The car which hit John's bicycle disappeared around the corner (*which* for a non-animate (and non-human) subject)

The bird which shat on my nose flew away (*which* for a non-human, although animate, subject).

Such are the rules. But how are they maintained? Do we always obey them, or are there cases where rule-observation is less 'correct' than breaking the rule? Let's consider some additional examples.

My cat, *who* believes that I'm a fool, enjoys tormenting me.

This sentence (which is due to George Lakoff in the article quoted above) is not all bad, or always bad. It all depends on the cat, on the speaker, and on what their relationship is. Given a special, intimate connection between human and pet, it may even be the case that *which*, for a cat of a certain quality and lineage, is totally inappropriate, and even unthinkable.

The same is the case in the following extract, describing a program (called 'CREANIMATE') that will allow children to create animals of their choice, using the computer.

> In a typical interaction, a student may indicate that he wants to create a bird that swims. The system may respond by discussing some existing aquatic birds such as ducks and penguins. It could display video sequences demonstrating how these birds use the ability to swim to help them survive in the wild. The tutor would try to get the student to refine his design by asking whether the bird will use *his* wings to swim, the way a penguin does, or *its* feet, the way a duck does. (Schank and Edelson 1990: 9; my emphasis)

Strictly speaking, the above is not only ungrammatical – reference ('anaphora') is made to a non-human being (a penguin) by the human pronoun his – but also inconsistent: ducks are also non-human, but they are referred to by *its*. But *why* is a duck 'it' and a penguin 'he'?

This is not a matter of mere human-likeness in general (such as: penguins are 'dressed up' in black ties, like noble corporate gentlemen at a social occasion). The real clue to the different conceptualizations is in the total (not just linguistic) *context* and its attendant conceptualization. According to this, 'hand-swimming' is considered to be typically human, as opposed to 'doggie-style swimming' (with all four feet). Penguins, who swim with their 'hands', are therefore practising 'human-swim', ducks which swim with their feet are like doggies, therefore they 'animal-swim'.

Notice furthermore that this is not a reference to the 'real world', as humans don't swim only with their hands or arms either, as everybody knows who practises swimming. It's the legs that really get you going (at least in the breast-stroke), but we don't see it as such: visually and conceptually, the arms are what is somehow characteristic of human swimming.[4]

What we are dealing with here is an instance of a more general case, in which extralinguistic factors very often enter in judgements of well-formedness', as Lakoff remarks (1971b: 330). And it is precisely those 'extralinguistic factors' that open the door for apparently ungrammatical behaviour on the part of the language users.[5]

In the next section, I will examine some of these extralinguistic factors under the general term of 'presuppositions'.

2.6   A PROBLEM IN SEMANTICS: PRESUPPOSITIONS

Another case in point is that of *presuppositions*. These can be defined as assumptions underlying a statement, which remain in force even though the statement itself is denied. As an example, consider the sentence:

John managed to sell his shares before the market crashed

compared to

John didn't manage to sell his shares before the market crashed.

In both cases, it remains true that John (seriously) tried to sell his shares. This is the case, even though the sentences have opposite meanings: in the first, he was successful, and sold his shares, in the second, he was not, and had to take a financial beating. It is said that the presupposition of both sentences – John tried to sell his shares – is true, irrespective of the truth value of the sentences above: in other words, it doesn't matter whether it is true or false that John sold his shares. The presupposition that John tried survives the negation in this case.

Many linguists believe that these, along with other properties of presuppositions, are inherent in the semantics of the lexical items in question. According to Karttunen (1971), a verb such as *to manage* implies (conventionally) 'trying (seriously)' (on conventional implicatures, see section 5.2.4 below). However, a purely logical or semantic account, based solely on the truth or falsity of sentences uttered in isolation, cannot possibly be the whole story. True, in many cases we are dealing with a presupposition that is inextricably (logically or conventionally) tied to the isolated lexical item in question: when the checker in the supermarket tells you to 'Hurry back [to the store]', the use of the word 'back' logically presupposes that at the time of returning to the store, you've been there before: otherwise you couldn't 'hurry back.'

However, most cases are not such clear-cut instances of semantic or logical presupposition ('entailment', as is the technical term for the latter), and therefore, in the case that we're dealing with, and in the particular context in which this utterance happens, we must appeal to a pragmatic account of presupposition. To see this, consider the following utterances (from Levinson 1983: 201):

John regrets that he failed the exam

John doesn't regret that he failed the exam.

Both sentences rest on the presupposition that John has failed his exam – and that there *in fact* has been an exam (which is why *to regret* is called a 'factive' verb, viz., one that entails (presupposes) its complement; see Gazdar 1979: 119, Levinson 1983: 188; the original reference is to Kiparsky and Kiparsky's 1971 seminal article).

But consider now:

John doesn't regret having failed, because in fact he passed. (Levinson 1983: 201)

In this case, we should have a logical contradiction, because the second half of the above sentence ('because in fact he passed') presupposes, in fact logically reduces to, 'John passed', whereas the first part, as we have just seen, presupposes that he failed. The facts clash: there are conflicting truth values involved in this conjunction of sentences.

The reason that a conjoined sentence such as the above does not strike us as illogical or inconsistent, however, is that we can easily conjure up a situation where a person would say exactly that. Imagine, e.g., that the sentence is said in a triumphant tone of voice, indicating that the utterer feels that he has trapped his or her interlocutor into believing that John had failed the exam. The latter may have said something to the effect that s/he is sure that John regrets his having failed, whereupon the former speaker utters the sentence in question. Moreover, in a case like this (as Talbot has pointed out; 1987: 183), the presupposition implied in the 'regretting' (viz., that there was an exam that John failed) is the one speaker's only: the other knows that John has passed, and thus doesn't even have to 'undo' (or 'cancel') that presupposition.

In other words, the presupposition here rests entirely on the context: it is pragmatic, rather than semantic, and 'its only plausible use [is] in interaction' (Talbot 1987: 183). This is the rule, rather than the exception.[6] Furthermore, since any interaction presupposes the presence of some interactants, that is, of persons who engage in (linguistic) interaction, the stage is set for examining the role that the user plays in scenarios such as the ones we've been looking at so far.

2.7 A World of Users

One of the factors that have been instrumental in shaping modern pragmatics is the renewed interest in the users of language, as compared to language as a system, language in the abstract.

But where does this interest come from? How can we explain it, and what does it mean? It certainly won't do just to register the fact that pragmatics is now a fully accepted part of linguistics (as compared to earlier); our query must go deeper.

Levinson (1983: 35ff.) notes several 'convergent reasons' for this phenomenon. First of all, there are the historical reasons: mainly, the earlier mentioned discontent with Chomsky's aseptic and abstract model of a grammar. But along with (and perhaps above) this, there are other, internal-linguistic reasons, such as the many unexplained (and indeed unexplainable) phenomena having to do with the existence of language in the real world, a world of real users.

This 'world of users' has come to play the same role in pragmatics as the concept of 'context' has done in more traditional linguistics (even though it perhaps seldom was recognized as such), namely, that of an *existential* condition. That is, the world of users is, for pragmatics, the very condition of its existence.

Consider once more the example sentence given above in section 2.4:

Getting married and having a child is better than having a child and getting married.

Our understanding of this utterance depends crucially on the actual circumstances in which its utterers live, in particular with regard to matters and manners of child-begetting and -rearing and to the general conditions of their (married) lives. These circumstances cannot be predicted from the language viewed as a logical (sub)-system, but can only be discovered by looking at the total human *context of use*.

Thus (borrowing Gazdar's *bon mot*; 1979: 115), I would presume that it indeed makes a lot of difference if we discover a copy of the Papal encyclical *Humanae Vitae* lying on the utterer's night-table, when we are in the process of judging the above statements; they could then be attributed either to complete ignorance of the facts of life, or to age-old wisdom: it all depends on the utterer's context of culture and life.

The role of the context has been most forcefully advocated in non-traditional linguistics, such as the kind of studies we normally associate with names like Malinowski, Firth and the different schools of anthro-pologically- and sociologically-inspired language studies (Goffman, Fishman, Halliday, Hymes, to name just a few). Here, pragmatics is more than merely an extension of linguistics on its own terms – the linguist's waste-basket. The context is not just a widening of the sentential perspec-tive: it is the total social setting in which the speech event takes place, as Bilmes has perspicuously remarked (1986: 127). In his words, 'the mean-ing of an utterance is determined in large part by how it responds and how it is responded to, by its place in an interactional sequence', namely, a context of use.

Even within traditional linguistics, the role of the context as an explanatory device has been made more explicit (one might say: 'contextualized') by pragmatics as a *user context*, that is, a context in which the users are the paramount features of interest, inasmuch as they are the *primi motores* of the entire linguistic enterprise, both in its theoretical (grammar-oriented) and its practical (usage-bound) aspect.

Here, one encounters notions such as the 'register' (allowing us to determine whether an utterance is to be considered formal or relaxed, whether or not it connotes social prestige, and so on); the modal aspects of the utterance (having to do with speakers' and hearers' attitudes towards what is said); questions of rhetoric (e.g. 'how to get one's point across') and similar issues that have been almost totally neglected by linguistics (as they have been, until recently, by mainstream philosophy ever since the demise of the Sophists); and so on and so forth.

Now, if we confront this world of users and usage with the world of *rules* so characteristic of traditional linguistics, we cannot but marvel at the gap between the two, as well as at the bizarre fact that the practi-tioners of traditional linguistics seemingly did not care too much about this situation. This holds both for the purely syntactic rules (see the case of *who* vs. *which*, discussed above) and for phenomena of more content-oriented nature: semantic rules, as discussed above in connection with presuppositions; speech acts (to be discussed in Part II of this book); as well as a number of other phenomena that may be subsumed under the general notion of 'human context', the chief extralinguistic factor in language use. In what follows, I will try to define this human context as part of the proper object of pragmatics (see section 3.3).

EXERCISES AND REVIEW QUESTIONS

1. The following is a (Spanish) conversation by electronic mail, in which the sender asks the receiver 'How are you?', but immediately continues with 'I'm OK', without waiting for the other's reply.

> [Alma to Robin:] ¿Hola Robin que tal? Yo bien, aunque con el sindrome de la computadora.
> ('Hi Robin, how are you? I'm OK, except for my computer syndrome')
> (e-mail from Alma Bolón to Robin Cheesman, 9 May, 1991)

Syntactically, neither of the above Spanish expressions ¿que tal? and yo bien strictly speaking contains a verb ('to be'). Still, what Alma is saying is clearly the same as Yo estoy bien, literally: 'I am well'; however, she says it without using the verb 'to be' (Span. estar).

To understand the second half of Alma's reply, literally: 'even though with the syndrome of the computer', it is necessary that we understand the first half to be of the form 'I am', because only in that way can we 'extrapolate' the verb into the construction 'with the syndrome...' where it is needed to make sense (a process called 'gapping' in syntactic theory).

Questions:

Explain this syntactic irregularity along the pragmatic lines of the 'duck'–'penguin' case in section 2.5.

Explain the apparent lack of a proper 'reply' to Alma's 'question'. Can you give English examples of the same?

Name some of the pragmatic conditions that govern this type of 'inter-change' (hint: consider the context).

2. Above, I have criticized the idea that language has to obey the laws of logic. Do you agree?

If you do, then what to make of the following cases? The first is an anecdote told about the famous inventor Thomas Alva Edison:

> After Edison had tried, for the longest time, to construct a dry cell battery that would generate as much current as the unwieldy wet cell ones, somebody asked him if he wasn't discouraged by the fact that he had had no results. To which Edison is said to have replied:
>
> 'No results? I now know of 963 things that don't work!'

Similarly, doubts occur to Alice, when she is told by the White Queen to try and believe that she, the Queen, is

> 'just one hundred and one, five months and one day'.
> 'I ca'n't believe *that*!' said Alice.
> 'Ca'n't you?' the Queen said in a pitying tone. 'Try again . . .'
> Alice laughed. 'There's no use trying,' she said: 'one ca'n't believe impossible things.'
> 'I daresay you haven't had much practice,' said the Queen. 'When I was your age, I always did it for half-an-hour a day. Why, sometimes I've believed as many as six impossible things before breakfast.' (Lewis Carroll, *Through the Looking-Glass*, in *More Annotated Alice*, ed. Martin Gardner, New York: Random House, 1990, p. 237)

Finally, what do you say about the following, uttered by a mother cooking spaghetti for her family, who are impatiently waiting for their dinner:

They are done whether they are or not (Rundquist 1992: 443)?

'Logically' speaking, this makes no sense: spaghetti are done when they are done, but not when they are not. In this sense, the utterance carries no 'information'. So what is the point of saying this? What sense does it make, and why?

3. On 4 October, 1992, an El Al cargo plane lost control and plummeted into an apartment complex in the Southwestern part of the city of Amsterdam, The Netherlands. More than 75 apartments were razed, and an unknown number of people killed; the official estimates ran as high as 250, but were later downscaled, as fewer bodies were found than expected. The day after the crash, the mayor of Amsterdam, Ed van Thijn, was on Dutch radio, where he was asked how many people, in his estimate, had been killed in the accident. The mayor replied:

'We expect 250 persons to be killed.'

Questions:

Was this what the mayor intended to say?

Can you guess what he really wanted to say?

How would he have said it, if he had been a native speaker of English?

Now, if somebody were to reason as follows:

'killed', for all practical purposes, is the same as 'dead', so the sentence 'I expect 250 persons to be killed' means simply 'I expect 250 persons to be dead',

would you agree?

If not, how would you argue against such a view?

What kinds of arguments would you be using: syntactic, semantic, pragmatic, or perhaps all three kinds?

3

Defining Pragmatics

3.1 Preliminaries

It seems safe to say that most definitions of pragmatics somehow or other have been inspired by, and pay a certain amount of lip-service to, Charles Morris's famous (and well-worn) definition of pragmatics as 'the study of the relation of signs to interpreters' (1938: 6). Today, in a less technical, more communication-oriented terminology, one would perhaps use words such as 'message' and 'language user', rather than 'sign' and 'interpreter'. In any case, pragmatics is the science of language inasmuch as that science focuses on the language-using *human*; this distinguishes pragmatics from the classical linguistic disciplines, which first and foremost concentrate on the results of the language users' activity: the structures that the grammar (the language system) allows them to produce. Or, in a different terminology, pragmatics is interested in the process of producing language and in its producers, not just in the end-product, language.

If pragmatics, as suggested in the previous chapter, can indeed be called a new paradigm (or programme of research), this carries with it, at least implicitly, an obligation to come up with a new definition of the object of that research. In the case of pragmatics, it isn't always easy to see what such a new definition implies with regard to the boundaries between the 'old' and the 'new' interpretations of the research object, language as a human product. Just to mention a few of the major questions: How can we delimit pragmatics *vis-à-vis* syntax and semantics (not to mention phonology)?; what is the role of pragmatics in the classical so-called 'hyphenated areas' of research (psycho-, neuro-, socio-, ethno-... etc. linguistics)?; and how about in newer research areas such as mathematical and computational linguistics, text linguistics, not to forget the vast field covered by the term 'applied linguistics'?

One could imagine that the proper domain of pragmatics would be what Chomsky has called *performance*, that is to say, the way the individual user went about using his or her language in everyday life. The practice of performance would then be defined in contrast to the user's abstract *competence*, understood as his or her knowledge of the language and its rules (as e.g. described in a generative-transformational grammar).

People who accept this opposition as a valid one simply divide the study of language into two, pretty much independent, parts: one is a description of its structure (as dealt with in the classical descriptions or grammars), the other, a description of its use (to be taken care of by pragmatics).

In Katz's words: 'Grammars are theories about the structure of sentence types ... Pragmatic theories, in contrast ... explicate the reasoning of speakers and hearers ... ' (1977: 19), trying to establish a link between what is said and the semantic 'proposition' behind it.

3.2   THE IMPORTANCE OF BEING A USER

Whatever the outcome of our preliminary quest for a definition, the language user seems to be at the centre of attention in pragmatics. Thus, we can talk about the 'user's point of view' as a common orienting feature for both linguists and philosophers dealing with pragmatics.

However, this is not sufficient to define pragmatics; witness the various pragmaticians' rather varying conceptions of that user's role, as well as of what is implied by the term 'use of language'. For instance, one can consider 'language use' to be whatever happens when users are 'doing things with words'; or, following a more restrictive procedure, one can demand that pragmatics refer *explicitly* to a user, whenever language is discussed.[7]

Furthermore, from a social-scientific point of view, a theory of language as a user's interest should rest on a theory of the user. The user always being a member of a particular human society, such a theory should comprise everything that characterizes the user as a person whose use of language depends on the rules and norms that are valid at any time, in any place, in the community in which he or she is living.

The above may seem to be a rather encompassing notion of the user in society, but it is a natural extension of the notion of pragmatics as a theory of use. For Levinson, it entails a 'very broad usage of the term [pragmatics]'; Levinson also comments, somewhat regretfully, it might seem, that this usage is 'still the one generally used on the Continent' (1983: 2).

In the words of another scholar, Ralph Fasold, this 'Continental approach' 'makes any aspect whatsoever of linguistic interaction a legitimate topic for pragmatic research'; in a way, he says (and quotes Verschueren (1987: 5)), this is a return to the view of pragmatics espoused by the aforementioned Charles Morris: that 'pragmatics is about everything human in the communication process, psychological, biological, and sociological' (Fasold 1990: 176).

In contrast to these broader uses of the term 'pragmatics', we find others demanding a minimum of strictly technical-linguistic involvement, before we can begin to talk about pragmatics in the true, linguistic sense of the word.

In Levinson's words,

Pragmatics is the study of those relations between language and context that are *grammaticalized*, or encoded in the structure of a language. (1983: 9)

Even though he does not say so explicitly, Levinson seems to detect a conflict between those language–context relations that are, and those that are not, 'grammaticalized' (the process of grammaticalization being understood as the expression of pragmatic relations with the help of strictly linguistic means, such as the rules of a grammar, operating on phonological, morphological and syntactic elements). This, in turn, implies making a distinction between the 'grammatical' and the 'user' point of view on the basis of how language and context relate, whether they do this with, or without, grammar's helping hand. The important notion of context, however, and the role it plays in the expression of grammatical and pragmatic relations, is not addressed.

3.3   CONTEXT

In section 1.3, we saw an example that showed the importance of the notion of context in sorting out ambiguities in spoken or written language. We noticed that context is a dynamic, not a static concept: it is to be understood as the surroundings, in the widest sense, that enable the participants in the communication process to interact, and that make the linguistic expressions of their interaction intelligible.

The difference between a 'grammatical' and a 'user-oriented' point of view is precisely in the context: on the former view, we consider linguistic elements in isolation, as syntactic structures or parts of a grammatical paradigm, such as case, tense, etc., whereas on the latter, we pose ourselves the all-important question, how are these linguistic elements used in a concrete setting, i.e., a context?

A definition of pragmatics that limits such a setting, as well as all references to any wider, 'extralinguistic' contexts, to what is (or can be) grammatically expressed has, of course, a big advantage: it excludes a number of irrelevant factors from the scope of our investigation. For instance (to take a classic example from Chomsky 1957), the presence of food in the mouth while speaking may be part of some context, yet it is not a linguistic factor, and maybe not even a pragmatic one.

But what about the ways we usually refer to things by using proper names, pronouns, articles and so on? 'John' is only a person in the context in which he is known as 'John'; 'the policeman' is an officer we either know, or are supposed to know. 'John is the policeman' makes sense only in a context where there are policemen that I know by their first names, or whenever I assign a policeman's role to John (as when I am distributing parts in an amateur theatrical performance).

Contexts differ markedly from language to language. This is frequently seen in cases where the same instructions appear side by side in two or more languages; the differences are often remarkable, both in the choice of wording and in the length of the message. Consider the following text in English and Spanish, found on a towel dispenser in a restaurant in Cadillac, Michigan:

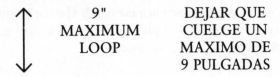

	9"	DEJAR QUE
	MAXIMUM	CUELGE UN
	LOOP	MAXIMO DE
		9 PULGADAS

(the Spanish text translates literally as: 'Allow to leave a maximum of 9 inches').

What is our first reaction to this different way of expressing the 'same' reality? One could perhaps think that the Spanish are more elegant in their ways of stating things; or that they are more verbose; or that they in general know little about modern restaurant gadgetry. The last explanation, though at first blush seemingly the expression of some feeling of racial or ethnic superiority, may contain a grain of truth, and lead us on to the explanation. The difference is in the *contexts* in which this message is encoded: US (or North American, generally), where English is used, vs. other, mainly Spanish-speaking environments.

As to the latter, one may safely surmise (without falling into the racial prejudice trap mentioned earlier) that more Spanish speakers than speakers of English will be unfamiliar with such gadgets as towel dispensers in restaurants. And that especially among the personnel who maintain washroom facilities in such places there may be a higher incidence of people who have not been exposed to the blessings of American civilization long enough to appreciate towel dispensers, toilet seat protectors and other salubrious devices found in American toilets. For such people, an explicit instruction of how to install and maintain the towel in the dispenser for proper functioning may be necessary and helpful. These people would clearly have a problem (as would perhaps some native English speakers) in deciphering the laconic language of the English instructions: having never seen a towel dispenser, or only very few, one is naturally baffled when mention is made of a 'loop' nine inches long. (Even in English, instructions on packages or wrappings for tools can be notoriously hard to follow unless one starts experimenting.) Only in the context of seeing the gadget and reading the explicit instructions, that is, placing the words in their proper contexts, does the whole thing begin to make sense.

But context is more than a matter of reference and of understanding what things are about, practically speaking. Context is also what gives our utterances their deeper ('true', but not in a philosophical sense of the word) meaning. Consider the following utterance:

It's a long time since we visited your mother.

This sentence, when uttered at the coffee-table after dinner in a married couple's living-room, has a totally different pragmatic meaning than the same sentence uttered by a husband to his wife while they are standing in front of the hippopotamus enclosure at the local zoo.[8]

The context is also of paramount importance in assigning a proper value to such phenomena as presuppositions, implicature (about which more in chapter 5), and the whole set of context-oriented features which were briefly mentioned in the previous section. I will give a few examples below that will show us why the 'strictly grammatical' definition of pragmatics must fail. First, an example of a conversational implicature, one of the most important notions in pragmatics.

By *conversational implicature* we understand, roughly speaking, the principle according to which an utterance, in a conversational setting, is always understood in accordance with what can be expected (for further discussion, see section 5.2.3). Thus, in a particular situation involving a question, an utterance that on the face of it doesn't make 'sense' can very well be an adequate answer. For instance, if a person asks me:

What time is it?

it makes perfectly good sense to answer:

The bus just went by

given a particular constellation of contextual factors, including the fact that there is only one bus a day, that it passes by our house at 7:45 each morning; and furthermore that my interlocutor is aware of this, and that he or she takes my answer in the spirit in which it was given, that is, as a relevant answer to a previous question. Notice, however, that there are no strictly 'grammaticalized' items in this interchange that could be identified as carriers of such information about the context. Hence, under the interpretation of pragmatics-as-strictly-grammatical, such relevant information about the users and their contexts is excluded from our considerations (more on this below, in section 5.2.3; see also Levinson 1983: 98).

The other example is that of *register*. By this notion, broadly speaking, we understand the ability that people possess to indicate and change their attitude towards their interlocutors, using linguistic means. Thus, e.g., we have the formal vs. the informal register, often linguistically expressed by the use of different address forms, such as French *tu* (familiar) vs. *vous* (formal), or by different verbal expressions, such as in Japanese, where the informal form of the copula 'to be', -*da*, alternates with the more formal -*desu* and the highly formal *gozaimasu*. Sometimes these alternations happen in similar, yet subtly different contexts. Thus, during the years that the Japanese National Railways operated the city loop (Yamanote) and other elevated lines in Tokyo, the engineers would routinely announce the upcoming station using -*desu*, whereas their colleagues on the private railways were under orders only to use the highly polite *gozaimasu*. (With privatization in effect for almost ten years now, the differences are gradually disappearing.)

Another case occurred on German television's Programme 2 (*ZDF*) on 26 March, 1992. The famous German poet and singer Wolf Biermann, whose escape to the West and subsequent 'de-naturalization' (he was deprived of his East German citizenship as a punitive measure) created quite a stir in the mid-eighties, was on a panel with his former friend and impresario Sasha Andersen, who still lived in the East, even after the Berlin Wall had come down.

In the course of the conversation, the discussion touched upon such delicate matters as Andersen's relationship with the *Stasi*, the German secret police. Biermann maintained that he had information showing that his friend had been an informer for the police, which Andersen denied. The latter also reminded Biermann of how he (Biermann) only had been able to work in the East thanks to Sasha Andersen's intercession and support; among other things, as a publisher and printer of Biermann's songs.

The most interesting feature of this conversation (apart from the topic) was that at a given point, the two friends started addressing each other by the formal *Sie* for 'you', whereas they before had used the familiar *du* (as they probably had been doing all their lives). Here, one suddenly experienced a total change of register, due to the fact that the context had changed: from a friendly one, in which one indulges in camaraderie and good-natured banter, it suddenly became a discussion on matters of (literally) life and death, where accusations and invectives were hurled across the table, much to the discomfort of whoever happened to watch the scene. There seemed to be a certain, critical point beyond which the familiar form *du* no longer could be tolerated, just as, e.g., water cannot exist as a liquid above a certain temperature. The critical context was never specified, yet both interlocutors spontaneously obeyed the unwritten rules of language use.

3.4   Towards A Definition of Pragmatics

As becomes clear from the examples quoted in the previous sections, restricting the field of pragmatics to 'purely linguistic matters' (Levinson) seems to lead to a rather unsatisfactory definition from a point of view that wants to include the whole context of human language use (even though it, of course, remains true that such a restriction strengthens the definition itself, as Levinson remarks (1983: 11)). But certainly not all extralinguistic factors can always and everywhere be safely excluded from a pragmatic evaluation. A truly pragmatic consideration has to deal with the context as a *user's* context, and cannot limit itself to the study of grammatically encoded aspects of contexts, as the 'grammaticalization requirement' seems to imply. (For more on this important notion of 'user's context', cf. section 4.3, and all of chapter 14.)

From what has been said so far, the following preliminary definition of pragmatics can be offered:

Language is the chief means by which people communicate. The use of language, for various purposes, is governed by the conditions of society, inasmuch as these conditions determine the users' access to, and control of, their communicative means.

Hence, *pragmatics is the study of the conditions of human language uses as these are determined by the context of society.*

To this definition, I will add two terminological remarks. First, I want to distinguish between a context which is primarily determined by society's institutions, and a context which is primarily created in interaction. The first I will call *societal*, the second *social*. (The conditions referred to in the above definition are properly societal, not social; needless to say that the social can only unfold itself in a societal environment.) Second, this distinction is akin to one which was introduced in sociology by the late Erwin Goffman some twenty-five years ago between 'systemic' and 'ritual' constraints, and which will be discussed at the end of the present chapter.

3.5   Pragmatics and The Rest

'To define' means to impose a boundary (cf. the Latin word *finis* 'end'; plural *fines* 'frontier'). 'Defining pragmatics' thus implies determining its frontiers with other, adjoining fields of research within (and possibly also outside of) linguistics.

Unfortunately, so far nobody has been able convincingly to postulate any such defining boundaries; nor have the definitions that have been offered given us any possibility of delimiting pragmatics clearly and neatly to everybody's satisfaction. A real 'definition' in this sense is thus just as impossible to provide as a 'grammatical' definition in the sense of the previous section.

Most authors either confine themselves to a strictly linguistically oriented definition (like the one I criticized at the end of section 2.2), or they resort to a definition that incorporates as much societal context as possible, but necessarily remains somewhat vague as regards the relation between pragmatics and the other areas of language studies, including the relative autonomy of these areas *vis-à-vis* linguistics proper.

It seems natural at this point to raise the question of why we need such clear, sharply demarcated boundaries at all, when pragmatics apparently is in a steady evolutionary flux and boundary markers, once placed, will have to be moved constantly anyway? Maybe a 'pragmatic' definition of pragmatics could be found which avoids both the Scylla and Charybdis of the above alternatives?

In the current literature, such an idea seems to have been received with some enthusiasm. The most prominent representative of this 'pragmatic eclecticism' is Geoffrey Leech, who advocates *complementarity* as his solution to the dilemma. This is what he says about the relation between pragmatics and its nearest linguistic neighbour, semantics:

> The view that semantics and pragmatics are distinct, though complementary and interrelated fields of study, is easy to appreciate subjectively, but is more difficult to justify in an objective way. It is best supported negatively, by pointing out the failures or weaknesses of alternative views. (1983: 6)

Leech distinguishes three possible ways of structuring this relationship: semanticism (pragmatics inside semantics), pragmaticism (semantics inside pragmatics) and complementarism (they both complement each other, but are otherwise independent areas of research).

As an instance of *semanticism*, one can mention the early suggestions for dealing with the 'presupposition problem' (cf. section 2.6). What the transformationalists called 'deep syntax' was in reality inspired by, and based on, semantics; presuppositions (which, after all, had a pragmatic background) were forced inside the semantico-syntactic chimera called 'semantax' in order not to disturb the unity and indivisibility of linguistics under the watchful eye of Divine Syntax.

In contrast to this, consider the way Austin dealt with this problem. For him, the only real issue at stake was the effect that our 'words' have when uttered, and the 'things' we can 'do' with them. In Leech's terminology, this means that the pragmatic aspect of language is the only really interesting one: clearly a case of *pragmaticism*.[9]

Finally, it seems plausible to assume that the main reason why Austin's work remained *terra incognita* for so many linguists for such a long time was precisely the same anxiety that radical views traditionally inspire in those who are concerned about territorial rights and privileges, and hence worry about boundaries. Obviously, being a syntactician or a semanticist, one wants to do linguistics in one's own, professionally established way; the moment other people start telling one what to do, one's territorial integrity is in danger. So, in order not to rock the boat, most traditionally-oriented linguists prefer to assign pragmatics (especially of the more radical variety, cf. our discussion above) to a quiet corner, preferably a little bit outside of linguistics 'proper'; here, pragmaticians can do their own thing, in 'complementarity and interrelation' with the rest, but still clearly distinguished from it. In this way, one can solve the delimitation problem in a complementarist fashion.

This latter alternative seems currently to be the preferred solution to the boundary problem. Levinson, discussing the relationship between semantics and pragmatics, remarks:

> From what we now know about the nature of meaning, a hybrid or modular account seems inescapable; there remains the hope that with two components, a semantics and a pragmatics working in tandem, each can be built on relatively homogeneous and systematic lines. (1983: 15)

3.6   THEORY AND PRACTICE

From a theoretical point of view, the tasks and functions of pragmatics can be characterized in different ways, depending on the view one has of linguistics as such, and of the place of pragmatics in linguistics.

Such a (more abstract) characterization will place emphasis on the function of pragmatics within linguistics, either as a 'component' (just as phonology, syntax and semantics are components of the linguistic system), or as a 'perspective'. By this, I understand something which is not an independent agency in its own right, but rather, pervades the other components and gives them a particular, pragmatic 'accent' (more on this below).

A practical characterization of the tasks and functions of pragmatics takes its point of departure in the traditional problems that linguistic research has grappled with over the years, and for whose solution one looks to pragmatics (cf. the discussions in the preceding chapter, sections 2.3 through 2.7).

Furthermore, pragmatics is often given the task of trying to solve the numerous practical problems that are inherent in the exercise of our linguistic functions. Many of these problems and problem areas have been opened up to pragmatics by 'outside agents': problems of conversation and turn-control (ethnomethodology; see section 11.2); problems of argumentation (philosophy); problems of language use in educational settings (applied linguistics); problems of interaction between humans and computers (computer software and design); and in general, all sorts of communication problems in anthropology, ethnography, psychiatry and psychology, in the public language inside and outside of social institutions, in rhetoric, the media sciences, educational sciences, and so on and so forth (see further chapter 14).

3.7 COMPONENT OR PERSPECTIVE?

Above, I broached the question of whether pragmatics should be considered a 'perspective' on linguistics and linguistic activities, rather than a component of linguistics proper.

The 'component view' of linguistics, popular ever since Chomsky's early works (1957, 1965) and maintained faithfully in all schools of generative-transformational grammar, despite all their internal differences, is essentially based on a 'modular' conception of the human mind (the different faculties are thought of as independent, but cooperating units – a conception which is quite popular among modern cognitive scientists and computer-oriented psychologists as well). In contrast, a 'perspective' on a human activity such as the use of language, and on the system underlying it, tries to emphasize certain aspects of that activity.

For instance, the pragmatic perspective on phonology will emphasize the societal aspects that are inherent in a certain phonological system, as compared to other, perhaps theoretically equivalent, but pragmatically radically different systems. As an example, think of the theoretical statements about Black English dialects of the 'inner city' being as 'good' as any other dialect of English (Labov 1966). These statements make little sense from a pragmatic perspective: the reason is that one simply cannot 'do the same things' with Black as with Standard English in any other surroundings than the inner city. In order to pursue any sort of career in 'mainstream' society, knowledge, and use, of the standard language is *de rigueur*.

The Belgian pragmatician Jef Verschueren has expressed this line of thinking in the following words:

> [We are dealing with] a radical departure from the established component view which tries to assign to pragmatics its own set of linguistic features in contradistinction with phonology, morphology, syntax and semantics. If pragmatics does not belong to the contrast set of these ... components of the study of language, neither does it belong to the contrast set of ... components such as psycholinguistics, sociolinguistics, etc. (each of which studies processes or phenomena which can be situated at various levels of linguistic structuring ... and each of which typically relates such processes or phenomena to a segment of extra-linguistic reality). (1987: 36)

What difference does it make whether we consider pragmatics to be a 'component' of linguistics, or look at it as a linguistic 'perspective'? In the component view of linguistics, each 'module' works within a properly delimited domain, with proper, well-defined objects, and with properly established, specific methods. Thus, phonetics and phonology busy themselves with speech sounds and phonemes, and leave syntactic objects such as sentences to the syntacticians; similarly, the syntactic component does not interfere in the workings of semantics except in a sideways fashion. (The components are not separated by watertight dividers, of course, as even the staunchest 'componentialists' will admit.)

In contrast, on a perspectivist view, the pragmatic aspects of the various divisions of linguistics would be emphasized. On this view, pragmatics could even be said to serve as an 'umbrella' for the modules of linguistics, its components; in the words of another modern pragmatician, the Finn Jan-Ola Östman, we should probably not be seeing pragmatics as 'belonging to the contrast set of psycholinguistics, sociolinguistics, etc., but rather as being the *umbrella* term for these and other (semi-)hyphenated areas in linguistics' (1988b: 28; my emphasis).

A natural extension of this view would be to let the 'component' and the 'perspective' conceptions exist side by side: after all, they both are metaphors, designed to expand, not to narrow our epistemological horizon. Thus, we could have a structural component (such as phonology, a part of the system of language) along with a structural perspective, i.e. a way of looking at language (in case, phonology) as a structured system. In the same vein, one could have a pragmatic component, understood as the set of whatever pragmatic functions can be assigned to language, along with a pragmatic perspective, i.e. the way these functions operate within the single units of the language system and of language use, respectively.

Summarizing this view, Östman uses an analogy:

[if] the unit of analysis in semantics [is] simply *meaning*: the meanings of words, phrases, larger constructions, prosody, and so on, . . . then by the same token, the 'unit' of analysis for pragmatics could be said to be *the functioning of language*. . . . (1988b: 28)[10]

3.8 THE FUNCTIONAL WAY

The notion of language as a functional whole is (not unlike other good ideas) by no means a recent one. As early as the mid-thirties, the German psychologist Karl Bühler elaborated his famous functional triangle of *Ausdruck*, *Appell* and *Darstellung* (roughly, 'expression' or 'manifestation', (speech) 'appeal' and 'representation') as characteristic of language (1934: 28–9);[11] and in the sixties, Roman Jakobson elaborated on this Bühlerian model by adding three more functions: code, channel and poetic quality (1960: 350ff.).

What these models of human language intend to impart is a feeling of the importance of the human user in the communicative process.

Messages are not just 'signals', relayed through abstract channels; the human expression functions as a means of social togetherness, of solidarity with, and appeal to, other users.

The result of adopting this way of looking at linguistic phenomena is vividly demonstrated by the fact that the different agendas which have been drawn up by the componentialists and the perspectivists can now be consolidated. Whereas representatives of the former line of thought are mainly interested in phenomena such as presuppositions, implicatures, deixis and so on (many of which will be discussed in detail later, in chapter 5), a typical 'perspectivist' will deal with concepts such as 'negotiability, adaptability and variability, motivations, effects, etc.' (Östman 1988b: 29). In a functional synthesis, all this can be brought together: the most important criterion for language as it is used is whether it fulfils its functions of communication and interaction, not what it sounds like, or which techniques it uses for getting its message across.

Neither can this be said to be a new idea. Already Austin and the early speech act theoreticians such as Searle realized that in speech acting, as in so many other ways of word(l)y behaviour, 'what you get is what you expect.' Asking a passer-by what time it is, a person may use a question of the type: 'Can you tell me . . .', or even 'Do you have . . .' (that is, the time). The questioner would certainly be greatly taken aback by an answer in the affirmative ('Yes'), without any further information being offered. The reason for this astonishment is that such a 'question' is really more of a 'request' than a question (cf. the 'polite imperative' of the type 'please tell . . .' or 'please give . . .' – expressions which, incidentally, are rarely found in situations like the above). Other examples, quoted endlessly in the linguistic literature, include such cases as requesting that a window be closed by remarking on the temperature in the room (type: 'It's cold in here, isn't it?'); requesting that the salt be passed by enquiring about one's neighbour's ability to do so (type: 'Can you pass me the salt?'); and so on.

Linguistic functions of use are best studied in situations where people interact normally, using language face to face. This leads us to consider such situations as the primary sources of information, when it comes to studying this functional aspect of language: among these, everyday conversation among people takes a front-row seat.

As we will see later, there are basically two ways of going about studying conversation and other basic linguistic interaction: in one, we can just study what's going on, trying to describe it as exactly as possible, and figuring out what the options are for participants to join in at any given point, and what their choices are of expressing themselves to their own and others' satisfaction. This line of approach is followed by the so-called conversation analysts (who will be discussed in greater detail in chapters 10–12).[12]

Another, more theoretical approach tries to go 'behind conversation', as it were, establishing the minimal conditions for successful interaction both on the linguistic, and also (and maybe even more importantly) on the hidden levels of societal equality or inequality among people, of prejudice and class feeling, education and culture; in short, the whole gamut of societal background information that is necessary to carry on a successful conversation, understood as 'the sustained production of chains of mutually-dependent acts, constructed by two or more agents each monitoring and building on the actions of the other' (Levinson 1983: 44).

The latter approach, needless to say, comes closer to what I have defined as pragmatics; in the present context of writing, it is the linguistic dimension of social interaction.

One could try to realize what is involved here by carrying out a thought experiment. Suppose one had to instruct two extraterrestrial beings in conversational techniques; what would one have to teach them? This problem, as Schank remarks, is astonishingly similar to that of figuring out what it would take to teach a computer to understand human language, or even to speak 'as' a human (Schank 1984: 91–2).The constraints that operate in these cases can be separated (following Goffman) into constraints belonging to the system, and constraints of a ritual nature,

> where the first label[s] the ingredients essential to sustaining any kind of systematic interweaving of actions by more than one party, and the second those ingredients that, while not essential to the maintaining of the interaction, are nevertheless typical of it – they are, if one likes, the social dimensions of interaction. (1976: 266–7)

The latter constraints are those that properly belong in the realm of 'metapragmatics', as we will see in chapter 13.

EXERCISES AND REVIEW QUESTIONS

1. One of the tasks of pragmatics is to explain how the 'same' content is expressed differently in different (cultural, religious, professional, etc.) contexts. Often, such contexts will be linguistically different, as is the case from language community to language community. The following is an example of this.

In the US, whenever an Interstate Highway starts climbing a hill, you will find that a new, 'slow' lane is added to the right of the (usually) two already existing ones. This lane is destined for trucks and other slower vehicles, to prevent them from clogging up the traffic in the faster lanes. On a sign posted well in advance of the widened pavement, you will read the following text:

SLOWER TRAFFIC KEEP RIGHT

However, in Canada the same situation is 'worded' differently:

KEEP RIGHT EXCEPT TO PASS

Can you say something about this difference in terms of 'context'?

Is there a difference in content?

Is there a pragmatic difference?

2. (Due to Alvaro G. Meseguer) During a strike among the crew personnel of the Spanish airline Iberia in 1990, the following document was presented to the travellers. Read the text, paying special attention to the first sentence. (For those not familiar with Spanish, it should be pointed out that the word *huelga* means 'strike'.)

Estimado cliente:
Debido a la huelga de nuestros Tripulantes de Cabina de Pasajeros,
Vd. recibirá a bordo un servicio distinto al habitual.
IBERIA está haciendo todo lo posible para reducir su incidencia en
nuestros clientes . . .
    Muchas gracias. Recibe un cordial saludo.

Dear Customer,
The industrial action being taken by our cabin crew means that the on-board services you receive will not be those which we normally offer our passengers.
IBERIA is doing everything possible to minimize the inconvenience to our clients. . . .
    Thank you very much. Sincerely yours,

      (sign.) Pilar Villanueva

Explanatory commentary:

As may be expected in the situation described, the above notice, by its bilingual nature, aims at an audience in which there are speakers of English as well as of Spanish. *A priori*, one would assume that the message to both classes of readers would be identical, and such is also the case, with one glaring exception: while the Spanish text uses the word *huelga*, 'strike', its English counterpart has 'industrial action'.

Questions:

Why do you think the English text avoids the use of the word 'strike' in this context?

How does 'strike' come across, compared to 'industrial action', if we assume that the point of the message is to 'fulfil the functions of communication and interaction', as I called it above?

What presuppositions can be identified in the use of 'strike' and 'industrial action', respectively?

Is there a difference of content between the two messages?

What kind of difference *do* we have?

3. Conversational implicatures often involve expectations, as in the case where I ask: 'What time is it?' – I don't expect an answer like: 'You just stepped on my toe.'

Consider the following interchanges:

(a)
A: Your name isn't really Misty Beethoven, is it?
B: You're right – it's Teresa Beethoven.

(b) (due to Bruce Fraser)
A: What's your name?
B: Betty Skymitch.
A: Spell it, please.
B: B – E – T – T – Y.

Questions:

What presuppositions are violated (cf. ch. 2)?

What kind of presuppositions are they?

What do these examples have in common?

Why are they funny?

4

Pragmatic Principles

4.1 INTRODUCTION: WHY PRINCIPLES?

Historically, there is nothing strange in the use of 'principle' as a concept in linguistics (as in many other branches of science). The term is simply part of the scientific language that linguists have been using ever since the days of the Neogrammarians. Thus, one finds the term in many standard titles of linguistics, old and new, and of widely varying content: from Hermann Paul's older work *Prinzipien der Sprachgeschichte* (1874; English translation 1891), through Louis Hjelmslev's theoretical exposition *Principes de grammaire générale* (1929) to contemporary dissertations in the Chomskyan tradition, such as Eric Reuland's *Principles of Subordination and Construal* (1979).

In contexts such as these, the word 'principle' usually connotes 'understanding' ('elements of understanding', or even 'prerequisites to understanding'), on all levels of linguistic sophistication, from the sharing of elementary knowledge to high-level, metatheoretical speculation.

Another, slightly different use of the term 'principles' is also found in the works of Hjelmslev. In what is probably his most important work, *Prolegomena to a Theory of Language*, Hjelmslev lays down three methodological ground rules for any future, sensible practice of linguistics: the principles of *simplicity, non-contradiction* and *exhaustivity* (1953: 15). These principles are simply conditions to be imposed on any scientific description of a language; as such, they are not to be confused with the rules of description themselves, as often happens in modern uses of the word (thus in Reuland 1979: 2, where 'principle' is equivalent to 'proposal for description'; or in the well-known parlance of post-Chomskyan grammatical writing, where the adjective 'principled' usually is merely a synonym for 'reasoned', or simply 'decent'). As we will see, these uses of the term 'principle' are different from what is usual in pragmatics.

4.2   PRINCIPLES AND RULES; THE COMMUNICATIVE PRINCIPLE

Another term that is frequently encountered in modern grammatical writing is that of *rule*. Even before Chomsky arrived on the scene, people knew that they had to look in the grammar to find the rules of the language; ever since Chomsky, a grammar is thought of as simply consisting of rules. The rules are the grammar, not to say: the language.

In earlier versions of transformational grammar, rules were thought of as exclusively syntactic in origin and function; it is for this reason (in order to create a contrast to, and a distance from, the transformational model of language description) that so many authors have advocated the use of the term principles, whenever it has been necessary or desirable to establish an explanatory framework on a higher level, such as that of semantics or of pragmatics (see on this Mey 1991b).

We can bring out the need for such a contrasting terminology by asking ourselves what a 'rule' (in the sense of Chomskyan grammar) possibly could do outside of the domain of syntax. Does it make sense at all to talk about a semantic or even a pragmatic rule? What would such a rule look like? What use is a semantic, or even a pragmatic rule? And what does it mean, as Leech has said (1983), that one uses rules in syntax, but principles in pragmatics?[13]

To answer this question, consider the prime property and chief power of a grammatical rule: its ability to *predict* (in connection with the other rules of the grammar) which sentences are correct, which incorrect. The syntactic rules contain all the information to establish ('generate') the entire set of correct ('well-formed') sentences of a language, and only these: as far as syntax is concerned, language is rule-generated.

But in what sense of the term could we say that the set of well-formed sentences (called 'the language' by Chomsky), is predicted by rules, where semantics or pragmatics are concerned? In semantics, the concept of well-formedness is controversial, to say the least. What a person is saying, and what this person *means* by what he or she says, is clearly an exclusive concern, not to say privilege, of that person; hence semantic rules only make sense outside of the context of actual language use (such as in a dictionary, or in fictitious examples). In the semantics of actual language use, the user 'rules the waves' (and, as the case may be, waives the rules). On the other hand, it is also true that the person who moves too far away from what is commonly accepted as 'normal' language use will have difficulties in being understood; hence the only sense that we can attribute to semantic rules is that of rules of usage, not of prediction.

The above reasoning applies *a fortiori* to pragmatics, where (as we have seen) the point of view of the user is paramount. Thus, the view, quoted above, that pragmatics has principles, syntax has rules, seems to be a good first approximation to a reasonable account of the difference between the two.

Still, there is more to the problem than a mere squabble about terminology. From the above, it should also be clear that we must look beyond terminology: the one, all-important factor in this connection is the fact that the users indulge in communicative activity when they use language; it is not too important whether or not they observe a particular syntactic (or semantic) rule. When people talk, they do this with the intention to communicate something to somebody; this, I will call the *Communicative Principle*. Even though this principle is not mentioned in the pragmatic literature (at least not under this name), it is nevertheless the foundation of all linguistic behaviour, and the minimal agreed-on premise of all investigation into the pragmatic activity of humans.

The above, of course, is not to say that users actually always communicate what they set out to, or what they think they do. However, this problem has nothing to do with the question of whether or not the users observe any rules of grammar. As Leech puts it, speakers 'often "mean more than they say"' (1983: 9), a fact which can be explained by appealing to a pragmatic principle or maxim (in this case, a conversational implicature; on which more in section 5.2.3). At other times, speakers un- or subconsciously express thoughts or feelings that they consciously would like to suppress – something which must be explained in an even wider framework, that of the psychological (and sometimes even pathological) aspects of language use.[14]

Let us consider some examples. Suppose I utter a sentence such as

Many of the delegates opposed the motion.

On a normal reading, such a sentence would convey the impression that although many delegates voted for the motion, a number of them were against, and voted accordingly. In fact, this is the interpretation that I, as the sender, want the receiver to accept. Normally, the sentence would thus not be taken to mean that all of the delegates voted against the motion, even though, strictly speaking ('many' doesn't say how many), such a reading could be consistent with the normal reading – especially if I complete my utterance by adding something like

In fact, all of them did.

The question is why anybody would say 'many' rather than 'all', if in actual fact there were no others? If I could have used the stronger expression ('all'), why didn't I?

What we're confronted with here is a pragmatic principle: speakers try to be understood correctly and avoid giving false impressions. If what I say is logically correct, and true according to some abstract semantic 'rule', but still confuses or misleads my hearer, then my utterance will not have its proper effect: I will be misunderstood.

There seems to be a general understanding that people, when they give out information, prefer to do so in the spirit of parsimoniousness. In Gazdar's terminology (1979: 56–8), we can talk about a scale of expressions, from stronger to weaker; an example is the following scale (adapted from Levinson 1983: 132):

all, most, many, some, few, none,

where the strongest 'scalar' expression occurs to the left, with strength decreasing as one moves right (though the ordering of 'some' before 'few' can be questioned from this point of view).

It seems to be the case that we, by using a weaker expression, exclude the stronger ones; that is, the use of 'many' implies that 'all' cannot be used, at least in a 'canonical' (that is, non-expanded) context.

The principle that is invoked here is a particular case of the general principle of cooperation, as originally defined by Grice (1975), and in particular of the maxim of 'quantity', by which we are supposed always to provide the suitable amount of information. In this spirit of cooperation, we will avoid giving our interlocutors either an over- or an underdose of information. When a vague expression such as 'some' or 'many' is used, we appeal to the others' understanding of ourselves as cooperative language users: we want them to (correctly) assume that we would have used a more rigorous expression (such as 'all' or 'none') if, and only if, there was indeed a need for it. (See below, section 4.4.1.)

Consider now the following. Since, in accordance with what was said above, the occurrence of 'many' implies that 'all' is out of the question, instead of the original

Many of the delegates opposed the motion

I could have uttered the sentence

Not all delegates opposed the motion.

This sentence is both more 'rigorous' and easier to verify than the original one; besides, as we have seen, it is implied in it (by conversational implicature, as the term goes); so why don't I just say this and avoid all misunderstandings?[15]

The answer to that question lies in the way language users go about their communicative business. Communication is not a matter of logic or truth, but of cooperation; not of what I say, but of what I *can* say, given the circumstances, and of what I *must* say, given my partner's expectations. Thus, in the case at hand, it is cooperative to prefer the 'vaguer' expression (e.g., 'many'), even though in theory, we could have chosen the more stringent 'not all'. To see this, consider the following situation.

The scene is a political meeting; a motion is proposed and carries by a show of hands. What is important here is that the motion carries; this is more important, under normal circumstances, than to know whether all, or exactly how many, of the delegates actually voted for the motion. In fact, as long as the secretary of the meeting has enough evidence for a majority vote, and nobody asks for a vote count, the question of unanimity is irrelevant to the motion's fate. Thus, I can safely say that 'a majority of the delegates' voted for the motion, even though in fact there *may* have been a unanimous vote. (A case in point would be where the vote was crucial in another connection, and a newspaper reporter had to rush to the nearest telephone to relay the message to his or her editorial office.)

Or, to elaborate a bit on Leech's example (1983: 9), I could be my political party's whip, and it be my responsibility to ensure that all the party members who are present toe the party line and vote to oppose the motion. Supposing now that I'm less than successful in my efforts at keeping the voters in line, I might want to de-emphasize this fact, e.g. by stating, in my report to party headquarters, that

... when the question was asked, many of our people voted against . . . .

In a situation like this, the party's executive secretary, criticizing me, might say something like

... but you didn't do your job properly: after all, not all of our people voted against, so . . . .

Logically speaking (that is, from a truth-conditional point of view), the second utterance is more rigorous than the first; further, as to the amount of information conveyed, it contains nothing new. *Pragmatically*, however, its effect in the context is strikingly different, when compared to the first utterance. The difference is in what these utterances emphasize, given the circumstances: after all, there *were* many delegates who voted against, even though not all did. Hence I may choose to counter the secretary's remark by saying

Well, but even so, many of them did oppose the motion.

What these examples show is that the pragmatic principles, unlike so many grammatical rules, operate in concrete contexts, rather than in the abstract space of linguistic speculation. The reason is (as we will see in the next section) that they are based on implicatures like the ones discussed here – not just logical or conventional, but pragmatic, or conversational.

4.3   Nature, Convention and Context

4.3.1   I: The general case

In contrast to strictly grammatical or syntactic thinking, pragmatic thinking is context-bound. No matter how natural our language facilities or how convention-bound their use, as language users we always operate in contexts. Therefore, the context looms large, and has to be taken into account whenever we formulate our thoughts about language as rules and principles.

Clearly, there is a built-in contradiction between the conventionalized and more or less rigid forms that the language puts at our disposal, and the spontaneous, individual expression of our thoughts that we all strive to realize. This is not only true of the more technical rules of the grammar (especially those governing the inflection of words and the structure of sentences), but also of what is usually discussed under the heading of 'principles' or 'maxims'.[16]

Meanings can be natural, as expressed in the old Scholastic saying *Urina est signum sanitatis* ('Urine is a sign of health'); that is, from a person's urine it is possible to conclude about the person's health; and this conclusion is immediate, natural and, in most cases, uncontroversial.

In contrast to such a natural sign as urine, language usually is not natural, but conventional: that is, normally there is no immediate, direct connection between a word and what it expresses.[17] If we had to rely on so-called 'natural signs' for our communicative purposes, our communication would be rendered extremely restricted and difficult, if not impossible.

Here, I want to return to what I said above on the topic of conventionality vs. spontaneity. The paradox of language is that what we call 'speaker meaning' is natural only inasmuch as the desire to communicate, and the need to express himself or herself, are a natural thing for every speaker. But it is not the case that we can 'read off' the meaning of an utterance in the same way, and as directly, as a physician is able to interpret the colour and other significant properties of a person's urine.

On the other hand, linguistic (or 'sentence') meaning is purely conventional, inasmuch as it is the product of the rules of the grammar, as we have seen. To operate within those rules, as well as within the communicative conventions (or 'principles') of society, is a task that language users acquire only gradually, and many of them only imperfectly. The paradox of pragmatics is, then, that language users must employ conventional, linguistic means to express what cannot be expressed directly, by means of natural signs. The invisible workings of the mind, the intentions of the speaker and hearers cannot be immediately expressed, in a 'natural' way, but must be coded in 'non-natural' carriers.

The paradox is solved by the fact that those carriers themselves (the 'media', one might say, in the proper sense of the word) are being 'conventionalized' through use. In fact, speech becomes so natural to us that we even use the adjective 'natural' to define a language that we perceive as being the opposite of truly artificial, e.g. logical or computer languages. But strictly speaking, there are no such things as natural languages; the only languages we have are the ones that have been developed as artifacts of society, among users and for users.

This leads us to an important conclusion as regards pragmatics. Since language is developed socially, its use is governed by society rather than by individual speakers. Language users do not decide, on the spur of the moment, which medium to choose in order to get their ideas or feelings across; they use the 'artificial' signs that 'natural' language provides them with, given the possibilities of their actual, historical context. The context determines both what one can say, and what one cannot say: only the pragmatics of the situation give meaning to one's words. Thus, one and the same utterance can obtain completely different, even diametrically opposed effects; well-known phenomena such as irony, sarcasm, metaphor, hyperbole and so on show us the richness and diversity of the life behind the linguistic scene, as compared to what transpires on stage through the official roles and costumes.

Here is an example of irony. If I say 'Great!' to the airline agent who has just told me that due to double booking I cannot get a seat on my plane and will have to spend the night in the airport, I am using this 'sentence meaning' in a quite novel way to express my 'speaker meaning': what I'm saying is something like 'This is the worst thing that could happen to me right now.'

However the above is not tantamount to a linguistic variant of 'anything goes.' Even if it is true that 'what the speaker means by any utterance U is not exhausted by the meaning of the linguistic form uttered' (Levinson 1983: 18), this does not mean, of course, that we cannot really or truly communicate. But how do we go about it? Levinson has this to say:

> How then is the full communicative intention to be recognized? By taking into account, not only the meaning of U, but also the precise mechanisms (like irony, or general assumptions of a certain level of implicitness) which may cause a divergence between the meaning of U and what is communicated by the utterance of U in a *particular context*. (Levinson 1983: 18; my emphasis)

In order to see this in some detail, consider the following conversation, as analysed by Levinson (1983: 48–9); here, we have some striking examples of the context's importance in understanding utterances, in this case as parts of a conversation:

(A and B are on the telephone, talking over arrangements for the next couple of days:)

A: So can you please come over here again right now.
B: Well, I have to go to Edinburgh today sir.
A: Hmm. How about this Thursday?

It takes us only a few moments to realize how many conditions, presuppositions, implicatures and other factual and contextual circumstances have to be drawn upon in this exchange in order for it to make sense. All of this cannot be accounted for by semantics or syntax, let alone by the so-called 'bare facts'. To take but a few examples: the time of the conversation ('today') must be understood as being different from 'this Thursday', but not only that: we can assume that the utterance 'this Thursday' only makes sense if uttered not on the Wednesday, or even the Tuesday preceding 'Thursday'; otherwise the speaker would probably have said 'tomorrow' or 'the day after tomorrow' (the 'preemptive tomorrow', as Levinson calls it (1983: 75)). Further, the place from which A is speaking is obviously not Edinburgh, but neither is it a place that is too far removed from either Edinburgh or the speaker's location; in addition, A seems to be in a position that allows him (cf. 'sir'!) to give orders to B; and so on. Levinson concludes that all these 'facts' are dealt with not on their 'face value', as 'bare facts', but as elements determining, and being part of, a pragmatic context:

> ['Facts'] are not, on a reasonable circumscription *—restriction* of semantic theory, part of the semantic content . . . Rather, they [and the corresponding inferences*] reflect our ability to compute out of utterances in sequence the contextual assumptions they imply: the facts about the spatial, temporal and social relationships between participants, and their requisite beliefs and intentions in undertaking certain verbal exchanges. (Levinson 1983: 49; *my note)

In other words (as we already saw above, section 3.3), context is the decisive factor in all of pragmatics. The next section will discuss this in some detail on the basis of the notion of metaphor.

4.3.2 II: The case of metaphor

Recently, a renewed interest in metaphors has stressed their importance as instruments of cognition. Metaphors have been assigned a central role

mental action or process of acquiring knowledge & understanding through thought experience + the senses.

in our perceptual and cognitive processes; in fact, 'we live by metaphors,' as the title of an influential study on the subject suggests (Lakoff and Johnson 1980).

Discussions on the aptness and necessity of metaphorical awareness usually concentrate on the problem of content: What does a particular metaphor express, and how? There is, however, another question that needs to be asked: How felicitous is a particular metaphor in a particular context (e.g. solving a problem, obtaining consensus, elucidating difficult subject matter, and so on)?

While metaphors are necessary for us to survive in the world we live in (as repositories of our past experiences and for guidance in dealing with new ones), it is also the case that precisely the use of one's metaphoric resources can be a hindrance to understanding other people, both actively (because I cannot grasp the other's metaphors) and passively (because the other party is unable to follow my metaphorical usage). Both dangers reflect a common origin: namely, the fact that metaphors represent certain ways of thinking that are rooted in a common social practice. As such, metaphors are conceptual means of dealing with the world which have become accepted within a given linguistic and cultural community.

Thus, metaphors are a way of life. No wonder, then, that different ways of life engender different metaphors, and that all understanding in life depends on, and even crucially presupposes, an understanding of metaphors.

Recently, researchers in various fields have stressed this importance of metaphors as a means of dealing with our world; as the key to our universe. In a thoughtful article on 'incommensurable concepts' and their comprehension through metaphor, Judge (1988) draws our attention to the multifarious uses of metaphor in different cultures and to the ways that such 'congealed forms' of thinking are relevant to mutual understanding. Judge speaks of a 'metaphoric revolution', by which he means a new openness to the diversity of beliefs and belief systems prevalent among the world's peoples and communities.

Such an openness is necessary to avoid the danger that lurks in the metaphorical background: to wit, a kind of conceptual or linguistic imperialism that downgrades all those who don't think and talk in the same way that we do (on this, see Phillipson 1991). Or worse still: we reject other ways of making metaphors as invalid, while we emphasize the correctness of our own. Metaphors are always charged with pragmatic explosives; they are 'loaded weapons', to use Bolinger's (1980) apt expression – itself a metaphor.

I will demonstrate the necessity of such a critical attitude by examining the metaphor that Judge, in the above article, has selected to explain the political processes characteristic of Western and westernized democracies. And I will show that despite his professed good intentions, he falls into his own metaphorical trap. Here is Judge:

> There is a striking parallel between the rotation of crops and the succession of (governmental) policies applied in a society. The contrast is also striking because of the essentially haphazard switch between 'right' and 'left' policies. There is little explicit awareness of the need for any rotation to correct for negative consequences ('pests') encouraged by each and to replenish the resources of society ('nutrients', 'soil structure') which each policy so characteristically depletes. (1988: 38)

The basic metaphor should be clear: Policy-making is a kind of farming, and just as in 'real' farming, one has to shift between different crops in order to obtain a maximum yield of the soil. Crop rotation should not be haphazard, though, but calculated in accordance with what we know about each crop's typical features and the particular structure of each patch of soil. Just as monocultural exploitation (that is, cultivating the same crops over and over again) is the root of all evil in farming, so the unchecked domination of any policy, left or right, should be avoided. The latter is the case when 'voters are either confronted with single party systems or are frustrated by the lack of real choice between the alternatives offered' (1988: 38). So, rather than let ourselves be frustrated by the seemingly haphazard changes in policy-making that come with democracy in its western(ized) forms, even when it is at its best, we should realize that the very life of the body politic is dependent on a system of rotation by which left and right policies alternate, without any of them becoming dominant for too long a period at a time.

Despite Judge's manifest and avowed intention to steer a middle course between the extremes of political commitment, he is unable to avoid the strong cultural and historical biases that are inherent in his own metaphor. Ironically, he thus demonstrates not only that the situation he set out to describe is real, but also (albeit implicitly and unwillingly) that his explanation is incomplete and his suggested solutions are insufficient.

Assimilating a change in policies between left and right to 'essential haphazard' crop rotation (1988: 38) leaves out the *content* of the policies in question – in the frame of the metaphor, what kind of crops rotate, and how we should plan their rotation depending on what they do to the soil.

Politics, as we see it happen in the world today, is no longer a matter of simple rotation. This much is obvious. But 'left' and 'right', in politics, were never simple alternatives or points on a scale, equidistant from some postulated origin. In politics, 'left' stands for planning, 'right' for turning loose the forces of so-called 'free enterprise'. In a conservative-type economy, the market forces are supposed to exert their beneficial influence for the common good, so that the economy, free from all outside interference and completely 'deregulated', is able to find its natural balance. However, what we see today is no longer an alternation between 'left' and 'right' policies, but rather, a battle between those who are willing to sacrifice everything for profit, and those who realize that in order to safeguard the scarce resources on our planet, we have to do some planning.

However, this battle cannot possibly, as Judge seems to suggest, be envisaged as a simple case of 'crop rotation', one alternative replacing the other, to be replaced again by the first, and so on *ad infinitum*. The limited resources of our finite world do not allow any of this kind of 'infinity': which is why the crop metaphor, in addition to being inaccurate on principled grounds, represents a very concrete danger. The forces of destruction that lead us towards the annihilation of the planet, if only by the simple depletion of its natural resources, leave nothing to rotate if they are allowed to proceed on their own devices. To have a crop you can rotate, you must have a place to plant a crop – this is the aspect that Judge's metaphor neglects.

From a pragmatic point of view, the biggest risk of using a 'wrong' metaphor is not that it promotes a 'wrong' conception of important issues. Pragmatically speaking, *all* metaphors are wrong as long as they are not 'contextualized', i.e. placed within the proper situation of use, and 'revitalized' continuously with regard to their applicability or non-applicability. Only the context of the situation that we want to character-ize metaphorically can determine the usefulness of a particular metaphor. The inherent danger of metaphor is thus in its uncritical acceptance, and continued use, by its users; the only way to deal with this danger is to continually go back to metaphor's roots. The task of pragmatics is to 'deconstruct' the metaphor, to unload the 'loaded weapon' of language.

4.4 SOME PRINCIPLES DISCUSSED

4.4.1 The Cooperative Principle

Traditionally in pragmatics, one dates the invention of the 'maxims' or 'principles' back to the work of Grice (in early lectures, and later, partly still unpublished writings; cf. 1971, 1975). The principle that Grice introduces has the general name of the *Cooperative Principle* (henceforth often abbreviated: CP); it consists of four sub-principles, or 'maxims', to wit:

The maxim of *quantity*:

1 Make your contribution as informative as required;
2 Do not make your contribution more informative than required.

The maxim of *quality*:

1 Do not say what you believe to be false;
2 Do not say that for which you lack adequate evidence.

The maxim of *relation*:

Make your contribution relevant.

The maxim of *manner*:

Be perspicuous, and specifically:
1 avoid obscurity
2 avoid ambiguity
3 be brief
4 be orderly.

These four maxims, or sub-principles, can be seen as instances of one superordinate (as Grice calls it) Cooperative Principle:

Make your contribution such as is required, at the stage at which it occurs, by the accepted purpose of the talk exchange in which you are engaged. (Grice 1975: 47)

To begin with, let's consider an example that shows how the Cooperative Principle works, not in the abstract world of principles, but in real life, in actual language use. When do we use the maxims, when do we fail to use them, and why are they necessary in the first place?

The answer, broadly, to the third question is: Because otherwise communication would be very difficult, and perhaps break down altogether. The following story shows the usefulness, even the necessity, of one of the Gricean maxims, that of quantity, in everyday conversation.

4.4.2 Dostoyevski and the rubber ball: A pragmatic anecdote

When my daughter Sara was about six years old, we stayed for a couple of days at the house of some friends. These people were lovers of books, and their whole living-room was filled with them: there were bookshelves all around, all the way up to the ceiling.

While Sara was playing, somehow her little bouncing ball managed to get itself lost behind a row of books on one of the lower shelves; but since she hadn't seen it disappear, she didn't know where to look for it. Meanwhile, the owner of the books, who was reading his newspaper in an armchair nearby, had observed the ball's wayward course. So, when Sara asked him if he had seen her ball, he replied:

Why don't you look behind Volume 6 of Dostoyevski's Collected Works?

Why is such an answer a non-cooperative one?

First of all, because it violates the maxim of manner by offering information in a manner which is not 'perspicuous'. For a six-year-old girl, the name 'Dostoyevski' doesn't have any meaning; at that, this particular collection of Dostoyevski's writings happened to be in Russian, so she couldn't even have obtained the necessary information by going to the shelves and trying to read the authors' names and titles off the backs of the books.

One could also argue that the answer given sinned against the maxim of quantity by containing, at the same time, too much and too little information:

Too *much* information for one who doesn't know anything about Dostoyevski, and for whom a book still is just another material object in her world, possessing a particular shape and colour, but not much more. Thus, an answer such as 'behind one of those fat brown books in the middle of the bottom shelf' would have been more informative, although it gives less 'information', says 'less'.

Too *little* information, because what is proffered is not enough for the little girl wanting to retrieve her lost toy.

On both counts, the adult interlocutor failed to observe the principal demand set up by Grice in the CP: namely, to cooperate with your conversational partner. In this case, that would have meant to be forthcoming with one's knowledge, rather than squirrelling away and niggardly handing out small nuggets of information in a manner that may have impressed some of his adult audience, but certainly alienated the young person considerably (and her parents as well; in fact, when the owner of the Dostoyevski collection had to get up from his chair and get the ball for Sara, we all thought: 'Serves him right').[18]

4.4.3   Politeness and other virtues

A criticism that is often offered of the maxims outlined above is that they can be interpreted as a moral code of behaviour: 'How to be a good conversationalist' ('good' in both senses of the word: 'expert' and 'virtuous').[19] And it is easy to understand why: obeying the rules of any game marks you as a decent kind of person (one who doesn't cheat), and probably gives you a better chance of coming out ahead of the others.

However, the moral aspect of the matter is not what has kept philosophers and linguists busiest. The former's avowed aim (adopted by many of the latter as well) is to construct a rational philosophy of language use; '[to] describe rational means for conducting co-operative exchanges' (Levinson 1983: 103; the saying is attributed to Grice). The underlying assumption here is that of a rational language user; I will have more to say on this later on, when discussing 'metapragmatic principles' such as Economy, Efficiency, Relevance and so on (see sections 4.4.6.2 and 13.3). But certainly the language user is not supposed to be virtuous in the *moral* sense.

For the moment, let's concentrate on another principle (or rather, set of principles): *politeness*.

First, one has to know what being 'polite' means. Leech has this to say on the subject: 'Some illocutions (e.g. orders) are inherently impolite, and others (e.g. offers) are inherently polite' (1983: 83).

This view assumes politeness to be an abstract quality, residing in individual particular expressions, lexical items or morphemes, without regard for the particular circumstances that govern their use. Being 'inherently' polite implies being always polite, without regard for the contextual factors that may determine politeness in a particular situation.

There are at least two things one could argue are wrong with such a view: first, that the social position of the speakers relative to one another may indicate different politeness values for individual cases. The existence of a social hierarchy (as in institutionalized contexts such as the schools, the military, religious communities, etc.) may preempt the use of politeness altogether. Rather than claiming that an order in the military is polite whenever the command structure is right, I'd prefer to say that an order is vindicated if it conforms to the demands of the military hierarchy; commands are neither polite nor impolite. The same goes for an exchange between participants in an institutionalized situation: the priest imposing a penance after hearing one's confession is neither polite nor impolite when he issues the order '*Ter Ave*' (meaning: 'I order you to say three times the 'Hail Mary' as a penance for your sins').

Second, the politeness of the order may depend on other factors, such as the positive or negative effects on the person who is given the order. Olga Kunst-Gnamuš (1991) has shown that this 'cost-benefit scale' is decisive in assigning politeness values even to 'bald' imperatives. Her statistics show that

> . . . the evaluation of the politeness of a request expressed in the imperative form depends on the evaluation on the cost and benefit scale stemming from the required act . . . (1991: 59)

In other words, I can use a 'bald' imperative if the 'order' is beneficial to my addressee ('Have another sandwich'), as opposed to an order which imposes a hardship on the hearer ('Peel the potatoes'). As a result of this relationship, 'requests to the hearer may be expressed directly in the imperative form without being considered impolite' (1991: 60; on 'bald' imperatives, see section 4.4.4 below).

According to Leech, the point of politeness, as a principle, is to minimize the effects of impolite statements or expressions ('negative politeness') and to maximize the politeness of polite illocutions ('positive politeness'); all the time, of course, bearing in mind the intentions that accompany all conversation.[20] Here are some examples, all provided by Leech (1983: 80):

Parent: Someone's eaten the icing off the cake.
Child: It wasn't ME.
    (with rising-falling intonation on the emphasized ME)

Leech's point, in providing this example, is that this parent's particular way of insinuating a possible misdemeanour committed by the child is considered to be more polite than a direct accusation. If the parent had said something like

You have eaten the icing off the cake

to the child, rather than relying on an implicature, the child would have been insulted, especially if the accusation in fact was incorrect. Thus, the parent's utterance, while violating the maxim of quantity under the Cooperative Principle, inasmuch as it is not as informative as possible, or maybe not even relevant at all,[21] obeys the principle of politeness, and thus rescues the Cooperative Principle 'from serious trouble', as Leech remarks (I'll come back to this below).
Similarly, in the following example:

A: We'll all miss Bill and Agatha, won't we?
B: Well, we'll all miss BILL.
    (intonation pattern as in the above example),

the principle invoked by Leech is, again, politeness, and not cooperation. By not mentioning Agatha, when you don't agree about her being missed, you're being more polite than by saying outright that you won't miss her.[22] So here, too, cooperation takes a back seat to politeness: B, in not offering any comment on a part of A's utterance, knowingly and wilfully sins against the maxim of quantity, but does so for reasons of politeness.
Notice that this 'flouting' of a principle, as Grice has called it, does not

necessarily imply that B is being 'nicer' in dealing with unpopular people like Agatha: politeness and being 'nice' are not necessarily connected. Actually, one could arguably maintain that the way the speaker in the above example treats Agatha in her absence is a lot *less* nice than baldly mentioning her as a *persona non grata* would have been – if for no other reason, then because Agatha's place in the exchange (even if she'd been there) is *a priori* and summarily excluded: she is not even mentioned in B's reply. One of the functions of politeness is to create a distance between the interlocutors (or to manifest an already existing distance, as in the case of social-hierarchical placements that have to be maintained through language use). But distance in most cases reduces the amount of verbal collaboration possible. The standardized replies in the military are but one example ('Sir! Yes Sir!'): yet another case of cooperation yielding to politeness.

What Leech has in mind when he talks about the Politeness Principle is a principle that is supposed to operate on the same level as, and to collaborate with, the Cooperative Principle and its associated maxims. However, it is not at all plausible that a PP (politeness principle) is indeed able, or even needed, to 'rescue the CP' (1983: 80); at the least, such an ability is not borne out by Leech's examples, and besides, as we shall see, the CP may not even need to be rescued.

Still, the observations that Leech offers on his various maxims, such as those of 'tact', 'generosity', 'approbation', etc. (1983: 131ff.), have a certain value in themselves as descriptive devices. The same holds for the other principles (such as the 'Irony Principle') that Leech postulates. While these principles are neither theoretically nor practically on the same level as the CP, one could make a point of subsuming them under the latter principle in some form or other, once one has agreed on cooperation as the basis of conversation. This is precisely what we are going to look into in the next section.

4.4.4 Do people really cooperate? 'Losing face'

The question raised in the title of this section could be completed as follows:

... and if yes, why and to what extent?

Actually, there seem to be two ideas involved here. One is that of cooperative behaviour as a kind of rationality ('without cooperation, communication wouldn't be possible, hence we had better cooperate');[23] The other is the notion of cooperation as what is minimally necessary to explain what is actually happening among people using language (if A says such-and-such, then B is supposed to react in a specific way, or: A's saying *implies* that certain things will be assumed to be the case by B, who will then act accordingly).

The first issue is one of moral philosophy and practical politics: Can people who have conflicting interests, and sometimes in fact are at battle with one another (such as Palestinians and Israelis, Iraqis and Americans, Sunnites and Shiites, Serbs, Croats and Muslims in former Yugoslavia and so on) really be supposed to adopt cooperation as the basis for conversational, and in general, communicative behaviour?

Levinson comments on this as follows:

> Are they [the maxims of conversational behaviour] conventional rules that we learn as we learn, say, table manners? Grice suggests that the maxims are in fact not arbitrary conventions, but rather describe rational means for conducting co-operative exchanges. If this is so, we would expect them to govern aspects of non-linguistic behaviour too, and indeed they seem to do so. [A number of illustrative cases from daily life follow here, such as: When asked to pass the brake fluid, you don't pass the oil, and so on.]
>
> In each of these cases the [non-cooperative] behaviour falls short of some natural notion of full co-operation, because it violates one or another of the non-verbal analogues of the maxims of conversation. This suggests that the maxims do indeed derive from *general considerations of rationality* applying to all kinds of co-operative exchanges, and if so they ought in addition to have universal application, at least to the extent that other, culture-specific, constraints on interaction allow. Broadly, this too seems to be so. (1983: 103; my emphasis)

In the next section, I will try and establish some criteria for real cooperation (Levinson's 'full co-operation') and show that this notion is a utopian one, inasmuch as in our pragmatic thinking we cannot operate on the fiction of a 'general . . . rationality'. But before I go into that, I want to say a few words about a concept that has attracted considerable attention in recent years, especially among people studying cooperative phenomena from a practical point of view (such as the 'ethnomethod-ologists' and conversation analysts; see chapters 11 and 12), namely, the notion of *face*.

'Face' is commonly believed to be derived from a vaguely Eastern notion of politeness associated with the expression 'to lose face'. In the established interpretation of this concept (due to Brown and Levinson 1978), the notion of face has two aspects: a positive one, by which a person's status as an autonomous, independent, free agent is affirmed; and a negative one, by which a person's immunity from outside interference and undue external pressure is stressed. As a comparison, think of the analogous definitions one could give of 'freedom': positive freedom is, e.g., the freedom to express myself, to vote, to travel, to choose my own company; negative freedom is to be free from oppression, from threats to my safety, from political persecution, police harassment, importuning sales people and so forth.[24]

In cooperative acting, people try to build up their interlocutors' 'positive faces', while trying to avoid posing threats to their 'negative' ones. This is especially important in linguistic interaction, since every engagement in conversation opens up the possibility of 'losing face': I may either be 'drawn out', and say something I didn't really mean to say or didn't have the intention of sharing with my interlocutor (as often happens in 'open-microphone' interviews), or I may be subjected to bullying treatment by someone who doesn't like me, who thinks my presence is unwelcome or who wants to exploit me for his own profits.

When face is being threatened in interaction, both faces, the positive and the negative one, come under attack. A request to help someone may, for instance, constitute a threat to my positive face ('What kind of crazy person is this who thinks I'm here to help her?' – actually a variant on the old theme of 'Am I my brother's [sister's] keeper?'; Genesis 4: 9), as well as to my negative face ('I don't want to be bothered'). My interlocutor can (especially if she knows me) think of how to minimize these face-threats, either by building up my positive face ('You're actually the only person in the world who could help me') or by catering to my negative face ('I know this is an imposition, but could you please help me?')

In the first case, my partner tries to make me feel appreciated, loved, indispensable; in the second, she shows me due respect by publicly stating that she realizes she is intruding on my privacy, and that she is sorry for that.

There is, however, a third possibility, depending on how well I know the person, and how much social distance there is between me and my interlocutors. This strategy is called 'to go bald on record' (as having requested help, information or whatever, as in the example above). The circumstances may force me to use a 'bald' imperative, as when I discover there is a bomb in the car, and I yell at my passengers: 'Get out of here, quick!' In a family situation, bald imperatives are frequent ('Pass the salt'); as noted earlier, when the request is to the addressee's benefit, we are more likely to go bald on record: 'Have a good morning', 'help yourself to some more bourbon' and so on.

Expressions that take the edge off face-threats are often called 'mitigation devices' (see, e.g., Fraser 1980); here, one also could include the techniques that we will study later on, when we talk about 'indirect speech acts' (chapter 7), 'pre-sequences' (section 11.5.1) and 'pragmatic acts' (section 12.7). In this connection, one such technique in particular deserves to be mentioned: the 'forgettable' request (named by me, after a frequent 'opting-out' expression: 'Forget it').

If somebody asks me for a favour without really making a formal request, for example, by 'dropping a hint' ('Gee, that ice-cream looks really good' – implying: 'Can I have a taste?'), the 'request' is made 'off record', as Brown and Levinson (1978) call it; hence I, the addressee, do not have to go 'on record', either, as acknowledging it and reacting to it. An appropriate off-record reply (amounting to a more or less polite refusal) would be: 'Yes, aren't they clever, those Swenson people?' ('Swenson' being the name of the ice-cream makers). Since my face was never officially threatened by this request, I don't have to deal with any implicit 'threat' to my face: the reply is just as much 'off record' as the request.

Alternatively, I could react by saying: 'Yes, why don't you get yourself one, too?' Here, the implicit request is more explicitly denied, and I show that I have detected the real reason for the other's remark. In this case, too, the hint is apparently lost on me – but not as completely as in the first case, though a lesser threat to my interlocutor's face is posed than if I were to go on record with an abrasive rejection ('Get lost,' 'Don't waste your time,' 'Leave me alone,' or 'This Bud is NOT for you').

In all these cases, what we're dealing with are different ways of preserving politeness while conserving one's integrity as an interlocutor and trying to be considerate of one's partner's face – all in one fell sweep.

Cooperation is a complex behaviour, and politeness could be defined as a strategy for cooperation with least cost and maximum benefit to all interlocutors.

4.4.5 Problems with cooperation

Despite the immediate plausibility of Levinson's 'general considerations of rationality applying to all kinds of co-operative exchanges', as quoted in the previous section, there are a number of problems that he does not touch upon. In the following, I will mention three of the most important problem areas.

First, there is the problem of the 'general rationality' of cooperation between humans, which is taken as a sort of general, inviolable and indisputable maxim. As has been pointed out by many authors (see, e.g., Leech and Thomas 1988: 15 for some references), this assumption is simply too broad and sweeping. I will not go into any detailed treatment of this question here, but refer to what I have written on the subject elsewhere (Mey 1985).

Second, there is the issue of the inter-cultural differences as to what people assume to be cooperative behaviour; in this respect, cultures can be very different, with disastrous consequences for the naive, would-be cooperative conversationalist.

Some linguists (e.g. Gazdar 1979: 54–5) have taken this to imply that cooperation, in the exclusive sense of the Gricean principles 'Be brief', 'Be perspicuous', etc., doesn't exist as such, but is always defined relative to a particular culture; as evidence, he adduces the case of the Malagasy (as studied by Keenan 1976), whose form of cooperation seems to consist in making their contribution as opaque, convoluted and non-perspicuous as possible. Gazdar takes this to mean that what for outsiders must appear to be a flagrant violation of the CP, in fact is a normal, or even highly-valued way of exercising the virtues of conversational cooperation in this particular culture. Yet, others (e.g. Green 1989: 96) have queried the presuppositions underlying this discussion, remarking that the proposed obscurity ('withholding of information') is highly context-determined: 'information [which] does not threaten the speaker's position in the community [or violates a taboo, as Green also mentions] . . . is not with-held.' Green concludes that Malagasy speakers abide by the CP, even if they sometimes have to let the maxim of quantity play second fiddle to that of quality.

The third issue is rather different from the first two, even though it has a superficial similarity with them. When one considers what happens in language use, one cannot help noticing that certain forms of behaviour are preferred (and hence rewarded), while others are subject to sanction. Practical cooperation clearly belongs in the former category, as in Levinson's example (1983: 103): we don't pass somebody the brake fluid if oil is what he was asking for; cf. also what the Bible says: 'Or what man of you, if his son asks him for bread, will give him a stone?' (Matthew 7: 9).

What happens, first of all, is that one encounters certain regularities in understanding that are not always directly dependent on, or deducible from, the semantic content of the utterances in question, and sometimes even contradict that 'official' content (as in American Black English 'he baaad, man').[25] Utterances are not simply objects in the physical world, nor do they belong exclusively to the domain of logic and philosophy (like the 'judgements' of the School). Utterances are linguistic objects: that means that they imply, first of all, other linguistic objects, other utterances; utterances are not simply subsumed under the laws of physics or logic, or allocated a place in the semantic universe by means of a simple indexing ('ostensive' or referential) function. The implications of linguistic objects, including their relationships to, and effects on, the world are much more intricate than perceived by most philosophers of language and logicians, and even by many linguists.[26]

Neither – and this is important to note – are we dealing here with *moral* issues: what is at stake here is simply what happens between language users. To take one of Levinson's (1983: 103) examples: if a car-owner tells a passer-by that he is out of gas, and the passer-by replies:

Oh, there's a garage just around the corner,

this is considered, in normal conversation, to imply that the car-owner will be able to obtain gas there and that the purpose of the remark indeed had been to enquire about the possibility of obtaining gasoline somewhere nearby.

But second, and more interestingly, the whole problem of 'flouting' a maxim should be rethought in terms of what people want to obtain by their linguistic behaviour, that is to say, in the light of the pragmatic aspect of cooperation (as I have already mentioned several times; e.g. in section 4.4.2, where I discussed the case of Sara's rubber ball, and how Dostoyevski could be brought to bear on that issue).

The general concept of flouting presupposes a desired effect of the violation of a maxim; in Sara's case the effect presumably was to impress the bystanders, or – who knows? – to educate a six-year-old. As Leech and Thomas (1988: 15–16) remark, 'we can make a blatant show of breaking one of the maxims . . . in order to lead the addressee to look for a covert, implied meaning,' thus gently nudging the listener or reader to the assumption of one or more conversational implicatures.

However, this flouting can also occur in even more profound and deliberate ways, especially when the intended pragmatic effect is, so to speak, postponed for better results.

Suppose that, when telling a joke, I start out by revealing the punchline. That won't do me any good, nor will my audience appreciate my observation of the maxim of quantity ('be as informative as possible'). I'm simply being a bad joke-teller. Or consider the author who, in telling a story, puts all his cards on the table. We do get the information, and it is as complete as can be – but do we like to be treated that way? Certainly not: as readers, we want to be fooled, up to a certain point (Mey 1993b). The author who plays it sincere cannot expect to be taken seriously: good authors always have something up their sleeves, and may allow themselves even deliberate omissions, misleading statements, uninformative or disinformative remarks: all narrative tricks, that serve to create an illusion which is conducive to the development of the plot.

The late Argentine writer Julio Cortázar was a past master of this gentle art of deception; in one of his novellas, *Clone* (1985), he leads us down a garden path of musical narrative, only to reveal, at the very end, that he all the time had been playing with a double deck of cards; in other words, that he had been deliberately flouting most of Grice's maxims. What happens in the novella is a modern reenactment of an historical tragedy: the double murder of Gesualdo's wife and her lover at the hands of her husband, the crazed Prince of Venosa. Cortázar executes this reenactment by assigning his protagonists the parts of the piece of music they are performing: they are clad, as it were, in the voices of a Gesualdo madrigal – except that this crucial musicological information is withheld from us until we have finished our first reading; whereupon the author takes us through a second reading, 'if we wish', where we are given all the necessary information.

On another occasion, in an uncanny 'spider story' (*Historia con migalas*, 1985), Cortázar enacts a ingenuous cat-and-mouse game with his readers, leading them down a garden path of morphological subtlety, based on the Spanish language's uninformativeness as to the gender of non-compounded plural verb forms and predicative constructions. Only in the last two lines is it revealed that the persons we had been thinking of as a 'normal' couple are in reality two 'black widows' who devour the men they come in touch with. (An analysis of this narrative masterpiece is provided in Mey 1992b.)

Thus, we see that 'flouting the maxims' can be many things, and that in the final analysis, there is no way of prescribing or proscribing a particular violation as useful or detrimental. Here, as in all other matters of linguistic consumption, the producer is judged by the willingness of his or her clientele to buy into the violated maxims: the proof of the pudding is, as always, in the eating.

⚹ 4.4.6 Rethinking Grice: Do we need all those maxims?

The question naturally arises whether it might not be possible to simplify the various accounts of the maxims having to do with cooperation. As Green remarks (1989: 89), the maxims have various weightings in people's minds. Thus, there is a greater moral value attached to the maxim of quality than to the others: 'violating it amounts to a moral offense, whereas violating the others is at worst inconsiderate or rude'.

One may also question the necessity of having all of the maxims around: couldn't they be simplified somewhat? Green mentions her doubts about the maxim of quantity, second part ('Do not make your contribution more informative than required'), and considers the possibility of including it in the maxim's first half ('Make your contribution as informative as required'); alternatively, she suggests (with Grice) including it under the maxim of relation ('Be relevant').

Similarly, in the case of the maxim of quality, one could argue that the second half of the maxim ('Do not say that for which you lack adequate evidence') might entail the first ('Do not say what you believe to be false'): if I never say anything which I have only inadequate grounds to believe, I necessarily will never say anything which I believe to be false.

As to the maxim of relevance, this has been the subject of two major efforts at rethinking Grice. The first is due to Horn (1984); the other to Sperber and Wilson (1986). The proposals are a bit alike in that they both concentrate on relevance; they are different in that the former keeps relevance within the general framework of Gricean theory, whereas the latter makes relevance the cornerstone of a new approach to communication and cognition, aptly described as *Relevance Theory* (RT).

The two proposals are also different as to the amount of attention they have attracted. Sperber and Wilson generated a lot of interest with the publication of their book, *Relevance: Communication and Cognition*; in the aftermath of its publication, a strong (albeit still rather local) movement has arisen (some would even call it a 'school'), within which RT is discussed and used as a model for further speculation and description (see, e.g., Blakemore 1990). Horn's neo-Gricean theory, on the other hand, has remained a more isolated effort, which has never attained a similar status; yet it deserves close attention for its painstaking analysis and elegant formulation of some rather original thoughts on the subject of maxims.

I will treat the two proposals separately below.

4.4.6.1 Horn's two principles

Horn focuses on a central problem in conversational cooperation: Some utterances, on a certain reading, have a clear and unambiguous meaning, other interpretations require a special effort on the part of the listener.

Thus, for example, if I say

I cut a finger yesterday (Horn's example (1984: 15), slightly adapted here),

the normal reading is that the cut finger is mine, and it takes some stretch of imagination to read 'a finger' as one that belongs to someone else.

By contrast, some seemingly very similar utterances require an extra effort in order to be interpreted along the lines of the 'normal' reading of the utterance above, whereas no effort is required to obtain the alternative interpretation. Thus, when I say

I'm meeting a woman tonight,

the woman is not 'mine' (whatever that implies); every other interpretation is just a joke (and is frequently exploited as such).[27] Why is this so?

It won't just do to make *ad hoc* adjustments and 'local' rules (such as that in the 'finger' case, a necessary condition would specify that there needs to be more than one: 'nose', as Grice remarks, would not qualify in this connection). The problem lies deeper, and it is Horn's merit to have suggested a plausible interpretation for cases like these by appealing to conversational maxims.

Horn postulates the existence of two principles in order to explain the curious phenomenon: that two utterances which (apart from their lexical differences) are remarkably alike in structure, can still have diametrically opposed meanings. The principles are: the *Q-principle* ('Q' for 'quantity'), telling us to 'say as much as we can'; and the *R-principle* ('R' for 'relation'), which says that we should 'say no more than we must.' If I state that I cut a finger yesterday, I invoke the R-principle to establish the fact that the finger is mine (I needn't say more; if I do say more, people may think I'm a member of the *yakuza*); whereas in the case of the woman, I invoke the Q-principle to make it clear that it is not my wife or regular girlfriend I'm seeing (if it had been either of them, I wouldn't have said what I said at all).

The differences become clearer when we think of possible replies to both sentences. Normally, when somebody tells me about a mishap like the finger case, my reaction will be one of commiseration; I might utter something like

That's too bad;

and not much more can be said on the subject.

However, in the case where a friend is using the second utterance above to tell me about his (or her) date, I probably will say something along the lines of

Oh? Who is she?

the inference being that there is a lot more to tell.

In other words: in the Q-case, I have provided as much information as I can, given the circumstances; in the R-case, I let the circumstances speak, and give out no more information than needed.

In Horn's system, the Q-principle covers the Gricean maxims of quantity$_1$ (being the first half of the maxim), whereas the R-principle contains within it the second half of the quantity maxim (quantity$_2$) plus the maxims of manner and relation. (Horn leaves the maxim of quality alone, since, as he says, we need that in any case unless we want to see 'the entire conversational . . . apparatus collapse' (1984: 12).)

Horn's principles are able to explain a variety of phenomena in the realm of politeness, negation, the lexicon and so on; they stand out as a worthwhile attempt to simplify the matter of pragmatic principles, bringing them to some common denominators.

4.4.6.2   Relevance theory

According to Sperber and Wilson, pragmatics needs only one principle, that of *relevance*, which says that every utterance creates in the addressee an expectation of relevance. The underlying assumption of RT – that, in any given context, we have to assume that what people say is relevant – makes sense as a further specification of the Gricean notion of cooperation; 'the principle of relevance is much more explicit than Grice's co-operative principle and maxims' (Sperber and Wilson 1986: 161).

In another sense, Sperber and Wilson feel (as do many other of Grice's critics, including the present writer) that the CP, when taken too literally, puts too much of a strain on our linguistic interaction. By contrast, the Principle of Relevance does not make claims about 'common purposes or set of purposes' (Grice 1975: 45, as quoted by Sperber and Wilson 1986); for relevance theory, achieving successful communication is a sufficient aim in conversation or other verbal interaction.

A 'successful communication' is here to be taken in the sense that I am recognized by my partners as one who has something to say that matters, something that is relevant. The successful communicator is one who makes his or her intention to convey information, to persuade, to make believe, etc. 'manifest' to both him-/herself and his or her partners. As Sperber and Wilson remark, 'the realisation that a trustworthy communicator intends to make you believe something is an excellent reason for believing it' (1986: 163). This 'mutually manifest assumption' of an informative intention is at the core of Sperber and Wilson's thinking; furthermore, it is a central trait of human communicative behaviour, even to the point that we cannot properly say that we 'follow' the principle of relevance: 'Communicators do not "follow" the principle of relevance; and they could not violate it even if they wanted to. The principle of relevance applies without exceptions . . .' (1986: 162).

Sperber and Wilson's approach is useful in many ways, because it forces us to rethink a number of central questions in linguistics, especially in semantics and pragmatics. The purpose of communication, according to the RT, is not to 'duplicate thoughts', but to 'enlarge mutual cognitive environments' (Sperber and Wilson 1986: 193).

Thus, ambiguity in expressions, that great crux of communicative modelling, is often thought of as a purely semantic affair; for example, in programs for automatic translation of text, we have to 'disambiguate' the expressions that are 'unclear', and do contextual guesses, by a sort of bottom-to-top procedure. For Sperber and Wilson, by contrast, everything is ambiguous, as long as it is taken by itself, but nothing is strictly ambiguous in its proper, cognitive environment, if we look at it top-to-bottom, so to speak (cf. Sperber and Wilson 1986: 205).[28] Building on the presumption of relevance, we have a context in which the utterance we're hearing or reading makes sense in that it is part of our mutually recognized, common cognitive environment. We are ready for something that will make sense ('is relevant') and we build our understanding around that assumption; by contrast, we are not equally ready for something that would not belong in such a common, cognitive environment. Information belonging to our common cognitive environment we call *accessible* information. (On accessibility, see Ariel 1990; Gundel et al 1993). Take Sperber and Wilson's example (1986: 168):

George has a big cat.

Here, the most common assumption is that we are talking about an animal such as a Maine coon cat, or any other big species of the genus *Felis domestica*; in order to arrive at the interpretation 'tiger, puma or lion', we must add something to that common environment, make it more specific (e.g. by building on the contextual information that George delivers wild animals to zoos and circuses). The latter interpretation would be less relevant, because it is less accessible in 'normal' circumstances.

RT is said to be able to account for all the phenomena that earlier had been assigned to the other maxims for their explanation. Actually, this may seem rather a tall order for any theory; but as if this were not enough, Sperber and Wilson also assume their principle to be without exception, indeed, irrefutable; in the end, being relevant may either be obvious, and hence not interesting, or the notion of relevance itself becomes so encompassing as to lose its explanatory force.[29]

Another serious problem lies in the fact that RT, despite its pronounced commitment to communication, says very little about real communicative interaction, as it happens in our society. As such, RT (just as much of traditional linguistics and linguistic philosophy) does not include, let alone focus on, the social dimensions of language, as I have argued elsewhere (Mey and Talbot 1989). Furthermore, the conceptual backdrop of Sperber and Wilson's theory is the familiar current orientation towards the computer as a metaphor for human thinking processes, combined with a tendency to see human mental processes as expressions of economically rational behaviour. Much of their thinking on human cognitive activities is thus either couched in terms of economic categories, or it relies heavily on the metaphor of information-processing by computer (as, e.g., admirably shown by Hinkelman in her comment on what she styles the 'relevance computer'; 1987: 721). Even the language Sperber and Wilson use to explain their theory is regularly borrowed from monetary economics ('cost-benefit relations') or from computer science, where increased 'processing time' is said to hamper understanding and put obstacles in the way of communication (see, e.g., p. 204). Thus, as Talbot remarks,

> ... people are depicted as individuals who confront unique problems in communication. In the real world, however, people are social beings who are working within pre-existing [societally-determined] conditions. . . .
>
> In Sperber and Wilson's model, differences between people are depicted solely as differences between individuals' cognitive environments. These differences are assumed to stem from variations in physical environment and cognitive ability between people. Considerations of culture and society are notably absent in the characterisation of individuals' cognitive environments. (Talbot 1994: 3526)

It is essentially under this latter, pragmatic aspect that RT, despite its many useful insights, falls somewhat short of its promises and the expectations it initially raised. In the end, it remains disconnected from everyday communication and its problems, such as these are brought to the fore in, e.g. discourse theory (see, sections 9.5 and 10.4.5).

4.4.7 A computer story

That cooperation, as described in the previous sections, is by no means a foregone conclusion when it comes to language use can be seen, among other things, from computer experiments simulating human linguistic capabilities. One such experiment is called 'Tale-Spin' (Meehan 1981); it consists of an attempt to construct a program that will understand the elements of a story and continue to create new stories on the basis of the original one.

Tale-Spin creates characters in an animal world that are endowed with certain human abilities (such as being able to speak) and have certain other human-like properties (as in Aesop's fables). Here are Joe Bear and Irving Bird acting out a very simple scenario: finding food.

> One day Joe Bear was hungry. He asked his friend Irving Bird where some honey was. Irving told him there was a beehive in the oak tree. Joe threatened to hit Irving if he didn't tell him where some honey was. (Meehan 1981: 217)

Clearly, in this situation Joe Bear has missed the point of Irving Bird's reply. He didn't understand the 'implicature' of the answer: that what he got was indeed an answer to his question about the availability of honey.[30]

Notice that the inferences we make in telling stories or hearing them are such that we may call them *implied*: they don't have to be stated explicitly, whenever normal conversationalists are around. The trouble with the program that runs Tale-Spin was that it had not been instructed to make those implications; again, being a cooperative conversationalist is not so much a matter of morals as of knowing how and when to make the right inferences about what is implied and what is not. The following chapter will deal with this problem in some detail.

EXERCISES AND REVIEW QUESTIONS

1. How would you read the following sentence, found inside a North American (AMTRAK, USA) railway carriage? (example due to Bruce Fraser)

All of the doors won't close.

Explain your interpretation in terms of 'scalarity'.

2. Consider the following father–daughter interchange (Rundquist 1992: 433)

[*A child walks into the kitchen and takes some popcorn*]
Father: I thought you were practicing your violin.
Child: I need to get the [violin] stand.
Father: Is it under the popcorn?

Questions:

What conversational implicatures are generated in this interchange?

Are any conventional implicatures present?

Is the child's reply an answer – if so, to what?

Which maxim is violated by the father in the last reply?

3. Discuss the following metaphor (from an ad for Avondale Federal Savings, 'For Four Generations of Homeowners', on radio station WBEZ, Chicago, 23 September, 1992):

These are the building blocks from which Avondale has grown, and that will continue to guide it into the future: friendly service, a quality product, and an unrelenting commitment to safety.

4. The following interchange is from Lewis Carroll's well-known book *Alice in Wonderland*, a work much loved by children, logicians and linguists alike (among the latter is Bruce Fraser, who brought the quotation to my attention):

'Take some more tea,' the March Hare said to Alice, very earnestly.
    'I've had nothing yet,' Alice replied in an offended tone: 'so I ca'n't take more.'
    'You mean you ca'n't take *less*,' said the Hatter: 'it's very easy to take *more* than nothing.' (In *More Annotated Alice*, ed. Martin Gardner, New York: Random House, 1990, p. 89)

Discuss this passage in the light of the concept of 'scalarity', mentioned in section 4.2.

5. The following is a report on a visit by Pope John Paul II to Chile in 1987. The report is entitled: 'The Papal Puzzle'.

After appearing on the balcony with General Augusto Pinochet, the pope visited the slums of Santiago, where he embraced 19-year old Carmen Quintero, still bearing the scars of the burning she received at the hands of Chilean security forces. Her companion, 19-year old Rodríguez Rojas, died of burns in the torching.

'Holy Father,' said Carmen Quintero, 'the military did this to me.'

'I know, my child,' the pontiff replied. This assuaged the persecuted, for whom it is comfort to know that the pope is aware of their sufferings. (*Washington Post*, 2 July, 1987, p. A2)

Questions:

Would you say that the Pope's reply to Carmen makes sense?

Is it relevant?

What is the journalist's comment supposed to do?

Rundquist (1992: 448) raises the question whether 'conversational inference [and by extension, such matters as relevance, politeness, etc.] is based entirely on a cognitive foundation', or if we should recognize a 'social component' as well. Can you comment on this view, taking your point of departure in the quote above?

Why is the article called 'The Papal Puzzle'?

PART II

Micropragmatics

5

Reference and Implicature

5.1 REFERENCE AND ANAPHORA

5.1.1 Introduction: The philosophy of reference

Let's suppose I'm in a foreign country, sitting in my hotel room at night. There is a knock on the door. I don't open the door, but ask: 'Who's there?' The visitor answers: 'It's me.' Now, what do I do?

Basically, there are two possibilities. Either I recognize the visitor's voice, and then I can decide whether or not to open the door. Or I don't, and then I'm in a quandary. What can I do with a voice that refers to a 'me', when I don't know who that 'me' is? Since a 'me' always refers to an 'I', and every 'I' is a 'speaking me', the utterance 'It's me,' is always and necessarily true, and hence totally uninformative, when it comes to establishing a speaker's identity.

In more technical terms, there is no known referent for 'me' by virtue of the linguistic expression *me* itself: of the referent of a 'deictic' word such as 'me' changes with the person uttering it.[31]

We're dealing here with a problem that is basically philosophical, but which has serious consequences both for theoretical linguistics and for our use of language; hence, reference is also a pragmatic problem.

We use language to refer to persons and things, directly or indirectly. In the first case (direct reference), we have names available that will lead us to persons and things: we know who 'John' is, we understand the meaning of 'tax return', and so on. But in the second case (indirect reference), we need to have recourse to other, linguistic as well as non-linguistic, strategies in order to establish the correct reference (as, in the above example, for the person who is talking through my hotel door). For instance, I can say: 'Me who?', or 'Who's talking?', or simply repeat my first utterance ('Who's there?'), maybe in an irritated tone, or with increased volume. Depending on the answer I get, I then decide what to do. If the other person says: 'It's a friend,' I probably will want to know more, as the reference of the indefinite article (*a*) is, by definition, left undetermined. If the person says: 'It's Natasha's mother,' and Natasha happens to be the name of one of my important contacts, I probably will open the door, especially if I have the additional information available that comes from (possibly) recognizing Natasha's mother by her voice.

In extreme cases, I will need substantially more reference-establishing documentation, as when the voice outside starts the conversation by pronouncing: 'Police. Open the door!'. In such a case, I will at least try to have my interlocutor show me a piece of identification, such as a plastic card or a tag, in order for me to be quite sure of the correct reference.

As the German psychologist-philosopher of language, Karl Bühler, expressed it more than fifty years ago,

Everybody can say *I*, and whoever says it, points to another object than everybody else; one needs as many proper names as there are speakers, in order to map (in the same way as in the case of the nouns) the intersubjective ambiguity of this one word into the unambiguous reference of linguistic symbols. (1934: 103; my translation)

According to Bühler (and in the spirit of the period), such an 'unambiguous reference' is demanded of language by the logicians. In the same spirit, some of the latter in all sincerity proposed that we should abolish words with 'unclear reference' such as 'I' or 'you', because there is no way of checking whether they correspond to something 'out there'; as their reference is always shifting. (Incidentally, this is why the Russian-American linguist Roman Jakobson has suggested calling such deictic words 'shifters'; more on this in section 5.1.4.)

5.1.2 Reference and indexical expressions

Traditionally, the proper nouns (from Latin *nomen proprium*, 'a name that belongs to somebody or something') are the prime examples of linguistic expressions with 'proper' reference: names name persons, institutions and, in general, objects whose reference is clear.[32] Still, it is possible to make reference to a certain person without using the 'proper' expression; the classic examples include reference made to Sir Walter Scott, either by the expression 'Sir Walter (Scott)', or by any of his attributes, such as 'the author of *Waverley*' (Rudolf Carnap's example). Similarly, one can refer to Napoleon as either 'the victor of Jena' or 'the loser of Waterloo' (Edmund Husserl's example).

A regular noun, however, despite its etymological affinity with the word for 'name', includes a certain indefiniteness in its naming: *cow* refers to any representative of the *genus bovinum*, and doesn't tell us anything about what a particular cow is called, what it might look like, where it might be in the pen, how many gallons of milk it yields per year, and so on and so forth. What we are missing here is something indicating what to look for, and where: an indexical expression, in short.

Indexical expressions are a particular kind of referential expressions, where the reference is not just 'baldly' semantic, but includes a reference to the particular context in which the semantics is put to work. Indexical expressions are basically pragmatically determined. The following example is due to Levinson (1983: 58):

I am six feet tall.

The meaning of 'six feet tall' is given by what the individual words mean, and any competent user of English will understand them as indicating a certain height of the person uttering the words. The problem is in the 'I am': how do we understand that the asserted height is indeed that of this particular speaker? That can only be decided by looking at the context in which the words are uttered. The context is responsible for fixing the 'coordinates' of the utterance; only after establishing them can we decide whether or not the utterance makes sense.[33] Such coordinates involve precisely the indexical elements that I have mentioned here; they include pronouns (especially personal pronouns), local and temporal adverbs, verb tenses and so on. In the next section we will see how these elements operate in a pragmatic context.

5.1.3 The pragmatic functions of indexicals

When we talk about the linguistic means of expressing an indexical relationship, we usually refer to the so-called deictic elements of the language. As we have seen, the function of such 'indexing' expressions (we can think of them as 'pointers') is to tell us where to look for a reference.[34]

In the linguistic and philosophic traditions, one usually mentions the categories of person, place and time in this connection. The philosophy behind this tripartition is that all 'indexing' or 'pointing' is done by living human beings, and that therefore all pointing expressions have to be related to the person who has uttered them, 'pointing' in a particular place and at a particular time.

Karl Bühler, whom I have mentioned earlier, has codified these relationships in the term 'index field' (German *Zeigfeld*; Bühler 1934: 149), which is centred around an 'origin' (i.e., the point of intersection of the main coordinates of a system). This origin, or base point, is what gives any speaker utterance its proper pragmatic meaning in a referential context of person, place and time: *who* is the 'I' that is speaking, *where* does he or she speak from, and *when*, at what point of time?

A word of caution is appropriate here: it seems natural to assume (as I have done at the beginning of this chapter, where I called the 'I' a 'speaking me') that speaker and 'I' are identical. This 'egocentrical organization' of deixis, as Levinson has called it (1983: 63) is not always and necessarily the case, even though it may be, at least in our culture, the 'default', the unmarked alternative. But one can imagine other possibilities.

Honorific expressions in many Far Eastern (and other) languages (such as Classical Chinese, Japanese, Korean, Javanese, etc.) provide some good examples.[35] Here, the 'centre point' for determining the honorific use of a particular expression is not necessarily and always located in the *speaker's* 'origin'. Speakers may downgrade themselves by using less honorific expressions about their own possessions, relationships, capacities, etc., taking their own 'origin' as the point from which these possessions, etc. are looked at and linguistically evaluated, using 'negative honorifics'. But in speaking about other persons' attributes and possessions, the origin shifts: now, it is placed in the intersection of the other person's coordinates. For instance, in Japanese I may refer to my daughter as *musume*, literally '[my] girl', whereas another person's daughter is called *o-joo-san*, literally '[your] honorable Miss daughter'; similarly, there are several sets of pronouns in the person category (I, you, etc.), all measured against the varying scales of social prestige and positive 'face', as I have called it earlier.

Some linguists have termed this change in perspective a shift in 'point of view'; the notion is important also in other contexts, e.g. narrative theory (in connection with the question of whose voice is being heard as carrying the narration, one of the major problem areas of modern fiction). Let me borrow an anecdote from Levinson (1983: 68) here to make my point clearer (the actual source is not Levinson himself, but a book of Yiddish jokes by Leo Rosten, *The Joys of Yiddish* (1968):

> A melamed [Hebrew teacher] discovering that he had left his comfortable slippers back in the house, sent a student after them with a note for his wife. The note read: 'Send me your slippers with this boy'. When the student asked why he had written 'your' slippers, the melamed answered: 'Yold! [Fool!] If I wrote "my" slippers, she would read "my" slippers and would send her slippers. What could I do with her slippers? So I wrote "your" slippers, she'll read "your" slippers and send me mine.'

This story illustrates, among other things, the importance of having the *right* point of view (as discussed above); furthermore, it shows how one can anticipate the way other people will construe the world in terms of *their* point of view.

Normally, when there is any doubt, we will add something to clarify the situation: for instance, when I say: 'To the left!', I can either specify it as 'To *your* left!', or leave the point of view implicit in the context, as happens at army training camp, when the sergeant gives orders to his recruits and shouts 'EEEYZZZ LEFT!' – which of course is understood as 'to their left', not his. Similarly, the Hebrew story's *melamed* would have been in trouble had he followed 'normal procedure': he had to use the equivalent of a military drill routine in order to get what he wanted from his wife – a true eye-opener on 'point of view', one might say.

All indexical expressions refer to certain world conditions, either subjective or objective in nature. Consider the case of 'time'. If I say: 'I saw him last week', my 'point of time', that is, 'last week', depends on the point of time I'm at now: that is, the time of my uttering 'I saw him last week.' Now, last week is, of course, the week that came before the current week, the week that is my point of time. I cannot use 'last week' for any old week that has come before some other week; it has to be the week that is 'last' from my current point of view. For a week that precedes (an)other week(s), in general, we use 'the preceding week' or 'the week before'.

The same happens with 'next', as in 'next week'. If we simply want to express the idea of 'following', we say 'the following week'; however, if this following week is indeed following the present week from the point of view where I am situated, then, and only then, can (and must) I use 'next week'.

Some languages codify these 'points of view' regarding time by giving them specific, lexicalized expressions. Japanese does this in the case of years, weeks and days; French has lexical pairs for days that follow, and precede, the current day, as well as for days that are not defined with respect to the current 'point of time': while *demain* means 'tomorrow', for 'the day after', the French use *le lendemain*. Similarly, *hier* is 'yesterday' in French, but 'the day before' is elegantly rendered by *la veille* (which is the same word, originally, as English 'vigil').

The problem is well known in connection with correspondence across the hemispheres. If I write to a colleague in Australia that I would like to teach at his university during the summer quarter, chances are that he will not know when to arrange my stay. Am I writing from my point of view (my 'summer'), or am I adopting his 'I-origin' for the time coordinates, in Bühler's terminology? And what does a colleague from New Zealand mean, who (while on a sabbatical in Europe) is telling a story that is supposed to have happened to her 'last summer'?

In such cases, the context can be made more explicit by adding some further coordinates, e.g. of place. If I say, 'last summer in Australia', there will be no ambiguity; or I can use the 'other's point of view' (as was common practice in letter-writing in Ancient Rome) in order to defer to my correspondent, by using the imperfect past tense in the closing sentence of my letter, and dating my letter with a *Scribebam* (literally: 'I was writing'): *Romae Idibus Martiis* 'Rome, March 13'. (For these and similar problems of 'point of view', see Mey 1993c.)

Similarly, speakers can use their 'own' past tense for present happenings, if such a happening is seen as the result of a past process, from their point of view. In Japan, on finding the house-key that you had been looking for frantically for the past half hour, you would exclaim: *Arimashita!* (literally: ['There it] was', not 'There it is', as one does in English); similarly, when something good has happened, especially in cases where a bad thing had been expected, one says *yokatta* (literally: '[it] was good'), rather than (as in English) 'That's splendid.' Danish has a similar usage: *Dér var det* (literally: 'There it was', much like the

Japanese *Arimashita!*); *Det var godt* (literally 'That was good', in the sense of 'Good for you' (or 'Good for him/her').

5.1.4 From deixis to anaphora

The cases discussed at the end of the previous section point up the need of referring to the context in order to establish the proper reference for deictic terms such as 'next' or 'last'.

The same happens with other deictic expressions: their referent cannot be identified unless we have a certain minimal context (up to, and including, sometimes extending beyond, the current point of view). If I say:

I need a box this big,

the reference is to a certain movement of the hands and arms indicating the desired size of the box; usually, this presupposes that one can see the speaker and identify his or her movements.

But what about

I met this girl the other day;

do we really wish to 'index' this particular person, or are we using 'this' simply as referring to 'a certain young female' whose identity needs no further introduction? (Either because her identity is of no interest to the story, or because it is already sufficiently established in other ways – the case of so-called 'reminder-that' (Gundel et al. 1993: 302), as in '... the Tri-State very slow, there is that overturned car at Touhy ...' (Shadow Traffic Report on radio station WBEZ, Chicago, November 1992), or in 'Gimme that old time religion').

The demonstrative pronouns of Latin exhibit a similar character. On the one hand, they serve to indicate the dimensions and distances of speaker space; on the other, they indicate speaker evaluations. The following Biblical example shows how (I quote the Latin, Vulgate text):

Tu es ille vir 'Thou art that [very] man.' (2 Samuel 12: 7)

These are the words spoken by Nathan the prophet, after he had told King David the fable about the rich, greedy landowner who virtually had stolen his poor neighbour's only possession, the ewe lamb that was 'unto him like a daughter', ate from his plate and 'lay in his bosom' (2 Samuel

12: 3). Here, we have a very strong deictic reference,[36] both of pointing and truly 'in-d[e]icting': '*You* are precisely the man I was talking about: *you* stole your neighbour's wife.' (David had in fact 'stolen' Bathsheba, Uriah the Hittite's wife, having placed him in a combat zone where there was not much hope of survival, and marrying her upon the general's death in action.) Compare this strong, deictic use with that of 'this' in the earlier example, 'I met this girl the other day', or of *ille* in the title of A. A. Milne's well-known children's book: *Nalle Ille Pu* ('Winnie the Pooh', in its Latin translation), and one notices the difference: almost no deictic indexicality, and total dependence on implicit contextual elements.

But, as we also see from the above example, a demonstrative pronoun often indicates other things than mere spatial or temporal relationships. In fact, the Latin pronoun *ille* belongs to the famous deictic triad *hic* (close to the speaker), *ille* (close to the addressee) and *iste* (away at some distance from speaker and hearer), while at the same time connoting positive or negative evaluations. Thus, *ille* connotes 'famous', 'superior', 'important' (as in the above example); *iste* 'puny', 'insignificant', etc., as in *iste sicarius* ('that two-bit thug'; Cicero, *In Catilinam* I). In the course of time, however, such demonstratives may lose their deictic power altogether, as in the case of *ille*, which survives in the Romance languages as the definite article (e.g. French *le*). What is left of deixis in such expressions is the function of referring (sentence- or discourse-internally) to earlier mentions of the noun that is preceded by the definite article in question. This referring is often called *anaphora*.

The case of the article is perhaps not the most characteristic instance of such an anaphoric use of language. For more typical instances we turn to the pronouns, whose very names suggest that they 'stand in' for, refer to, something else.[37]

Pronominal referents are identified by their anaphoric relations; this well-known phenomenon is discussed in innumerable treatises on grammar, both of the scientific and of the practical kind. Here is an example:

The man was walking softly; he carried a big stick

where *the* marks a known referent ('the man' has been spoken of earlier, or is identified in other ways); *he* refers anaphorically to the immediately preceding noun.

Note that we are dealing with a kind of 'floating-point indexing': the references depend on, and sometimes change with, the presence of the referred terms. Moreover, this presence has to obey certain rules of proximity (cf. the discussions in the literature about how far away a pronoun can occur from its referent and still be perceived as anaphorical).

What is most interesting for us, however, is the pragmatic aspect of anaphorical (or pronominal) reference. The so-called 'antecedent' (i.e., that which precedes the pronoun and to which the pronoun refers) can be of different kinds, depending on the kind of text we're dealing with. The technicalities do not interest us here; suffice it to say that a pragmatic approach to anaphora tries to take into account not only what the anaphorical pronoun is referring to, strictly speaking (this can be a noun, a piece of text, even a situation) but, beyond that, what 'hidden dimensions' there are in anaphorical reference; that is: what kind of (mostly implicit) value-judgements accompany a sentence- or text-anaphoric expression?

An interesting case in this respect is the reference that holds between gender-marked articles and pronouns and their corresponding nouns. The old controversy about the 'generic masculine' has been actualized in the past decades under the influence of the feminist movement: it should no longer be acceptable to refer to female persons by the masculine gender, nor to 'mixed' sets of humans by the so-called 'generic masculine' alone. While there are quick-and-easy solutions to this problem in English (the 'generic plural', or using 'combined pronouns' such as 's/he', or the perhaps a little more awkward 'he or she'), languages such as Spanish have no options here.

In Spanish (as in the other Romance languages), every noun has its specific grammatical gender, and referential expressions must agree in gender with the anaphorized ones. If I say *los profesores* 'the teachers', then I have already made a choice (since I also could have said *las profesoras* 'the female teachers'); if I choose to spell out the gender distinctions (*los/las profesores/as*, or use the heavier technique of repetition: *los profesores y las profesoras*), then I still encounter the problem of reference in the corresponding pronouns: do I say *ellos* or *ellas*, or, again, both? The problem is a pragmatic one, and not just a matter of grammar: what is at stake is not simply correctness in observing the grammatical rules, but the ways these rules reflect the patterns of domination that are at work in society. Whereas the grammarians only tell us to avoid 'syntactic clashes' (Casares 1947), pragmatics informs us about the clashes of interest between different groups in society, and specifically about the ways in which these clashes are expressed in the language (including the syntax), and in the way the language (including the syntax) is used by its speakers.

Anaphora may not always obey the strict referential rules of grammatical theory, as in the case of the so-called 'lazy pronouns' (the expression is due to Barbara Partee (1972)) and other elements with ambiguous 'local reference', that everybody accepts and understands correctly because in a given context, they are unambiguous. Thus, in the classic examples (originally due to Lauri Karttunen (1969) and others), such as

> He's been to Italy many times but he still doesn't speak *the* language

or

> The man who gave *his paycheck* to his wife was wiser than the man who gave *it* to his mistress (Partee 1972: 434)

we understand the anaphora to cover references that aren't 'really' there. 'The' language does not refer to any language that has been mentioned previously; however, we understand it immediately as 'the language of Italy', since Italy has been mentioned. Similarly, in the other example, despite the fact that *it* grammatically refers to the paycheck the man did not give to his mistress, but to his wife, pragmatically we understand *it* to refer to the paycheck the man gave his mistress, not his wife.

As to the 'syntactic clashes' that were mentioned earlier, consider the following Spanish example:

> *la catedrático* ['the female (University) professor'].

Here, the real-world reference is to a woman (manifested by the feminine article *la*); as such, it conflicts with the masculine gender of the head noun *catedrático*. Rather than condemning this violation of the rules of syntax, as does the Spanish academician Julio Casares, who remarked that such a 'syntactic clash [would be] insupportable' (1947: 303; quoted Kjær Nissen 1990: 14), the pragmatically oriented linguist turns his or her attention to the real-world reasons for such a 'clash'. The true concern of pragmatics is not whether the rules of grammar have been observed, but whether or not the use of those rules serves to reveal the implicit conditions that govern such a use: in the above case, the existence of a linguistically underprivileged segment of the population, the 'invisible professional women', who have to borrow their titles from their male colleagues.

The observation that language operates under a set of implicit conditions and assumptions is by no means restricted to the case of reference and anaphora. In the remainder of this chapter, we will look into cases where the very existence of such implied relationships has given rise to an important, independently motivated concept in philosophy and linguistics: that of implication, and its pragmatic variant, implicature.

5.2 IMPLICATURE

5.2.1 Introduction: What is an implicature?

The word 'implicature' is derived from the verb 'to imply', as is its cognate 'implication'. Etymologically, 'to imply' means 'to fold something into something else' (from the Latin verb *plicare* 'to fold'); hence, that which is implied, is 'folded in', and has to be 'unfolded' in order to be understood. A *conversational implicature* is, therefore, something which is implied in conversation, that is, something which is left implicit in actual language use.[38] This is the reason that pragmatics is interested in this phenomenon: we seem to be dealing here with a certain type of regularity, and one that cannot be captured in a simple syntactic or semantic 'rule', but perhaps may be accounted for by 'some conversational principle' (Bilmes 1986: 27).

Of course, this is only a first approximation. To obtain a satisfactory account of the phenomenon of implicature, we must appeal to specifically pragmatic explanations, building upon specific pragmatic principles. The trouble is that the principles themselves are rather 'com-plicated', and have to be unfolded, 'ex-plicated', in order to make sense. The following is an attempt at performing this task.

5.2.2 Implications and implicatures

The use of the term 'implication', as distinguished from 'implicature', usually indicates a rather narrowly defined logical relationship between two propositions. Let these propositions be symbolized as p and q; then the logical implication is the relation 'if p, then q', or:

$$p \rightarrow q.[39]$$

If–then relationships are well known also in daily life, and can be expressed in everyday language. Suppose I have a hedge that needs cutting, and a son who might do the job, given the necessary inducements. Let the 'proposition'

you cut my hedge

be symbolized by p, and

I'll take you out to dinner

by q. Then the logical expression $p \rightarrow q$ will stand for

If you cut my hedge, I'll take you out to dinner.

Supposing that I say this to my son, he will have a rightful grudge against me if he cuts the hedge, yet I refuse to make good on what he considers to be a promise. And his grudge is not only rightful: it is also 'logical': $p \rightarrow q$, or: p 'implies' q, as one could also say. So far, so good.

But what if my son does not cut the hedge? Then, it will be OK for me not to take him out to dinner, and he will have no claim on me. However, logically speaking, I *could* still take him out to his favourite hamburger joint: from the non-truth of the first proposition (p), I cannot conclude the non-truth of the second (q). Logically, non-p does not imply non-q.[40]

As we see from the above example, a logical implication (or the lack of such an implication) does not have to correspond to what in everyday life we understand by 'implies'. In the above case, we would say that my son's not cutting the hedge 'implied' his not getting a dinner, just like his cutting 'implied' his being taken out. However, logic and everyday life do not always look at things in the same way. This is why we need another term: in addition to the logical implications, we will speak of conversational implicatures. They will be discussed in the next section.[41]

• 5.2.3 Conversational implicatures

To know what people mean, you have to interpret what they say. But interpretation is a tricky affair; misunderstandings are always possible and sometimes seem to be the rule rather than the exception. As Leech remarks, 'Interpreting an utterance is ultimately a matter of guesswork, or (to use a more dignified term) hypothesis formation' (1983: 30–1). We can show this using Leech's own example.

Suppose one of my aunts has a birthday, but I don't remember the exact date. I can ask another member of the family, e.g by uttering

When's Aunt Rose's birthday?

and the person I'm asking may answer

It's sometime in April.

'Sometime in April' means, strictly speaking, that it could be any day in April, between, and including, the 1st and the 30th. However, this is speaking 'strictly', or, if one prefers, 'logically'. In real life, such an answer means a lot more: on hearing that it's 'sometime in April', for one thing, we understand that it probably is not on the first or the last day, or even on one of the first or last days of the month. People born on April 1st usually are remembered for that particular lack of luck, and in general, when it comes to remembering birthdays, we seem to be able to do better than just an unspecified 'sometime' in a month; we would say, for instance, 'sometime in early April', 'in the middle of April' or 'at the end of April'.

All these possibilities, logically speaking, imply 'sometime in April'. But, although logically, it's OK to say 'sometime in April' even though the actual birthday is on the 1st, around the middle, or perhaps on the 30th of the month, if the speaker knows when it is, and does *not* offer this information, the answer 'sometime in April' will strike the recipient as somewhat bizarre. In everyday life, we may even accuse the speaker of bad faith or of withholding essential information: if he or she knew the exact date, why did s/he choose such a vague expression?

All other things being equal (and in particular, the speaker not being liable to allegations of ill will), the answer 'Sometime in April' will tell us, by conversational (as opposed to logical) implicature, that the only thing the speaker remembered about Auntie's birthday was the month in which it occurred, and that the speaker honestly didn't know whether it was at the beginning, the middle or the end of that month. But how do we go about constructing this additional knowledge; how does a conversational implicature come about?

Clearly, in analysing an utterance such as this, following strict semantic or logical criteria will not help. Neither will it do just to guess: the 'guesswork' that Leech talks about will have to be of a somewhat qualified nature. Besides, in everyday life we cannot philosophically deduce meanings; in this sense, all understanding implies some qualified guessing depending on the context; that is, the circumstances of this particular question, the persons involved in the situation, these persons' backgrounds, etc. And the more we know about this context, the more well-grounded our 'guesswork' is going to be.

As a matter of fact, however, people normally do qualify as guessers. Or perhaps we should say: it is their language that qualifies their guesswork, by an intricate set of mechanisms that have very little to do with logic and semantics, but are grounded in the pragmatic principles (or maxims) that were mentioned earlier, and which will be discussed in more detail in later chapters. Here, let's consider some further illustrations of the difference between logical and conversational implicatures. The following example is adapted from Leech (1983: 85).

If I want to express the fact that one of my children has had her hand in the raisin box by uttering:

Alexandra ate some of the raisins;

then my allegation clearly has a limited scope. So, if in the course of the (presumably somewhat heated) conversation that follows, I inadvertently were to say to my daughter:

But why did you have to eat all those raisins?

she will rightfully accuse me of manipulating the truth (on manipulation, see further chapter 14, especially section 14.4). There is a clear (and, on the face of it, both logical and conversational) opposition between 'some' and 'all'.

However, on a strictly logical interpretation, 'some' does not exclude 'all': there is a sense in which 'all' can be said to be a very special case of 'some' (cf. the case of the negative 'not all', discussed above in section 4.2). How, then, do we interpret the 'raisin case' in accordance with the intention of the speaker and the understanding of the hearer: that some but not all of the raisins were eaten (presumably by Alex)?

The answer is similar to that given above: there is a conversational implicature at work here that tells us that if a speaker says 'some', he or she does not mean 'all', because in that case, s/he would have said so. *Saying* 'some' conversationally implies that I do not mean 'all', because if I did mean 'all', I would have said 'all': we are dealing with a 'scalar' implicature in the sense defined by Gazdar (1979: 56); see above, section 4.2.

This does not mean that I cannot undo (or 'cancel', as it is called technically) this 'implicature' in conversation; precisely because it is implied by the context, another context can 'ex-plicate' it again. This happens whenever I abrogate the implicature by adding more context; the im-plication is then 'explicated',[42] since it is explicitly denied. Thus, I can say

Alex ate some of the biscuits,

and add, as an afterthought:

– in fact she ate *all* of them.

Here, the added context undoes, 'cancels', the first sentence's implicature: 'some' turns out to be 'all', after all!

Loosely speaking, the 'context' is the sum total of everyday language use, of what people say to each other in their daily conversation. Since, furthermore, it is this conversational context that decides whether the contradiction between the quantifiers 'all' and 'some' is a logical or a pragmatic one, the term 'conversational implicature' is well chosen. There is, however, another kind of implicature, called 'conventional'; this will be the topic of the next section.

5.2.4 Conventional implicatures

It is possible to consider everything that is not covered by strict truth-conditional logic as belonging to the phenomenon of 'implicature'; in this sense, implicature is a broad cover term, a 'pragmatic waste-basket', to use that well-known terminology.

However, not all implicatures have to be conversational, that is to say, dependent on the context of a particular language use (or 'conversation'). There are certain expressions which, taken *by themselves*, implicate[43] certain states of the world that cannot be attributed to our use of language, but rather, are manifested by such use. The examples given at

the end of section 5.1.3 may serve as examples. For instance, the word
'last', taken by itself, means 'the ultimate item in a sequence' (e.g. 'the last
page of my manuscript' – a conventional implicature); but it may also
mean 'that which came before what is present for me now, at the time of
speaking' (as in, e.g., 'last winter' – a conversational implicature).

Consider also the case of 'speaking with an accent' – be it a dialectal
('provincial'), or a more exotic, foreign one. In itself, an accent is like a
'natural sign' (cf. 'urine as a sign of health', discussed above, section
4.3.1): just as my urine shows something about my health, whether I
want it to or not, my dialect reveals where I am from, independently of
my will.[44] However, when accents are perceived as socially 'inferior'
(which is true, in general, of 'oppressed' language forms and languages;
on this, see Mey 1985: 25–6, and below, chapter 14), the problem is not
so much that such accents in themselves are considered 'inferior'; what is
a dialect in one generation may become the speech of the ruling classes in
the next, as history has demonstrated over and over again. Rather, the
problem with such deviant language forms is in what they imply: a
socially lower standing, a lack of culture and education, and in general
a lot of negative features having to do with the fact that speakers with
an accent usually do not 'belong' in the socially 'received' world of
language use.[45] Since such 'implicatures' cannot be changed by invoking
another context, they are standardized by convention, and hence called
'conventional'.

One can wonder whether conventional implicatures have anything to
do with pragmatics; some authors (including Levinson) seem to be of the
opinion that they do not, since they are, so to speak, 'automatic' and
therefore non-cancellable: once a Galilean, always a Galilean (the exception confirming the rule, Professor Higgins' Eliza, notwithstanding). Cf.:

> Conventional implicatures are non-truth-conditional inferences
> that are *not* derived from superordinate pragmatic principles like
> the maxims, but are simply attached by convention to particular
> lexical items. (Levinson 1983: 127)

For some authors, this 'attachment' takes the form of unavoidable,
even 'logical' conclusions, such as when Leech remarks that on hearing a
sentence like

Sally is the secretary,

we automatically conclude that

Sally is a secretary. (1983: 90)[46]

The notion of a 'conventional implicature' being non-cancellable, automatic and almost 'logical' is open to criticism, however. First of all, one should resist the temptation to believe that anything in linguistics, and especially in pragmatics, can be explained by 'laws' (as we have seen in the first chapter of the present work). No matter how conventional the implicatures, it is still the case that the conventions which govern their use are culture-specific, historically developed and class-related; in other words, conventional implicatures may clash with conventional uses. The well-known examples of dialect use, or of the contrast between 'polite' and 'impolite' forms of address (such as the French *vous* vs. *tu*) are only valid in certain, well-defined contexts. For instance, it is quite all right to use the 'non-polite' form (*tu*) when asking for a drink in a Québec bar, whereas no one would ever do so in France: the 'implicature' in this case is cancelled out by the culture. Neither is it possible in such a context to 'exploit' the implicature to obtain a special effect (e.g. of being impolite in a surrounding where politeness is required, or vice versa).[47]

In other contexts, a conventional implicature may be exploited. The most frequently quoted instance of this 'exploitation' is the English word *but*. Even though strictly logically speaking, the value of *but* in conjoining two phrases or sentences is the same as that of *and* (that is, the conjoined sentences with *but* have the same truth conditions as those with *and*; the one is true in exactly the same cases as the other), the conventional implicature that is exploited creates a feeling of contrast: what follows *but* is perceived as being somewhat in contrast with what precedes, whereas in the case of *and* no such implicatures are generated. Notice that there is no strict, universally valid law that would impose *but* rather than *and* in any particular context; in many cases, the two are almost interchangeable. The Bible is rich in examples of this; the Biblical 'and' functions often like a 'but', cf. Genesis 14: 21–2: 'And the king of Sodom said to Abram . . . But Abram said to the king of Sodom . . .'; 15: 2–3: 'But Abram said . . . And Abram said . . .', and so on. It is perhaps worth noticing that in Hebrew, the particle *wa* fulfills both functions, and that even in English, we may join phrases and sentences without a formal conjunctive device: constructions like the classic 'asyndeton' (the 'conjunctionless conjunct'). A well-known example is Caesar's *Veni, vidi, vici* 'I came, I saw, I vanquished'; sentences conjoined by a semicolon or colon are other instances in kind. In particular, the colon is interesting from this angle in that it occupies a place in between 'and' and 'but' – the true sense emerges only in the given context (just as in the case of Hebrew *wa*), and in many cases, the connection is kept intentionally vague by the author or speaker. As Bilmes (1986: 50) remarks, quoting the late Harvey Sacks,

> Conversational rules are not analogous to scientific laws. The laws of physics are never violated . . . [c]onversational rules are usually obeyed, and when they are broken, the breach is 'observable', 'noticeable' (Sacks).

EXERCISES AND REVIEW QUESTIONS

1. Deixis (due to Jan-Ola Östman)
The passage below contains the opening paragraphs of Bruce Chatwin's short novel *Utz* (London: Chatto and Windus, 1988).

> An hour before dawn on March 7th, 1974, Kaspar Joachim Utz died of a second and long-expected stroke, in his apartment at No. 5, Široká Street, overlooking the Old Jewish cemetery in Prague.
> Three days later, at 7.45 a.m., his friend Dr Václav Orlík was standing outside the Church of St Sigismund, awaiting the arrival of the hearse and clutching seven of the ten pink carnations he had hoped to afford at the florist's. He noted with approval the first signs of spring. In a garden across the street, jackdaws with twigs in their beaks were wheeling above the lindens, and now and then a minor avalanche would slide from the pantiled roof of a tenement.
> While Orlík waited, he was approached by a man with a curtain of grey hair that fell below the collar of his raincoat.
> 'Do you play the organ?' the man asked in a catarrhal voice.
> 'I fear not,' said Orlík.
> 'Nor do I,' the man said, and shuffled off down a side-street.

Questions:

What types of deixis are found in the above excerpt?

Make an inventory, and try to establish a preliminary classification.

(Hint: you can proceed either by looking at the *type* of deixis, or at what the deictic elements refer to in the text.)

Why is the notion of *context* so important in determining deixis?
Is the difference between co- and context of importance here? Why?

2. In January 1993, the CTA (Chicago Transit Authority) vehicles (buses and suburban trains) carried big outside ads for a device called 'The Club', a means of blocking an automobile's steering wheel, thus protecting the car from being stolen. The picture of the installed club carried the following text:

> Beware of imitations!
> ## THE CLUB!
> Anti-theft device for cars
> ## POLICE SAY:
> 'USE IT'
> OR LOSE IT

Questions:

What does the 'it' in 'Use it' refer to?

What about the 'it' in 'Lose it'?

How do we know which is which?

How is this different from that other well-known slogan:

America: Love It or Leave It,

also often seen on means of transportation?

Do you have any idea as to the original possible context of the expression 'Use it or lose it'?

3. An ad for Miller Lite Beer runs as follows:

MILLER LITE
IT'S IT AND THAT'S THAT

(*Reader*, Chicago, 28 August, 1992)

Question:

What do 'it' and 'that' refer to here?

4. A popular 1940s tune ran:

> Open the door, Richard,
> Open the door, Richard,
> [*percussion rolls to imitate knock-knock-knocking*]
> Richard, why don't you open that door?

Questions:

What does the deictic element *that* refer to here?

What do we call this kind of deixis?

6

Speech Acts

6.1 HISTORY AND INTRODUCTION

6.1.1 Why speech acts?

The impressive success of certain theoretical developments in linguistics in the sixties (mainly within the framework of transformational grammar, following Chomsky's classic works: the 1957 *Syntactic Structures* and its 1965 companion *Aspects of the Theory of Syntax*) made it difficult for other workers in linguistics and the related sciences to have their voices heard. This was in particular the case with those philosophers of language whose interests always had been directed more towards the semantic than the formal-syntactic aspects of language.[48]

Much of the semantic work done by philosophers of language during the sixties and early seventies rested upon the 'truth-functional' definitions of semantics in the Carnapian tradition and continued by philosophers such as David Lewis (e.g. 1969). Other semantically-oriented philosophers eventually joined hands with the formal syntactics tradition; Richard Montague and his school are the prime exponents of this development (called 'intensional semantics').

None of these directions of research will be dealt with here, as they are not directly relevant to pragmatics. Rather, I'll focus on what happened in another branch of philosophy, with origins in the British tradition of thinking about language, which in the course of time came be known as 'speech act theory'. Its main developers were the British philosopher John L. Austin (whose posthumous *How to Do Things with Words* (1962) had an enormous impact on linguistic philosophy, and thereby on linguistics, especially in its pragmatic variant), and the American John R. Searle, who had studied under Austin at Oxford in the fifties, and who became the main proponent and defender of the former's ideas in the United States, and subsequently world-wide.

The main problem that was raised in this fledgling pragmatic tradition was that of the limitations of a semantics based on truth conditions. If we look at language as it is actually used, we see that the examples proposed as illustrations of their theories by the philosophers working in the truth-functional tradition are mostly limited to one particular class of sentences, the so-called declaratives. In order to be true or false, a declarative sentence must contain a proposition about the world. In the case of a sentence such as

It's cold outside,

we can go outside, if we wish, and test the truth or falsity of the 'declaration'; but what if I say:

Happy Birthday?

In this case, I can talk about the truth of my feelings, or about the truth of the fact that I actually did pronounce those words, but not about the truth of the wish 'Happy Birthday', or any other wish (e.g. 'Good luck', 'Congratulations', 'Well done', and so on). The reason is that wishes are not propositions: they are 'words that do things' in the world, to paraphrase Austin. In brief, they are *speech acts*.

The present chapter explores which criteria (different from the truth-functional ones) we need for dealing with these other (and, incidentally, most frequently occurring) human utterances.[49]

6.1.2 Speech acts: Language in use

Many linguistic theories take their premises in some rather simple-minded assumptions about human language: that it is nothing but a combination of 'sound and meaning' (thus in most descriptive grammars), or that language can be defined as a set of correct sentences (thus in most generative-transformational thinking). The basic flaw in these theoreticians' conceptualizations is their disregard of language as *action*, an action which produces 'speech acts', as they have come to be called with a somewhat infelicitous but by now well-entrenched terminology (infelicitous, because 'speech' connotates the oral medium of language production – by no means the only medium in which 'speech acts' may occur).

As Searle puts it:

The unit of linguistic communication is not, as has generally been supposed, the symbol, word or sentence, or even the token [roughly: the occurrence] of the symbol, word or sentence, but rather the production or issuance of the symbol or word or sentence in the performance of the speech act. (1969: 16)

Furthermore, the speech act is not performed in the solitary philosopher's think-tank, but in actual situations of language use:

To take the token as a message is to take it as a produced or issued token . . . [S]peech acts . . . are the basic or minimal units of linguistic communication. (1969: 16)

Finally, one has to recall that this 'production' presupposes a 'producer' and a 'consumer', human agents, whose intentions are relevant and indispensable to the correct understanding and description of their utterances. Such utterances cannot be equated with the incidental, non-use-oriented constructions of most grammarians and philosophers:

When I take a noise or a mark on a piece of paper to be an instance of linguistic communication, as a message, one of the things I must assume is that the noise or mark was produced by a being or beings more or less like myself and produced with certain kinds of *intentions*. If I regard the noise or mark as a natural phenomenon like the wind in the trees or a stain on the paper, I exclude it from the class of linguistic communication, even though the noise or mark may be indistinguishable from spoken or written words. (Searle 1969: 16)

6.1.3 How speech acts function

The first thing one should notice is that speech acts are actions happening in the world, that is, they bring about a change in the existing state of affairs (hence the label 'performative utterances' which originally was attached to them).[50] For instance, if I say to a (newborn) human: 'I baptize thee "in the name of the Father, and of the Son, and of the Holy Ghost"' (cf. Matthew 28: 19), then this human being is from now on and forever a Christian – provided I took care to let my words be accompanied by the flowing of water (not sprinkling, as it is practised in certain new-fangled mass religions) on some part of the infant's body. And if I belong to those who believe in the power of baptism, the world as a whole will now have changed as well: there will be one more Christian among the living. This type of insight, viz., that words can change the world, is not only of importance in a religious context (in principle, such changes in the state of the world are subject to one's beliefs or may depend, as in the case of miracles, on the strength of one's faith); it is an essential part of speech act thinking as well. And as such, it has become an important linguistic discovery.

The classic distinction between the different aspects (or 'forces') of speech acts is due to Austin (1962). First, we have the locutionary aspect: this is simply the activity we engage in in saying something, e.g.

It's cold in here.

In addition, this utterance has a 'force': by saying this sentence, I make a statement, a declaration. (On the face of it, the above utterance is neither a question, nor a promise, nor a threat, etc.) This particular, declarative aspect of the speech act is said to be its illocutionary force.[51]

However, if by saying

It's cold in here

we obtain further effects (which can range all the way from making an announcement to an attempt to have people leave the room), we are talking about the perlocutionary effects of an utterance. These ultimate effects are, of course, dependent on the particular circumstances of the utterance, and are by no means always predictable. By contrast, the illocutionary force is, for many pragmaticians, bound up with the very form the utterance may have: statement, question, wish, etc.

In Levinson's words, the *locutionary* aspect has to do with 'the utterance of a sentence with determinate sense and reference'; the *illocutionary* aspect with 'the naming of a statement, offer, promise, etc.

in uttering a sentence, by virtue of the conventional *force* associated with it'; whereas the *perlocutionary* aspect deals with 'the bringing about of effects on the audience by means of uttering the sentence, such effects being special to the circumstances of utterance' (Levinson 1983: 236).

Without going into too much detail, we can safely say that the second aspect, the illocutionary force, is what has occupied speech act theorists most (even though, from a pragmatic point of view, the perlocutionary aspect is the most interesting one, and, as we will see, the one that contains the key to the understanding of what people use their illocutionary acts for).

Another question that has drawn much attention in early speech act thinking is that of the conditions that must obtain before a speech act can be said to have an illocutionary effect; that is to say, before it can be said to 'count as' a particular speech act, and not as some irrelevant remark out of context.

For a speech act to happen 'felicitously' or 'happily', as it usually is called, and to prevent it from 'misfiring', several conditions (called 'felicity conditions') have been proposed. Here is what Searle has to say about a particular speech act, that of 'promising' (I will come back to this particular speech act in detail in sections 6.1.4 and 6.2):

> In order to give an analysis of the illocutionary act of promising, I shall ask what conditions are necessary and sufficient for the act of promising to have been successfully and non-defectively ['felicitously'] performed in the utterance of a given sentence ... [E]ach condition will be a necessary condition for the successful and non-defective performance of the act of promising, and taken collectively the set of conditions will be a sufficient condition for such a performance. (Searle 1969: 54)

As an example, consider the following case. I utter the words:

I hereby pronounce this person dead.

What kind of conditions have to be fulfilled for this to be a valid speech act of 'pronouncing'? First of all, we have to be certain that the person enunciating these words actually has the power to do so, and second, we have to have the right circumstances for the uttering. For example, it won't do to 'pronounce' my neighbours 'dead' in a dispute over garden boundaries. I can *wish* people dead, but I cannot *pronounce* them dead (except in an imaginary world, where my words have this kind of magical effect, as when children at play say 'Poof – you're dead').

The correct circumstances (or 'appropriate', as Austin called them), are, in this particular case, that I am a doctor, and that somebody has been brought in to the hospital after a traffic accident, and that I, as a doctor, have to determine whether the person in case is alive or dead. I am given this authority and duty by my being on call at the emergency unit and having been requested to produce such an official utterance, which then is entered into the official report as: 'The victim was pronounced dead on arrival [at the hospital].' In any other circumstances, the would-be speech act 'misfires'.

Or take the following case, where the 'misfiring' happens at the other end, so to speak. If I say to a friend:

I'll bet you ten dollars that the buses won't run on Thanksgiving,

then I can only claim my money (in case my prediction was correct) if my friend has 'taken on' the bet. For her to do so, she has to perform a corresponding speech act expressing 'uptake' (in this case, of a bet), such as

You're on.

Without these, there is no felicitous act of betting: some (or all) of the parties involved will not have had the right intentions and/or conduct.[52]

Famous (or perhaps one should say: notorious) cases of (sometimes intentional) misfiring of speech acts are found in connection with the laws governing the Roman Catholic institution of marriage. According to Canon Law, an intention (whether or not expressed before or during the ceremony) not to consummate the marriage or not to have children, or even the withholding of one's intention to get married (the so-called *reservatio mentalis*) is sufficient to render the marriage null and void.

This, clearly, is a most important aspect of the speech act of 'pronouncing' marriage vows, as it is almost the only way a Catholic can be released from his or her vows (divorce is not permitted according to Canon Law). Historically, the difficulty has of course always been to establish the appropriate (failure of) intention: here, the mighty of the earth have had the advantage of being able to produce such evidence with the help of underlings willing to testify under oath that the King in fact had said such and such on the eve of his marriage to the Queen he now wants to get rid of – irrespective of the truth of the matter (England's Henry VIII and his Cardinal Wolsey are, of course, the classic case).

6.1.4 Premises to promises

For various reasons, some of them historical, certain speech acts have always been favourites in expositions and discussions of speech act theory and speech acts; among them are the speech acts of 'promise' and 'request'. While the next section will be devoted in its entirety to a discussion of 'promising', the present section clears the ground for such a discussion by pointing out a number of current misunderstandings concerning the wording of promises, as well as of other speech acts.

One of the problems with speech acts is that the very wording of the act can lead to misunderstandings. To put it succinctly: Is the word *promise* a necessary element in the speech act 'promise'? Or, in more general terms: Do I have to use a so-called 'speech act verb' to perform a speech act?

We are all familiar with the problem in everyday life. We assume our friends will make the reservations for the restaurant because that's what they promised (or so we believe). However, when we get to the restaurant, there is no table; and our friends maintain that they never said they were going to make a reservation, or if they had said so, they didn't think it was so important, and so on and so forth.

The big question, of course, is: Can one trust people to keep a promise even when they haven't used the word 'promise'?

The answer to this question may not be where we think it is to be found, in the area of practical, everyday organization of our lives. Our friends may have different ideas about 'promising' than we have; but first of all, the very idea of 'promising' may need some adjustments.

Consider how children are prone to literalism: for them, a promise is only one that has the word *promise* in it; just as a 'lie' is only that which is called a *lie*. But in normal, adult contacts it should not be necessary to be so formalistic. Nor is such an attitude helpful: if we want to be secure in our expectations, then we should concentrate on the people who promise, rather than on what they say.[53]

We are confronted here with a veritable hedge of tangled and almost impenetrable conditions, and conditions on conditions. On the one side of the fence, there are the orthodox 'speech act verbers', for whom a speech act is only valid on condition that there is a valid speech act verb present (as we so often see it happen among children). On the other side, we have the people who point out that some of our most binding promises are given without the verb *to promise* ever coming into play, as in the standard Christian marriage ritual. Worse even: if I say 'I promise' in answer to the question: 'Wilt thou have this woman for thy wife?', I do *not* meet the felicity conditions for this kind of promise; in Austin's words, I fail to execute the procedure completely and correctly.

What is it that 'counts as' a promise, to use Searle's expression (1969: 36)? Something counts as something only within a specified set of rules. Thus, physically overthrowing the king in a game of chess only counts as 'winning' if it has been preceded by a situation of (actual or impending) check-mate.

Similarly, if I utter a warning, e.g.,

There is a policeman at the corner,

that will only and truly count as a warning if I utter it in a situation where somebody is about to perpetrate a break-in or some other crime. Without that context, or in another context, the utterance could count as an assurance, a dare, a hint as to where to ask for directions, a warning not to put that car in the space for the handicapped in front of the shop, and so on.

Similarly, a question such as

Can you pass me the salt?

(to take an example already mentioned) only counts as a question under very specific circumstances; normally, we will let it count as a request (if I merely answer 'Yes' without passing the salt, I'm defaulting on the correct 'uptake' of this particular speech act).

These phenomena have been the object of much debate over the years, and many efforts have been made to reduce speech acts to the exercise of 'speech act verbing', or at least, to deal with speech acts in terms of what 'the language' (read: English) has to offer in the line of major categories of such verbs. Thus, Searle (1979) distinguishes five classes of illocutionary acts, based more or less on what we, as speakers of SAE (Standard Average European languages, to borrow Whorf's term (1969:

138ff.)) find normal and acceptable.⁵⁴ However, to stay with the 'promise' example, there are dozens of ways to make a promise in any particular language, and it is not even certain that all or any of these fit into every scheme that we can put up for illocutionary acts, based on a particular language such as English.

Furthermore, the very use of a particular 'speech act verb' is often excluded from use in performing that very speech act: I seldom declare anything by 'declaring' (except in Dickensian elderly ladies' speech); also, we have to be very careful in extending restrictions and allowances in this respect across languages, even within SAE usage (see also sections 9.4 and 13.5). A 'promise' in Danish, for instance, is not the same as one in English: even the Danish speech act verb *at love* 'to promise' has a rather different sphere of usage than the corresponding English verb 'to promise'. If I say, e.g., to my American car mechanic

But you said you would have it ready by 4 o'clock,

the use of the word 'promise', rather than 'said', would sound strange in this context (unless of course, the mechanic had made a formal commitment, equal to a promise). Not so in Danish, however:

Men du lovede den skulle være færdig kl. 4
('But you promised it would be ready by 4 o'clock')

is what one would say in the most neutral of contexts, without any formal promise even having been hinted at.

We conclude, with Searle, that it is the context which determines whether an expression 'counts as' a speech act (1969: 52). Therefore, we understand a 'question' such as

Is there any salt over there?

as a polite request (properly, a 'pre-sequence' to a speech act of requesting, that serves as the speech act itself; see below, section 11.5.1). However, that does not entitle us to postulate an 'underlying' speech act verb, whenever a request is uttered that does not formally correspond to the speech act's 'canonical' expression in the form of a specific verb. Such hypothesizing would in most cases lead to an undesired proliferation of speech acts beyond any rationale; a case in point is the notorious 'performative hypothesis' from the earliest transformational heresies.[55]

The remainder of the present chapter will be devoted to the discussion of one particular speech act, that of promising.

6.2 PHYSIOGNOMY OF A SPEECH ACT: PROMISING

6.2.1 Introduction: The problem

Talking about speech acts, we run into a problem of a rather general character, having to do with the way different languages organize their locutionary (or illocutionary, or even perlocutionary) economy. Questions ranging under this heading are, typically:

- How can we determine a speech act?
- How many speech acts are there, and how are they expressed in language?
- Are there such things as 'universal speech acts', i.e. speech acts that are found across languages, or even in all languages?

The first of these questions will be dealt with exemplarily in the present section by choosing a model speech act, promising, and exploring the conditions governing its use. Here, I will follow Searle's exposition (1969: 57ff.), adding a critical commentary in the last section of this chapter.

The other two questions will be discussed on and off in the remainder of this book, and especially in chapters 7 and 8.

6.2.2 A speech act's physiognomy, I: Conditions

Being a philosopher, Searle is interested in many details of a more technical-philosophical nature that needn't bother us here (he characterizes his presentation as following a 'complicated way'; 1969: 57).

Searle's first question is: What conditions can be formulated for a speech act to 'count as' a promise? He lists nine of these; they will be dealt with in the present section.

His second question is: What rules govern a successful use of this speech act? There are five such rules, according to Searle; I will discuss them in the next section.[56]

Condition 1 Normal conditions must obtain for input and output. By this, one means that speakers know how to deal with the language: they must of course speak it, and not have any special handicaps (deafness, etc.); furthermore, they must abstain from what Searle calls 'parasitic use of language' such as jokes and acting.[57]

Condition 2 The promise must have a content (Searle: 'the propositional content'): that which remains as the 'kernel' of the utterance after we've done away with the promise part. Thus, in

I promise I'll be there tomorrow,

the propositional content is for me to be there tomorrow (or more precisely, the day after today).

This condition bears clearly the imprint of a propositional idealization; I'll come back to this problem in section 6.2.3.

Condition 3 At the moment of uttering, the content of the promise must have to do with a future, possible action of the speaker. Clearly, one cannot promise a thing that has happened in the past; neither can anybody promise anything in another person's stead (which of course is not the same as promising to try and *make* somebody else do something). Furthermore, the promise can be positive or negative: in the latter case, I promise not to do a certain thing, or not to do anything at all (cf. promises to 'cease and desist').

Condition 4 Clearly, what is being promised must be to the advantage of the 'promisee'. The difference between a promise and a threat, according to Searle, is that 'a promise is a pledge to do something for you, not to you . . . a threat is a pledge to do something to you, not for you' (1969: 58). Searle takes this condition fairly seriously: even though the promiser uses the *words* 'I promise', there is no promise unless it is to the advantage of the promisee. Besides, the situation must be of such a nature that the promiser is certain of the promisee's needs, so that the latter agrees as to the beneficial effect of the content of the promise, and so on.

From this, it would follow that a threat remains a threat, in accordance with the above, even though its wording is that of a promise:

If you don't behave, I promise there's going to be trouble.

Condition 5 The content of the promise must not be something which clearly is going to happen anyway: I can't promise anybody that the sun will rise tomorrow. As Searle rightly remarks, 'A happily married man who promises his wife he will not desert her in the next week is likely to provide more anxiety than comfort' (1969: 59).

Conditions 4 and 5 are often called (in accordance with Searle's terminology) preparatory conditions, that is, conditions that must have been met before we can begin to talk about promises.

Condition 6 This condition has to do with the sincerity of the promiser in carrying out the act of promising. This implies that the sincere promiser must intend to carry out the act that he or she promises to do; without that intention, we have no sincere promise.[58]

The condition we are dealing with here is appropriately called the sincerity condition.

Condition 7 This condition can be said to be the cornerstone of Searle's philosophy of promises: A promiser intends to put him-/herself under the obligation of carrying out the promised act. This is more than just intending to carry out the act: only if the intention is corroborated by this recognition of an inevitable obligation can one properly speak of a promise. This, according to Searle, is the essential condition for any promise. Conversely, if a prospective promise does not have this property of the speaker being sincere in his or her intention, as well as being serious about his or her obligations, then we do not have a promise: '. . . if a speaker can demonstrate that he did not have this intention in a given utterance[,] he can prove that the utterance was not a promise' (Searle 1969: 60).

The last two conditions have to do with the 'semantics' of promising, in particular with the effect that promises obtain, given the conventions of use in a particular language community.

Condition 8 Here it is stated that the normal conditions of language use must apply, such that the uttering of words like *I promise* have as their effect that the 'promisee' now understands that a promise is being made; or, more technically, that the utterance conventionally produces this understanding in the promisee: 'The speaker assumes that the semantic rules (which determine the meaning) of the expressions uttered are such that the utterance counts as the undertaking of an obligation' (Searle 1969: 61).

What is being postulated here by Searle is basically that the circumstances of uttering a promise must be conventionally right. Suppose that, in a certain linguistic or cultural environment, or in a particular, socially recognized situation, the words *I promise* conventionally never mean just that, or perhaps cannot even be uttered; then we wouldn't have a promise on our hands, no matter how much we 'promised'. One can think of situations where promises are made under 'duress', or in a recognized state of non-responsibility (to children, in drunkenness, etc.).

We try to capture such situations by saying, e.g., 'Never trust a drunk's promises,' or, as many parents undoubtedly would agree, 'promises to children don't count.' What is difficult to see here, however, is that Searle's choice of the term 'semantic' is right; in a more modern view, this is a clear case of the pragmatics of promising cutting right through both the syntax and the semantics of the speech act. Something similar is the case with the ninth condition.

Condition 9 This final condition says that '. . . the sentence uttered [must be] one which, by the semantical rules of the language, is used to make a promise' (p. 61).

Here, too, the emphasis on semantics is a bit disturbing, especially since Searle intends this ninth condition to be a 'wrap-up-condition': all of 1–8 must obtain, and the ninth condition itself is imposed on 'the semantical rules of the dialect spoken by S and H' (1969: 61; for 'S' and 'H', read 'speaker' and 'hearer', or 'promiser' and 'promisee').

Again, this is not a matter of semantics, or of semantics alone: the pragmatic conditions governing the use of the language are the ones that mainly determine the (promissory) validity of the utterance (whereby the utterance 'counts as' a promise). (I will return to these pragmatic questions later; see also the following sections.)

6.2.3 A speech act's physiognomy, II: Rules

According to Searle, our next task is to extract a set of rules from the above conditions for correct 'promising' behaviour. First of all, we must make a distinction between different kinds of rules: 'constitutive' and 'regulative'. Let me illustrate the distinction by an often-made analogy with the game of chess.

In this game, there are rules that have to do with the actual performance of the players: these are called *regulative* rules. The other kind of rules are called *constitutive* rules (because they 'make up', constitute, our game of chess: without them, the chess game is impossible). An example of a regulative rule of chess could be that players are not allowed to 'undo' a move; another could be that they can only use a certain amount of time for a certain number (e.g., 40) of moves (this is a common rule at chess tournaments), or that they are not allowed to touch the chess-pieces unless they intend to make a move, and so on.

The constitutive rules determine what counts as a move for the individual chessmen: thus, pawns move one square except for the first time, when they can move over two; the knights 'jump' across the board, whereas the bishops move diagonally, etc. Another kind of constitutive rules are the ones defining the number of chessmen, the number of squares on the board, etc. The latter kind of rules can be used to define (within certain limits) different kinds of chess, some of which are, or have been, recognized in other cultures and times as legitimate variants of the game. However, in any particular game, we must play the game according to *some* set of rules (if we want to play chess at all), and these rules cannot be varied: we must obey the regulations that are in force, and this, again, can be called a 'regulative' rule. (I will come back to the question of regulative vs. constitutive rules below, in section 6.2.4.)

In the case of the speech act 'to promise', we have four regulative rules that we can distill from the conditions in the previous section; in addition, we obtain one constitutive rule, as we will see. As to the conditions themselves, Searle says, only conditions 2–7 are specific to the speech act of promising; 1, 8 and 9 hold for all speech acts, and are not proper to promises.[59] The rules derived from them are said to govern the *force* that is present in the promise; recall here the earlier use of the term 'illocutionary force' as characteristic for a particular speech act. Now the time has come to characterize the linguistic means for the use of such a force; in Searle's terms, we're talking about the rules for using a so-called 'illocutionary force indicating device' (henceforth for short called 'IFID').

Rule 1   Only use a promissory IFID when the content of the utterance is about something which is to happen in the future.

This rule captures conditions 2 and 3, above; it is called the (propositional) content rule.

Rule 2   Only use the promissory IFID when the promise contains something that the promisee actually wants to happen to him or her.

Rule 3   Only use an IFID for promising when the content of the promise does not concern the occurrence of an already scheduled, self-justifying or natural happening.

Rules 2 and 3 are called the preparatory rules, in analogy with the preparatory conditions (4 and 5) above.

Rule 4   Only use a promissory IFID if you intend to carry out your promise.

This is clearly the sincerity rule, corresponding to the sincerity condition (6) above.

These four rules together make up the 'regulations' for promising. But what is it that makes a promise a promise? That is done by the fifth rule.

Rule 5   Only use a promissory IFID on condition that the promise is uttered, and recognized (accepted) as creating an obligation from the promiser to the promisee.

This, finally, is the 'count as', or essential rule, corresponding to the essential condition (7) above.

6.2.4   The pragmatics of rules

To the above rules, as proposed by Searle, I want to add a pragmatic comment. It should be clear from the above exposition-cum-discussion that we are faced with a curious paradox: Even though speech act theory, by its name and pretensions, should be a theory of action, it is in reality a philosophical theory of, or about, propositions. Classical speech act theory only nominally focuses on action; in reality, it is still proposition-bound. Bickhard and Campbell express this concisely and to the point:

> Speech act theory focuses on the 'action' inherent in an utterance (e.g. Austin 1962; Searle 1969), but it is still an action (a message transmission, not an *inter*action) based on an encoded proposition. (1992: 428)[60]

We may find this paradox aptly demonstrated in the remark by Searle himself, quoted in section 6.2.2, that a promise should not be about things that are going to happen, or should happen, anyway. The example that is given strikes us as a trifle humorous, but why? The reason is that we here are faced with a paradox, a clash between a condition (4) which then is absorbed into rule 2, a regulative, preparatory rule for the use of

IFIDs, and another condition (5) (captured by rule 3) which seems to belong to the essence of promising, in that it bars us from promising whatever is going to happen anyway (and, we might add, that which we cannot under any circumstances control). This is why we smile when we read Searle's somewhat naïve observation on the hapless husband who promises to be faithful to his wife.

The promise of fidelity (as enshrined in the marriage vows) is indeed something that should not have to be reiterated every time one goes off on a trip; however, the facts of life tell us that even if such a promise were given, in many cases it wouldn't be kept anyway. The constitutive rule (5) according to which a 'promise is uttered and accepted as creating an obligation from the promiser to the promisee' is subject to a regulative rule that tells us how to deal with these promises in actual life. Promises once given should not need to be renewed; but promises once given *are* broken, even so. A pragmatic view on promising accepts this as a fact of life, and recognizes that the regulative and the constitutive rules perhaps are not as easily separable as was implied above.

Let's pursue the analogy of chess. Clearly, if you play chess according to the rules, you have a valid chess game. But chess is not one and the same activity for everybody: the champion plays a very different game than the amateur; and the rank beginner, who has merely internalized the rules and remembers everything about the game that he was taught, has no clue as to how actually to win.

Similarly, the IFIDs of speech act theory only indicate illocutionary force; they don't put the force to work. To do that, we need a pragmatic act, an act that lifts the speech act out of the domain of abstract describing into the realm of concrete acting. For example, the speech act of requesting has in its constitutive rule a stipulation that the requester wants the requestee to do something for him/her. But this doesn't mean that we always, in actual fact, can or may request anything at all, or certain things in particular. The sanctions embodied in the regulative rules ('What is an allowable request?'; cf. 'What is a correct way of playing chess?') derive from the fact that we, in our daily lives, want people to do things for us that are necessary and beneficial to us. We cannot request things that are blatantly unreasonable (even though we may daydream about going to our boss and requesting that he double our salary).

The reason that a particular request cannot be put into action is not contained in the constitutive rule as such; yet, it derives from it, just as the sanctions that derive from the Fifth Commandment ('Thou shalt not kill') derive from the constitutive character of the Ten Commandments (whether they are seen as the embodiment of Divine Law, or as the expression of a basic respect for human life, property, truth, etc.). As Giddens remarks, 'all social rules have both constitutive and regulative (sanctioning) aspects to them' (1979: 66).

Again, we're confronted with a chicken-and-egg problem: the regulative rules define what the constitutive rules say they do; but the constitutive rules determine the weight that is given those rules in the daily exercise of them.

This paradox cannot be resolved within the context that Searle and other speech act theoreticians can offer us, as this context is firmly anchored in the truth-functional, or propositional, tradition of studying speech acts. In my book *Whose Language?* (1985), I have argued for a context-oriented, pragmatic view of language, as used by humans and for humans. This pragmatic view should not be 'walled off' from the rest of linguistics, or treated as a separate component (to be added to truth-conditional semantics or speech act theory following Searle; see Bickhard and Campbell 1992: 429). Rather, we should use an interactive perspective, in which the role of the user is no longer added on, but is an integrated part of our theorizing. Applied to the case of promising, this means that we cannot, in all decency, talk about promising in the abstract: every promise is a promiser's promise, promised to a real-life promisee. The conditions of use for promises should, therefore, include these users, promisers as well as promisees, and their conditions of interaction (for more on this, see Mey 1985: 40ff.).

Similar things can be said about the other speech acts. Take once more the case of requesting: there are some absurd cases around of requests that are not really about the thing they request, or indeed about anything at all, but still are counted as requests, or in general, expressions of a certain pragmatic reality; for instance that the requester acknowledge his lowly status, as in the military: 'Request permission to address my captain . . .' (where the request strictly speaking is taken for granted, otherwise it couldn't even be uttered), or in certain religious orders, where one *must* request 'permission' to take an afternoon snack, even if one doesn't feel like having one, and where the request in reality boils down to a recognition of the fact that the member of the order (being duty-bound by a holy vow of obedience) cannot do anything except in subordination, i.e. per request and by permission (*venia*). In these cases, the constitutive element of the speech act is almost totally subsumed under the regulative one, and one understands why these paradoxes have led people like Giddens to want to abolish the distinction altogether. Only a pragmatic approach to speech acts can resolve these paradoxes.

With regard to the other two questions raised in section 6.2.1, it seems justified, as Searle does, to generalize that which is common to all speech acting, and 'factor' it out, as he calls it:

> ... some of these rules seem to be just particular manifestations as regards promising of very general underlying rules for illocutionary acts; and ultimately we should be able, as it were, to *factor them out*, so that they are not finally to be construed as rules exclusively for the illocutionary force indicating device for promising as opposed to other types of illocutionary force indicating devices. (1969: 63; my emphasis)

However, we should always keep in mind that the nature of speech acting varies according to various linguistic uses, not only across languages, but also, and not least interestingly, within a single language (cf. the remarks above). Hence, the existing speech acts of English can only give us an approximation to the general problems of speech act theory, especially the difficult problems of the cross-language equivalencies and universal, inter-language inventories of speech acts. The following chapter will consider one aspect of this problem: the so-called 'speech act verbs'.

EXERCISES AND REVIEW QUESTIONS

1. Consider the following utterance:

I promise not to keep this promise

What would Searle say of such an utterance? Does it qualify as a promise? Why (not)?

2. Suppose you come across a street sign or billboard whose text simply says:

DO NOT READ THIS SIGN

What kind of speech act are we dealing with here?

Can one take this order seriously? Why not?

What could it mean?

3. Consider the following utterances:

Sit down

Please sit down

Please have a drink

Please have a nice vacation

Please be good to me (conventional translation of the Japanese expression of greeting *doozo yoroshiku*)

Questions:

How would you characterize the above utterances from the point of view of the speech act of 'ordering'?

How would you rank their illocutionary force?

4. Consider the following speech acts:

I promise (hereby) to set fire to your house

I hereby warn you that you will be awarded the Nobel prize in literature

WARNING: Your lawn will turn brown in November

UNDER PENALTY OF LAW: DO NOT REMOVE THIS TAG
(text on tags attached to all bedding material purchased in the US prior to 1981)

Questions:

What is the problem with these speech acts?

Do they all suffer from the same irregularity, or are they irregular in different ways? Which (in either case)?

Can you think of any conditions that make any of these speech acts acceptable?

5. Consider the following text, found on a package of American brewers' yeast in the 1920s:

> Do not mix the contents of this package with 2 qts of lukewarm water.
> Do not add 1 lb of sprouted barley.
> Do not put in a warm spot (74 degrees) for 7–10 days.
> Do not skim.
> Do not put mixture in copper pot and heat.
> Do not condense vapors.
> Do not consume end product.
> Do not get caught.

What speech acts are these (if any)?

What would Grice have to say about the above text?

6. Here's a little puzzle:
Between British Rail's Waverley and Haymarket stations in central Edinburgh, Scotland, the train (travelling in the direction of Haymarket) enters a tunnel. On entering the tunnel, the astonished traveller notices a big red billboard, about 4' by 6', with large white lettering saying:

DO NOT ENTER
UNLESS
IN FULL POSSESSION

Questions:

What kind of a speech act are we faced with here?

Establish the context for this speech act in order to make it meaningful.

Who is addressed here, and what is the person addressed supposed to do/ not to do? (Hint: use such cues as the location of the sign, its appearance, visibility, wording, etc.)

What do you think 'possession' is supposed to mean?

7

Speech Act Verbs and Indirect Speech Acts

7.1 SPEECH ACT VERBS

7.1.1 Introduction: Why speech act verbs?

In the previous chapter, I raised three questions, two of which remained (at least in part) unanswered. The first question was:

How many speech acts are there, and how are they expressed?

This question has to do with the problem of the so-called 'speech act verbs', which is the name linguists have given to those verbs that somehow or other seem to be the natural way of expressing a particular speech act.

The second question was:

Are there universal speech acts, i.e., speech acts that are (necessarily and always) found in any language whatsoever?

This question deals with the typology of speech acts and the various ways a particular speech act can manifest itself in different languages.

The two questions will turn out to be intimately related but not, for that, any easier to answer. It seems reasonable to start with the first question, since it constitutes a necessary preliminary step towards solving the 'universality' problem: we simply need to know what we are talking about when we discuss speech acts and the ways these speech acts can be realized in various languages across the world. In chapter 8, we will look more closely into the universality of speech acts.

7.1.2   The number of speech acts, and how they are expressed

Many suggestions have been offered as to the number of (principal) speech acts that any particular language has to offer. The differences in opinion have to do with, among other things, the demands that one places upon classificatory criteria.

Some linguists stipulate that there have to be strict syntactic-morphological or semantic criteria telling us whether or not we are dealing with a 'real' speech act. In this way, one may obtain a rough-and-ready typology of speech acts, either by following the traditional syntactic classification of verbal 'mood' rather closely (indicative, subjunctive, imperative, optative, etc., are thus all typical expressions of some speech act), or by relying heavily on broad, semantic distinctions. As an example of the latter kind we can study the five-part classification, offered by Searle (1977: 34–8), who divides the illocutionary (i.e. speech) acts into: *representatives* (the point of which is to represent a state of affairs; which have a word-to-world fit, i.e. the intention is to make the words fit the world; in which a belief is expressed; and in which any proposition can occur), e.g. statements; *directives* (the point of which is to direct the hearer towards doing something; which have a world-to-word direction of fit; in which a wish is expressed; in which the proposition is a future act done by the hearer), e.g. orders; *commissives* (the point of which is that the speaker commits himself to doing something; which have a world-to-word direction of fit; in which an intention is expressed; in which the proposition is a future act done by the speaker), e.g. promises; *expressives* (the point of which is that a certain psychological state is expressed; which have no direction of fit; in which a wide range of psychological states can be expressed; in which the proposition ascribes a property or act to the speaker or the hearer), e.g. congratulations; *declarations* (the point of which is to bring something about in the world; which have both a word-to-world and a world-to-word direction of fit; in which no psychological state is expressed; in which any proposition can occur), e.g. an excommunication.

Searle, in the classification given above, is mainly concerned with what he calls the (illocutionary) 'point' of the speech act in question, along with what he calls its 'fit'. What does Searle mean by that?

'Fit' expresses the fact that our words both *match* the world we live in, and that they, at least potentially, though not always visibly, are able to *change* that world (for more on this relationship between language and world, see section 14.8). The fit, can, moreover, have one of two 'directions': words to world, or world to words. In the first case, my language is 'fitted to', or even 'fit for', my environment, as when I describe a piece of scenery, tell a story that I have played a part in, represent a state of affairs (e.g. in a report), etc.; the direction of fit is 'words to world'. Searle's examples comprise mainly the so-called 'representatives'.

In the second case, the world is 'fitted to' my words. That is, through the use of words, I make the world fit my language: I change the world in accordance with my directions, as given through my use of language. Examples here are 'directives' and 'commissives'.

There are two further possible cases, in which there is either no direction of fit at all, as in the case of 'expressives', or a bidirectional fit, as in the case of the so-called 'declarations'. When I merely express my emotion, there need not be any strict correspondence between what I say and what the state of affairs is like. This is typically the case when people 'get emotional' (representing themselves), or 'hysterical' (when they characterize a state of affairs in terms that are thought of as too 'expressive').

The other case is where both directions of fit are possible and coexist. This occurs in the (rather few) cases where I use my authority and power to create a state of the world that is both based on the previously existing state, and changes it to a new state. Typically, this happens when in the Catholic Church, the priest administers the sacrament of penance (usually called 'confession'): the confessor must 'fit' his words of absolution to a condition in the world (in this case, in the penitent), one of 'being sorry for one's sins' (and saying so, having enumerated them in front of the priest); technically this is called 'a state of (perfect) contrition'. But at the same time, the words spoken operate on the world (in this case, the sinner) in that they expunge the mark of sin from the sinner's soul and, if necessary (e.g. in case of a mortal sin), restore the soul to its pristine state of grace.

While the classification given by Searle thus mainly rests on features of representation (one of the senses of 'meaning', hence a semantic trait; cf. Lyons 1977: 5), some of them also are rather close to what one would refer to, in syntax, by the classical term 'moods', such as 'indicative' (Searle's 'representatives'), or 'imperative' (Searle's 'directives').[61]

Classifiers such as Searle belong to the category Verschueren (1979: 10) has called the 'lumpers': those who lump together their speech acts into a few, large categories. Opposite them, we have the 'splitters', that is to say those who split up their speech acts into a great number of classes; that number may be 'between five hundred and six hundred' (1975: 10). The individual speech act realizations may range from 1,000 to 9,999 (as Austin has suggested), or even go up into the tens of thousands, all depending on our patience and acumen in making the necessary distinctions.[62]

Whatever the number of hypothetical speech acts, languages have historically shown their preferences for certain, well defined exemplars of the species, and expressed this preference by bestowing the honours of specific, linguistic expressions on such acts; such expressions go by the name of speech act verbs (henceforth SAVs).

7.1.3   Speech act verbs and performativity

Traditionally, a number of languages associate some kind of activity with the word for 'verb' itself. Thus, Danish has, in its traditionally purist grammatical nomenclature, an autochthonous term for the (morphological category) 'verb': *udsagnsord*, literally: 'word for predicating [about the subject]' – a term that clearly harkens back to the classical grammatical term 'predicate', denoting the role of the verb in the sentence. Another Germanic language that has fallen prey to the pranks of purist grammarians is Dutch; here, the verb is called *werkwoord*, literally 'work word', as if it were the verb that was doing whatever work had to be performed in the context of the sentence – and all by itself. A similar 'dynamic metaphor' is encountered in the Japanese term for 'verb': *doo-shi*, literally 'move-word'.

It thus seems natural to look for linguistic expressions of activity ('work') among the members of the category 'verb', and to call those that are found to denote speech acts, 'speech act verbs'. This also makes sense historically: Austin's first 'discovery' of the phenomena of speech acts happened in a strictly 'verbal' environment, the classic examples being institutionalized speech act verbs such as 'to baptize', 'to invest', 'to dub', 'to sentence' and so on.

There is, however, a certain asymmetry in the relationship between SAVs and speech acts (SAs) proper: first of all, not all SAs are represented by a specific SAV, but may be represented by several (with the sole exception of the 'purest' and strictly institutionalized SAs, such as 'to baptize'). Thus, an SA such as 'to order' may be expressed in various, often indirect ways (see section 7.2) – by a direct 'ordering' verb, by a 'normal' verb in the imperative or even by a circumlocution:

I order you to shut the door

Shut the door!

You will shut that door,

where all three utterances express the same order.

Second, and conversely, not every SA has a corresponding, custom-made SAV of its own. The act of pronouncing a jury's finding is called 'to render a verdict'; however, (in English at least) there is no SAV 'to *verdict'.[63] Apparently, not all SAs are on a par with regard to SAVs.

To see this a little more clearly, consider the case of the so-called 'performative verbs' (often called 'explicit performatives', since most verbs perform something anyway, but presumably implicitly).

The uttering of a sentence of the type

I promise to come

carries out two separate functions: on the one hand, it tells the world that the speaker, in this case 'I', has performed something, namely, a promise of 'coming'; on the other, it binds me, the speaker, to my promise: the utterance 'I promise to come', when uttered by a speaker, *explicitly* performs this promise for the speaker.

Now consider the same sentence in the past tense:

I promised to come.

Here, the second function, the 'explicit performative', is absent. What this sentence does is describe a state of affairs that has happened once upon a time; it is not a promising utterance, hence not an SA of promising, despite the use of the word 'promise'. Similarly, when I say

He promised to come,

I have not in any way performed a promise for the person referred to by 'he'.

The above must not be interpreted to imply that one cannot perform an SA without having an explicit performative at one's disposal. It just serves to demonstrate the differences that obtain between SAVs with respect to their use and usability. One could say that the 'explicit performatives' are the most extreme cases of SAVs, in that they can perform, and necessarily perform, certain SAs for which they are designated (given that the proper conditions are met, among which are, in our case, the use of the present tense and of the first person).

But couldn't we generalize the argument, and maintain that, properly speaking, all verbs, inasmuch they express an 'activity' of some kind, in principle are SAVs?

Such a generalization would not hold water in most cases, even with SAVs that otherwise are beyond any suspicion of non-performance. Consider the following pair of sentences:

I believe in God

I believe that the Earth is flat.

While the first utterance is an 'act of faith', typically performed by an SAV 'to believe', as in the *Credo in unum Deum* of the Nicene Creed, the second is no more than the expression of a (rather unsubstantiated) opinion or 'belief'. I might as well have said (and would perhaps have been better off saying) that I suppose, or think, or conjecture, that the world is flat. However, such is precisely the 'normal', everyday use of the verb 'to believe', and we should perhaps not even call it an SAV in such an everyday context.[64]

Among the more standard SAVs (i.e. the ones having, among other things, the privilege of always being quoted by the established speech act theoreticians) we find such verbs as 'to announce', 'to declare', 'to enquire', and so on.[65] But are these always 'performative', i.e. performing something? If a person says:

I hereby declare this bridge to be opened,

then (provided he or she is endowed with the proper authority) there is some kind of performance: that of opening a bridge. But what if I say:

He declared himself to be innocent/that he was innocent/his innocence?

One would be hard put (especially in the context of the judiciary) to accept this utterance as containing a performative verb: any criminal could let himself off the hook by this kind of verbal magic.

Many speech act theoreticians, having noticed that sentences such as the above often contain, or may contain, an adverb such as 'hereby', as in

I hereby declare the bridge to be opened,

have used this adverb as a practical criterion for a true, 'performative' SAV. Compare also the fact that one cannot easily or felicitously utter sentences like

I hereby love you

or

I hereby know that the Earth is flat.[66]

However, the fact that one can legitimately say, e.g.,

I hereby declare my innocence

seems to indicate that the use of 'hereby' at best is an indicator of SAVs in general, not of performativity; and also that the two categories, SAVs and performatives, in most cases do not coincide.

Finally, there is the strange category of verbal expressions that have the property of denying what they are doing, or doing what they explicitly are denying. Consider

I don't want to bother you, but could you please have a look at my program?

or

I'm not threatening you, but if I ever see your face again around these parts . . .

Here, the speaker explicitly 'performs' an act of not wanting to bother or threaten the addressee, while he or she in actual fact does precisely that (and probably wants to as well). Conversely, in such cases, the use of the verbs 'to bother' or 'to threaten', taken by themselves, would not have the same effect as it had above; one would hardly consider utterances such as

I am (hereby) bothering you . . .

I (hereby) threaten you . . .

as particularly expressive or performative of the acts of 'threatening' or 'bothering', and perhaps not even of anything at all.

We may conclude that performativity is a property that is not specifically bound up with SAVs; in Verschueren's words, we are dealing with a performativity 'continuum', running all the way from 'institutionalized' SAVs such as 'to baptize', to everyday verbs that occasionally can take on a performative character, such as the ones cited in the last two examples above.

7.1.4 Speech acts without SAVs

What was said in the last paragraphs of the preceding section could lead, rather naturally, to the tentative assumption that we may not even need SAVs as a special category of verbs. Indeed, since performativity is all over the verbal spectrum (albeit primarily residing in a small set of institutionalized verbs), we clearly do not need an SAV to perform a speech act, and in many cases, we cannot even properly perform the very speech act that is 'officially' expressed by the verb, by making explicit mention of the appropriate verb. Two cases may serve to illustrate the point.

The first is that of the so-called 'Speech Act Formulae' (SAF; Verschueren 1979: 6). These are verbal expressions that in all respects behave like SAVs, except that they are not 'regular' verbs, but rather, stylistic or other variations on a common semantic theme. For instance, I can say

I want to express my gratitude for your valuable assistance

or, with the same effect (in another, more relaxed mode)

I want to thank you for your help.

Similarly, one has expressions such as 'to express one's intention', 'to utter a warning', 'to make up one's mind' and so on, where a simple verb could render the same service of 'notifying', 'warning', 'deciding', etc.

Often, too, individual languages handle the 'same' semantic units in entirely different ways when it comes to expressing a certain verbal notion. Examples include 'to study' (or Danish *at studere*) vs. French *faire ses études* (but also *étudier*) or Japanese *benkyoo shimasu* (literally: 'to do study'); expressions for 'please': French *s'il vous plaît*, Danish *vær så venlig* ('be so kind'), Portuguese *faz favor* ('do the favour'), Japanese *o-negai-shimasu* ('grant the honourable request') and so on. Even though closely related expressions may be found from one language to other, related ones, the languages in question do not always avail themselves of such options; the verb 'to realize' exists in a French form as *réaliser*; however, to express the verb's meaning 'to become aware of', French uses *se rendre compte*.

The second case is somehow related to the first; it has to do with 'verbless expressions' of the kind 'Thanks'. One can doubt whether we are dealing with a verb here, let alone an SAV; witness also the fact that in many languages other than English, the speech act of 'thanking' has a substantive (singular or plural) as its regular expression. As examples, we have Danish *tak* (a singular/plural), cf. *en stor tak* 'a big thanks', *mange tak* ('many thanks'), *tusind tak* ('a thousand thanks'); Finnish *kiitos/ kiitoksia* (singular/plural 'thanks'); Czech *díky* ('thanks', a plural) and so on. Still other languages alternate with, or even prefer, a form of the verb 'to thank': Dutch *bedankt* ('[you are] thanked'); Swedish *tackar* '[I] thank [you]' (along with *tack*, of the same use and meaning as Danish *tak*); Czech (along with *díky*) *děkuji* ('I thank'); cf. also the English expression *thank you* (perhaps for 'I thank you', the 'full' speech act, which under normal circumstances would seem to be overdoing it slightly). Similarly French has the (almost totally deverbalized) (*Je vous souhaite un*) *bonjour*; a Hungarian equivalent is *Jó napot kivánok* (literally '[A] good day wish I').

7.1.5 An historical speech act paradox: 'Thank you for what?'

It seems clear from what I have said so far that speech acts, as well as SAVs, only make sense when we see them used in their proper contexts. As isolated lexical items, or members of a set, they have very little to tell us. The context, however, is not a sterile hull containing a dried-out seed: we make the speech acts come alive, like the dry bones contemplated by the Prophet in the field of Megiddo (Ezekiel 37: 7–8) with or without the help of SAVs, by continually varying the context and expanding it to suit our communicative purposes.

What I have said above is nothing new; I will illustrate it both with an historical speech act anecdote and with a classical quotation. The quote is from a work by the Danish linguist Louis Hjelmslev:

> The so-called lexical meanings in certain signs are nothing but artificially isolated contextual meanings, or artificial paraphrases of such meanings. In absolute isolation, no sign has any meaning; all sign meaning originates in a context, by which we either understand a situational context or an explicit context; the distinction is, however, without meaning, since we in an unbounded or productive text (a living language) always can transform a situation context into an explicit one. (1943: 41; my translation)

That is to say: even if one observes an SAV in some supposedly linguistic connection, one should not believe a speech act to be taking place, before one has considered, or possibly created, the appropriate context.

Next, the anecdote.

In 1976, the Israeli colonel Bar-Lev, on a special mission to Uganda, placed a telephone call to that country's dictator Idi Amin in order to 'thank' him for his cooperation during a successful operation in the airport of Entebbe (special units of the Israeli army had freed the hostages held by a Palestinian guerrilla group after a hijacking). The following is a transcript of this telephone conversation, as found in Verschueren (1980: 65–6).[67]

Bar-Lev: Sir, I want to thank you for your cooperation and I want to thank you very much.

Idi Amin: You know I did not succeed.

Bar-Lev: Thank you very much for your cooperation. What? The cooperation did not succeed? Why?

Idi Amin: Have I done anything at all?

Bar-Lev: I just want to thank you, sir, for the cooperation.

Idi Amin: Have I done anything?

Bar-Lev: I did exactly what you wanted.

Idi Amin: Wh— Wh— What happened?

Bar-Lev: What happened?

Idi Amin: Yes?

Bar-Lev: I don't know.

Idi Amin: Can't you tell me?

Bar-Lev: No, I don't know. I have been requested to thank you for your cooperation.

Idi Amin: Can you tell me about the suggestion you mentioned?

Bar-Lev: I have been requested by a friend with good connections in the government to thank you for your cooperation.
I don't know what was meant by it, but I think you do know.

Idi Amin: I don't know because I've only now returned hurriedly from Mauritius.

Bar-Lev: Ah . . .

Idi Amin: . . . in order to solve the problem before the ultimatum expires tomorrow morning.

Bar-Lev: I understand very well, sir . . . Thank you for the cooperation. Perhaps I'll call you again tomorrow morning? Do you want me to call you again tomorrow morning?

Idi Amin: Yes.

Bar-Lev: Very well, thank you sir. Good-bye.

In order to understand what is going on in this conversation, we should recall that the Israeli paratroopers actually operated inside another sovereign country, Uganda, contrary to international laws and conventions (no state of war existed between Israel and Uganda). The only way this operation could have a semblance of legality was to 'legalize' it by directly involving the head of the Ugandan state, the dictator Idi Amin. However, the clever politician had (maybe following a leak or a direct hint) seen fit to decamp for Mauritius, thus leaving the field wide open for the Israeli operation.

On coming back from his visit, Idi Amin finds that the 'embarrassing' situation has ceased to exist: the hijackers have been liquidated, and the hostages freed. Moreover, Idi Amin has not lost 'face' (on this, see section 4.4.4), because he obviously cannot be held responsible for what people did in his absence. But if he isn't responsible, then he cannot accept a 'Thank you' from the Israelis either. The Israeli commander, on the other hand, is highly concerned about the international image of the state of Israel. Actions like these tend to confirm the impression, already existent in much of the Third World, of Israel as an aggressive nation, without respect for international law and order. Therefore, the best thing for Israel to do is to involve the Ugandans *post factum*, so to speak, and obtain an official 'absolution' from their head of state: if it can be said that Idi Amin knew about the impending Israeli strike, and even better, if he had said he would cooperate, then Israel cannot be accused of international terrorism and adventurism.

So the Israel colonel tries to involve Idi Amin in an act of 'thanksgiving', by which the Israeli operation would be acknowledged as a co-operation, hence more or less legalized.

But also, and conversely, if Israel is not to blame, then Uganda must be: for having allowed the Israelis to enter Entebbe airport and free the hostages, killing the hijackers. For Idi Amin, this blame must be avoided at all costs, which is what explains his 'hedges', pretended ignorance and in general, his non-cooperative behaviour.

What we see in this conversation is an instance of the well known, symmetrical and synchronized speech acting that we are familiar with from other occasions, such as greeting, thanking and so on. This special case is called 'imposition and avoidance'. The various 'thank you's represent an endeavour to put co-responsibility, and hence blame, on the other party, whose professed ignorance should be read as an effort to reject and avoid the imposition, by not allowing himself to be thanked. Hence, the question that Verschueren raises (in his account of the episode): 'Did Bar-Lev thank [Idi] Amin?' may be rephrased as: 'Did any speech act of the symmetrical, synchronized kind occur?', and the answer is: 'Yes, there was such a symmetrical interchange, but it had nothing to do with thanking.' The surface acts were not performed as *bona fide* speech acts of 'thanking', but as manipulatory manoeuvres of 'blaming'; whereas the acts of professing non-knowledge were counter-manoeuvres of 'rejecting an effort to blame'.

And since no thanks were involved, the answer to our question above is doubly negative: first of all, the surface 'thanking' was not successful, because the 'uptake' was absent; but also, on a deeper level, no thanking was involved at all (see also the parallel case of the 'failed bet', discussed in section 9.5).

As we see from this example, surface verbs (or other forms) do not always and necessarily tell the truth about what they are doing. Often, we may have to disregard the surface form of a verb, when trying to determine what kind of speech act we are confronted with. But not only can speech act verbs substitute for one another, given the occasion; the speech acts themselves can be used in ways that have nothing, or not much, to do with what they 'really' stand for. These so-called 'indirect' speech acts are the topic of the next section.

7.2   INDIRECT SPEECH ACTS

7.2.1   Introduction: The problem

If I say to somebody

Could you move over a bit?

I do not expect that person to 'answer my question' with

Yes

or

Yes, perhaps I could

and not budge an inch. On the contrary, I would consider such an 'answer' highly inappropriate, even though I did indeed utter a question (formally characterized as such by word order, intonation, etc.) of the 'Yes/No' type. By contrast, if the person did move, but never 'answered' my question (such as might be the case if the scene happened to be a cinema or concert hall), I would be perfectly happy with his or her reaction (or 'answer').

The reason for this apparent incongruity is found in the character of my 'question'. It was never intended as an enquiry into the physical or moral degrees of freedom of my interlocutor; what I told him or her was simply to move over, but I did so indirectly: hence the expression *indirect speech act*.

7.2.2   Recognizing indirect speech acts

Here is an example originally due to Searle (1975: 61). Suppose somebody says to a friend:

Let's go to the movies tonight

and the friend answers:

I have to study for an exam.

What is this person trying to tell his/her interlocutor? And how do we know?

Searle himself suggests a comparison:

> The problem seems to me somewhat like those problems in the epistemological analysis of perception in which one seeks to explain how a perceiver recognizes an object on the basis of imperfect sensory input. The question, How do I know that he has made a request when he only asked me a question about my abilities? may be like the question, How do I know it was a car when all I perceived was a flash going past me on the highway? (1975: 82)

Still, this does not really solve our problem: How can we know, in the example above, that the second utterance in fact is a rejection of the proposal contained in the first, while seeming to be completely unrelated to it and not containing any overt or hidden expression of negation, denial or rejection, or even a mention of the rejected offer?

There are basically two ways of approaching this problem. The first one is the philosophical-semantic one; it is based on strict reasoning and certain basic principles, such as the ones we became acquainted with at the beginning of chapter 4. This is the approach followed by Searle and a number of other semanticists and philosophers of language; below, I will give a short résumé of Searle's reasoning.

The other way of looking at the problem is more genuinely pragmatic, in the sense that it takes its point of departure in what people actually say, and 'do with their words'. It assumes, and with a certain right, that it cannot be just by accident that in our daily use of language, indirect speech acts abound, and in some cases (as we have seen above, section 6.1.4, in the case of the 'promise') are far more numerous than direct ones. Also, the occurrence of the imperative in orders or requests is dispreferred in many languages, including English, despite its status as the 'genuine' expression of the speech act 'order' or 'request'; Levinson remarks that 'most usages [of requests] are indirect' (1983: 264), whereas 'imperatives are rarely used to command or request' (p. 275). I will deal with both approaches in the following two sections.

7.2.3 The ten steps of Searle

Searle views the phenomenon of indirect speech acting as a combination of two acts, a primary illocutionary act (in our example above, rejecting a proposal), and a secondary one (in this case, making a statement), where the primary act operates through, and in force of, the secondary one:

> [The utterer] performs the secondary illocutionary act by way of uttering a sentence the LITERAL meaning of which is such that its literal utterance constitutes a performance of that illocutionary act. We may, therefore . . . say that the secondary illocutionary act is literal; the primary illocutionary act is not literal . . . The question is, How does [the listener] understand the nonliteral primary illocutionary act from understanding the literal secondary illocutionary act? (1975: 62)

In order to answer this question, Searle builds a ten-step pyramid of reasoning at whose summit he places his conclusion as a logically necessary keystone.[68] The steps go as follows (A will denote the proposer, B the rejecter; both are assumed to be male):

Step 1   A has uttered a suggestion (to go to the movies); B has uttered a statement (about studying for an exam). These are the bare facts of the case.

Step 2   A assumes B to be cooperative in the conversation situation, that is, his answer is taken to be relevant, in accordance with the maxim of relevance under the Cooperative Principle.

Step 3   Relevant answers in the situation at hand (where a suggestion/ request is being made) are found among the following: acceptance, rejection, counter-suggestion ('Why don't we make it tomorrow?'), suggestion for further discussion ('That entirely depends on what's on') – and perhaps a few more, depending on the circumstances.

Step 4   None of the relevant answers in step 3 matches the actual answer given, so that the latter, taken at face value, must be said not to be one of these (this follows from steps 1 and 3).

Step 5   We must, therefore, assume that B means more (or something entirely different) by uttering his statement than what it says at face value. That is to say, his primary intention (see above) is different from his secondary one. This follows from steps 2 and 4; it is the 'crucial link' in the argumentative chain: unless we can distinguish the primary from the literal, there is no way of making sense of indirect speech acts, says Searle (1975: 63).

Step 6   Everybody knows that one needs time to study for an exam, and that going to the movies may result in precious study-time being lost – something many students cannot afford. This is factual, shared information about the world, carrying the same weight as the facts mentioned above, under step 1.

Step 7   Hence, it is likely that B cannot (or doesn't want to) combine the two things: go to the cinema and study; this is an immediate consequence of the preceding step.

Step 8   Speech act theory has taught us that among the preparatory conditions (see above, section 8.2) for any speech act having to do with proposals (such as in the above case) are the ability, and willingness, to carry out such a proposed act.

Step 9   From this, A can infer that B's utterance in all likelihood is meant to tell him that he cannot accept his proposal (this follows from steps 1, 7 and 8).

Step 10   We must conclude that B's primary intention in mentioning his exam preparation has been to reject A's proposal (from steps 5 and 9).[69]

7.2.4   The pragmatic view

Starting out from the observation that indirect speech acts (despite their name) in many cases are the most common, 'direct' realizations of what we have come to know as 'illocutionary force' (see section 6.1.3), one could ask whether it would not be wiser to concentrate on the pragmatic aspects of that force, rather than to try and establish watertight semantic and syntactic criteria for individual speech acts and speech act verbs. Such an approach would have the advantage of being closer to what people actually do with their words; the drawback would be that in such an approach, the original insights about speech acts (such as Austin's, as discussed in chapter 6) could be lost.

However, on closer look, such a drawback is not real. A truly pragmatic approach would, in every case, concentrate on what users do; but it would not stop there. Users are part of a world of usage: they are never alone in their use of language, but use their language as members of a speech community that reflects the conditions of the community at large.

Among those conditions are the official institutions which society has created for itself: the legislative, the executive, the judiciary, and other organs of the state; the various religious organizations such as sects and churches; human social institutions such as marriage, the family, the market and so on. In all such institutions and bodies, certain human agreements and customs have become legalized, and this legalization has found its symbolic representation in language.

In this way, language transcends the historical boundaries of the 'here and now', as well as the subjective limitations of the individual's knowledge and experience. Language, in symbolizing human life, standardizes and codifies it. Thus, we are able to speak of language as defining, indeed 'constructing' social institutions (and to maintain, on the other hand, that the social reality, in a deeper sense, is the basis of the phenomenon of language (for more on this, see section 14.7)). We can, in fact, speak not only of the 'social construction of reality' but of a 'linguistic construction of social facts'.

Berger and Luckmann (1966), whose ideas I am closely following here, state that

[l]anguage . . . constructs immense edifices of symbolic representations that appear to tower over the reality of everyday life like gigantic presences from another world. Religion, philosophy, art, and science are the historically most important symbol systems of this kind. To name these is already to say that, despite the maximal detachment from everyday experience that the construction of these systems requires, they can be of very great importance indeed for the reality of everyday life. Language is capable not only of con-

structing symbols that are highly abstracted from everyday experience, but also of 'bringing back' these symbols and appresenting them [presumably: 'abstractly presenting them to us'] as objectively real elements in everyday life.' (1966: 40)

As examples, we can think of the language of the law, or legal language; the language of the church, or religious language; the language of institutionalized aggression, or military language; and so on. In these languages, people have seen fit to standardize certain linguistic symbolizations in order to perform certain, appropriate functions that are pertinent to the existence and survival of the institutions and their members. Thus, we find there is language defining the institution of marriage, prescribing the correct ways of entering a binding matrimonial contract; there is language establishing the correct exercise of the judiciary power as it is embodied in the shape of judges, juries and courts of justices, by allowing only certain, well-defined expressions to be used and 'sentences' (in the double meaning of the word) to be pronounced; and so on (see further section 8.2.10).

It is important to note that the real performative value of a 'prime' linguistic symbol, such as the SAV 'to baptize', is actually fairly restricted. The performance of the act of baptizing is closely bound up with the utterance of precisely the words 'I baptize thee . . .' (cf. section 6.1.3). This particular language both guarantees, and vouchsafes, the exercise of a highly specific speech act, but it can only achieve it inasmuch as it is the performance of a highly institutionalized and empowered societal function.

On the other hand, in the more normal cases we find language use that relies heavily on interaction in order to be effective, even in institutional surroundings such as the court, the classroom, the hospital, the physician's office, etc. Here, the case of doctor–patient 'conversation' comes to mind as a particularly good, and well-studied example. A number of authors, such as Lacoste (1981), and Treichler, Frankel, Kramarae, Zoppi and Beckmann (1984), have shown that the power of language in a situation such as the medical interview depends on two factors: one, the power that one 'brings with one', in virtue of one's status, e.g. as a physician or a patient; two, on the successful negotiation in the course of the interview. This latter relation, while still asymmetrical, is also mutual: the doctor has to rely on the patient for obtaining crucial information, just as much as the patient depends on the doctor for obtaining the remedy he or she seeks for his or her ailments. An interesting circumstance (which is perhaps not emphasized enough in the research by Treichler et al.) is that the exchange of information becomes more effective in an environment of *reduced* unilateral power; a medical student who 'converses' with the patient ('out of curiosity', as he says) after the 'real' interview by the physician, is able to elicit vital information that would have helped the doctor immensely in his diagnosis, had the latter had access to it. Clearly, this shows that when all is said and done, the power you bring with you is a major factor in determining your position as a negotiator and your success (or lack of it) in the negotiation process. (Similar observations have been made by Wodak-Engel (1984) and by O'Barr (1984) with regard to courtroom hearings.)

In a way, one could say that classical speech act theory has put the cart before the horse: the case of the performatives, paraded for inspection on every occasion, is a very special one indeed, and one that is very far removed from 'normal' use of language. When it comes to real-world interaction, successful performance is not exclusively due to the power inherent either in the user or in his or her words; to a high degree, this power resides in the society, but mediated and negotiated in the institutional setting of a particular societal context.

Also when it comes to more mundane problems (such as: How to characterize a question? or: What is a proper answer to a question?), the criterion of strict 'performativity' is ruefully inadequate; in our everyday language use, the only decent characterization of a 'good' answer to a question is: 'One which all the participants in a particular context of question-asking and -answering find acceptable'.[70]

But does that imply that we do *not* 'perform' things with words? By no means. However, we perform in many ways, and the 'performative verbs' are not even a major tool in this respect, as we have seen. With regard to indirect speech acts, our original topic in this chapter, the conclusion must be that they are not 'abnormal' cases (either in theory or in practice); rather, the problem is with the cases which earlier were thought of as 'normal' and which seemed to conform to the standards of speaking with the proper illocutionary force. As pragmaticians, we must ask, first of all, when exercising our power of speech, what *effects* our speech acting has, or can have, when performed in actual social, institutional and other surroundings. This, again, will force us to revise whatever classifications we have adopted of speech acts and of their ways of being expressed. The next chapter will go into some detail with respect to this.

EXERCISES AND REVIEW QUESTIONS

1. Consult again the account (in section 7.1.5) of the telephone conversation between Colonel Bar-Lev and President Idi Amin.

Questions:

How many speech acts can you identify in this text?

What types of speech acts do you recognize? (Use Searle's criteria)

What speech act verbs ('SAVs') are found in this text?

Can you identify any indirect speech acts? Can you suggest an alternative wording to any speech act occurring in the text?

2. Consider the following utterances:

Do you know what time it is?

Do you have the correct time?

Can you tell me how to get to the men's (ladies') room?

Do you see the salt anywhere?

It's cold in here.

Isn't this soup rather bland?

Questions:

What kinds of speech acts are we dealing with here?

Discuss the indirect speech acting that is observed in these examples (note: for finer distinctions, see also section 12.7.2).

3. The famous sage-cum-buffoon Nasreddin Hoca, a figure familiar in popular culture from Serbia to the Middle East, reportedly once had a visit from an importune neighbour, who wanted to borrow a length of rope. This is how the Hoca managed to get out of the bind without offending his neighbour too much:

Neighbour: *Efendim*, could I borrow your rope?
Hoca: Sorry, my friend, the rope is in use.

Neighbour: But I cannot see anybody using it.

Hoca: Of course not, my *harem* is using it.

Neighbour: *Hocam*, what could your *harem* possibly be doing with
　　　　　a length of rope?

Hoca: They're putting flour on it.

Neighbour: *Allah Allah*! How could anybody be putting flour on a
　　　　　rope?

Hoca: Clearly, that's what one does when one doesn't want to let
　　　one's neighbour have it.

　　　(Anonymous, *Nasrettin Hoca'nın letaifi* ['Stories of
　　　Nasreddin Hoca'], Istanbul 1956)

Questions:

What speech acts are being used here?

Why does the Hoca have to explain what he is doing?

Discuss the Cooperative Principle on the basis of this example.

Notes:

Hoca is originally the same word as the Arabic *hadji* 'pilgrim who has
visited Mecca'; in Turkish, it is used as synonymous with 'sage, teacher'.

Hocam, Efendim: the suffix *-m* denotes the first person singular posses-
sive: 'my' (cf. in French: '*mon général*' as form of address to a four-star
officer).

harem means both the actual collection of wives that are allowed a man
under Koranic law and the location where these wives are found (the
usual interpretation in Western texts).

Allah Allah: exclamation of astonishment etc.: 'for God's sake'.

8

Speech Acts and their Classification

8.1 Introduction: The Problem

In his 1977 article 'A classification of illocutionary acts', Searle states the following:

> The primary purpose of this paper is to develop a reasoned classi-
> fication of illocutionary acts into certain basic categories or types.
> (p. 27)

In saying this, Searle takes exception to Austin's original classification (into 'verdictive', 'expositive', 'exercitive', 'behabitive', and 'commissive' acts; 1962: 109ff.). Among other things, Searle criticizes Austin for operating with overlapping criteria, for having incompatible elements within his categories and for including elements in his categories that do not satisfy the definition of the category. But mainly, Searle is unhappy about the fact that Austin apparently does not see that there is a difference between speech acts and speech act verbs, and that the existence or non-existence of the latter cannot (and should not) be a criterion for the existence or non-existence of a particular speech act.

Similarly, Leech criticizes Austin for committing the grave error of supposing that 'verbs in the English language correspond one-to-one with categories of speech act'; in other words, again a confusion of speech acts and speech act verbs. In Leech's words,

> [Austin's] classification (into 'Verdictives'[,] 'Exercitives',
> 'Commissives', 'Behabitives', and 'Expositives') is a prime example

of what I have . . . called the 'Illocutionary-Verb Fallacy' . . . (1983: 176)

a fallacy that is closely connected to the problems I have discussed in several of the preceding chapters (cf. especially sections 6.1.4 and 7.1.3) under the heading of 'performativity' and its pitfalls.

Before I say a few things about Searle's own classification (which in many regards, even in a partially identical nomenclature, replicates Austin's), let us have a look at the background for Searle's criticisms, as they are spelt out in the article mentioned above.

8.2   SEARLE'S CRITERIA: ACT, FORCE AND POINT

When trying to establish the differences between the different speech acts (as, e.g., in the categorization proposed by Austin), one soon discovers that there are many levels at which speech acts can differ. Searle puts it as follows:

> . . . there are several quite different principles of distinction: that is, there are different kinds of difference that enable us to say that the force of this utterance is different from the force of that utterance. (1977: 27)

This being conscious of 'differences that make a difference' should keep us from identifying speech act verbs with speech act types; however, in reality we hurry to conclusions of precisely this kind as soon as we observe two different speech act verbs performing what seemingly are different speech acts but in reality may be the same: e.g. 'to order' and 'to command'. Especially when doing cross-language comparisons, we tend to see such differences in speech acting whenever the other language's speech act verbs are different from what we are accustomed to. To take a very simple example from two well-known, closely related European languages, German and English: whereas German has two verbs describing the action of 'asking' (*bitten*, when you ask for a favour; *fragen*, when you're asking for information), English has only one: 'to ask'. When evaluating such cases, we have to ask ourselves how much of the difference is due to authentic differences with regard to illocutionary point, and how much to variations in forcefulness, politeness, directness of expression, etc. in speech-acting.[71]

Compare also the naïve enthusiasm that many first-time second language (L_2) learners display for the 'richness' of the (however partially acquired) new language acquaintance, as compared to the 'poor' relative in the old country. One frequently hears such learners, after they have become relatively competent in the foreign idiom, say something like; 'Now that I've learned L_2, I just can't say anything in my own language any more without feeling totally inept' (where L_2 stands for the newly acquired, 'second' language – usually English).

The psychological explanation of this phenomenon is that, as you expand your horizon, taking in the different dimensions of another culture, you acquire a language to deal with those differences. It is not always easy, or even practically feasible, to 'feed back' those new experiences into the 'old' language. A new wording process, geared to the new realities, is taking place in the L_2 learner; the old (L_1) wording will be experienced, and quite rightly so, as inadequate for these new processes. The result is similar to the 'moving trains' effect, by which we perceive ourselves as moving, whereas in reality it is the other train pulling out of the station. In the same way, we experience the new language as 'better' only because it is differently oriented (and, of course, better oriented towards our current state of mind-in-the-world).

More or less the same as what has been said here about the 'point' of a speech act verb can be said about its 'force'. Here, too, inter-cultural differences show up. For example, when an American wants to draw his interlocutors' attention to the fact that he has been misunderstood, he may try to clear up the misunderstanding using a speech act of 'self-correcting', e.g. by saying

I'm afraid I didn't express myself too clearly.

Compare this with what a Frenchman might say in a similar situation:

Mais vous ne comprenez pas! (literally, 'But you don't understand!').

If uttered in (American) English, such a speech act might be understood literally, as a statement about the others' level of comprehension, hence possibly about their intelligence, adequate behaviour and cooperation (or lack of such qualities). An American may feel insulted if thusly appraised; yet, there is nothing in the French expression that connotes an insult, or an intention to detract from the other party's mental or intellectual capabilities. In fact, the French speech act represents the same underlying intention as does the American English one: to set a misunderstanding straight, without going into any details: 'If you didn't understand what I said, the reason must be that I didn't express myself too clearly.'

Thus, the difference in speech acting reduces to the question of how to treat the other person's 'face' (cf. section 4.4.4): in the English example, I preempt the threat to the interlocutors' face by blaming myself, whereas the Frenchman goes 'bald on record' as stating the fact of non-understanding. The conclusion that the others must be dumb is not conversationally implied in the French speech acting, whereas it clearly would be in a direct English translation.

Searle tackles the problems connected with the different kinds of speech acting and their relationships to illocutionary verbs by first stating a general warning:

> Differences in illocutionary verbs are a good guide, but by no means a sure guide to differences in illocutionary acts. (1975: 28)

Next, in order to be on the safe side, he enumerates all twelve different dimensions along which speech acts can be different. Among these twelve, he selects a few to guide him in his final determination of the typology of speech acts, to be discussed in section 8.3.3. Here, I will briefly discuss, and comment on, Searle's twelve 'dimensions'.

8.2.1 Illocutionary point

If we ask ourselves what the point is of giving an order, the answer will be something along the lines of: 'to make somebody do something' (or, in the case of a negative order, 'to make somebody stop, or refrain from, doing something'). This is the illocutionary point of the speech act 'to order'.

Similarly, the illocutionary point of a descriptive speech act is to represent reality, somehow or other.

As to promises, we have seen (in section 6.2) how their essential condition is to create an obligation in the speaker that is recognized as such by the hearer; this obligation, then, constitutes the 'point' of promising.

The other speech acts can be described along the same lines as to their illocutionary point.

Searle takes great care to distinguish this 'illocutionary point' from both 'illocutionary act' (the general concept of speech act) and 'illocutionary force'. For the latter distinction, compare the difference between an 'order' and a 'request': these are different speech acts having the same point; however, they are distinguished by a difference in illocutionary force.

8.2.2   Direction of 'fit'

As we have seen above, in section 7.1.2, the term 'fit' conceptualizes a relation between the 'word' (or, generally speaking, 'language') and the 'world' (or, generally speaking, 'reality'). Hence, the 'fit' is between language and reality, and it can be construed either from language to reality, or from reality to language: we either 'word the world', or 'world the word'. In the first case, my utterance is a correct description of a state of affairs in the world (as when I say: 'My checking account is $7,000 in the red', and this is really the case); in the second case, I may express a wish, issue an order, etc., producing a change in the world (as when I say 'I wish I had $7,000 to put into my account', or 'Please transfer $7,000 from my savings to my checking account').

Thus, in speech acting, either language is fitted to reality, or reality is fitted to language. Either way, a change takes place as a result of the use of a speech act; paraphrasing Wittgenstein's famous dictum that 'uttering a true sentence changes the entire world,' we could say that my utterances, by being uttered, perform a change in the world. However, it is not true, as we have seen, that they, for this reason, constitute a special class of speech acts called 'performatives' – a hypothesis rightly dismissed by Leech in his discussion of the 'Performative Fallacy' (also called the 'Illocutionary Verb Fallacy'; see section 8.1). Neither is it the case that, at the other end of the pragmatic spectrum, speech acts operate by the very fact of being said, and effect the change they're implying in their wording (except in special cases, the true performatives, which operate *ex opere operato*, like the words spoken in the baptism ceremony). A well-known folk saying captures this wisdom in the old adage: 'Saying it don't make it so'; maybe this is what Searle had in mind when he maintained that certain speech acts (such as declaratives) merely represent a 'correct fit', while others (such as commissives) 'twist' the fit (e.g. to the advantage of the speaker).

8.2.3   Expressed psychological state

This criterion lets us view a number of seemingly different speech acts under the same angle ('the difference that does *not* make a difference'). Thus, a state of mind, such as a 'belief' (Searle's example), can be expressed in a number of different ways, using different speech acts:

> If one tries to do a classification of illocutionary acts based entirely on differently expressed psychological states . . . one can get quite a long way. Thus, *belief* collects not only statements, assertions, remarks, and explanations, but also reports, claims, deductions, and arguments. (1977: 29)

Conversely, one cannot usually express a psychological state using a speech act (e.g., of 'believing') without being in that particular psychological state (and not in some other, e.g. opposite, state). Doing otherwise would lead to the famous paradox that bears Moore's name:

> The cat is on the mat but I don't believe it.

Here, I utter something about myself in relation to reality: I hold the 'belief' (in the weak sense discussed earlier) that the cat is indeed on the mat (and not, e.g., on the sofa); but then I go on to say that I don't 'really' believe it.[72]

These three criteria are Searle's most important ones; however, the remaining nine deserve to be mentioned as well.

8.2.4   Force

If one compares the sentence

> I suggest that we go home now

with

> I insist that we go home now,

the difference between these two utterances is clearly one of 'illocutionary force' (also interpretable as: speaker's involvement in what is uttered).

8.2.5   Social status

This criterion could also be subsumed under the heading 'micro-social relations' (as opposed to 'macro-social', on which see section 8.2.10). Any utterance has to be situated within the context of the speaker's and hearer's status in society in order to be properly understood. This general principle of pragmatics (on which I will have more to say in chapter 14) is applicable to speech acts as well; it seems proper to call this awareness of societal conditions a 'preparatory condition' in the sense defined above (section 6.2.2).

Consider the 'alternative' that is offered in the following utterance (spoken by a teacher in class):

Either you shut up or you have to leave the classroom.

This is by no means a real alternative in the sense that the student is free to choose whatever s/he prefers; given the social status of the teacher and his or her place in the institution, 'school', the sentence contains an indirectly threatening speech act.

8.2.6   Interest

In any speech situation, the interlocutors have different interests, and worry about different things. The speech acts that are being used in any situation should reflect these interests and worries, as a preparatory condition. Thus, e.g., it would be highly inappropriate to use a speech act of 'congratulating' in a situation where somebody had lost a close relative, a good friend or a beloved pet; any such speech act would be construed as an insult or as sarcasm. Similarly, one's eagerness in offering advice or critique should be carefully measured against the ability or willingness of the interlocutor to accept such advisory or critical remarks.

8.2.7   Discourse-related functions

In many cases, speech acts explicitly refer to the context in which they are being uttered, as a precondition to their proper functioning and their being 'taken up' correctly. Thus, we may refer to what has been said before, or to what is coming later on, the latter being mostly restricted to cases of 'planned discourse', such as written composition or oral rhetoric (on discourse, see sections 9.5 and 10.4.5).

As a rule, these functions are realized through the use of so-called 'sentence adverbials':

By the same token, . . .

In contrast to this, . . .

Similarly, . . .

etc.

We also can use speech acts to realize these goals of 'discourse economy' by uttering, e.g.,

Let me say it like this: . . .

To conclude, . . .

I must register an objection here . . .

or by employing the well-known courtroom speech act of 'objecting' (familiar from a number of famous TV-series):

Objection (Your Honour)!

These and other 'metapragmatic' utterances (on this term, see chapter 13) are often subject to severe constraints; e.g. I cannot 'conclude' for somebody else, nor can I 'insinuate' on my own account: 'I conclude' is only a valid speech act for the speaker him-/herself (as was the case with 'to promise'). An utterance such as 'So, you conclude that . . .' is a speech act by which I express my evaluation of my interlocutor's utterance as a conclusion; it is not the other's speech act of concluding.

8.2.8 Content

This criterion allows us to separate out speech acts in accordance with what they are 'about': for instance, in the dimension of time, past events can never be the object of predictions, only of statements and narrative acts. Thus, in Classical Greek drama, the messenger can only report the death of the protagonist in the past, whereas the chorus may predict the fatal ending in the future. Once the event has come to happen, we are no longer allowed to use the speech act of predicting.

8.2.9   Speech acts or speech act verbs?

An order need not be expressed by a speech act verb of ordering; similarly, most statements are not prefaced by anything that even remotely resembles the speech act verb 'to state'. When it comes to institutionalized speech acts, however, the situation is different, as we have seen above: here, a particular speech act verb usually is *de rigueur*. (I refer to the discussions on this topic in section 7.1.4; see also section 8.2.11.)

8.2.10   Societal institutions and speech acts

Societally institutionalized speech acts were among the first to be discovered by Austin (1962). Since then, we have come to realize that such acts are relatively rare occurrences in everyday speech; yet, the concept of the societal institution as a 'macro-social' factor has been valuable not only as a classificatory criterion, but also as a way of looking at what speech acts really do, and how they are able to do what they do.

Rather than re-hashing the classic examples (such as the launching and naming of ships, the sentencing of criminals in court, and so on), let me illustrate my point by referring to a short story, 'The Breakdown', by the Swiss author Friedrich Dürrenmatt (1956).

In this story, a travelling salesman meets three people in the dining-room of a hotel in a little provincial town where he has to spend the night, because his car has broken down. For some reason, the three gentlemen seem to be overjoyed to see him, and invite him for a late supper at the home of one of the three. During and after the meal, the conversation becomes more and more focused on the hosts' past occupations, respectively as attorney general, judge and trial lawyer; in the end, the trio enacts a mock 'court' session, in which the travelling salesman (who by now has lost any sense of the dimensions of time and space) is condemned to the severest penalties for his past misdeeds.

What is truly interesting here is the way in which societal institutions are re-instituted through the use of speech acts. By force of their earlier occupations, the three gentlemen manage to create the illusion of a court session in which the accused ends up confessing his crimes and accepting his sentence. Not only do the institutions allow for, and determine, the illocutionary point of the appropriate speech acts, they are themselves construed through the macro-social use of the appropriate language.

Here, it is fitting to recall that institutions like the judiciary and its concrete manifestations, such as the different kinds of courts, come about through the combined workings of language and societal relationships.

The societal relations are expressed in the institutions that people have created to take care of the daily exigencies of the common life in a regulated, predictable and universally acceptable way. Thus, while the individual members of society may have no wish or right to kill each other, a way of putting people to death institutionally can be made acceptable through the institutions of ritual sacrifice, war and capital punishment.

However, this is only the one side of the institution as a societal phenomenon. The other side is language. Language is used to record what has been going on, and accepted, in the context of society, in particular, of its institutions. For example, the practice of law in Roman society (a practice which survives in segments of modern legalistic thinking, especially in the far northwestern reaches of the Northern hemisphere such as England, Denmark or Norway) was based on cases (hence the use of the term 'casuistry', literally: 'case-based reasoning', for 'finding a good case to argue your point of view'; the negative connotations are of later date). The logic of societal institutions thus becomes embedded in cases. But cases need to be recorded to be useful. And how can one record a case without the help of language?

Records may initially have been in oral form, but as soon as writing was invented, among its first practical uses were bookkeeping and case-recording. The elaborate records of past cases have resulted, in the legal domain, in such egregious collections (called *corpora*) as the famous *Corpus Iustinianum*, or the *Corpus Iuris Canonici*, to name just two of the historical mainstays of legal thinking, which were originally descriptions of cases and how they were resolved.

With time, the preservative role of language in recording cases becomes more and more a prescriptive one. The roles that are prescribed for the exercise of the societal functions are given in terms of words pronounced ('speech acts'), words recorded ('transcripts'), and words handed down in written form to the next generation ('laws'). 'Law' becomes synonymous with 'written law' – which is why we still call it 'to read law', or 'to read at the bar', when a person studies in the legal domain with the intention of obtaining authorization to practise as a lawyer.

The significance of Dürrenmatt's little game episode is that it shows us the quasi-independence of the 'law' (as embodied in roles and their corresponding language) from the societal anchoring that shores it up, as far as the individual subject goes. The hapless traveller who fell into the clutches of the quasi-practising legal trio was every bit as 'damned' as he would have been had he been condemned by a regular court. Indeed, the court needn't even be there at all; as long as we're aware it's there, it can stay in the background, as in the case of Josef K in Kafka's The Trial. As Berger and Luckmann say,

Only through . . . representation in performed roles can the institution manifest itself in actual experience. The institution, with its assemblage of 'programmed' actions, is like the unwritten libretto of a drama. The realization of the drama depends upon the reiterated performance of its prescribed roles by living actors. (1966: 70)

What Berger and Luckmann do not say, however, or maybe do not even see, is that the language embodying the law takes on a life of its own (as we have seen above, section 7.2.4): the speech act of sentencing not only creates a state of affairs (the person sentenced is now going to jail), but it also creates and re-creates itself (the sentence pronounced confirms the reality of the legal system). A law that isn't practised is no law; a judge who does not sentence is no judge; a district attorney who does not prosecute is not a proper district attorney, and a chief of police who never makes an arrest is not a good policeman (witness Police Chief Bastian in Thorbjørn Egner's (1960) well-known portrayal of 'people and robbers' in Kardemomme City). This is the psychological, sociological and pragmatic relevance of the legal 'joke' perpetrated on the traveller in the Dürrenmatt story.

8.2.11 Speech acts and performatives

As we have seen, only certain speech acts can be said to have a performative character; that is, the property of doing what they explicitly say. This criterion has been discussed extensively in section 7.1.3.

8.2.12   Style

For most people, the way we say things – that is, mainly (but not exclusively) the speech acts we avail ourselves of when saying certain things – are often more important than the contents of what is being said. I'll never forget the time when a colleague of mine, in response to a question in a seminar, told the questioner: 'I don't understand the status of your question.' In the context, this answer 'counted as' (to use Searle's expression) a put-down: what was said had this particular effect because of, among other things, the style of answering.

Similarly, a simple question like

What do you mean by that?

can be the famous piece of red cloth that sets off some people's wildest aggressions ('What do you mean, "What do you mean?"?!'), while others perceive nothing but an innocent query. *Le style, c'est l'homme*, 'The style is the (hu)man', as the French proverb has it; speech acts are not excepted from this tendency. Still, it is the case that particular speech acts in certain cultures are considered to be inherently more aggressive than others; linguistic fieldworkers report that it can be difficult to elicit answers to questions in foreign languages because the asking of questions in the other cultures is perceived as belonging to different universes of discourse – at times merely stylistic, at other times painfully realistic (cf. our 'exam questions', or the modern revival of earlier methods of 'strict interrogation').

8.3   On Searle's Classification of Speech Acts

8.3.1   Introduction

As I said above (section 8.1), Searle finds fault with Austin's taxonomy of speech acts for various reasons (inconsistency, incompleteness and so on). His twelve criteria discussed in the preceding section are supposed to lay the groundwork for a better classificatory procedure. Let us consider the resulting taxonomy, and then compare it to the one suggested by Austin.

8.3.2 Searle's speech acts

First of all, it should be noted that in his taxonomy Searle uses only four of his twelve criteria, namely:

- Illocutionary point
- Direction of fit
- Psychological state
- Content.

Two further conditions essential for a pragmatic understanding of speech acting are not covered by Searle and hence are not included among the twelve criteria above; these are:

- Reference to a speaker or a hearer ['S', 'H']

(speakers and hearers do occur in Searle's early descriptions of the individual speech acts; however, they are never explicitly introduced), and

- Contextual conditions (i.e. the framework in which a speech act has to be performed to be valid).

These conditions will be discussed further in chapter 14.

The five categories that Searle (1977: 34) ends up establishing are:

- Representatives[73]
- Directives
- Commissives
- Expressives
- Declarations.

I will discuss the five in this order.

8.3.2.1 Representatives (assertives)

These speech acts are assertions, in the classical sense of Frege, and thus carry the values 'true' or 'false'. This is their 'point'; as to 'fit', they should, of course, match the world in order to be true.

The problem with assertions is that they often, perhaps even always, represent a subjective state of mind: the speaker who asserts a proposition as true, does so based on his or her belief – thus, the belief may have different degrees of 'force'. It makes a difference whether I postulate something or merely hypothesize; however, the point of the speech act remains the same.

On a closer look, though, there seem to be many 'asserting' statements for which the 'true/false' criterion does not hold. Is a complaint true or false? We usually say that a complaint is justified, if and only if the content of the complaint is truthful, i.e. represents the world in a true manner; but that is not the same as saying that the complaint is true. Hence, the status of this particular criterion is somewhat uncertain: Searle (1977: 35) admits that strictly speaking it is neither necessary nor sufficient (the same criticism, incidentally, that he had earlier directed at some of Austin's classifying characteristics).

8.3.2.2   Directives

As the name suggests, these speech acts embody an effort on the part of the speaker to get the hearer to do something, to 'direct' him or her towards some goal (of the speaker's, mostly). This is their illocutionary point; at the extreme end of this category, we have the classical imperatives.

As to the 'fit' that these speech acts represent, there is also a clear 'direction' in the other, technical sense of this term, namely, from words to world: the world is adapted to the uttered words. Thus, imperatives (at least in intent) change the world in that they (hopefully) make things happen in accordance with my wishes.

Directives differ in force, from pious wish to peremptory, harsh order. (Austin had placed them under either 'exercitives' or 'behabitives'; see below, section 8.3.2.5.)

8.3.2.3   Commissives

This class turns out to be more or less identical with Austin's of the same name; Searle calls it 'unexceptionable' (1977: 35). Like directives, commissives operate a change in the world by means of creating an obligation; however, this obligation is created in the speaker, not in the hearer, as in the case of the directives. As an instance, compare the difference between a request and a promise: the first is a directive, the second a commissive. As to their 'direction of fit', they are identical (world adapted to words). However, the 'direction' of the obligation created (or maybe better, its 'locus') is different: whereas the promise creates an obligation in the promiser, the request does so in the requestee.

One can ask whether it would be useful to lump these two speech acts, requests and promises, together into one category of 'obligatives'. For Searle, the problem with this suggestion is in the nature of the obligation: requesting somebody to do something does not create the kind of obligation that a promise does.

However, one could perhaps consider the act of promising to be a particular kind of request, one directed towards the speaker, and having a particular 'promising force': thus, the difference between directives and commissives would be reduced to one of illocutionary force. Such a hypothesis would square well with the varying degrees of force that one has to assign to promises anyhow: as we have seen above, there are great differences in the ways people use promises from culture to culture, something which has been the cause of much misunderstanding and has given rise to a number of cross-cultural prejudices (such as that of the supposedly 'unreliable natives'; for more detail, see Mey 1985: 40–2).

8.3.2.4 Expressives

These speech acts, as the word says, express an inner state of the speaker which, insofar as it is essentially subjective, says nothing about the world. Saying 'Excuse me' when stepping on a person's toe (to use Searle's example) has nothing to do, causally or in terms of consequences, with the act of stepping as such: the words 'Excuse me' do not change anything here, done is done, and both stepper and 'steppee' will have to live with the consequences of this particular change in world conditions: a stepped-on toe. In this sense, the criterion of 'fit' cannot be said to operate. (However, as we will see below (section 8.4.2), there is another sense in which we can speak of 'fit', and here world-conditions do play a role.)

One might ask why on earth people would bother to utter apologetic expressions when committing social and other gaffes, when the evil is done anyway and cannot be reversed – especially in cases where an evil intention seems to be foreclosed. People do not normally step on other people's toes for fun, or with premeditation; and if they indeed should so do, they certainly will not apologize (except perhaps for fun, or in hypocrisy).

This is certainly a point to take into consideration when discussing the speech act of 'expressives': because of its subjective character, this speech act is also subject to limitations and changes according to different conceptualizations of social guilt behaviour. In Japan, e.g., it is not customary to say *Sumimasen*, 'Excuse me', when stepping on people's toes in the subway; on the contrary, apologizing for such a (mostly unavoidable) social blunder would make people suppose that one had indeed had evil intentions. In the same vein, only the good Lord can, strictly speaking, apologize for bad weather; common humans can only be bothered or irritated by it.

Another matter is the *truth* of the expressive speech act – or rather, the truth of the 'embedded proposition', called (somewhat misleadingly) a 'property' of the speech act by Searle. If I congratulate somebody on an exam, the presupposition is that there has indeed been an exam, and that the person has passed (unless I'm being ironical, or even sarcastic). The offering of condolences in the case of a bereavement is an expression of sorrow, supposed to be present in the speaker and to be in sympathy with the state of sorrow in the hearer; this naturally presupposes that the hearer indeed has suffered the loss I offer my condolences for (again, barring hypocrisy and the like).[74]

8.3.2.5 Declarations

Actually, this is in a way the 'original' category of speech acts; the 'declarative' in, e.g.,

I declare this bridge to be opened

is the declaration that changes the state of affairs in the world with respect to the bridge. What earlier was a 'not-yet-opened' bridge now becomes an opened bridge. Similarly in the case of

I declare you to be husband and wife,

the marriage candidates cease to be just an ordinary (albeit loving) pair of people, and become a married couple. In Searle's words:

Declarations bring about some alternation in the status or condition of the referred to object or objects solely by virtue of the fact
that the declaration has been successfully performed. (1977: 37)

Austin used this distinction to establish what he saw as the main
divider in speech act theory: the difference between locutionary and
illocutionary acts. On the face of it, an utterance such as

I just resigned

is as much a declarative statement as

You're (hereby) fired;

however, the big difference is that while the former utterance is a purely
descriptive statement (which does not change my universe of employment, only reports such a change), the latter is the fatal utterance termi-
nating my relationship with the firm; in the first case, I choose my words
such that they fit the world, whereas in the second, the speaker fits the
world to his words.

    In this way, Austin arrived at the first, main distinction between purely
'constative' and 'performative' verbs, a distinction that later came under
much attack, as we have seen in section 7.1.3. The reason for this attack
is that even the simplest, most neutral statement still has some effect on
the world in which it is enunciated. And this effect is obtained by some
sort of illocutionary act (which one could call 'enunciative'). The difference between such acts and the original, 'performative' ones would then
be either in the change they operate on the world, or in their respective
forces (as in the case of the directives discussed in section 8.3.2.2), or
both – but *not* in the performative quality of one of the members of the
distinction. And this is precisely the insight Searle maintains Austin
arrived at in his book *How to Do Things with Words*:

The main theme of Austin's mature work, *How to Do Things
with Words*, is that this distinction [between locutionary and
illocutionary acts] collapses. Just as saying certain things constitute
[sic] getting married (a 'performative'), and saying certain things
constitute [sic] making a promise (another 'performative'), so saying certain things constitute [sic] making a statement (supposedly a

'constative'). As Austin saw, but as many philosophers still fail to see, the parallel is exact. Making a statement is as much performing an illocutionary act as making a promise, a bet, a warning, or what have you. Any utterance will consist in performing one or more illocutionary acts. (1977: 37)

When we focus on the 'fit' between world and words, however, the declaratives seem to occupy a privileged place. Even though 'declaring' that you've been fired may be a perfectly acceptable illocutionary act, it still isn't the act that changed your employment situation. That declaration has to obey other conditions, such as being uttered by a person in power (I'll return to this in the next section).

Interestingly, in cases where changes of the latter type are really important in the context of society, the two speech act types are assigned to (theoretically at least) independent societal institutions. This is the philosophy underlying the separation of powers in modern, secular society, or (as in the judiciary) the separation of the power of 'declaring' in the first sense (as performed by the jury in rendering a verdict: 'Guilty/ Not guilty'), and that of 'declaring' in the second sense (as performed by the judge in sentencing: 'To be hanged by the neck until dead').

Notice especially that the judge's declaration (in the latter sense) does change the world for the accused, and that the sentence, once executed, cannot be undone. Still, the judge has not 'declared' (in the first sense) the person to have committed the crime of which he or she stands accused; that speech act, being separated from the execution of the sentence, can at any time be undone. This is the ultimate sense of rehabilitating the victims of 'persecutive speech acting' in the world of politics: The truth cannot, and should not, be allowed to die, even if people can.

8.3.3   A preliminary conclusion

8.3.3.1   Restating the problem

I began this chapter by referring to various criticisms that have been offered of Austin's original theory of speech acts, and in particular of his classificatory categorization. Another classification was suggested by one of Austin's critics, John Searle; this classification, which supposedly avoids the weaknesses inherent in Austin's, was the subject of a detailed examination in the preceding sections.

The question is now: Has Searle's proposal been successful, and if not, what is the reason?

I will divide this question into two parts: first, an internal criticism of Searle's classification, and second, some remarks of a more general nature, leading into a discussion of the feasibility of classifying human speech acts on the basis of their 'surface form' alone.

8.3.3.2   Searle and Austin

Searle is undoubtedly right in criticizing Austin for the deficiencies in his classificatory schema. For instance, the categories that Austin establishes are not mutually exclusive, as their criteria often overlap (e.g., the speech act of 'describing' belongs at the same time in the category of 'verdictives' and in that of 'expositives'; cf. also the problems with 'declaring' that we discussed in section 8.3.2.5). Further, there is, in Austin's work, a rather general confusion between the notion of 'speech acts' and that of 'speech act verbs'; the definitions of speech acts that Austin provides are too wide; and so on.

But, in order to do due justice to all parties, one should not forget that Austin himself was not always happy with the classes of speech acts he proposed: among others, his 'behabitives' caused him a lot of trouble. And even though in his description of the individual speech act he often ended up describing particular speech act verbs in English, the importance of his discovery, namely that language is an instrument of action, not just of speaking, is not restricted to a particular language, nor has it diminished over time.

When it comes to evaluating Searle's classification, the first thing one notes is that in many respects it resembles Austin's. Thus, Searle, like Austin, distinguishes five classes of speech acts; and one of Searle's classes, the so-called 'commissives', is more or less conceptually identical with, and extensionally coterminous to, the class defined by Austin under the same name. In Searle's exposition, much is made of all the different criteria that one could employ in order to establish a coherent and consistent taxonomy; but when it comes to applying the criteria, only a few of them are used, and not even these are applied exclusively all the time by Searle's own admission (cf. the case of 'complaining', discussed in section 8.3.2.1 under the speech act category 'representatives' ('assertives')).

However, in one respect Searle's taxonomy is superior to Austin's: it is more oriented towards the real world, inasmuch as it takes its point of departure in what actually is the case (that people perform a speech act whenever they use language, irrespective of the 'performative' criterion), and that therefore the interest of linguists and philosophers should centre on the illocutionary aspects of language use, rather than on the dubious distinction between locutionary and illocutionary acts (which Searle, by the way, never accepted; cf. 1969: 23).

If one wants to criticize Searle and his categorization, one cannot overlook the fact that both he and Austin, as philosophers, had certain objectives in describing language which, for linguistic purposes, did not always seem that relevant. Over the years, with the development of pragmatic linguistics, these shortcomings have become more and more apparent; the next section will discuss some of them.

8.4   THE CASE AGAINST SPEECH ACTS: THE PRAGMATIC VIEW

Both Austin and Searle operate on the 'one sentence–one case principle'. That is to say, in order to illustrate their theory, they use examples that are characteristic of what they see as the 'case' under discussion, such as, e.g., a particular kind of speech act. I will, in the following, show the shortcomings of the 'case approach' by discussing some 'cases': that of the Austinian 'promise' and that of the 'stepped-on toe' (from sections 8.3.2.3 and 8.3.2.4 above); throwing in an historical *cause célèbre* for good measure.

8.4.1   Promise revisited

Austin, in discussing promises, limits himself to one single instance, one isolated utterance of promising; Searle does the same. However, if we look at promises from a slightly wider perspective, we notice that the context in which a promise is made is of the utmost importance for its status as a promise and for its binding effects. Take the case of a young person promising his or her parents not to smoke before the age of eighteen. In this case, the societal conditions surrounding the execution of such a promise can be exceedingly difficult (peer-group pressure, work conditions, etc.). In such a context, a more explicit act of promising (rather than simply saying 'I won't smoke until I'm eighteen') makes sense.

Similarly, in the case of the 'vow' against the 'promise', it is the societal context that motivates the distinction. The vow is a solemn public promise with great illocutionary force, and should only be used in contexts where society imposes a need of such a unique promising, invoking sanctions of all kinds, and promising select, often recognizable, social status to the promisers (as in the case of monks and nuns, or of the Vestal virgins of ancient Rome). We could say that this societal context is a kind of 'preparatory condition' on vows, and in general, any kind of promise – a contextual condition that obliges both promiser and promisee to enquire whether there exist conditions that would create certain rights and obligations either to accept the promise or reject it. Why is a promise made to a person about to die considered more binding than a regular promise? Can I accept a promise from a person who evidently is not able to realize what the promise is all about? (As a child, I promised my mother I would never leave her; luckily, she never held this against me.)

Indeed, for promises as for other speech acts, with regard to their preparatory, felicity, essential and other conditions, the condition above all conditions is the human condition: 'Felicity's condition', to quote Goffman (1983: 53).

All this may seem fairly obvious. But how then to explain that we are only able or willing to admit the importance of such factors at times when we are motivated by other considerations, such as the need of being 'pedagogical' or 'adult' with regard to one's children, not wanting to bind them to promises they evidently cannot ever keep? Clearly, the problem is not one of being 'nice' or 'adult' about one's promises: it touches the very core of the speech act and the conditions for its valid and legitimate use.

Factors such as these are never brought to the fore in Austin's or Searle's discussions. In all probability, they would reject the inclusion of contextual factors among the criteria for categorizing speech acts (cf. the fact that even though Searle mentions the institutional character of speech acting, he does not utilize this criterion; cf. section 8.2.10). However, from a pragmatic point of view there is no doubt that we should pay attention to such conditions when describing speech acts and, in general, people's use of language.

The reason for this is that if the societal conditions for a particular speech act's being realized are not met, there simply is no speech act, no matter what is said or written. In the legal tradition, this insight has furnished us with the category of 'promises under duress', which aren't promises at all; other speech act categories show similar examples. The next section discusses one such (historically rather notorious) case of 'frustrated speech acting'.

8.4.2 Of bulls and briefs

A famous instance of a speech act that didn't quite make it is found in the story of the suppression of the Jesuit order in the late eighteenth century. The instrument of this suppression was a so-called 'Papal brief'; for documents such as Papal bulls and briefs to be valid as a legal instruments (e.g. of proclaiming an interdict,[75] of condemning a heresy and so on), they have to be read publicly in the presence of those whom they concern. Without such a reading (called a 'promulgation'), the document is null and void, as far as its legal effects are concerned.

The history of the *Compañía de Jesús* (Society of Jesus, the Order of Jesuits founded by Iñigo (St Ignatius) de Loyola in 1536) provides us with an interesting case of non-operative Papal speech acting. In the year 1783, after much pressure from a number of European (in particular, the Portuguese and French) governments, the Holy See decided to dissolve the Jesuit Order world-wide. Without going into the particulars of this rather unique event in the history of the Church and in the practice of Canon Law (other 'suppressions' of religious orders having been mostly local, such as that of the Carthusians by Emperor Joseph II of Austria-Hungary in 1782), one can safely say that the disbanding of the Jesuits was a political act, rather than a disciplinary measure of strictly religious character.

However, the interesting point about the particular legal instrument that was created by Pope Clement XIV in the form of the Papal brief *Dominus ac Redemptor* (1774) was that it could not be promulgated world-wide, as intended by the Pope. In Russia, the strong-willed and hard-headed Empress Catherine the Great was not going to allow the intrusion of any papal nonsense onto her territory – which, at the time, after Poland's third partition, contained most of 'Polonia Maior and Mazovia', i.e. the parts of Poland that were closest to Russia. In those newly acquired parts of the Czarist empire, which was predominantly Roman Catholic, there were several Jesuit residences; and these continued to function without special interference from the Orthodox Church or the Russian authorities. Thus, Poland's partition, a disaster to the nation, became a blessing for the Jesuits: since the brief never was promulgated in any of the Polish Jesuit 'houses', these residences could not formally be dissolved, and continued in effect to exist until the Order's glorious restoration (by means of Pius VII's Papal bull *Sollicitudo omnium ecclesiarum*) in 1814.

To this happy ending of the story, a few comments should be added from the point of view of speech act theory. First, there are those Papal 'speech acts': not only may their different nomenclature seem puzzling to the lay person, but why was a 'brief' used for the Jesuit Order's suppression, as against a 'bull' for its restoration?

The answer to this question is of some theoretical, but mainly of a practical interest. One could argue that, in a general way of speaking, there is a different force at play in the various illocutionary acts that these acts contain (bulls are more forceful than briefs). However, as to the perlocutionary effect of these Papal 'speech acts', there seems to be only little difference: at any rate, things couldn't possibly have been worse for the Jesuits, even though their suppression only happened by way of a brief, rather than a bull.

The real and most important difference between the two instruments of 'ordering' is of a quite different, pragmatic nature. It is contained in the 'felicity conditions' that govern the issuing by a Pope of a particular legal instrument: whereas a brief requires only two signatories to be valid, a bull needs twenty. Given the controversial nature of the Papal act, it seems clear that His Holiness Pignatelli preferred not to have to shop around for too many signatures, and stayed with a brief, rather than do it the bullish way.

Papal bulls offer other interesting examples of 'legalistic speech acting'. At the end of each bull, all the various speech act verbs that have been used throughout the bull are repeated in their nominalized forms. For instance, if the bull has 'commanded' somebody to do something, then at the end will be found the phrase: 'Let nobody dare to go against this command'; if there has been a speech act of 'revoking', then the corresponding verbal noun ('revocation') is mentioned in the Bull's final clauses; the verb 'abrogate' is matched by the noun 'abrogation'; and so on. Correspondingly, the final clauses of any Papal bull are of the following, standardized form:

If anybody should be so bold as to go against these letters of command, admonition, abrogation, revocation ... let him know

that he will incur the wrath of Almighty God and of His Holy
Apostles St Peter and St Paul. Given in Rome, at the Holy Apostles
Peter and Paul's, in the Year of Our Lord . . . , in the . . . th year of
Our Pontificate.

We see how, using a final, compounded nominalized speech act, the
bull wraps up the entirety of its legal illocutionary force in one fell sweep
of 'threatening-by-telling': 'Let him know . . .' ('We're only telling
you . . .').

8.4.3   Once more: Stepping on toes

In section 8.3.2.4, I discussed the speech act of 'excusing oneself'. There,
I remarked on some of the cultural differences surrounding this act, and
offered some observations from a Japanese context.

The problem lies deeper, though, than first assumed. In Searle's interpretation, excusing oneself does not change the world: there is no real
contextual effect to this 'expressive' speech act, and the only valuable
criterion is that of sincerity (in the utterer) and that of truth (in the
propositional content of the excuse, namely its object).

However, what Searle (and most other speech act theoreticians) do not
see is that there are other factors involved in changing the world than
those having to do with propositional content, and that changes of this
kind may well be the real purpose of the speech acting. Take the example
of apologies. In certain parts of the world, such as West Africa, the use
of an 'excuse me' (or equivalent expression) does not connote any guilt
or direct responsibility on the part of the speaker (as it would do in our
culture). If I see somebody falling off his bicycle in Ghana, and I happen
to be passing by, it would be perfectly all right for me to utter 'Sorry' or
something like that, even though it wasn't my fault that the rider lost his
balance. Similarly, in Japan one can utter *Sumimasen* (the multi-purpose
'Excuse me') in situations where an excuse would be highly inappropriate
in our culture, such as when we are offered a gift, or when we accept an
invitation.

What happens in these cases is in reality an adjustment of the 'fit' that
we have talked about so much above: a realignment of the world in the
wake of a temporary disturbance in which the speaker and the hearer
have been somehow involved (as spectators, as givers or receivers of gifts,
as some who have undergone wrongdoing and so on). The speech act of

'excusing' serves to ensure that all social and psychological mechanisms are set back to 'normal', and the green light is given for further, safe interaction at the 'unmarked' level: 'Business as usual'.

EXERCISES AND REVIEW QUESTIONS

1. Consider the following text (from a Bankruptcy Court Order, Northern District of Illinois, Eastern Division, by Judge Jack B. Schmaetterer, *in re* the petition for relief by the well-known bicycle manufacturing company Schwinn (28 December, 1992):

> Enclosed is a form of a Proof of Claim. Each Proof of Claim must be filed . . . *on or before 4:30 p.m. Chicago, Illinois time, on January 6, 1993* . . .
> PLEASE TAKE FURTHER NOTICE THAT . . . ANY HOLDER OF A CLAIM WHO FAILS TO FILE A PROOF OF CLAIM ON OR BEFORE 4:3O P.M. CHICAGO TIME, ON JANUARY 6, 1993 . . . SHALL BE FOREVER BARRED, ESTOPPED, AND ENJOINED FROM ASSERTING SUCH CLAIM (OR FILING A PROOF OF CLAIM WITH RESPECT THERETO) . . .

Questions:

What kind of speech act(s) do we encounter here?

How many are there?

Are we looking at speech acts, speech act verbs, or what? (Discuss the question in terms of illocutionary point and force.)

Why do you think the judiciary uses this kind of language? (see section 8.4.2 for a hint).

2. Compare the following two warnings, appearing on the brown paper wrapping bags that the OLLB (Ontario Liquor Licencing Board) provides its customers with to hide their purchases in when venturing out into the street:

(English) 'Don't drink and drive'

(French) 'Si vous buvez, ne conduisez pas' [lit. 'if you drink, don't drive']

Questions:

What is the illocutionary force involved here?

Is there a difference between the English and the French text in this respect?

If so, what is the difference?

If not, why the different wording?

Here is another variant of the French text:

'Si vous buvez, ne prenez pas le volant' [lit. 'if you drink, don't take the wheel']

Ask yourself the same questions as above.

In addition, explain what 'to take the wheel' means, and how it is related to 'to drive'.

Do you have any suggestions as to why, and in which context, the latter expression might be preferred?

3. On presidential promises

On 14 January, 1993, US President-elect Bill Clinton spoke to journalists in the wake of rumours that he might go back on some of his promises made during the electoral campaign. This issue came up with particular force after a number of Haitian 'boat people' had been stopped and turned back from the coasts of Florida, and Clinton had reversed his earlier stand, made during the campaign, according to which he wouldn't turn away any Haitian refugees. When cornered by some rather insistent journalists, Clinton came up with the following statement:

I think it would be foolish for the President of the United States, for any President of the United States, not to respond to changing circumstances. Every President of the United States, as far as I know, and particularly those who have done a good job, have known how to respond to changing circumstances. It would clearly be foolish for a President of the United States to do otherwise. (National Public Radio broadcast, 8:00 a.m., 15 January, 1993)

Three days later, on Sunday 17 January, National Public Radio news analyst Daniel Schorr read a mock 'pre-inaugural statement' ascribed to Bill Clinton, in which he made the President-elect take back all his promises before the inauguration 'so he wouldn't have to break them afterwards'. Schorr/Clinton concluded his 'address' with the words:

'Campaigning is not the same as governing.'

Questions:

What can one say about promises made during an electoral campaign, if you look at them from a Searlian point of view?

And from a pragmatic point of view?

How do you evaluate the sentence: 'Campaigning is not the same as governing'? Do you agree? Why (not)?

Going back to Clinton answering the journalists, is there anything in his choice of words that strikes you as unusual?

If you were to assign Clinton's words an illocutionary label, what would it be?

How about their 'force'?

Is 'force' a significant factor here, pragmatically speaking? In what way?

Do 'illocutionary force' and 'pragmatic force' always go together? (let's define 'pragmatic force' as more or less the same as 'perlocutionary effect', for the time that it takes you to provide an answer to the question).

PART III

Macropragmatics

9

Introduction to Macropragmatics

9.1 INTRODUCTION: CO-TEXT AND CONTEXT

In parts I and II of this book, I have concentrated on the pragmatics of the lesser units of human language use: from questions of implicature, deixis, anaphora and reference up to and including speech acts. All the time, I have maintained that a truly pragmatic view on language cannot, and should not, restrict itself to these 'micropragmatic' contexts (as one could call them), but will have to expand into what I will call 'macropragmatics'.

There are two ways of understanding this term.

One is the *extensional* way of simply enlarging the scope of the units we're looking at: rather than examining isolated sentences or utterances, we consider those same sentences and utterances placed in the contexts in which they belong, and from which they originally were culled in order to illustrate the points made in the previous chapters.

This, again, can be understood in two ways: either as extending the scope of the individual utterances making up the text; in this way, one defines the *co-text*, as it is called (see the next section). Or, alternatively and in addition, we may consider those utterances in their natural 'habitat', so to speak; in the latter case, we're dealing with the larger *context* in which people use language, in particular for the purpose of conversation.

The other way of dealing with 'macropragmatics' is to dig down to the *intensional* base of pragmatics, putting emphasis on those factors that, albeit not explicitly expressed in any text, still determine the form of that text in ways that are difficult to analyse, or even see, with the naked eye.

Basically, what these questions and problems amount to is the eternal query of 'whose language' we're speaking, and why (Mey 1985). Raising this question amounts to starting an investigation into the societal parameters of language use. Furthermore, the problems envisaged here will have to be framed against a background of a deeper understanding of familiar concepts such as rules, utterances, speech acts, contexts and so on. Such questions will properly be treated under the heading of *metapragmatics*, broadly understood as: 'reflections on the language users' use'.

From this point of view, the present part of my book naturally falls into, first, a number of chapters dealing with so-called 'conversation analysis'. (Questions of 'text linguistics' proper will be dealt with only briefly in the present book: see section 9.2.) After that, a chapter will deal with metapragmatic questions of various kinds. Finally, in a concluding chapter we will look more closely into the social conditions of language use; unfortunately, we will only be able to skim the surface of the problem.[76]

The present chapter will present an overview of the entire macro-pragmatic problematic, starting from the single utterance (or sentence) up to and including the notion of 'discourse'.

9.2   FROM SENTENCE (PAIR) TO TEXT

Most people will agree that single sentences, or pairs of sentences (as exemplified in the standard conversational interchange: greeting–greeting, question–answer, and so on), are not sufficient as a framework for a pragmatic theory, and that we have to extend our vision to what is loosely called the 'text'. However, not all are agreed on what a text is, and how to deal with it.

'Text theory', as such, is not an invention of the last decades. Although most linguists of the traditional observances have concentrated their attention on describing units of 'sub-text' size, even structuralists such as the Dane Louis Hjelmslev held that the proper object of linguistic analysis was the text (cf. Hjelmslev 1943: 18).

In more recent times, we have witnessed the rise of so-called 'text grammar'. In its more primitive version, a text grammar is no more than a grammar of anything that extends beyond the sentence. For some text grammarians, the text is indeed nothing but an extended sentence, bound together by certain special, somewhat strange 'punctuation marks', called 'sentence connectives'. This is the view advocated by, among others, Katz and Fodor in their early (and influential) article 'The structure of a semantic theory':

> ... discourse [i.e. text] can be treated as a single sentence in isolation by regarding sentence boundaries as sentential connectives. (1963: 181)

Others, thus van Dijk, in his early writings, or Petöfi (e.g. 1976), distinguish between 'composite sentences' and 'sequences of sentences', in this way extending the theory of speech acts to comprise the text, or part of it, under the concept of a 'macro speech act', that is a speech act that is spread out, so to speak, over several utterances to form a

> ... global speech act performed by the utterance of a whole discourse, and executed by a sequence of possibly different speech acts. (van Dijk 1977: 215)

Even though we now know that a text is neither a pair or some simple sequence of sentences, nor a sequence of utterances each representing an individual speech act, such early endeavours should not be peremptorily brushed off as nothing but clumsy efforts to go beyond the limitations of the sentence. These approaches, for all their weaknesses, represent an important historical step towards widening our outlook on human language production, by recognizing the insufficiency of describing language as consisting of small, isolated units of description, and trying to transcend these by looking at larger units, called 'text'.[77]

The trouble, however, with such endeavours is not only that they do not go far enough: ironically, the very assumption that they operate under – that a text somehow is an ordered sequence of some smaller units – prevents these approaches from *ever* going far enough. In text production, it is impossible to tell exactly when a certain sequence is 'long enough' to qualify as a text. Text is produced all the time: the production of text literally never comes to a stop, as long as there are text producers. Hence, there is no such thing as a sufficiently long, or even a 'longest' sentence (an insight that early generative-transformational grammar had already come to); *a fortiori*, there is no longest text, or body of texts.

Pursuing any extensional conception of text grammar, we find our-selves in a kind of double bind: on the one hand, we think of a text as an (infinitely expandable) sentence or sentence-like object; on the other, such an abstract, theoretical construct will never match the concrete, finite reality of spoken or written texts. If we ask how we can escape this impasse, the answer is simply that the text, as discussed in the above framework, is not a particularly helpful or interesting concept in under-standing human speech behaviour. What we need to do is to transcend the limited approach that sees texts as collections of language produc-tions and ascribes these productions to a single individual uttering sen-tences, or even to pairs of individuals exchanging standardized text units such as questions and answers, orders and acknowledgements, promises and acceptances, and other simple conversational repartees.

By widening our perspective to what (in the widest possible sense) surrounds spoken or written utterances, we also obtain a better under-standing of what the utterances are really about; as we know, utterances only make sense when they are quoted in their proper context.

Usually, one defines the co-text of a (single or multiple) sentence as that portion of text which (more or less immediately) surrounds it. (Unfortunately, there are no agreed limits as to what 'immediately' is supposed to mean here.)

However, such a co-text of utterance is insufficient for our under-standing of the words that are spoken, unless it includes an understand-ing of the actions that take place as part of, and as a result of, those words. In order to understand people's linguistic behaviour, we need to know what their language use is about; that is, we must look further than the co-text of utterance and take the whole of the linguistic scene into our view. This means that we must extend our vision from co-text to *con-text*: the entirety of circumstances (not only linguistic) that surround the production of language.[78] What does this mean? A first approach could go as follows.

9.3 From Speech Act to Conversation

In Part II, I spent a lot of time talking about speech acts and about the ways they are used to express our aims and intentions: what we want to 'do with our words', as Austin put it. In the present chapter, I want to situate those speech acts in the context in which most of them normally and naturally occur: in interchanges between two or several 'conversationalists'.

Such a context should not be restricted to what, technically speaking, is a co-text. It will not only have to go beyond the individual speech act and its expression, but even beyond what many linguists, especially speech act theorists, have traditionally assumed to be the ideal (and correct) frame for their theory: the two-person, two-utterance 'interchange' (A says something to which B replies). In the framework of so-called 'conversation analysis' (CA), the various mechanisms determining people's use of language in an extended, open conversational setting are explored: Who holds the right to speak (often called the 'floor', because that's where 'common' people traditionally stand when they speak in public); what kind of rules are there for either yielding or holding on to the 'floor'; what makes a particular point in the conversation particularly appropriate for a 'turn' (one speaker leaving the floor, another taking it); and so on?

Conversation analysts have deployed a wealth of insights into these matters, and have elaborated an impressive arsenal of techniques for the description and explanation of the mechanisms of conversation, as we will see in the following chapters. However, with all due respect for their findings and results, the framework in which they operate is strictly that of a co-text, in the sense defined above; put in another way, CA is a minimalist approach, which allows only so much hypothesizing as is strictly required to explain the phenomena at hand.

While such a parsimonious attitude to theory building undoubtedly has its merits, it also causes certain deficiencies inasmuch as it leaves out all 'contextual' considerations (in the sense of 'context' I talked about a moment ago). In particular, the social aspects of this extended context have no place to go in such a framework; which is what explains some of the weaknesses of the CA approach.[79] The following section will deal with these aspects; for a more in-depth treatment of the social aspects of text production and consumption, see chapter 14, below.

9.4   SOCIETY AND CONTEXT

Linguistic behaviour is social behaviour. People talk because they want to socialize, in the widest possible sense of the word: either for fun, or to express themselves to other humans, or for some 'serious' purposes, such as building a house, closing a deal, solving a problem and so on. This basic fact implies two other, equally basic facts:

One, that we have to look at what people *really* say when they are together, when they socialize (or: express themselves as social beings); and

Two, that any understanding that linguists can hope to obtain of what goes on between people using language is based, necessarily and uniquely, on a correct understanding of the whole context in which the linguistic interaction takes place.

Let me illustrate this by an example. Suppose we are witness to the following interaction between two 'conversationalists' (the example is due to Levinson 1983: 292):

> A: I have a fourteen year old son
> B: Well that's all right
> A: I also have a dog
> B: Oh I'm sorry

On the face of it, this is a pretty strange conversation. In fact, it makes no sense at all, unless we happen to know what the context is: A is trying to lease a flat, and mentions the fact that he has a child. The landlord doesn't mind children, but when he hears that the prospective tenant also has a dog, he indicates that A's prospects as a future lease-holder are rather dim, by uttering 'I'm sorry.'

Now, if one asks what exactly the landlord is sorry about, it is clearly not the fact that A has a dog. Rather, it has something to do with the fact that the regulations for the block of flats do not allow tenants to have pets; so A either has to give up his dog, or he must renounce getting a lease. In the first case, the owner of the flat is sorry for A, while in the second case he may be sorry for himself as well, if A looks like a good prospect as a tenant.

9.5   SOCIETY AND DISCOURSE

The preceding section emphasized the importance of the social context of language use. Such a context naturally presupposes the existence of a particular society, with its implicit and explicit values, norms, rules and laws, and with all its particular conditions of life: economic, social, political and cultural. All these factors together are often referred to by a metaphorical expression: the 'fabric of society'. To call attention to the fact that this 'fabric', as the supporting element for all societal structures and the necessary context for all human activity, operates, and becomes visible, through our use of language, we choose to employ the term *discourse*.

This term (which perhaps has suffered from overuse lately) thus serves to indicate not only the immediately perceptible context of, e.g., a conversation, a job interview, a medical consultation and so on, but also the hidden conditions that govern such situations of language use. How do people use their language in their respective social contexts? What are the degrees of freedom that they enjoy in their use of language, and what are the constraints limiting that use?

Discourse is different from text in that it embodies more than just the text, understood as a collection of sentences (see above); discourse is what makes the text context-bound, in the widest sense of the term. But discourse, in this understanding of the term, is also different from conversation. Conversation is one particular type of text, governed by special rules of use, as we will see. These rules govern a use of language – social – which figures among its most important functions: conversation is what people most naturally do, do socially, and, so to speak, do all the time; it is the most widespread form of language use and, in a sense, the embedding of all our linguistic activities, both in our personal history and development and in our daily lives.

Thus, while it seems natural to use the term 'discourse' specifically in connection with conversation, discourse and conversation are not the same. For some, 'discourse analysis' includes the analysis of conversational language use (see Stubbs 1983); but 'conversation analysis' should not (as is often done) be used as more or less synonymous with 'discourse analysis' (more on this distinction in the next chapter).

To round off this section and chapter, let's consider the following case showing the difference between a discourse-oriented approach and one that is exclusively based on the semantics of the individual expressions and on the speech acts that they represent:

A: I bet you $500 that Swale will win the race.[80]
B: Oh?

In this conversation, some linguists would claim, A has performed a speech act of betting (in the strict linguistic sense), just by uttering the words 'I bet.' Yet, in another, equally valid, pragmatic and discourse-oriented sense, he has not: B has not 'risen to the bet', as one could say, by uttering 'You're on,' or something along that line. Instead, B utters a noncommittal, uninterested 'Oh?' Consequently, there has been no 'uptake', as it is called in the terminology of speech acting; hence, one or more of the conditions necessary for felicitously performing a bet have not been fulfilled, and so there has been no bet (for a detailed discussion and an adverse opinion, see Kasher 1982).

This example shows how the context is all-important when it comes to using language properly (which is not the same as 'correctly', in the sense of the grammar). Any speech act (be it of promising, requesting, betting or whatever) depends on a social convention as its premise; in the case of the bet, this premise is the acceptance of the bet by a proper recipient, a 'co-better', who has to signify his or her uptake of the bet by using one of the prescribed formulaic expressions for this occasion (such as 'OK', 'You're on', etc.) As Levinson puts it,

the utterance . . . does not succeed without the interactional ratification typical of conversation. (1983: 285)

Contrast now this discourse-oriented view of the speech act with a typical semantics-based approach (as advocated by Kasher 1982). The latter would typically claim that only the rules for the use of speech acts proper are of a linguistic nature, whereas we have other sets of rules for such acts as placing bets: these rules do not belong to the system of the language, but should be called 'extralinguistic'. Discourse, by the same token, would be a narrowly linguistic concept, not a pragmatic one.

This distinction would entail that we have to divide up the context of use for speakers into a linguistic (grammatical) and an 'extralinguistic' (pragmatic) one. Such a division between grammar and discourse, however (which was implicit all along in the structuralist view of linguistics) does not seem fruitful from a pragmatic point of view (more on this below, in chapter 13).

EXERCISES AND REVIEW QUESTIONS

1. The following examples all rely on a broader context for their under-standing; the immediate co-text is not sufficient. Indicate what such broader contexts, in your opinion, could look like.

(a)
A: Let's go to the movies.
B: I'll bring the toilet paper. (Bruce Fraser)

(b)
A: (in store) Good morning. Do you have anything to treat complete loss of voice?
B: Good morning sir. What can I do for you today? (Bruce Fraser)

(c)
A: Did you get to look at those dresses?
B: No, I didn't come that way. (Amy B. Tsui)

(d)
'Road Legally Closed. Proceed At Your Own Risk' (Connecticut road sign)

(e)
'Frida is a real Friskies cat. She can't wait to come home and have a bowl.' (advertisement for Friskies cat food)

(f)
'A Meal To Remember' (road sign for the 'Golden Rooster' restaurant on Chief Justice Cushing Highway in Scituate, Mass.)

(g)
'We don't make compromises, we make Saabs' (radio spot on station WBFT, Chicago, 26 August, 1992)

2. Consider the following dialogue:

A: She's the type to take control, show strength and affirmation.
B: Actually she falls apart. She fell apart when her mother died.
A: Who wouldn't?
B: She fell apart when Steffie called from camp with a broken bone in her hand . . .

A: Her daughter, far away, among strangers, in pain. Who
   wouldn't?
B: Not her daughter. My daughter.
A: Not *even* her daughter.
B: No.
A: Extraordinary. I have to love it.
   (Don Delillo, *White Noise*. New York: Viking/Penguin 1986,
   pp. 19–20. My emphasis)

Questions:

How would you characterize the coherence of this text in terms of the co-
text (in particular between the individual 'turns' of the dialogue)?

What makes for the 'surprise' effect (most clearly demonstrated in A's
'even' near the end?

How much would providing an extended context help to understand the
dialogue? For instance, would it help to know that the person that is
talked about ('she') is married to B? Or that A has a crush on her?

What could one say about the relationship between A and B on the basis
of this text?

3. Consider the following text:

   The telephone rang.
   'Is that Dr. Bailey?'
   'Yes.'
   'Is Roland Michell there?'
   'It's for you.'
   'Who?'
   'Young, male and well-bred. Who is that, please?'
   'You won't know me. My name is Euan MacIntyre.'
      (A. S. Byatt, *Possession: A Romance*. London: Vintage, 1990,
      p. 432)

Questions:

What do you make of this conversation?

In particular, who are the different conversationalists, and who are
referred to by the various 'who's' and 'you's'?

How are the different turns marked?

Do you find anything unusual in the turn-taking?

10

Conversation Analysis: Basic Notions

10.1 INTRODUCTION: FROM SPEECH ACTS TO CONVERSATION

What can we use the theory of speech acts for, when it comes to conversation?

Historically, speech act theory has been useful as an 'eye-opener', making us see that we can do things with our words – that our words work for us in speech acts. But how these words work, and how, or where, these speech acts are used, is not immediately evident, and cannot at any rate be derived from a formal framework, in the way that correct sentences are supposed to be 'deduced' in a grammar.

The main reason for this is that there is no such thing as a 'correct' conversation. Conversation is what happens: when people use language together, their speech acting only makes sense in a common context. The most important thing about speech acts is their function in conversation; it is not crucial what the speech acts represent 'officially': what counts is how the conversationalists use them. An example will illustrate this. Imagine that the following remark is made by one conversational partner to another:

Why can't you shut up?

On the face of it, we could believe that this was a question. And it could be (perhaps);[81] but in any normal context of conversation we would consider this a (rather unpleasant kind of) order.

Now, let's ask ourselves if the above is the only, or only 'correct', way of ordering the other person to keep his or her tongue. Clearly, such a question makes no sense: There are simply dozens of ways of putting such an order into words. Moreover, if we look a bit more closely at what's happening, we see that the majority of those commands are not formulated as commands at all, but as questions, remarks, statements, doubts, hints, etc.; and that, moreover, nearly all of them avoid using the word 'order'. Here are a few of the innumerable variants on the above theme:

I strongly suggest you shut your mouth

Sometimes it's a good idea to shut up

How about if you just shut up[82]

I wonder if you really should do all that talking

I wouldn't say more, if I were you

Remember that proverb, 'Speech is silver . . . ?

and so on and so forth.

All such utterances boil down to one big order: to close one's mouth, say nothing more, keep silent, or what have you – yet, there is among them not one 'true' speech act of ordering (in the sense of 'SAV-expressed'; see section 7.1.4).

We can deal with this 'disorder' because we know how to evaluate things in context: as born conversationalists, we understand the words that others speak, the way they are intended to be understood (with certain limitations, about which later). Furthermore, we not only are *able* to do this; as conversationalists, we are placed under the *obligation* to operate contextually, that is, to recognize conversational content and intention almost in spite of their eternally varying surface shapes. Conversation is not only a human right (Ruiz Mayo 1990); it is a human duty.

At the basis of all conversational activity is society. Human social life and work are what necessitate conversation in the first place; and conversation, in its turn, is shaped by human life and work. Thus, our conversational society is a society of mutual use (and sometimes, indeed, abuse); hence, the user is the central figure when language is put to a conversational, social use. In fact, Levinson even goes as far as to state that 'conversation is the *prototypical* kind of language use' (1983: 284; my emphasis). In other words, it is not enough to operate with the mere notion of text, understood as a sequence of concatenated, 'interwoven' pieces of language (as one does in most 'text grammars'; cf. the Latin etymon of 'text', *textus* ('woven; a text'); that notion just is not strong enough. What we're interested in is not the notion of text as text, of text as a piece of 'fabric' in its own right, but the text as part of a larger, *social* fabric, in which not only words are woven together, but human acts and lives.

As we have seen earlier, text as subsumed in this larger fabric is often called discourse. While 'discourse' naturally includes 'conversation', the two are not identical, as we saw above; in the context of the present chapter, 'discourse' is frequently taken as opposed to 'conversation'. The next section will discuss the distinction between the two in more detail.

10.2 DISCOURSE ANALYSIS VS. CONVERSATION ANALYSIS

According to Levinson, 'Discourse analysis' (DA) is the kind of conversation analysis that comes closest to the classical model of grammar as traditionally oriented towards syntax, with a little admixture of semantics. For many linguists, DA simply means: 'old-fashioned', grammar- and speech act-oriented analysis of spoken language.

Naturally, in such a framework, the concepts of rule, well-formedness, and so on have their natural place. One could say that DA is yet another, simple extension of the grammar, in the same sense that I earlier (section 9.2) talked about 'text grammar' as being, for certain linguists, the proper way of doing an extended linguistic analysis, by viewing any text (including conversation) as a collection of well-formed sentences, and the text itself as a well-formed 'super-sentence'.

As to the methods used in DA, these are similar to those of classical, syntax-oriented grammar: one singles out a few, short sentences as examples, and builds one's theories on, or around, these isolated sentence tokens, taken as representative of language (in particular, syntax) as such. The empirical basis of such analyses usually is a great deal of introspection, supplemented by field work in the corridors and offices of Linguistics departments as well as at assorted linguistics parties world-wide. Favourite elicitation methods include questions such as: 'Tell me, can you say X in Y?', where X is a word, construction, phrase or sentence in a language Y, which your interlocutor is supposed to know something about, or maybe even speak.

As we have seen earlier, the organization of a 'text grammar' based on such principles is very much like the one that we know from sentence grammars; except that the grammatical categories now are called 'discourse categories', and that their sequences are kept together by their semantic connectedness (often called 'coherence'), as well as by their (syntactic and other) structural connectedness, also called 'cohesion'.[83]

By contrast, the conversation analysis (CA) approach bases itself on the observation, gathering and analysis of large masses of data, in particular of actual pieces of language use, and especially of all kinds of conversations as they take place in real life. Thus, CA research has been responsible, among other things, for elaborate methods of transcribing conversation, something which is not a trivial task at all if one wants to get *everything* down on paper, and not just the 'words, all the words, and nothing but the words' (for examples, see chapter 6 of Levinson 1983; also below, at the end of chapter 11 (Exercise 1)).

With respect to methodology, one could say that whereas DA operates deductively, CA uses inductive techniques: in the latter, the data are the exclusive foundation and heuristic basis of the hypotheses. In other words, CA theorizing is 'data-driven'; by contrast, DA could be said to be 'rule- or grammar-driven'. Depending on one's own methodological biases, one could use these labels as neutral descriptive terms or as invectives; much depends, as everywhere else, on one's own theoretical background, on the goals for one's description and even on one's temperament.

Therefore, it seems a bit harsh to call the DA approach 'fundamentally misconceived' (as Levinson does; 1983: 288); at any rate, it is no more 'misconceived' than is 'classical' transformational grammar. Neither can it *a priori* be excluded that DA, like classical transformational grammar in its various avatars, has something to contribute when it comes to understanding human texts in all their aspects, grammatical as well as use-oriented.[84]

As a descriptive method for analysing conversation, however, there is not much that this type of discourse analysis is relevant to, or useful for, inasmuch as it is mainly based on abstract rules for generating text and on strictly syntactico-logical concepts of connectedness. The next section will consider some of the weaknesses of such approaches.

10.3   THE HANDMAID'S TALE: WEAKNESSES OF THE PHILOSOPHICAL APPROACH

Traditionally, philosophy has had a high standing on the scientific status ladder. In part, this had to do with the fact that it ranked next highest in the hierarchy established in the Scholastic tradition, that is, close to theology, as its main auxiliary discipline: *ancilla theologiae*, the 'handmaid of theology'.

From a more worldly perspective, philosophy has always been associated with a deeper understanding of the doubts and uncertainties that beset humans in an ever-changing world: the quest for the final answer to 'Man's eternal questions', *sub luce aeternitatis*, in the light of eternity. In particular, the 'eternal truths' of philosophy were considered superior to the vicissitudes of lowly human life and thinking; thus, one came to consider the criterion of ('eternal') *truth* as the all-important one in dealing with the products and workings of the human mind.

Truth functions were also among the first to be formalized in the history of philosophy, and truth-functional approaches to philosophical thinking have had an enormous influence not only within the discipline itself, but also on the related human sciences, not least those connected with (our thinking on) language.

These historical observations may be useful if we want to explain why philosophy (in particular epistemology, that is, the philosophical sub-discipline dealing with the way we take cognizance of our environment, and utter so-called 'judgements' on its state of affairs) has been so influential. But why should grammar, and in particular syntax and semantics, have been so strongly affected by these philosophical ways of dealing with the world?

Consider the fact that for the longest time, philosophy was mainly concerned with logical rules and truth functions; any grammatical thinking consistent with this would thus have to be part of a grammar dealing in 'rules' and 'correctness' (among other things, in the interest of preserving 'truth' in the face of grammatical changes, and of establishing truth-equivalences among sentences or 'judgements').

In the hierarchical view, sketched above, grammar could be said to have functioned as a 'handmaid to logic', just as philosophy itself had been to theology; it is this ancient relationship which hovers in the wings, whenever people start talking about such and such an expression or sentence being 'wrong' because it isn't 'logical'. Add to this that philosophers (as well as the majority of classical linguists) always have been more interested in form than in substance, and the stage is set for many of the contemporary approaches to text and discourse.

In order to illustrate some of the weaker sides of the philosophical-grammatical approach, especially when it comes to discussing the rules of language *use*, consider the following example showing the relative value of the logical/truth-functional method in dealing with actual language.

According to a thesis originally due to Frege and known as the 'compositionality principle' (see also above, section 2.6), truth values for combined (i.e. syntactically conjoined) expressions, such as compound sentences, are supposed to be directly read off from the combined truth functions of their components. Thus, a sentence consisting of two main clauses connected by *and* is considered to be true if and only if both of its components show the value 'true'.

Consider now an example due to Levinson (1983: 288). A says to B:

How are you?

And B retorts, not too politely:

To hell with you.

Suppose now we conjoin these two utterances using the word *and*:

How are you and to hell with you.

Such a sentence, if we indeed could imagine ourselves (or anybody at all) saying it, is not a correct paraphrase of the conjunction of the original utterances. The sentence (supposing it did occur in actual discourse, e.g. in the course of a report on a domestic quarrel) would not have the same truth conditions as those valid for the conjunction of its components.[85]

Not only can a truth-functional view in no way help us to explain and understand what goes on in actual discourse (be it a report on a conversation, as hypothetically in Levinson's construed example, or a piece of actual conversation), it is also woefully inadequate as an explanation of the production of such discourse (e.g. in dialogue). What is interesting about a text is not whether it expresses truth or falsity: most texts don't express either, and nobody cares (except in courtrooms and other contexts where there is a penalty on uttering certain non-truths). When we use language, we have other things to worry about than just (or mainly) truths. Hence, the truth-functional view is inadequate for explaining any kind of discourse (and not only 'non-dialogic text', as Levinson seems to imply; 1983: 288), precisely because it reduces the language to a piece of formal machinery and the user (if the user is indeed allowed to be present at the creation of the text in question) to a manipulator of built-in truth tables.

10.4 THE ROLE OF PRAGMATICS IN CONVERSATION

10.4.1 Deixis and shifters revisited

If one asks for the reason why in the end neither speech act theory nor conversation analysis, by themselves, are able to provide a complete account of the human use of human language, the answer is that no theory that leaves the user out of account will ever be able to account for users' use. Not even at the basic level of primitive tool-making and -using can one pretend to give a satisfactory description of what is being made or done, unless one knows the manufacturers/users of the tool and understands what they had in mind when they were making or using it.[86] In later chapters, I will have ample opportunity to expand on this view; let me here briefly summarize its importance in a CA connection.

From a pragmatic point of view, the presence of actual or potential conversational partners is a necessary condition on any use of language in conversation. On the intuitive level, this is borne out by the fact that people actually gesture while speaking on the phone: they need to make the presence of their conversational partner explicit to themselves, even though their partner cannot see them, nor they their partner. The smiles and the gestures continue to exercise their functions of maintaining and supporting the conversational context, whether or not there are any conversational partners physically present.

A classic instance of this 'invisible partnership' is found in a famous example, originally due to Fillmore (1981: 151). A person speaking on the phone is giving instructions to his conversational partner; in the course of the conversation, mention is made of a certain box, the size of which the conversationalist indicates by using the American English word *yea*. Now, an expression like *yea* belongs to a group of words that make no sense without the corresponding gesture indicating the exact (or more or less exact) measure that the *yea* stands for. Therefore, since the partner cannot see the gesture, the utterance

I need a box *yea* big,

when spoken on the phone, is essentially meaningless; generalizing from this conversational use of the 'shifter' *yea* (especially when combined with the corresponding gesture, indicating size), we may infer that conversation only makes sense when we keep our conversational partners in mind.

The same holds for what is often called the 'telephone smile': your partner in a telephone conversation is unable to see you, hence in principle, it's meaningless to bestow a smile on her or him; still, everybody does it. Another matter is that in certain cultures, where smiling is one of the paramount social mechanisms, a 'phoney smile' may actually be so vigorously executed as to be audible (as happens in Japanese, especially in the case of such female conversationalists as switchboard operators, elevator girls and airline agents).

The well-known case of the 'shifters' (i.e., pronouns and adverbs that change their reference in proportion to the speaker's, or the entire context's, centre of orientation; see sections 5.1.1 and 5.1.4) also serves to illustrate the importance of partner presence in any normal conversation. To use an example provided by Levinson (1983: 55), it is useless to say to one's partner, e.g.,

Meet me here a week from now with a stick about this big

without some conversational 'anchoring' of the pronouns and adverbs (*here, now, this*) in question. 'Deictic' pronouns such as *this* or *that* presuppose a 'centre' of orientation; if nothing is said, we assume that the centre is in the neighbourhood of the speaker, or has somehow something to do with the speaker (and analogously for adverbs of time and space).

Thus, the conversational participants and their common 'coordinates' are an integrated and necessary part of the language act; hence the assumption of the always already 'co-present conversational participants' that Levinson (1983: 284) singles out as essential to the pragmatic organization of texts. That such an organization is not restricted to the deictic aspects of a text (such as have been focused on here)[87] will be the topic of the next three sections.

10.4.2   Presuppositions Revisited, I: Semantic

As we already saw above (section 2.6), a presupposition such as

John failed the examination

in the utterance

John doesn't regret that he failed the examination

can be 'undone' by adding

. . . in fact, he passed it.

Such 'defeasible' presuppositions (or 'cancellable', as Grice calls them; cf. Levinson 1983: 114) have been the centre of much attention in the pragmatic literature. I will not go into details here, but only remark that the connection between presuppositions and conversation, alluded to in the title of the present section, rests precisely on the fact that conversation is a pragmatic activity, and that conversely, presuppositions cannot be explained on the basis of a logico-semantic theory alone; in fact, Gazdar even talks about the 'irremediable inadequacy' of semantics-only based accounts of presuppositions (1979: 89).

While truth-conditional explanations of presuppositions focus on 'what is the case', testably, and thus can be shown to be true or false, e.g. in testimonial evidence or in 'judgements' (the term itself harkens back to the judiciary environment), the fact that people in conversation may have an 'argument' need not imply that their standards of correct language use must conform to what is acceptable in strict truth-functional terms only. Indeed, truth or non-truth is, in most cases, uninteresting as a topic of conversation: the important thing is what we communicate to our listeners. What is or what is not the case is only marginally relevant to the purpose of conversation; language use, of which conversation is such an egregious instance, is not about cases or facts or truths as such, but about what people think and feel, or think and feel others think and feel about cases, facts or maybe even truths; in short, about the world in which they live, and about their lives in this world.

There is another reason that logico-semantic accounts of presuppositions turn out so unsatisfactorily when applied to real language use. As we all know (and as the conversation analysts have demonstrated over and again, as we will see in the next chapters), human conversation does not happen in nice bundles of isolated, or even conjoined, utterances. Humans, when conversing, do not abide, first and foremost, by the rules for grammatical correctness and formal philosophical argument; rather, they follow the rules that are embodied in the practice of human conversing, in the co-authorship of 'common talk', as 'conversation' is called in Danish (*sam-tale*), or in Japanese (*kai-wa*).

This means that an utterance by itself is never enough of a meaning-carrier to be analysed as to its truth value or other significance. What has happened prior to the utterance, and what is going to happen afterwards, is of as much, if not more, importance as what is talked about within the frame of the utterance itself. In a pragmatic view, the importance of the entire context of uttering cannot be overestimated, as we will see later (chapter 14). And in this sense, every presupposition can be undone, given time and context. What is more: even truths are not truths unless they are framed in a context where a truth is expected. Saying a truth in a context of lies is tantamount to lying, as the famous case of the two rabbis illustrates.[88] (Cf. also the story of the *melamed* and his slippers, told above, section 5.1.3.)

To see this even better, let's consider the case of what are called 'pragmatic presuppositions'.

10.4.3 Presuppositions revisited, II: Pragmatic

As we saw in the previous section, the notion of presupposition, originally devised as a purely semantic one, does not hold up to the expectations that we may have of it as pragmaticians. For one thing, semantic presuppositions deal with truth or falsity; they are defined as 'holding' (that is, being true), even if the sentence containing the presupposition is false (see the examples in section 2.6). Such a 'truth-conditional' definition of presupposition fails on several pragmatic counts: first, there is more to utterances than their abstract truth value; second, utterances are spoken, and cannot be considered in isolation – hence we must introduce the speaker, as well as the listener(s), as relevant factors in any situation in which language is used; and third, people do not live their lives by truth conditions alone: 'truth' is more often than not a philosophical pursuit; real people have other concerns as well. 'What is it to me?' is a legitimate question here; another pertinent question is: 'What good does it do?' Such questions cannot be answered by a purely semantic theory of presuppositions.

Characteristically, one of the first to discover this pragmatic fact was, again, not a linguist, but a philosopher, Robert Stalnaker. Stalnaker introduced the term 'pragmatic presupposition' in an influential early article (Stalnaker 1977 [1974]); what he did was to establish the fact that an utterance, in order to be correctly interpreted, also with respect to its truth or falsity (which was what Stalnaker, being a philosopher, was mainly interested in), needs a context.

Take every philosopher's favourite example:

The cat is on the mat.

This utterance, regardless of whether it is true or false (whether or not there is a certain cat on a certain mat), presupposes that there is some cat, and some mat: the one that the sentence refers to, the one that we are speaking about. But the sentence doesn't tell us a thing about the context in which it could be uttered; neither does it say anything about what this particular cat means to its (his? her?) owner. The latter may have said this sentence in despair: 'The cat is on the mat!', thereby conveying a message to his or her household, or to the person in the household who was closest by; the message may have been the equivalent of 'Quick! Joey is doing it again – get him off Aunt Euphemia's mat!' (said about a particular cat who, under certain conditions and in particular contexts, such as being in an agitated state of mind, sees fit to spray on a particular mat, a precious heirloom after a much cherished, long deceased great-grandaunt). This utterance is quite different from the 'same' sentence pronounced by the philosopher who uses it as an example in one of his abstract musings about the nature of presupposition.

Speaking of cats, the following notice could be found on a lamp-post in Evanston, Illinois, one day in August of 1992:

FOUND: GREY CAT
LOST SINCE JULY
PHONE: 491–7040

What do we make of this? Suppose the usual, semantic presuppositions hold: we know that there is a cat, and that the cat is grey. We know furthermore that people when they say things like 'Grey cat found' usually speak the truth; when they put up a sign like the one above, they normally do not play tricks. This we can conclude by way of conversational implicature (see section 5.2.3). Similarly, by a conventional implicature (see section 5.2.4), we can safely assume that the author of the message is the same person as she who actually found the cat (the utterance 'found' conventionally implies 'found by someone' – usually the utterer).

In the terminology of speech acts, the message counts as a speech act of informing the community about the fact that a cat has been found; and it also counts as a speech act of offering; namely, to give the cat back to its owners (that's why there is a phone number included in the message). But we still have a long way to go before we can understand the real 'meaning' of this rather strange message.

We need, first of all, to explain the situation itself: What do people do when they find a cat? Or maybe even more fundamentally: what do cats do when they start touring the neighbourhood, and find themselves new homes? (I'm not asking *why* they do it; that is beyond our pragmatic universe.) In our society, there are a number of unwritten conventions that deal with 'pet behaviour', understood both as the behaviour of the pets themselves, and that of the humans dealing with them. As to the latter conventions, it is tacitly assumed that on finding a stray cat on the streets, or on discovering that you have aquired a new houseguest who turns up every morning and asks for milk and loving care, you do something about it: you ask around who might have lost a cat, you insert an ad in the local free paper or you put up notices around your house.

These are all pragmatic presuppositions: they have to do with the world in which the language users and their cats live, conditions that can be subsumed under the label 'common' (or 'shared') knowledge, as it is often called in the literature.

However, this 'nomer' is also a misnomer: the 'knowledge' we are speaking about has not just to do with 'knowing things', but should rather be understood in the broader sense in which the Bible talks about 'knowing' (as, e.g., in 'carnal knowledge'). In Caffi's words, '[p]ragmatic presuppositions not only concern knowledge, whether true or false: they concern expectations, desires, interests, claims, attitudes towards the world, fears etc.' (1994a: 3324).

Furthermore, the word 'shared' in the expression 'shared knowledge' contains a possible misunderstanding as well. Take the example of the 'grey cat', above. The last sentence of the message had me truly puzzled: 'Lost since July'. What is that supposed to mean? How could the person who wrote the notice at the end of August have known that the cat had been lost for two months? Did the cat speak to him or her in human words, like cats do in fairy tales? Or did the person possess preternatural insights, or have a revelation, or did he or she conclude from the state of emaciation the poor animal was in, that it had been on the road since July? 'Lost since July' conventionally implies that there was a time before which the cat was not lost; but how can one determine that point of time with sufficient confidence to go officially on record, on a lamppost on a public street, as maintaining this to be 'true'?

Clearly, at this point, if no more information is available, we must give up. The 'shared knowledge' that we possess does not allow us to deal with all the implications and presuppositions of the sentence, either in a truth-functional or in a pragmatic sense.

Semantic presupposition theory (and this still partly includes, despite its name, Stalnaker's original notion of pragmatic presupposition) is concerned with what is true or false, and intends to link sentences together on the basis of this criterion. A serious theory of pragmatic presupposition goes several steps further, and asks impertinent questions of the type: How is this utterance to be understood in the context of its users, on their 'common ground'?

In particular, it is important to know *why* people say things, and why they say them the way they do. In the 'cat' example, the pragmatic presupposition is that pet lovers will do anything to save a cat from a fate worse than death: living in an animal shelter on borrowed time. But consider now the following example, an advertisement in the 'For Sale' section of the Chicago weekly *Reader* (29 August, 1992):

MOVING OUT OF country. Everything must go. Husband, dog, microwave, tv, vcr, personal word processor, appliances. Great deals. Call Ori, 312-404-2391.

For brevity's sake, let's disregard the obvious presuppositions here (such as: there are certain items for sale, 'moving out of country' means: 'leaving the US'), along with the usual conversational implicatures (the author of the ad intends to sell certain items: 'must go' means in this context: 'I want to sell'; something which also can be independently inferred from the fact that the ad appears in the 'For Sale' section of the paper). Even so, there are still a number of pragmatic presuppositions that have to be sorted out.

One of these is the institution of the 'Sayonara-sale', best known from Japanese contexts, where servicemen and others going back to the US, or whatever their home country happens to be, will sell absolutely everything they have. Apparently, the current sale, too, represents a 'good-bye' (Japanese *sayoonara*): to a previous life, to the current place of abode, to a lot of possessions – which is precisely the difference between this type of sale and, say, a regular garage or yard sale, where one usually only sells things one doesn't need any more, or at least can do without.

In the case of this 'Sayonara-sale', however, another pragmatic presupposition seems to emerge, conflicting with the first one: in our society, one does not usually sell husbands; and dogs only under very restricted conditions. So, how to sell a husband? Is the ad to be understood as a polite invitation – to whoever happens to be first in line or on the phone – 'to take this husband of mine off my hands'?

In fact, none of these pragmatic presuppositions seems to be able to explain the story behind the ad. The theory of conversational implicature has taught us that in such a case, we must try to figure out what the implied motives of the ad writer could have been; for example, by trying to establish a suitable context in which this 'sale scenario' could happen. One such scenario could be that of the joke: the whole thing could be a spoof, with nothing to it, and the ad writer would be a prankster (or pranksteress). However, we run up against yet another pragmatic presupposition here: in US society, there are certain things you don't joke about, at least not in public; among them are marriage, death, defecation, sex, religion and money.

But now what if the ad were *meant* to announce an upcoming divorce? In this case, we would be able to assign the proper speech act (of 'announcing') to the ad, but pragmatically, it still would be a strange situation: an advertisement such as this one is not a usual way of telling your friends that you're splitting up. So, depending on the circumstances, this could indeed be a very nasty way of saying that your marriage was on the rocks (especially if hubby didn't know he was up for sale).

What we can learn from trying to analyse these seemingly so innocent texts is, one, that pragmatic presuppositions are necessary in order to understand what people are doing with their language; two, that we need

to use our faculty of conversationally implying along with that of pragmatically presupposing; and three, that it sometimes is impossible, even
with the best of wills and the cleverest of techniques, to ferret out all the
pragmatic presuppositions, and make the correct implicatures that we
need in order to make sense of what is being said or written. ('What else
is new?', somebody might say at this point.)

The chief moral to be gathered from the above is that the 'shared' or
'mutual knowledge' which conversation presupposes is not always given;
indeed, only through conversation are we able to build up this knowledge, to supplement it, to refine it. In this way, too, the presuppositions
can be brought out into the open, if necessary. But notice that there is an
important difference between our dealing with presuppositions as opposed to with conversational implicatures: valid presuppositions remain
mostly implicit, valid implicatures arise in the course of conversation.
Normally, we don't have to go 'presupposition-hunting' in order to
understand an utterance: questioning them is a dangerous sport inasmuch as it may involve the 'face' of my conversational partner(s). Contrariwise, in the case of conversational implicatures, we are able to
understand the utterance only if we make the proper inferences, based on
our conversational activity. Also, while we are obliged to act on those
inferences, the nature of this action, precisely because its necessity is out
in the open, is subject to discussion. What is conversationally expected or
requested, may be refused or denied without conversational penalty: our
action can be a negative one, and the conversational implicature rejected.

Whereas pragmatic presuppositions (as all presuppositions) are here
to stay, once they are accepted (and not explicitly cancelled), conversational implicatures share the shifting framework of conversational interaction. We may put presuppositions to work to create an implicature; but
we cannot use an implicature to create a presupposition. As Caffi remarks, in her lucid treatment of the subject, 'presuppositions are
grounded on complicity . . . communication is somehow like sitting
down at the card table: presuppositions can be a bluff' (1994a: 3321, 3323).

10.4.4 Speech acts revisited

Earlier, I said that the study of speech acts has been instrumental in
paving the way towards a better understanding of our use of language.
That is an historical fact; however, the record of speech act theory as a

help towards understanding and analysing 'real' language use has not always been impressive.

The problem of language use is as old as language itself: How to connect the words of our language with the things of our world? All human language activity consists in 'doing these things with those words', that is, uniting what is said with what is done, joining speech acts with real-world activity.

But beyond that, the problem with speech acts is how to isolate and identify them in relation to the actual words being uttered (the 'utterances'); as we have seen, this is not an easy task. In particular, there certainly is nothing like a simple, one-to-one correspondence between the words uttered and the speech acts performed; and here, I'm not even thinking of what comes about in the world as the result of our speech acts (their 'perlocutionary effect', as it was called in section 6.1.3).

In order to explore the role that speech acts play in conversation analysis, we may focus on their function as elements in a dialogue: requests can be granted or refused, promises can be accepted or rejected, threats can be acknowledged or ignored, questions are normally answered, greetings returned and so on. Everywhere, the appropriate speech acts involved in these situations of language use enter the scene, play their roles and exit again. In this way, they seem to provide a kind of mini-scenario for what is happening in language interaction, and they suggest a simple way of explaining the more or less predictable sequences that we all know from normal conversation. Rarely, if ever, is a greeting not returned (except by oversight); a congratulation is normally not rejected; and so on. Thus, speech acts seem to play a structuring role in the baffling diversity of human talk. But certain conditions have to be fulfilled in order that they can play this role, most of which are not normally met in the classical conception of speech acting.

Among these conditions, Levinson enumerates the following: the existence of a well-defined set of speech acts; a clear definition of their respective illocutionary forces; a clear, preferably univocal assignment of the individual speech acts to utterances or portions thereof; and an agreed understanding as to the effect of speech acts in their contextual setting.

None of these conditions can be said to be fulfilled in normal contexts of language use, as we have seen over and again in the preceding. To take just one example: in the case of engaging in a bet, we certainly can enumerate a number of expressions that would count as correct verbal 'uptake', but there are at least as many unpredictable, never heard before, and sometimes not even verbalized ways of recognizing a bet that still (given the circumstances) would count as correct uptakes. Here, as always in language use, it is the result that counts: once an utterance is placed in its proper, linguistic co-text, as well as in its entire real-world context, its effects are visible, and the nature of the speech act that was performed becomes transparent.

Such a situation, however, cannot be (re)constructed in the linguist's or speech act theoretician's abstract world: we have to turn to the real world of language as it is used (among other things, in conversation). As will become clear in the following chapters, sequencing in conversation is by no means a simple succession of speech acts, as one may be inclined to assume on the basis of the sometimes rather naïve examples that have been provided by the theoreticians. There is far more to speech acting than speech acts, and the reason is that all speech act activity ultimately underlies the laws of ('is subsumed by', as I will call it below) the greater universe of discourse.

10.4.5 Discourse revisited

In section 9.5, I drew attention to the fact that text and discourse are not synonyms; neither are conversation and discourse, although in some terminology the two are often confused. In the present section, I will attempt to expand the view on discourse sketched above to comprise the entire gamut of human language use, especially as it becomes visible in conversation.

Foucault has characterized discourse as the practice of making sense of signs. This practice transcends the mere interpretive activity of 'understanding': the 'making sense' should be understood as an active *creation* of meaning, '. . . practices that systematically form the objects of which they speak' (1972: 44). Thus, the space in which these objects are created is the medium of creation outside of which nothing happens, hence no discourse is possible: the discursive space is a fertile *tohuwabohu*, ready to accept the impact of the Word, of language (cf. Genesis 1: 2; John 1: 14).

The emphasis that Foucault places on practice is what makes discourse different from mere text, or even conversation. Practice names its own conditions, but these conditions are not the well-known restrictions of grammatical rules or truth conditions; rather, they embody the whole of the human sociality. Discourse, as practice, is society's own practice: the space that Foucault mentions as the locus of emergence and transformation of various objects (1972: 32) is society. Humans constitute and transform their social relations in discourse; discourse is, in Mumby and Stohl's words,

> the ensemble of phenomena in and through which social production of meaning takes place, an ensemble which constitutes *society as such*. (1991: 315; my emphasis)

Seen under this angle, the use of language in conversation becomes more than an idle pastime, a way of getting to know your neighbours, of 'passing the time of day', as the somewhat old-fashioned expression has it. Discourse is a function that transcends the individual user: by its creation and re-creation of society's bonds, it enables the single individual to exist and to co-exist with other individuals. If it is true that objects can be arranged in a system according to a true/false evaluation of their distinctive features (as is done, e.g. in phonology for the classification of the phonemes), or according to their distributional properties (as in classical morphology and syntax), and if the same objects can be said to form structures, that is, meaningful wholes in which the single classified items derive a surplus of meaning from their being structured into the totality, then the transcendental character of discourse is in its conditioning effect: discourse is what makes possible the enabling of both system and structure as 'the [discursive] space on which various objects emerge and are continuously transformed' (Foucault 1972: 32), in their everlasting creation and re-creation.[89]

Discourse, however, is not to be considered in isolation from the systems and structures that support it and whose fulfilment it constitutes. That means that in a very real sense, 'discourse' has to do with 'speaking', and in particularly, speaking *about*; (the French *discours* is often used in the sense of 'address, speech' as in, e.g., *les discours chez Thucydide*, 'the speeches in Thucydides'). The way society speaks about itself is, furthermore, characterized by the relations of power that obtain in a given society. Power structures discourse, and discourse supports the power it has created. The following may serve as an illustration.

Current social discourse in the US is blind to the issue of class, and focuses instead on such variables as race, gender, income, education and the like. The tenet of the 'classless society' pervades all discussions on issues of social equality, discrimination, minority rights and so on. 'Class is for European democracies or something else – it isn't for the United States of America. We are not going to be divided by class' (President George Bush; quoted Navarro 1991: 1).

When we focus on some particular aspect of US society, however, as for instance the relationship between mortality rates and class, it becomes clear that class issues indeed are important: fatal heart diseases strike about two and a half times more frequently among workers in the steel industry than among corporate lawyers (Navarro 1991: 4; the figures are 86 vs. 37 per 10,000, according to the latest available (1986) US census).

While it is true, of course, that one finds relatively fewer blacks among corporate lawyers than among steel workers, it is nevertheless the case that the white steel worker has a mortality prognosis that is much closer to that of his black co-worker than to his race-mate's in the upper echelons of society. This fact may then be exploited by the corporate structure (big companies, organized medicine as represented by the AMA, the American Medical Association, or the government) to prevent the establishment of a universal health care for all of the disprivileged: if one succeeds in creating the illusion that white workers' health prospects are better than the black population's, a major incentive for an across-the-board health reform is neutralized in the awareness of a large segment of the class which needs it most: the American workers.

What we see here illustrates the double aspect of discourse that we mentioned above: by speaking (or not speaking) about some vital issues, or by speaking about them in a special way, categories and attitudes are created that are conducive to keeping the power alive that created the 'discursive space' in the first place. Participation in discourse happens on the premises and conditions of the powerful: as a result, those that are powerless are *ipso facto* disempowered to change their powerless condition, since their only way of speaking ('discoursing') about power is that imposed upon them by the powerful.

On the other hand, keeping totally out of society's discourse (by rejecting the current structures and isolating oneself from whatever is happening on the societal scene) is no solution either. J. M. Coetzee, the South African novelist and critic, has beautifully illustrated this in his novel *The Life and Times of Michael K* (1984). Michael K is an illiterate 'blue collar' worker (his race is never specified, in keeping with the official 'colour-blindness' of official South African literary discourse)[90] who, after the death of his mother and the loss of his employment as a city gardener, 'opts out' of the oppressive society around him. His defenselessness is not just a matter of being underprivileged and poor and (probably) black: what keeps him down is his inability to articulate his needs and wants in a language that is acceptable to the oppressors. By contrast, his inner language, as depicted by Coetzee, is of great poetic richness and expressivity. However, by not speaking to anybody, by not speaking about anything, by not understanding what is going on about him, and in the end, by not wanting to have any part in the official discourse, the man is in the end reduced to a mere chattel: a poignant illustration of the importance of practising discourse, and the terrible consequences of opting out even of daily conversational routines.

The next chapter will go into more detail on the technicalities of these routines.

EXERCISES AND REVIEW QUESTIONS

1. Consider the following ad:

Blue Cross
What Went Wrong?

Prepared by the Health & Law Project
University of Pennsylvania
Sylvia Law, Principal author

'Here is must reading for legislators and anyone with the slightest interest in health and hospital insurance. Professor Law's important study of the Blue Cross presents some shocking facts and figures . . . she examines the development of Blue Cross into a web of local hospital insurance agencies . . . [and] arrives at the conclusion that the Blue Cross is not serving the public well.'

(*The New Republic*, 29 June, 1974)

Questions:

If I ask: 'What went wrong?' what are the two immediate presuppositions?

What is the answer to the question 'What went wrong?'

How do we go about determining where in the *text* to find the answer?

How do we know that this is the right place to find the answer, in the *'real world'*?

Which of the presuppositions that you have discovered are semantic, which are pragmatic?

2. The following two cases have to do with the well-established North American tradition of tipping for services rendered.

(a) A sign detailing the rights and duties of employees and customers, on display in Edward's Shoe Shop on Sherman Avenue in Evanston, Illinois, tells us as item #5:

EMPLOYEES ARE ALLOWED TO ACCEPT UP TO U.S. $50.00
AS A TIP

(b) One Sunday afternoon in January of 1993, having missed the Clark Airport Coach, I am approached by the driver of a livery car, who offers to take me to Toronto International Airport for the modest fare of $30 (Canadian). Since it is cold, and my plane is about to leave, and the next bus won't leave until half an hour later, I accept. Upon arriving at the airport, I tender the driver $40 (Canadian). Whereupon he says,

'How much change do you want back on this, sir?'

Questions:

What are the presuppositions (semantic and pragmatic) in these two cases?

What do the two cases have in common, and how are they different, both from the viewpoint of presuppositions and from the viewpoint of speech act theory?

Are these 'smart' moves? Which of the two is smarter?

Can you suggest alternative expressions from the point of view of:

   the store owner
   the employers
   the taxi-driver
   the customer/passenger?

3. Justifying the 1989 Panama campaign, President George Bush, in a TV newsreel interview, said the following:

'When American servicemen's wives are being sexually molested, this President isn't going to sit with his hands in his lap.'
(From the documentary film *The Panama Deception*, directed by Barbara Trent, written and edited by David Kasper; Empowerment Project, 1992)

Questions:

How would you account for the deictic 'this' in 'this President'?

What does such a form for 'self-deixis' usually connote?

11

Conversation Analysis: Part I

11.1 INTRODUCTION: WHAT HAPPENS IN CONVERSATION?

As we saw in the preceding chapter, conversation is a way of using language socially, of 'doing things with words' together with other persons.

We can look at this use of language from two points of view. The first is that of content: then our attention will focus on what the conversation is about, the topics discussed and how they are brought into the conversation; on whether or not these topics are overtly announced or perhaps presupposed, or hidden in other ways; on what kinds of topic lead to other topics and why; and so on. Here, we also focus on the topical organization of conversation and how the topics are managed, either by overt steering ('Let's see, what is all this talk really about?', said, e.g., at a meeting), or by covert manipulation, often in the form of indirect speech acting (e.g., in the course of a tax audit, 'I don't want to suggest that the Internal Revenue Service shouldn't be talking about my credit rating'). A further point to be considered is the function of conversation in creating an 'ambiance', a context in which the conversationalists are able to pursue their (overt or hidden) goals; this is usually the function of what is called 'small talk' or 'chit-chat'.

Alternatively, one can focus on the formal aspects of conversation: How conversation works, what rules are observed, how 'sequencing' is achieved (gaining and leaving the floor, turn-taking, pausing, interrupting and so on). These aspects are often structured, in the framework of speech act theory, in pairs such as questions and answers, summonses and compliances, advice and thanks, and so on (often called 'adjacency pairs'; see section 12.4), which are seen as conversationally coherent on account of their underlying speech acts.

The present chapter will discuss some of these formal aspects; conversational content will be taken up in the next chapter.

11.2   THE ETHNOMETHODOLOGICAL APPROACH

In the midst of the theoretical turmoil that followed in the wake of Chomsky's 'revolution' in the late fifties and early sixties, a group of non-professional language workers were looking at what people did with their words when they were not busy producing sample sentences for curious linguists. These 'non-linguists' of various observances felt that the professionals' 'custom-made' utterances were unnatural, since they were not embedded in actually occurring talk; actual talk, by contrast, they typically found to occur in everyday conversation.

The main point these so-called 'ethnomethodologists' (who were the first to explore this area of linguistic activity) wanted to make was that, contrary to the received bias of 'official' linguistics, conversational talk was not in the least incoherent or irregular; the absence of a formal set of rules for generating the set of 'all and only correct' conversational utterances was not tantamount to conversation being un-ruled, or even unruly. The rules that conversation was found to obey, however, turned out to be more like the rules that people had devised for other social activities: they were the practitioners', the local folk's, rules, and they resembled the rules that had been discovered by researchers in anthropology (especially its sub-field, ethnomethodology) for all sorts of social interactions much more than they resembled linguistic rules. As Bilmes (1986: 184) puts it, '[a]lthough rules are "real", even for the ethnomethodologist, there is a sense in which they are a resource for the member but not for the ethnomethodologist' (on 'members' resources', see Fairclough 1989: 11, 24). Hence, such rules are 'people rules', rather than linguists': they belong to society's, rather than to science's, practitioners. In other words, conversational rules are rules of discourse, in the widest sense of the term (see section 10.4.5, above).

Not surprisingly, the main focus of attention for the conversation analyst thus became, from the very beginning, the organization and structuring of conversation, and not so much its 'correctness' (form- or content-wise). To capture the (mostly unconscious) structuring that people practise when carrying on a conversation, it was necessary to develop a technique that was in many respects rather different from the classical transcription techniques of linguistics.

To name but one example: laughter is usually not considered a linguistic phenomenon; however, in conversation, laughter often plays an extremely important role, either as a means of marking off a sequence (telling one's conversational partner that one has 'got the point' of a joke), as a signal of embarrassment ('I don't really want to pursue this point any further'), as a weak kind of apology or as whatever else fits the context of a particular conversation. Since in linguistics there were no accepted ways of transcribing laughter, the ethnomethodologists naturally had to create their own transcription systems and devices. For them, transcribing conversation was not a matter of rendering all phonetic nuances in the most faithful way, in order to describe and classify the phonemes of a language and their variants, but rather a technique that should be able to help us identify the ways in which people establish the 'traffic rules' of talk, using linguistic (as well as other, e.g. gestural) means.

The metaphor of 'traffic rules' is a highly appropriate one in this context, since the main point of conversational structure is to keep the flow of conversation going, to avoid conversational 'accidents' ('clashes') and conversational 'traffic jams', in which the participants feel themselves gridlocked in sterile verbal exercise. Also, the techniques of good conversation management include some form of 'road assistance', by which a conversation that has halted, or has trouble maintaining the proper speed, can be helped along.

All such traffic rules and repair mechanisms find their embodiment in what Sacks and his followers have called the 'management of the conversational turn' (see, e.g., Sacks, Schegloff and Jefferson 1974). The next section will discuss this concept in more detail.

11.3   Turns and Turn-Taking

According to Sacks, the basic unit of the conversation is the 'turn', that is, a shift in the direction of the speaking 'flow' which is characteristic of normal conversation (in opposition to, e.g., the conversational monologue, that well-known party horror). Furthermore, in normal, civilized,

Western-type conversation, conversationalists do not speak all at the same time: they wait for their 'turn', also in this sense of the word.

Yielding the right to speak, or the 'floor', as it is often called, to the next speaker thus constitutes a turn. But how do people go about allocating turns to each other or themselves? This is where the so-called 'turn-taking mechanisms' come into the picture. On the one hand, there are natural breaks in every conversation: a speaker has to pause for breath, or runs out of things to say, or simply declares his or her contribution to be finished: all those points in the conversation are places where a natural 'transition', a relay of the right to speak to the next speaker, may occur. Such points are technically called 'transition relevance places', or TRPs, in ethnomethodological parlance.

A TRP can be exploited by the speaker holding the floor, either directly, for the purpose of allocating the right to speak to another conversationalist of his or her choice ('Now, we'd like to hear Jim's view on this'), or indirectly, by throwing the floor wide open to whoever feels like getting into the fray ('Any other opinions or further comments on this matter?'). Alternatively, the speaker may just ignore the TRP and continue past it; in the manner of certain old-time conversational practitioners, speakers ignore a natural TRP that would have occurred at the end of, say, a sentence (with the corresponding intonational pattern before a full stop), and instead, create an 'unnatural break' (e.g. in the form of a mid-sentence pause). Such a break is not perceived as a TRP by the other participants, and thus allows the speaker to continue full speed across the next upcoming, 'real' TRP. Other speakers employ the technique of 'masking' a TRP by emitting a more or less 'threatening' sound at potential transition points (such as 'Aaahhm'), thus warning other speakers of their intention to continue past the TRP as soon as they have got their breath.

All such mechanisms of 'selection' (self- or other-) are among the most important moving parts of the 'turn management system', the conversational machinery owned and operated by the actual and potential floor-holders and -getters.

On the other hand, the non-floor-holders in a conversational situation are not mere silent bystanders. First of all, their contribution to the conversation is an important element of the 'traffic management' that I talked about. Depending on differences of culture and language practices, the phenomena that are often gathered to the common denominator of 'back-channelling' may vary in shape and frequency, but are always of great importance for the flow of conversation. The 'back-channeller' provides support for the speaker in the form of short utterances ('I see,' 'Right' and so on), or of various, more or less articulate noises (regular phonetic ones as well as others).

Certain languages have specialized in back-channelling of the latter kind; thus, Japanese reportedly has some 150 different back-channel devices (called *aizuchi*), varying from regular utterances such as *hai* or *ee* ('yes') and *soo* ('I see') to vocalic and consonantal sounds of great variety, including grunts and (oral or nasal) sucked-in breaths.[91]

Bystanders can also directly intervene in the conversation, for example by taking the floor, preferably at a TRP, so as not to be accused of interrupting the speaker, as there are strong cultural taboos in many language communities against usurping the right to speak, not only in a formal, official or religious context, but also in everyday conversational practice. 'Wait for your turn' is a warning that is instilled as a maxim in children from a very early age in our society; nevertheless, the rule may not be entirely universal. In other cultures, the anathema of interrupting is not felt so strongly, and consequently not inculcated so forcefully.[92]

11.4 PREVIEWING TRPs

If it is true, as the old proverb has it, that *gouverner c'est prévoir*, 'to govern is to foresee,' then managing the conversation has a lot to do with one's ability to foresee what's going to happen around the next bend in the road, the next turn. While chapter 12 will deal with the content-related aspects of this management, let me here point to some of the formal aspects of what sometimes has been called 'predictability'.

One clearly identifiable case of predictability is that of the so-called 'adjacency pairs': these are typically questions/answers, requests/offers or requests/denials and so on: given one part of the pair, the other is normally predictable. Since such adjacency pairs often have a content component, I will treat them below, in chapter 12.

Other, more or less clearly attributable 'turn signals' consist in changes of speed of delivery (this is, among other things, why we often are able to predict the end of somebody's speech at a public occasion) or of intonation and word-choice patterns, as in certain stylized types of conversations and other discourse (such as Rhythmic American Poetry, or 'rapping'). 'Opening up closings', as it is often called (after the article of that name by Schegloff and Sacks 1973) similarly prefigures a point where the conversation between two partners is expected to end, and others can have their say. In particular in telephone conversations, signals such as 'OK', 'well', or other 'summarizing devices' often announce an upcoming ('pre-sequence' of) closing, a 'pre-closing' (on 'pre-sequences', see section 11.5.1); usually, such signals, too, are accompanied by marked changes in intonation and/or speed that are as difficult to describe as they are easy to detect.

Furthermore, such 'final', or intended-to-be-final, markers can be used as manipulative devices, not only preventing others from joining the conversation, but signalling that one's next TRP should be considered as the end-point of the entire interchange. A speaker may say something like

To sum this all up, let me add a last comment . . .

or

Concluding our discussion, we should not omit to . . .

in order to tell the other speakers that in his or her opinion, enough has been said on the matter. Such ritualized pre-closing signals are available for those leading meeting in conventional, standardized environments, where they can routinely pronounce phrases such as

Let us all pray (*towards the end of an invocation*)

None higher? First . . . Second . . . Third (*at auctions*)

Are you ready for the question? (*closing the discussion at a meeting*)

and so on.

But also in everyday conversations, such pre-sequences are common; and many, if not most of them have a ritualized character that wholly or partially excludes a 'normal' reaction. For example, ritualized pre-sequences, such as greetings of the type

How are you?

followed by the predictable

Fine, and you?

have in reality lost their original content of 'enquiring about somebody's health', and serve only as signals for possible openings of conversations; hence, they have become purely formal devices. Still, these formal pre-sequences can be 'revived' at will by conversationalists who choose to ignore their 'pre-character' and will answer a 'first pair part' of greetings (on this, see section 12.4.2, below) like the above by a lengthy and detailed account of their bodily and mental state of health.

Often, such misunderstandings are caused by inter-cultural differences in the nature of the greetings: a formally more elaborated enquiry as to the health of the greeted person, such as

How are you feelin' this morning Ma'am

tends to elicit an elaborate response more easily than, e.g., one of the above cited forms. An amusing instance of such a 'cultural misunder-standing' is found in the following extract from David Lodge's novel *Paradise News*:

The waitress, whose name, Darlette, was displayed on a badge pinned to the front of her apron, put a jug of iced water on the table and said brightly, 'How are you this evening, sir?'
'Oh, bearing up', said Bernard, wondering if the stress of the day's events had marked him so obviously that even total strangers were concerned for his well-being. But he inferred from Darlette's puzzled expression that her enquiry had been entirely phatic. 'Fine, thank you', he said, and her countenance cleared. (1992: 129)

Here, the problem lies in the nature of the greeting, 'How are you this evening, sir?' For Bernard, a British tourist in Hawaii, this is a question about his well-being, to be answered in some (admittedly perfunctory) manner. For Darlette, his answer is baffling. Her question had not been a real question, but an instance of 'phatic communication', in Roman Jakobson's terms (1960).[93]

Similarly, if somebody asks us if we are doing anything tonight, we expect the other person to come up with suggestions as to what we possibly could do together. Innumerable jokes are built around failed expectancies of this kind (possible answers other than 'What have you got in mind?' or 'Let's get together' could include, e.g., 'Bruce is coming around,' 'Mind your own business,' or even a flat 'Of course, I'm always doing something'). The fact that in certain cultures, the mere expression of admiration of another person's property may be construed as a pre-sequence to the obligatory offering of that property as a gift, followed by the equally obligatory acceptance of the property by the other party, points to the strength of such conventional predictability.[94] In these cases, we are watching a natural transition to the more content-oriented turn-allocating mechanisms that will be the subject of the next chapter.

11.5   PRE-SEQUENCES AND INSERTION SEQUENCES

11.5.1   Pre-sequences

As already indicated in the previous section, certain utterances are usually (even, in some instances, always) felt to be 'precursors' to something else (another utterance, or perhaps a sequence of utterances). The classical examples are the so-called 'attention getters', such as

Hey

You know something?

Excuse me

and so on, to which the usual answer would be

Yes

What?

or something in the same vein.

After this initial exchange has been concluded, the real business can be dealt with. Utterances which serve as 'precursors' to others are often called *pre-sequences*. They can be considered as purely formal tools of conversation management, but usually, they are more than that, and occupy a position which is midway between the formal and the content-related aspects of conversation.

Thus, some of the most frequent pre-sequences are of the type sometimes called 'enquirers'. These usually precede a request of some kind;

their function is to make sure that the request about to be made is indeed within the limits of the possible, from the point of view of the requestee. For example, before purchasing an item in the shop or requesting information, help with a task, or any favour at all, we enquire about the available possibilities of obtaining that item, information, help or favour.

For instance, a well-known pre-sequence in shopping would be

I wonder if you have . . .

Do you by any chance have . . .

Does your shop carry . . .

(some item X, that I might want to purchase).

When the sales clerk answers in the negative, the sequence usually comes to an end then and there (unless some information is offered or given as to where else to buy the desired item). However, if the answer is affirmative, the 'pre-sequence' usually (though not necessarily) changes its 'type' from being a pre-sequence of an informatory kind to being a prelude to an act of buying. This act can, under the circumstances, be rather unavoidable, depending on the item (and, of course, the social conditions of the purchase). Thus, it may be all right for an American restaurant guest to enquire

Waiter, do you have any oysters on the half shell tonight?

and subsequently, after the waiter has checked and come back with an affirmative response, to decide to have not oysters after all, but lobster. In France, however, a request such as

Are there any Coquilles St Jacques?

would bind the guest to consume a portion if the waiter is able to confirm that there are indeed scallops on the menu (Max Silberztein, personal communication).

Further pre-sequences include pre-announcements (such as 'Whatdoyouknow'), pre-invitations (e.g. 'Are you doing anything tonight?'), pre-threats ('Watch it'), and numerous others (see Levinson 1983: 346ff.).

Since pre-sequences in a way have a life of their own – that is, they are not always counted as sequences on a par with any following, independent sequences, to which they play an ancillary role – they may appear to be half-submerged, somewhat 'under the surface' of the conversation, so to speak. The following exchange is an example:

Are you doing anything tonight?

Why are you asking?

I thought we might see a movie.

Well, no, nothing in particular. What do you want to see?

In this sequence, the pre-sequence ('Are you doing anything to-night?') is interrupted by the question 'Why are you asking?', which is answered first, before the answer to the pre-sequence question is made available. Such overlapping of sequences runs counter to the normal situation, where utterances stay 'in line', that is, one turn is completed before the next turn is started upon. Whereas overlapping is rather normal in the case of pre-sequences, it is by no means limited to that case. The phenomenon in question is usually captured under the label of 'insertion sequences', about which more in the section following.

11.5.2   Insertion sequences, 'smiley's and repairs

Even though the requirement of immediate neighbouring (or 'adjacency'; on this, see section 12.4.2) typically holds for two utterances belonging to the same exchange, there are cases where such immediacy is not maintained; the resulting overlapping, however, does not damage conversational coherence. The general name for this phenomenon is *insertion*; one of the most frequent instances of insertion is *repair*.

In an insertion sequence, the normal flow of conversation is not stopped; conversationalists behave as if they were aware that the 'turns' in their talk are operating at different levels, and thus the main stream of conversation may continue its course, even though part of it is shunted off in order to let the conversationalists attend to actual or possible upcoming difficulties. After the obstacles have been removed, conversation continues as before; the turn-taking counters have not been affected by the insertion sequence. Typically, in the middle of a conversational

exchange, one may be presented with a greeting, or a request for information, or an order, none of these having anything to do with the topic
of the exchange.

In the following exchange (from Halliday 1978), different conversational goals are being pursued: greetings, buying/selling, exchange of
information about the weather (maybe just a case of 'passing the time of
day'), good-byes. All these actions are intertwined, rather than following
each other strictly in sequence. Thus, e.g., in the buying sequence below,
the conversationalists insert a 'weather information exchange'. Notice
also the pre-sequence that 'preempts' (see below, sections 12.4.3 and
12.6) the actual act of 'buying/selling', replacing it by an indirect speech
act of 'enquiring about the availability of the item to be purchased'.

> Morning Tom!
> Good morning, sir!
> Have you got a *Guardian* left this morning?
> You're lucky; it's the last one. Bit brighter today, by the looks of it.
> Yes, we could do with a bit of a dry spell. You got change for a
>   pound?
> Yes, plenty of change; here you are. Anything else today?
> No, that's all just now, Tom. Be seeing you.
> Mind how you go. (Halliday 1978: 219)

Normally, one does not perceive attending to such 'other business'
(greetings, requests, orders etc.) as interfering with the business at hand;
it is similar to telling your party on the other phone line that you're busy,
or uttering the standardized phrase (valid in all sorts of situations): 'Just
a moment please'.

Consider the following sequence:

> Father (*on the phone to university*): So I think I'll be in tomorrow,
>   when Peter is a little better. And if you could tell the ethics
>   committee . . .
> [*in a loud voice*] HEY STOP THAT RIGHT AWAY
> Secretary: You want me to stop WHAT
> Father: Sorry, I was talking to the cat – Hold on
> Secretary: ???
> Father: The damn cat was fixin' to sit on the baby's face.

While there is no proper 'sequencing' of replies in this conversation, if we know the situation, its coherence is obvious, despite the interruption caused by the insertion sequence.

In cases where the insertion sequences deal with non-related, non-life-threatening matters, though, the reaction may be different.

The classic case is the shop scenario, in which the shopkeeper or clerk picks up the phone and starts talking to a customer on an incoming line right in the middle of your interchange, and most of the time without so much as offering an apology to you. This is usually perceived as non-cooperative behaviour, especially in cases where the inserted conversation tends to go on and on, or turns out to be a private, non-business-related call. Interestingly, and perhaps in part due to the relative newness and relatively recent common availability of telephone service, as yet we seem not to have been able to develop a generally accepted way of conversationally dealing with such situations.

Another consideration is the following. There is a crucial difference between normal and telephone conversation in that the former utilizes a great number of non-verbal communicative methods for regulating the interchange: think of the role that eye contact plays in establishing or changing turns, or of the importance of body postures that tell the other person something about what you're going to say next (like getting up from your chair as a body-language pre-sequence to saying good-bye). In contrast, there is no established way of communicating such signals by telephone. Telephone conversations remain largely an unexplored field, despite the pioneering work of Schegloff and Sacks in the early 1970s (see Schegloff 1972, Schegloff and Sacks 1973).

The same holds, *mutatis mutandis*, for another new conversational medium: the electronic message service, better known as 'e-mail'. In this medium, only the writing component can be used to represent language: no sounds or visual cues are available; yet, by the speed and immediacy of the electronic medium, the illusion of a real conversation is created (different from the customary slowness and distance in other form of written communication, such as letters). The way people have been dealing with this problem indirectly points up the importance of body language as an accompanying and modifying feature in all conversation: the need for an e-mail substitute for such language made computer buffs invent the 'smiley', a combination of (regular ASCII symbols and alphanumerical) characters, standardized to express a certain feeling or attitude towards what is being written (in some cases, the attitude is the equivalent of a smile, hence the name; the original 'smiley' was developed as a vertical implementation of the ubiquitous smiling figure of the seventies :). Putting a 'smiley' next to what you're writing means something like: 'Don't take this too seriously'; in other words, a 'smiley' is a visual mitigating device (there are reportedly well over a hundred 'smileys' around among computer users, and a whole new 'smiley' subculture is developing).

As we see from the examples given, sequences may be interrupted, or even stopped altogether, whenever other business needs to be attended to (which may or may not be related to the conversation at hand). Evidently, natural disasters, or even minor mishaps (like the cat example above) need immediate attention, and require that the conversationalists adjust their interchange to the emergent situation in the outside world. In general, although interruptions and insertions may happen at all times during all kinds of conversations, many of the actual phenomena are related to a particular culture (for instance, the above-described 'telephone intrusions' are much more familiar in the US than in Europe), and cannot be properly understood without some insight into the particular pragmatic presuppositions that are at work.

Whenever normal sequencing is not observed (either by non-adherence to strict adjacency, or by 'non-sequiturs' of a more pragmatic kind, or both), the phenomenon may be of sufficient interest to the interlocutors for a repair sequence to be initiated. One distinguishes between self-initiated repairs (where the speaker momentarily leaves the current floor, and erects a temporary structure where repair operations can be performed), and other-initiated repairs (mostly consisting in corrections offered to the speaker, e.g., 'You mean of course . . .', sometimes inserted directly into the speaker's discourse, correcting his or her vocabulary or pronunciation, questioning the utterance's presuppositions and/or setting them right, and so on).

Repairs are often strategic devices: correcting oneself, in particular, can be a way of gaining time to think, or a means to prevent somebody else from jumping into the conversation at an upcoming TRP. Sometimes, what seems to initiate a repair sequence by force of a request for information, an apology, etc., contains in reality a speech act of a totally different kind.

As an example, consider the other-initiated repair in the following conversation between a Macho Male (MM) and a Feminist Female (FF):

MM: So I was trying to pick up this chick when . . .
FF: Excuse ME, did I hear that right?
MM: Awfully sorry, I mean, *woman* . . .
FF: PICK UP?
MM: Awfully sorry, I mean, *meet* . . .
FF: So you're trying to imply that there actually are women
around who would go out with a MALE CHAUVINIST PIG
LIKE YOU?

In this case, both repairs are other-initiated; the speech acts of 'asking for confirmation' or 'excusing' are in reality threats, acknowledged as such by the speaker in his apology-cum-repair. The dialogue ends with a rather heavy-handed 'presupposition correction'.[95]

11.6 PREFERENCE

Imagine you're in a foreign country, where you speak and understand some of the language, without being fluent. You're staying in a friend's house and the phone rings. What do you do?

My guess is that you leave it alone. Not only are there the difficulties in speaking a foreign language on the phone (always more complicated than in face-to-face interaction), but what are you expected to say? And even if you know how to deliver the first line (the 'first pair part'; see section 12.4.2) of a telephone interchange, what does the other person say in return? And what comes next?

A typical telephone exchange in English could go like this:

Caller: [*phone rings*]
Respondent: Hello
C: May I speak to Alexander Kirkwood, please
R: Just a moment, please.

There are, of course, numerous variations on this scheme – but as a general rule, there is minimally a two-part interchange before the caller can proceed on business. Let's consider some of the possible variations of the first pair part: R may start with a self-identification (either by name or by phone number), in addition to the 'Hello'; the initial formula itself may be more or less explicit, in accordance with local and familial custom. Thus, in Italian, one says *Pronto*, 'ready [to take your call]'; in Czech, the opening gambit is *Prosím*, 'I beg [the favour of your call]'; in Spanish, one says simply *Diga*, 'Say [your message]' or the more old-fashioned *Mande*, 'Command [me to answer you]'. Some of my genteel Norwegian acquaintances answer the phone by naming themselves by their family name, followed by the sentence *Værsågod*, literally 'Be so kind' or 'Please [say something]'.

The follow-ups (the 'second pair parts'; see section 12.4.2) of such opening sequences are more controversial. For instance, does the caller have to offer proof of identity beyond a (perhaps recognizable) voice? How does it feel for the respondent to have to deal with an unidentified caller? Many respondents prefer to know who their caller is before they go any further into the conversation; on the other hand, many callers prefer to remain anonymous as long as they don't know who is at the other end of the line 'Do I have the party with who I am speaking?' (as Ernestine used to say in her famous telephone opening in the long-defunct show *Laugh-in*).

In general, what we notice is that there are relatively uncomplicated cases where the second pair part of an opening is expected in the context and goes straight through, whereas other sequences trigger a need for checking, backtracking, 'mental searches' ('I know this woman/man, but where did I meet her/him and what the hell is her/his name?'), and so on.

This observation does not hold for telephone interchanges only, but for all conversational interaction. Take a first-part greeting such as 'How are you?' Here, a second part in the form of a simple return greeting (e.g. 'Fine – and you?') is expected, whereas a lengthy account of sleepless nights or boring highway travel on the way to work are clearly to be avoided.

The next question is whether we can say anything about the form that such interchanges preferably take.

Consider the following two conversations:

(*In the liquor store*)

(a)
Sales clerk: You're over 21, aren't you?
Customer: Yes.
Sales clerk: OK, here's your beer.

(b)
Sales clerk: You're over 21, aren't you?

Customer: Well, er, yes, my birthday was actually yesterday,
          and my brother is coming over to celebrate . . .
Sales clerk: May I see your ID?

The customer's return in (b) is clearly problematic, given the circumstances (the case may serve as an illustration of what happens to those
who break the First Rule Of Dealing With Authorities: 'Never volunteer
information' – actually an instantiation of Grice's maxim of quantity; see
section 4.4.1). The fact that superfluous information is offered in the
second part of the turn makes this type of answer inappropriate, as well
as ineffective. As a result, the salesperson gets suspicious and wants to see
an ID.

But the story doesn't end here. If we look more closely at the
customer's utterance in (b), we notice a couple of other things. The
elaborate response in case (b) is in stark contrast to the simple 'OK' in
(a). In (b), there is hesitation in the customer's reply, and he starts his
sentence over again ('false start': 'er'); there is an expletive ('yes'), there
is a so-called 'hedge' (showing a certain insecurity: 'Well'); there is a lot
of irrelevant information (what does the sales clerk have to do with the
customer's birthday and/or his brother's visit) – all this is against the
norm and beside the point, and serves as an indicator of something being
'glossed over', conjured away by talk.

Generalizing from these examples, we get the following picture: in
conversational interchanges, not all second pair parts are of equal structural complexity. Some are extremely simple, such as acknowledgements
or confirmations ('Yes', 'OK'), others show various degrees of structural
build-up (like elaborate excuses, long explanations, etc.).

Here are some further contrasting instances; this time the interchange
has the form of a request and an (indirect) denial:

(Simple-structured second pair part):

A: Could you help me lift this box, please?
B: OK (goes over and helps A lift box)

(Complex-structured second pair part):

A: Could you help me move tomorrow morning?
B: Well, er, let me see, I have to take Cindy to nursery school and

take my mother-in-law who has just broken her arm to the doctor and Fred my handyman is coming over to fix the attic window, so . . . couldn't we make it some other day, perhaps, or does it have to be tomorrow?

It turns out that such negative responses to requests share a more complex structure, as compared to the positive ones. On a closer look, there is a general ranking present here (one that is not only valid for requests): from structurally simpler to structurally more complex, corresponding to the ranking 'acceptance–rejection' in the case of requests. In other words, one has to work harder, use more linguistic resources to say 'No' to a request than to say 'Yes' – the 'No' may have to be shored up with lots of background material intended to avoid giving the impression that one does not just decline to perform the requested action, but rather that the refusal is due exclusively to circumstances beyond one's control – which then have to be specified. This specification takes time and requires a greater effort – something which may surface as hesitation, pauses, 'repair' (starting over again after a false start) and so on.

The term that is used for this ranking is 'preference'; another, perhaps more suitable term would be 'marked'. 'Marked' sequences are structurally richer and more complex than 'unmarked' ones; the unmarked items are often termed the 'default': it's what we do when nothing else is specified, like driving along at 55 mph when there are no stop signs around, children to watch, speed signs to observe, and all the traffic lights are green. Marked behaviours (like making a turn, going at excessively slow speeds, stopping in the middle of the highway, not driving on when the light turns green and so on) have to be announced, preferably before they happen (e.g. by turning on one's signals). Marked behaviours are, furthermore, dispreferred because they require more effort on the part of the other users. And finally, they're sometimes lacking in effectiveness.

Some of the features mentioned above appear also in other contexts where dispreferred responses turn up. Most conspicuous are pauses (self-interruptions, possibly followed by self-repairs with or without explanation, e.g. 'what I really want to say is, er, yes . . .'), the already named 'false starts', repetitions, wordiness, but also features of a 'prosodic' kind: speed of delivery, stress, intonation, irregular breathing (both in- and out-); maybe even such extralinguistic features as flushing, trembling and the like. All such phenomena could lead one to believe that the whole matter of preference had its original seat in the physio-psychology of the individual language user. However, as Levinson remarks, this is not so: preference is a format of utterances, not a psychological state of the uttering individual. And he defends himself against accusations of circularity by pointing to a well-established correlation between the external phenomena I just mentioned and the facts of '(dis)preferredness': we find 'recurrent and reliable patterns' of correlation between the two domains, that of 'preference' and that of the 'kind of action' performed. Thus, e.g., in the case of offers or invitations, an acceptance is in preferred format, whereas refusals normally are in dispreferred format. Here is an illustration of the correlation that Levinson has in mind (1983: 336):

FIRST PARTS	request	offer/invitation	assessment	question	blame
SECOND PARTS					
Preferred	acceptance	acceptance	agreement	expected answer	denial
Dispreferred	refusal	refusal	disagreement	unexpected (or non-)answer	admission

On the whole, one can say that certain kinds of responses are always and definitely preferred, while others are usually and more or less definitely dispreferred. Among the latter, we find such telephone openings as 'Who are you?' or 'There is nobody here'; for second pair parts, we can think of silence, or heavy breathing, or even responses that carry too much information (as in the liquor store case quoted above), and therefore do not allow the gradual building up of a conversation. Here's an example of such an (unsuccessful) informational overload on the second pair part of a telephone greeting:[96]

[*Phone rings*]
Bruce: Hello
Caller: Hello, I'm Julie from the *Patriot Ledger*. How are you today?
Bruce: I'm fine, thanks, but I already take two newspapers and I think a third would be superfluous.

Here, the caller, by providing full self-identification and affiliation information, precludes further business; if she hadn't mentioned the name of the newspaper, she probably would have been able to continue the conversation and perhaps persuade Bruce to subscribe.

While the phenomenon of 'marked' or 'dispreferred' response sequences is probably universal, the way these markings are realized is not. In his treatment of 'preference organization', Levinson concentrates on the morphological and syntactic properties of 'marked' utterances. The prosodic properties of such utterances are not treated specifically (although some are included: e.g. pause, and others mentioned in passing, such as 'in-breath', p. 337).

Some languages have extensive prosodic means of signalling preference; breath mechanisms are often employed in this connection. Scandinavians preferably manifest assent by producing an in-breathed *ja* ('yes'); the Japanese show the difficulties involved in what they are talking about by sucking in their breath sharply, either though the mouth (producing a hissing sound) or through the nose (producing what sounds more like an inverted snort; the behaviour seems to be restricted to males). In contrast to the Scandinavian pattern, however, the utterance itself is not breathed in Japanese (as in the case of the implosive Scandinavian *ja*), and for good reasons: too much breath would be lost in the process to continue normal conversation. So, what happens is that one hears the 'hiss' (here reproduced as a number of <<'s, the number indicating length), followed by the utterance in question; e.g. <<<< *taihen desu* 'it's hard, terrible, etc.' In usual conversation, this prosodic marker for 'dispreferredness' occurs frequently as a short, nasal breath intake of different strength, often almost inaudible, and usually accompanied by a slowing down of the tempo and a lowering of the voice pitch. Here is an example:

(*A wants to pass on some concert tickets to B, because he can't go himself*)

A: . . . *konban ongaku-wa kippu-ga arun-desu-ga, doo-desu-ka*
    (I got tickets for tonight's concert, would you be interested?)

B: *Soo desu-neee* << . . . [*slow delivery, pitch descending, then a short moderate nasal in-breath, followed by a pause*]
    (Well, I don't know . . .)
    koo-yuu ongaku-wa doomo-neee <<<< . . . [*slow delivery, pitch and intensity decreasing, penultimate syllable inaudible, sharp nasal in-breath, followed by a pause*]
    (That kind of music, you know . . .)
    Katoo-san-ni agetara doo-desu-ka. Kurashikku-ga suki-da-soo-da-kara . . . [*lively speed, high pitch, engaged intonation*]
    (How about Miss Kato – wouldn't it be a good idea to offer her

the tickets? She is probably more interested in classical music).
(Mizutani and Mizutani 1986: 237)

As we see from this interchange, the physical, audible markings of 'dispreferredness' in Japanese are of a very different kind than we are used to in English – yet they are extremely effective, and very useful in helping one to structure one's preferences. Small wonder, then, that so many Japanese carry this marking device over into other languages, where the effect is rather grotesque (our usual association with a sharp breath intake through the mouth is one of extreme emotional upset, of approaching physical danger, or of physical pain). While preference as a phenomenon of conversational organization is probably universal, its individual manifestations in different languages may display a great deal of variation.

EXERCISES AND REVIEW QUESTIONS

1. The following extract from a conversation transcription (due to Jan-Ola Östman) looks the way you would find it in works and articles on conversation analysis (CA). Among the transcription conventions that are used in CA (and which actually occur in the extract below) are:

! exclamation mark: exclamatory intonation
? interrogation mark: rising intonation
= equal sign: no gap between utterances
– dashes: pause
:(:) colon(s) (after vowel): (degrees of) lengthening
underlining as in syllable: stressed syllable or word
// double slash: point of overlap (corresponding to point where next turn
   begins)
[left square bracket, vertically across two or more lines: alternative way
   of marking overlap
(for a full account of transcription conventions in conversation analysis,
   see Levinson 1983: 369–70).
The lines are numbered for easy reference.

   1. A. There was an astonishing traffic in Walnut Creek // today
   2. C. Oh, Bobby! // Did you like the you know – Bishop's Bloom-
      ing Market=

3. A. Huh?
4. A. [Well?
5. B. =I [went with her?
6. C. To<u>day</u>?=
7. B. =Yeah?
8. D. Oh exc<u>use</u> me? – is that the <u>new</u> one=
9. C. Yeah [the one on <u>North</u> Street
10. D. [=that they were gonna open last=
11. A. =<u>That</u>'s the one –
12. A. Anyway? – They had a <u>hu::ge</u> no a <u>ma:r</u>velous parking // lot
    there=
13. B. For three hundred [cars
14. A.   [=with space for <u>three</u> hundred // cars
15. C. So, did you <u>find</u> yourself a typewrit // er?
16. B. A <u>tape</u>-recorder [dear!
17. C.   [A <u>tape</u>-recorder?
18. A.   [Oh <u>no</u>? They were <u>fa:r</u> too expensive //
    for me=
19. C. Oh yeah?
20. A. =<u>Well</u>? – These days <u>every</u>one's affected by the <u>oil</u> crisis,
    <u>aren</u>'t they?

In this piece of conversation, four people, called here A, B, C and D, are
having an after-dinner conversation in the host's living-room. Two of the
people have been shopping at the new mall; the two others did not come
along. They exchange experiences and comments, and contribute 'small
talk'.

Questions:

In what way can we say that the conversation is typical of a particular
kind of people?

Who are the shoppers; who did not go?

Who is the host?

Who is 'Bobby'?

Who went out to buy ('find') what?

Did this person find and buy what he/she was looking for?

Who is most impressed by the new shopping mall?

Who is wowed by the number of cars that fit in the ('marvellous') parking lot?

Who is male, who is female among the conversationalists?

Who is interrupting most (least) in this conversation?

Who is saying most (least)?

Who of the four know each other, and how well?

Are any of them strangers to each other?

Are any of the four married (to any of the others)?

Does any of the four have a social position that is markedly different (higher, lower) from any of the others?

What is the topic of this conversation?

What are the intentions of the conversationalists?

What are the respective ages of the conversationalists? (roughly, within ten or fifteen years).

How would you characterize this conversation in terms of 'lively', 'dull', 'interesting', 'not interesting', 'engaged', 'uninterested'? How about the conversationalists?

From a CA point of view, how would you characterize this conversation? Frame your answer in terms of such concepts as: turn-taking, adjacency pairs, TRP's, and other CA concepts that you may find useful.

Is this a typical conversation? Why (not)?

Can you find any of the rules that you have found in CA writings to be observed/broken/irrelevant in the extract at hand?

For each of your answers, indicate where you think the text shows that your answer is correct, or at least reasonably motivated.

2. The following dialogue occurred at the US Immigration Service check-point in Lester B. Pearson International Airport, Toronto, Canada, on 10 January, 1993:

Immigration officer: Where do you live?
Passenger: Evanston, Illinois.
Officer: Are you an American citizen?
Passenger: No, I'm a resident.
Officer: May I see your Green Card?
Passenger: (hands over card)
Officer: (examines card, punches something into his computer, hands back card) Do you have a driver's license?
Passenger: Yes.
Officer: OK, pass on.
Passenger (somewhat astonished): But don't you want to see it?
Officer: No, just pass on.

Questions:

Why was the passenger astonished?

What kind of question was it the immigration officer 'really' was asking?

What kind of question did he ask?

12

Conversation Analysis: Part II

12.1 INTRODUCTION: FROM FORM TO CONTENT

The previous chapter concentrated on the formal devices conversationalists have at their disposal for structuring their talk, measuring their
interventions and controlling the 'floor'. As became apparent in that
discussion, these formal devices (in particular those having to do with
what will be called 'sequencing' in the following), often are inseparable
from what the forms in question express. A request is followed by a
compliance or a rejection, not only on the formal level: there is a reason
for pairs occurring together, to wit, the fact that both members of the
pair deal with the same content (roughly speaking).

In the following, we will first examine some of the content-oriented
mechanisms of conversation. Doing this, we will also obtain a first
understanding of the pragmatics involved here; a fuller discussion of this
aspect, however, will be reserved for later (see section 12.7).

12.2 COHERENCE

Intuitively, we are able to distinguish coherent talk from incoherent
babbling. Linguists of all kinds have endeavoured to give a reasoned
explanation of this immediate experience, and one of the ways they have
approached the problem has been by introducing coherence as a defini-
tional term. Conversation, like discourse in general, is said to be governed by the *Coherence Principle*:

... in order for an utterance to form a coherent sequence with the
preceding utterance, it must either fulfill the illocutionary intention
of the latter, or address its pragmatic presuppositions. (Tsui 1991:
111, 120)

I will address the matter of illocutionary intentions below, in section
12.5 (pragmatic presuppositions were discussed earlier, section 10.4.3).
The pragmatic aspects of coherence will be discussed in later sections
(12.6 and 12.7; cf. also 12.4.2). For now, let me provide a piece of text
that shows no coherence at all, although it is locally organized as a
sequence of 'turns'.

The following interchange (between a psychiatrist and his patient, an
80-year-old educated middle-class woman) is taken from Rosenbaum
and Sonne (1986); it is a typical instance of 'schizophrenic discourse', or
even 'discourses', as they say (1986: 18ff.).

I[nterviewer]: Is it something you have experienced?
P[atient]: No, yes, it's been said to us.
I: Aha.
P: Yes, it's been said.
I: Who said it to you?
P: Well, I can hardly remember who. There are many young gentle-
    men here, many young people who have been separated, and
    they have said it – they have told something about it. Yes.
I: Where are these young people?
P: Well, they are three hundred things after all, so we are, we had
    people all over space, yes. There were . . . the whole of space was
    filled with people and then they were put into three skins at our
    place.
I: Three skins?
P: Yes, they were put into the body, but I think that two of the skins
    are ready, they should be ready, they should be separated. And
    there were three hundred thousand who had no reason, or soul, or
    reason. But now they are so . . . now it seems that there are some
    who have neither soul nor reason and they had to be helped, and
    people have to be helped, I can't do it here in this where we are, we
    have to be in . . . if I am to take care of these things. These . . . that's
    what the ladies say, they are aware . . .
    . . .

P: I've helped them in Øster Søgade [a major thoroughfare in central Copenhagen] we helped them in that way.

I: In Øster Søgade?

P: Yes, we helped them in that way there and there were many who slid away and many who were helped. Yes.

I: There were many who slid away and many who were helped?

P: Yes, I don't know how many, I don't know. But there are many trisks and svilts, I think there are most trisks and svilts [meaningless English words calqued on equally meaningless Danish ones; cf. 'trilms', below]. That is those who are made out of svilt clay.

I: Out of svilt clay?

P: Yes, it is out on space. They make them in trilms.

I: Trilms?

P: By trilms. And then they go through three levels. Some only go through two. Some go through three. Yes. When they make them. (1986: 9ff.)

The coherence in this piece of conversation is strictly 'local', as conversation analysts would say; it turns around the local, formal organization of the talk by referring to items that have been mentioned in the immediately preceding context. Thus, there is a certain amount of what Stubbs (1983: 126–7) has called 'text cohesion';[97] but for the text to proceed in a minimally ordered, flowing fashion, the interviewer's 'prompting' role is all-important: whenever the patient halts, the interviewer repeats some of her last words, so as to get her started again.

However, it is difficult to say what 'text cohesion' (or even 'text coherence') really is 'about' in this interchange: what is the content of this piece of conversation? What are, e.g., 'trisks' and 'svilts' and 'trilms'? Or what about 'sliding' – into what? (later, it turns out that the people slide into 'sugar-pools').

Although it is, of course, strictly true that one never completely knows what the other party is going to say in a conversation, it seems clear that the above 'conversation' is so incoherent and unpredictable (despite its textual cohesion) that the only way to make it continue is for the interviewer to repeat some of the words that have just been uttered by the patient, more or less like a Rogerian therapist, or his or her computer equivalent, ELIZA, would do.[98] The interviewer just keeps the speech flow going, without having an inkling of *where* it's going.

As the interviewee herself remarks at a later point in the conversation, it is as if there were a sound tape playing in her head:

> P: ... we have a tape that speaks. It's a tape speaking now ... It's an old tape speaking.
> I: It's an old tape speaking?
> P: It's an old tape speaking when ...
> I: When you are speaking now?
> P: Yes, that's a tape too. ... (Rosenbaum and Sonne 1986: 12)

The 'tape metaphor' nicely symbolizes the 'text cohesion' that after all is present in this piece; however, there seems not to be much of a coherence in the sense defined by Tsui.

Contrast now the following interchanges, all of which, at first blush, seem to lack 'text cohesion'; yet in a larger framework, they end up making sense (Tsui 1991: 115).

> A: What's the time?
> B: (a) Eleven.
> (b) Time for coffee.
> (c) I haven't got a watch, sorry.
> (d) How should I know.
> (e) Ask Jack.
> (f) You know bloody well what time it is.
> (g) Why do you ask?
> (h) What did you say?
> (i) What do you mean?

Of all these answers, only the first two properly qualify for the coherence test that was suggested in the previous chapter ('request for information – compliance by giving information'). However, this does not make the rest of the answers irrelevant, inasmuch as they all make sense in *some* current context (that is, they address some common presuppositions in the pragmatic background of the speaker and hearer, as we will see below, section 12.4.2). For example, take the 'coffee' reply: people usually have coffee at the same time every day; hence 'time for coffee' equals some, more or less precise, indication of real clock time. Similarly, if one happened to live in the East Prussian city of Königsberg towards the end of the 18th century, a way of telling the time, '12 noon', would be to reply: 'Professor Kant just walked by'; Kant's daily noontime constitutionals on the city walls were so punctual that people could use them to set their watches by.

So, in normal conversation, even totally unexpected answers come as no surprise, once we're able to place them in the proper context, either in physical reality or in the universe of discourse. If we're unable to do either, we may ask ourselves if the person we're talking to perhaps suffers from some psychiatric disorder, or alternatively whether he or she intends to convey a totally different content than what we seem to perceive (e.g., 'I don't want to talk to you,' 'Get lost,' or some other such message).

12.3   SEQUENCING

The examples in the preceding section show that the mere fact of utterances following each other is no guarantee of coherence. Yet, sequencing (as I called it in section 11.5.2) plays an important role in the structuring of our conversations, not only on the level of formal signals, but also on the level of what the utterances mean, or of how they function. As Levinson remarks,

> ... rather, the units in question [the utterances] seem to be functionally defined by the actions they can be seen to perform in context. (1983: 293)

Conversely,

> ... the violation of the rules [governing coherent sequences] results in incoherent discourse which is *noticed* and attended to by interlocutors, and ... the violation of these rules can usually be accounted for. (Tsui 1991: 111; my emphasis)

Clearly, in the case of the schizophrenic discourse quoted in the previous section, some of these rules have been violated; this is something we notice while unsuccessfully trying to understand that conversation. Sequencing, then, clearly cannot just be a matter of a sequence of utterances; in particular, conversation is built up (as are, in general, texts) in a live environment, between living users. It is not constructed according to some abstract rules of 'text syntax' or conversational coherence: such rules are at best re-constructions of what actually has happened. Hence, even though

> ... conversations are (in part) composed of units that have some direct correspondence to sentences (Levinson 1983: 294),

the analytical methods of sentence and text grammars, as well as their conceptual structures, have only limited validity in the domain of conversation.

Still, it remains a fact that conversation is characterized by a certain amount of 'pair-wise structure'. The word 'conversation' itself suggests a certain similarity to ritually performed and metrically codified verbal exchanges, such as we know from the chorus of Classical Greek drama. Also in monastic antiphonal psalmody and hymn-singing, the parties alternate in responding, the pairs being marked in the text by the symbols '℣' and '℟', for *versus* and *responsorium*, respectively. Here, the term *versus* (from the Latin verb *vertere*, 'to turn'; cf. also how we refer to the two sides of a page: *recto* and *verso*) recalls the turning and returning of the lead in chanting that is so characteristic of choral psalmody (just as turning the pages is characteristic of reading). In the same vein, 'conversation' consists in people's paired (turn-wise) 'con-laboration', along with the repetitions and extensions that the turns naturally lead to. Such 'paired utterances' (Levinson 1983: 293) seem to be at the basis of the sequencing rules, in particular as manifested in so-called 'adjacency pairs', about which more in the next section.

12.4 ADJACENCY PAIRS

12.4.1 A little bit of history

Adjacency pairs were to conversation analysis what speech acts originally were to pragmatics: a discovery that became the starting-point for a whole new approach (theoretical in the case of speech acts, more practically-oriented in the case of adjacency pairs). This, one could say, is a first historical link between conversational analysis and speech act theory.

Another original discovery in conversation analysis (mainly due to Harvey Sacks in early lectures, recently (re)issued in his *Lectures on*

Conversation (1992)) was that conversation is an orderly affair: it doesn't just proceed at random, but obeys certain well-defined rules governing what follows what, who can speak when and so on. In other words, coherence, or 'text cohesion', is rule-governed.

Certain early text theoreticians (such as van Dijk, Petöfi and others) interpreted these 'rules' in strictly 'grammatical' terms; their text grammars were modelled on the then current (1970s) model of generative-transformational grammar, the so-called 'Revised Standard Theory'. Others, looking at texts (especially conversational texts) from the point of view of how people actually talk, didn't bother too much about grammatical orthodoxy, and tried instead to use some of the recently introduced concepts of speech act theory in their description of human interaction in conversation. This is the other historical link between speech acts and conversation analysis.

12.4.2 Types of adjacency pairs

Adjacency pairs are defined as two subsequent utterances constituting a conversational exchange. Pairs are characterized by their type. The type of a pair is given by a common illocutionary intention (or 'force', as Austin called it); pairs can thus be, e.g., 'greeting–greeting', 'order–(verbal) compliance', 'request (e.g. for information)–providing the requested item (e.g. information)' and so on.

Classical conversation analysis (see, e.g., Sacks, Schegloff and Jefferson 1974) distinguishes between the 'first pair part' and the 'second pair part' of any adjacency pair. For instance, the first pair part may be a summons; then what constitutes the second pair part has to be an utterance which deals with compliance (either positive or negative), as in the following exchanges:

Could you please close that window?

Sure

and

Could you please close that window?

No way.

Clearly, the second pair part could be one that contained more information (e.g., 'In a minute', or 'No, I'd rather have it open'); but that wouldn't affect the type of exchange or adjacency pair.

In general, the notion of 'type' is useful when it comes to predicting what the answer could be, and how it is managed: in a way, it defines the 'base-line' for the second pair parts that are possible. But it also does more.

Following the theory of adjacency pairs, given a first part of a pair, a second part is immediately relevant and expectable.[99] Furthermore, according to Schegloff (1972), if a second pair part is not found in the context of the conversation, then the first pair part is judged officially not to exist, and the first speaker may repeat the first part (e.g. by reiterating the summons, maybe with some emphasis: 'I asked you to close the window', 'Would you PLEASE close that window?' and so on). Such repeated first parts do not normally occur in conversation (e.g., one doesn't repeat a greeting, unless one wants to make a point: 'I have not been greeted').

The absence of a second pair part is noticeable, and has certain conversational effects, as in the case of 'pretending it didn't happen'. Suppose somebody makes a socially impossible request, such as asking the boss's wife for a date at the company outing. The painful silence which ensues makes the unfortunate requester feel embarrassed; yet it is also a means of telling him (by not giving any indication that anybody has heard what he said): 'Listen, you did something unfortunate, but we're prepared to pretend it didn't happen.'

Formally, one can express the same 'denied reality' using an explicit (and strictly speaking, self-contradictory) second pair part such as 'We didn't hear that, did we?' And an even stronger second part would contain an indirect speech act of reprimanding: 'I don't believe what I'm hearing'. In such cases, as noted earlier, the most effective way of stating is *not* stating (explicitly) what is really being expressed: that the speaker is a socially incompetent oaf.

The difference between the strict notion of 'adjacency' (based on the 'type' of interchange) and a more relaxed view (based on the pragmatic effect of the reply, viewed as an understanding of what the interchange really is about) reminds us of our earlier distinction between 'direct' speech acts and 'indirect' speech acts. While 'primitive speech act theory' (as outlined originally by Austin) put great emphasis on the actual verbs expressing speech acts, later developments allowed for speech acts to be realized in all sorts of 'indirect' ways (cf. the classic example: 'It's cold in here,' pragmatically understood as a request to close the door or a window).

In such a pragmatic view, neither the adjacency pair itself nor the speech act making up its 'type' are focused upon; rather, it is the entire (linguistic as well as social) user behaviour that has to be explained. This view will be elaborated below, in chapter 14.

12.4.3   Problems with questions

A question together with its answer is typically an adjacency pair – but what is its 'type'? To answer that, one has to know what constitutes a legitimate answer to a question.

Consider the following interchange:

Q. Is Lars there?
A. You can reach him at extension 3402.

Strictly speaking, this pair does not constitute a regular 'question–answer' type: the information requested by the speaker (whether or not Lars is 'there', i.e. at the listener's location) is not given, except indirectly. By contrast, the 'regular' possible answers, such as: 'No, he isn't,' or: 'I'm sorry, he isn't,' or simply 'No,' would merely provide the information requested; an addressee giving such 'regular' answers to the original question would stay strictly within the bounds of adjacency pair typology, yet be very uninformative in his or her answer.

One is tempted to say that the easiest way out of this dilemma is to assume that whatever follows a question simply *is* the answer. Here, it is important to notice that the 'second part' of a conversational pair (in general, of a sequence) cannot strictly be defined by its content, or by its 'classical' speech act character. As Levinson aptly remarks, there is no speech act of answering, no 'answerhood', except as a notion that is so vague and all-encompassing that it is useless for describing what actually occurs as answers to questions; cf.:

. . . significantly, there is no proposed illocutionary force of answering. (1983: 293)

In other words, 'answering' is not a speech act; it can only be defined on the basis of, among other things, the preceding question.

Another way of explaining the 'answerhood' of the above reply is to say that the question in reality was not about whether or not Lars was at the given location, but just represented another way of asking: 'Do you know where Lars is right now?', or simply: 'Where is Lars?' In that case, we could still maintain that the type of the pair was safeguarded and that therefore, the question–answer pair was coherent, also from the point of view of illocutionary intent.

In a strict adjacency pair typology, such an interpretation of the speech acting involved here is not recognized as useful. For given that the point of the original speech act was the extraction of some information about Lars's whereabouts, a 'bald on record' answer of the kind 'No (he isn't)' is anything but helpful. By contrast, an answer that specifies where I can reach Lars ('extension 3402') provides me with the information I need; given that knowledge, I don't even care any more whether or not Lars is at the original, presumed location.

Conversation analysts have tried to solve the problem of 'unexpected second pair parts' by invoking the distinction between sequences and pre-sequences (introduced above, section 11.5.1). Thus, in the case of the question

Is Lars there?

we are dealing, not with a request for information, but rather, a pre-request for something else (permission to speak with Lars, a request for being put in touch with Lars and so on). This pragmatic coherence, as it is sometimes called, cannot be explained in a strictly sequential framework (Jacobs and Jackson 1983a: 65). In a way, one could say that the question whether Lars is there enquires about a 'felicity condition' for the real request: clearly, if Lars isn't there, then it makes no sense to try and talk to him 'there'. The clever interlocutor perceives this, and infers that the real reason for enquiring about Lars' location is the speaker's desire to see him; therefore, he neglects ('preempts') that original question and answers what he thinks is the 'real' request by indicating where Lars may be reached:

You can reach him at extension 3402.

Conversely, there are cases where a pre-request mistakenly is interpreted as 'the real thing'. A good example of this is the following, due to Jacobs and Jackson (1983b: 302):

> (*A customer walks up to a cheque-cashing counter*)
> Customer: Can I cash a cheque?
> Attendant: I'll be right there.
> Customer: That's okay. I was just wondering whether it was too late or not.

Here, the first utterance is interpreted as a pre-sequence to a cheque-cashing encounter, where it in reality was a request for information. The uptake has been too quick: cooperation took the form of second-guessing. Sometimes this results in paranoid reactions, as in the delightful example also provided by Jacobs and Jackson (1983b: 301–2; here slightly adapted):

> (*The scene is Sally and Scott's house in Champaign, Illinois, where Sally and Scott both teach at the University. Sally is trying to get a plane out of Champaign, and has just finished talking to her travel agent on the phone. She sits down in the living room, wearing a coat to leave for the university. Scott is in the next room, preparing for his class; he has heard some of the conversation, looks up from his books and asks:*)

> Scott: Could you get out of here?
> Sally [indignant]: What do you *mean*, could I get *outta here*?!?
> Scott [laughing]: No, uh, heh-heh-hehhhh, could you get outta Champaign, er . . .

The above is an example of 'paranoid uptake': again, the second pair part is OK in the actual pair sequence (when Scott's utterance is interpreted as an indirect speech act of 'asking someone to leave'), but makes no sense as a sequel to a sincere request for information (which in fact it was, witness Scott's laughing reply).

To come back to the problem: Given a question, what can the answer be?, we note that a strictly sequential adjacency concept, based on a narrow speech act typology of 'questioning', does not provide a useful response. Any question can have numerous 'answers', all of them relevant to the (possibly hidden) point of the question. Here is a further illustrative example:

Q. What does Joe do for a living?
A. (i) The same as always
   (ii) Oh this and that
   (iii) I've no idea
   (iv) What's that got to do with it?
   (v) He doesn't (adapted from Levinson 1981: 483)

Here, all five answers are 'to the point', meaning that they make sense as answers (depending on the context, naturally), even though they do not provide any 'real' answer to the question, except in some vague, evasive way.

But notice that while only answer (i) strictly qualifies as a 'typologically acceptable' reply, it contains no information whatsoever about Joe's business (except in the case of a questioner who is more or less familiar with Joe and what he usually does for a living). As to the other answers, they state (appropriately, with respect to the question) that Joe doesn't do anything in particular for a living (ii); that the addressee doesn't know the answer (iii); that the question is rejected by the addressee as improper or irrelevant (iv); and that Joe is a lazy bum (v). All these answers are (again dependent on the context) perfectly acceptable, yet they are not in accordance with the theory of 'adjacency'. The reason may be that adjacency itself perhaps is not that cogent a notion; the following section will look into this.

12.4.4   Coherence and adjacency

The reason that our notion of coherence isn't upset by the answers quoted at the end of the previous section[100] is that all these replies are perfectly good answers, in a way: they somehow deal with the content of the question, since they address not only its illocutionary force, but also its pragmatic presuppositions.

Adjacency is usually defined as having to do with the illocutionary character (type) of the 'adjacency pair'. However, for discourse to be coherent, it is not enough, or even necessary, that an utterance and its predecessor or successor, combined into an adjacency 'pair', abide by the strict rules formulated by the conversation analysts and based on an orthodox speech act interpretation of the utterances in question.

According to Levinson, pairs are important because they 'steer us' towards a good understanding: 'given an answer, the question is relevant' (1983: 293). But also, conversation is much more than just combining pairs in sequences (not to mention the fact that those pairs can easily expand into 'threes', 'fours' and so on, and that 'sequence' in this sense does not have to entail 'immediately following or preceding'). Tsui's 'Coherence Principle' (quoted in section 12.2), with its double emphasis on both illocutionary force and pragmatic presuppositions, is stronger than, and hierarchically superior to, the notion of paired adjacency. Adjacency is a case of coherent sequencing, but not all sequencing needs to be defined strictly in terms of adjacency.

Of the two components that make up the coherence principle, 'pragmatic presuppositions' have been discussed in detail earlier, in section 10.4.3; I will come back to this topic in a broader, pragmatic context below, section 14.5. As to the other component of the principle, 'illocutionary force', this will be examined more closely in the next section.

12.5   CONVERSATION AND SPEECH ACTS

As I said above, the discovery of the 'paired' structure of conversation had a similar impact on the study of conversation analysis as the development of speech act theory did on the understanding of human linguistic behaviour (in particular, as this understanding is now realized in pragmatics). Obviously, the regularity with which certain speech acts manifest themselves as *acts* (cf. Austin's original discovery of institutionalized speech acts of the type 'I baptize thee', etc.), has a certain parallel to the discovery of what Levinson calls 'obvious regularities' in speech act behaviour: 'answers follow questions, greetings follow greetings, etc.' (1983: 289).

Consider now the following conversational exchange, in which John says to Mildred (at a party they're both attending; example modified from Levinson, 1983);

It's getting late, Mildred.

Among Mildred's possible answers, we could imagine at least the following three:

Are you really that bored?

Do you want to go home?

So?

Now, if we want to determine the 'type' of this exchange pair, we have
to find out what John's utterance really stands for: is it a statement about
the time of day (of course relative to the usual coordinates: 'late' is not an
absolute indication of time, such as, e.g., '00:15 GMT'); an expression of
boredom ('Let me tell you frankly that I'm bored out of my mind'); an act
of vengeance or punishment (Mildred may have been flirting with John's
neighbour); a secret code for 'Remember to take your pill'; or something
entirely different?

In other words, we must try to establish the 'illocutionary force' of
John's remark. What kind of speech act does it represent? A statement,
admonition, request, threat, confession? – it all depends on such things
as: how well Mildred knows John (whether they are married, or just
dating); what sort of a party it is (a formal dinner, or just a drop-in or
gate-crashing affair); and so on. To borrow a terminology originally
developed in another context: one must know the script for this particular interaction in order to assess the contextual value of this particular
utterance. A 'party script' would include presupposed information about
people's conversational behaviour at parties: they may joke, fight, argue,
flirt, discuss linguistics, eat potato chips, get drunk and so on; alternatively, they may even enjoy themselves.[101]

Now, the funny thing about Mildred's possible answers in the above
conversation is that they all, in a way, are OK; that is: in the context, they
make sense.[102] Especially if we look at their possible effects, they must
certainly be valid, in the sense of *effective* answers: John may get upset,
and just walk off, or he may hand Mildred the car keys, or they may
continue the conversation (which in all likelihood then is going to turn
into an argument, with its appropriate, but unpredictable speech acting
and its inappropriate, but equally predictable ending).

The above shows, first of all, that speech acts are not particularly good
tools to work with, when it comes to understanding an utterance in
context: which speech act one actually is looking at depends very much,
if not exclusively, on that particular context.

Second, the problem of classifying conversational adjacency pairs in
terms of 'illocutionary force' is a problem in itself (see above); however,

the 'force' problem certainly is not going to be less thorny if we limit ourselves to situating those pairs in their immediate appropriate co(n)texts, without taking their effects (perlocutionary and otherwise) into account.

One could be tempted to conclude that what really counts is how a speech act functions: if John's remark to Mildred functions as a statement (a 'reminder', to be precise), then it *is* that speech act (or some variant of the speech act 'statement'); if it functions as an expression of boredom, then it *is* that expression, and so on. In other words:

> ... the units in question seem to be functionally defined by the actions they can be seen to perform in context. (Levinson 1983: 291)

Taking this as our point of departure, we see how the discussions about the type of conversational interaction in reality are a bit beside the point. What is important is not what a speaker (more or less arbitrarily) decides to question, order, request, etc., but the effects the 'speech act' in question (however widely interpreted) have on the development of the conversational interaction.

Austin was already aware of this, when he talked about the 'uptake' as a necessary condition on the 'happiness' (or felicitousness) of speech acts. We may extend Austin's conditions to include also the qualifying conditions that are valid in a particular context, and ask: 'What does an individual utterance end up meaning, when considered in its total context?' For example, is a particular request (e.g. 'asking for a match') really a speech act of 'asking', or maybe a come-on remark, a plea for human understanding and sympathy or a prelude to armed robbery?

12.6   Beyond Local Organization

Rather than base ourselves on a typology of speech acts in order to achieve a classification of adjacency phenomena, we must look for an explanation outside a framework that bases itself on speech act theory proper.

Whereas Sacks and the original ethnomethodologists assumed 'speaker's intention' (a psychological notion) to be constitutive of the 'type' of interchange, a more pragmatic view would stress that whatever happens to be the outcome is the most important aspect of any situation. In the case of questions, whatever is answered, is 'the' answer, and it is the conversation analyst's task to find out what this answer means, rather than to rule a particular answer 'out of order'. Hence, any typology of conversational pairs (if indeed we can operate with this concept) is determined, not in accordance with the speaker's production of the utterance only, but by the cooperative work that speaker and hearer put into the production of the entire conversation, including this particular pair.

For this reason, it is important to identify a motivational point of view (typical question: 'Why do people say this or that?'), as opposed to a pragmatic point of view (typical question: 'How do people manage to get something done by saying something?'). True, we ask questions to obtain answers, but what *are* the questions?

Levinson (1981) has remarked that we should not overestimate the importance of conversational organization the way it is set up in the adjacency pair model. First of all, people do a lot more in conversation than produce pairs of utterances. In fact, once we take a look at real conversation, we see that the paired sequences (greetings, questions–answers, requests–compliances, etc.) do not account for anything like the majority of interchanges. The most important things in conversation are not those that can be expressed in this kind of rigid structure. Second, even in the paired model, the second pair part is not nearly as predictable as the conversation analysts would have it. Consider again the question discussed in section 12.4.3:

What does Joe do for a living?

Among the (many) possible answers to this question, Levinson suggests:

(i) Do you need to know?
(ii) Oh this and that
(iii) I've no idea
(iv) What's that got to do with it?
(v) He doesn't (1981: 483)

This set of answers could be supplemented by an utterance such as the following, representing a 'normal' answer:

He works in a library;

alternatively, one could imagine a response of a non-verbal kind (snickering), or no response at all (silence; I'll come back to this in a moment).

What a question is, therefore, and what it can expect to get as an answer is not just a matter of analysing the question itself, or of determining a possible set of answers, however large, that could or should be considered, but of finding out what, *in a given context*, makes sense as an answer. This, perhaps, is the deeper sense of the folk wisdom embodied in the saying 'Don't ask questions and you'll be told no lies': understood as an admonition to weigh the value of exercising one's privilege of questioning against the likelihood that the answer is not only unpredictable, but quite likely not to be the one I want, or even, at worst, a wrong one.

A good example of a second pair part that would be extremely hard to define, both under the conversation-analytical assumption of adjacency and under any kind of speech act based theory of question-answering, is the non-answer, silence. Here is an example, again due to Levinson:

Johnny, did *you* smear Susie's face with paint? (1981: 479)

In this utterance, the context determines how we are to interpret the fact that the 'accused' chooses not to answer; in fact, Levinson says, Johnny's silence 'can be heard as an affirmative reply' (but also, of course, as a refusal to answer, perhaps because Johnny doesn't want to squeal on his brother, or because Susie did something really bad to him first, such as smearing paint all over the picture he was doing for Mummy's birthday, and so on). Just as 'the relevant utterance units that can function as conversational contributions can be just about anything, including nothing' (Levinson 1981: 479), the speech acts involved can be any at all or none. Neither of the two approaches, strict adjacency or speech act-based, thus seems to be up to the exigencies of an explanatory account of what happens in conversation.

What does seem to make sense is to ask what *works*. After all, people get along in many ways; and questions do seem to get answered somehow, requests granted, information provided and so on. How to explain this?

The answer, as expected, must be found in a properly understood notion of context. From a pragmatic point of view, the only reasonable claim that can be made about adjacency, and in general, about conversational sequencing, is that these notions, if they are to capture actual conversational behaviour, must be 'contextualized' in order to yield fertile hypotheses about such behaviour. That is to say, they must take into account both the organizational aspects of the (not only paired) sequences and their 'outcome', that is, the pragmatic, or perlocutionary, aspect (cf. section 6.1.3). Basing oneself on a typology of speech acts for a classification of adjacency pairs, as is the usual thing to do in conversational analysis, is neither better nor worse than speech act theory's efforts at classifying speech acts by illocutionary force alone. While speech act theory may provide important clues for our understanding of human linguistic behaviour, it cannot be decisive in assigning the correct contextual value to people's utterances.

We know what functions as a question because we know how to ask a question. The art of asking questions is precisely in knowing that questions take on entirely different shapes, according to the different circumstances under which they are asked, the persons they address or the subject matter they question. And conversely: what seems to be a simple question may function in an entirely different way in a particular context: as an indirect speech act (cf. chapter 7), as an accusation or insinuation, based on a conversational implicature (cf. chapter 5), and so on. The examples are well known, and most of them by now also well-worn: questions that function as orders or requests, enquiries that double as advice, confessions that operate like hidden threats, 'trap-questions' and so on. Let's consider again one of those classic examples, the 'trap question':

When did you stop beating your wife?

In answering a loaded question such as the above, I must first convince myself that what a possible, adequate answer really should address is not the question of the 'when', but of the 'that': the assertion that I really beat my wife up from time to time is included as a presupposition in the question as to when I stopped beating her.

Second, I must realize that also, depending on the particular context in which the question is asked, partial answers, vague circumlocutions, evasive reactions, *non sequitur*s of all sorts or even silence, may function either as admissions of guilt, or as rejections of the question's presupposition.

Let's say my answer to the above 'question' is:

I never had a wife.

This would amount to a denial of the presupposition that I have a wife ('in order to beat a wife you must have one').

I could also say:

But I'm not in the habit of beating anybody,

thus implicitly (and at least partially) denying the presupposition of wife-beating ('I'm not a "beater-upper", hence not a wife-beater').

The same happens if I explicitly undo the presupposition by answering:

I never stopped because I never started.

In a particular context, however, such as a courtroom interrogation, this kind of reply might have the interrogator push for a more forthcoming answer, that is, one that would lead to the recognition of the implied guilty behaviour:

Just answer the question: When?

Here, the non-cooperative context preempts the possibility of a 'free' answer: the set of possible answers is narrowed down to those that will fit into the prosecutor's efforts to build a case against me.

However, if the interchange occurred in the course of a family row, and my brother-in-law, who thinks he knows all about my marriage, is cross-examining me in front of my wife and assorted relatives, I would probably prefer to remain altogether silent. Such an 'eloquent silence', perhaps combined with ugly and threatening looks or with 'charging behaviour' (moving forward, leaning over, looking the other straight into the eye and so on) could, under the circumstances, function as a valid, and perhaps more effective reply than a verbal answer, either in the form of a direct riposte ('Why don't you please drop dead'), or in the form of an explicit denial (as in the above case), or even, finally, as a formal vote of no confidence in the presuppositions which the other is trying to push on me. I may even try to bring those hidden presuppositions out into the open by saying things like 'Is that supposed to mean . . .'; 'Are you trying to insinuate . . .'; – only to have them promptly denied by their creator: 'Of course I didn't mean that;' 'You must be crazy;' 'Stop that paranoid behaviour of yours;' and so on.

A discussion of the societal aspects of these presuppositions, and how they fit into a pragmatic framework, will be provided in chapter 14.

12.7 Pragmatic Acts

12.7.1 Some cases

Earlier (in section 1.2), I introduced the concept of pragmatic act as being different from that of speech act. The example I gave there, 'indirect denial', prefigured some of the characteristics that are associated with the concept of 'pragmatic', rather than regular 'speech' act. Another frequent pragmatic act is that of 'co-opting', a technique that is especially frequent, not to say over-used, in advertising: this consists basically in seducing the 'hearer' through promised identification with some prestigious environment or a set of 'right people': young, smart and rich. (I'll come back to this below, section 12.7.3.)

Before I go on to define the concept of a pragmatic act, let's consider some further examples. Jacobs and Jackson (1983b: 285) refer to a situation related by Carl Bernstein and Bob Woodward in their famous analysis of the Nixon scandals, *All the President's Men* (1974). One of the authors, Woodward, is exposed to what Jacobs and Jackson call a 'conversational influence attempt' (for short, and perhaps not so amazingly, 'CIA'). Woodward perceived this 'CIA' as an effort on the part of the Nixon lawyers to 'strike a deal': they seem to offer him some information that he could use in his reporting, in exchange for his keeping out of some particularly sensitive areas (Bernstein and Woodward 1974: 328–9).

The point of the story is that at no time is such an offer explicitly made. And when Woodward voices his impression, the three lawyers protest their innocence in unison: Nothing was further from their minds, such a course of action would be totally reprehensible and immoral and so on. Woodward then muses that the only way he could have perceived the offer was because he had been listening for it. He was 'set up', so to speak, by the context: in such-and-such a context, when such-and-such is said, the wording *counts as* an attempt to bribe (to use classical speech act terminology), and is understood as such.

The case is analogous to the trick that I was taught on going into Mexico in the old days: when the policeman pulled you over, you had to be sure that there was a $20 bill tacked to the back of your driver's licence: whether or not this 'counted as' a bribe depended entirely on whether the policeman in question was 'set up' to expect a bribe (and was willing to accept it: the 'uptake', as I have called it, is essential here). Thus, no bribe was offered, technically speaking, except possibly in retrospect: if the policeman had taken the money, then there had indeed been an effort on my part at bribing him. However, if the policeman had proceeded to arrest me for allegedly attempting to bribe an official in function, then I could have proclaimed that I had never had the slightest intention of offering a bribe, but that the bill somehow had got stuck to my license in the Mexican sun.

What we see here illustrates three things:

One, for sequences like these to 'count as' a particular pragmatic act, the circumstances must be right (the 'setting up' effect);

Two, there need not be any speech act involved (either of bribing, making a request, of whatever else); it is the context that determines what the pragmatic act is;

Three, without 'uptake', there cannot be a pragmatic act, either; however, the uptake can be cancelled (depending on the context) by subsequent acts, either by explicit verbal denial or by some other (pragmatic) act (for instance, the policeman could try to stuff the money back into the driver's pocket if he has a suspicion that this might be a 'sting' operation).

An amusing instance of how to exploit such a 'setting up' is found in the well-known comedy by the Norwegian-Danish playwright Ludvig Holberg, *Erasmus Montanus*. Erasmus, a village lad with philosophical aspirations, newly created *Baccalaureus Philosophiae* at Copenhagen University, irritates everybody in his village by trying to involve them in the absurdest of philosophical 'disputations'. His favourite approach is to 'demonstrate' that people are not people, but stones, bulls, roosters, etc. In between, he preaches that the world is round, not flat (as everybody in the village believes), losing his sweetheart to Dame Philosophy in the deal. Having alienated the poor girl, and having made his mother cry because he has 'proven' that she in reality is a stone, he eventually gets entangled in a discussion with an army recruiter passing through the village. (Unbeknownst to him, some of the villagers have conspired with this lieutenant to try and rid themselves of Erasmus by having him inducted into the army.) During the conversation, the recruiter success-fully involves Montanus in a proposition according to which children should beat their parents. He feigns disbelief in Montanus' disputational qualities, and wagers a ducat on his not being able to prove such a ridiculous proposition. The other rises to the bait, and produces an elegant syllogism proving his point:

'what one has received he ought, according to his ability, to return. In my youth I received blows from my parents. *Ergo* I ought to give them blows in return.' (Act V, Scene 2 Holberg 1914: 172)

Upon which the lieutenant proffers the agreed-on ducat, which Erasmus, being an honest person, refuses to take – it had only been a joke, he says. The lieutenant insists – his honour is at stake, and as a gentleman and an officer, he must pay his debts. Erasmus finally agrees to take the money, and in the same instant, the recruiter clamps the manacles on him and declares him to be properly inducted into the Royal Army. No matter how Montanus tries to argue that he did not take the ducat as press-money (*'distinguendum est inter nummos'*, i.e. 'one has to distinguish between money and money'), and that hence his 'uptake' did not count, the officer has the last word, and 'proves' that Erasmus Montanus now is a true soldier ('Whoever has taken press-money is an enlisted soldier. You have done so, *ergo* – ') and, aided by his corporal, drags him forcefully away, to the amused discomfort of poor Erasmus' fellow villagers.

Clearly, the effects of the 'setting up', that is, of the contextual condi-tions in this case are such that there is only one possible outcome of the situation. The uptake cannot be rescinded retroactively, except by an extralinguistic agency, a *deus ex machina*: At the end of the play, the poor lad is liberated from military service, having recanted and promised 'never to bother any one with disputations any more' (p. 176).

Pragmatic acts are not necessarily or exclusively acts of speech – in the cases above, there were no specific uses of language that could 'count as' a particular illocutionary act such as 'bribing', 'co-opting' or 'denying'. This is not to say that there is never any language involved in these cases;

only that there are no *specific* speech acts that can be held accountable for the action. 'Fishing for compliments', for example, or 'soliciting invitations' can perfectly well be performed verbally without ever saying anything that could be pointed out as 'a speech act' of soliciting a compliment or an invitation. Jacobs and Jackson (1983b: 303) give the following example of such an interchange ('soliciting an invitation'):

> (*Fran, one of Sally's friends, has called Scott, Sally's husband, on the phone after Sally (who recently had a baby) had returned from her vacation. The baby is two-and-a-half months old*)
> Fran: How's the *baby*?
> Scott: Oh, he's fine. He's starting to crawl now.
> F: Oh *really*?
> S: Well, not really *crawling*. He just sorta inches along.
> F: Wow! I haven't even seen him yet.
> S: Yeah, he's down in Granite City right n//ow::
> F: Oh, with//Sally's folks.
> S: With the grandparents.
> (*3 second pause*)
> S: Jus' a second Fran, I've gotta get my hot dogs off the stove.
> F: Okay.

In this case, nothing is said anywhere about 'coming over'; neither is the word 'invitation' ever mentioned; but even so, the tenor of the conversation is clear. Fran tries to secure an invitation from Scott to come and see the baby; Scott doesn't want to commit himself (or maybe Sally) to what he sees as a somewhat importunate intrusion into their private sphere.

Levinson (1983: 279) has the following example of 'fishing for compliments':

> (*Interviewer to candidate for job*):
> Would you like to tell us, Mr Khan, why you've applied to Middleton College in particular?

Here, the interviewer's intention is clear: he wants to give the applicant an opportunity to say something nice about Middleton College. Mr Khan cannot very well say that it was the only place he thought he had a chance, or that it was the only job offering in the *Higher*: he knows damn well he is expected to say something positive about the institution he is applying to; it's all part of the game.

Levinson (1983: 264) suggests that we might add what he calls an 'indirect force' to the literal force of utterances in order to explain these 'indirect effects'. However, this won't do as an explanation. First of all, most usages of speech acts happen to be indirect, so this extra addition will not be sufficient to separate out what I have called 'pragmatic acts'. Second, such an addition seems totally *ad hoc*, and there is no motivation for adding a particular 'force' beyond what we can read off from the indirect pragmatic aspects of such situations. The suggested addition is thus typically a case for Occam's razor.

What I would propose, instead, is to consider these cases in the light of a theory of action that specifies, for any given situation, the limitations and possibilities that the situation is subject to, or opens up, as the case may be. What is wrong with speech act theory, in general, as has often been remarked, is that it has no theory of action; or if it does, action 'is thought of atomistically, as wholly emanating from the individual' – to quote an author (Fairclough 1989: 9) who, among others, has singled out precisely this trait as one of the main weaknesses of traditional pragmatics. Human activity is not something that is performed by the individual, setting 'goals' and devising 'strategies', or charting out courses of action like a captain on his ship, a Platonic rider on his beast of burden. Rather, the individual is situated in a societal context, which means that she or he is empowered, as well as limited, by the societal conditions under which she or he lives. The idea of the person as a 'free agent', engaging freely in all sorts of 'free enterprise', and deciding freely on means and ends – that idea never was anything but fiction, even in the days of Enlightenment and pristine undiluted capitalism, when 'Live Free Or Die' seemed to be a serious alternative.

The final example is the classic case of 'doing nothing', as in the old joke:

> Mother (*calling out the window to child in yard*): Joshua, what are
>   you doing?
> Joshua: Nothing . . .
> Mother: Will you stop it immediately!

Joshua's pragmatic act in this interchange could be described as trying to get out (by 'opting out') of a conversational minefield. Clearly, since there is no speech act 'to nothing' (although the philosopher Martin Heidegger did invent a word for it: *'Das Nichts nichtet'*, literally: 'The nothing nots'; which can happen only in German), the next best thing is to use words that say as little as possible, in fact 'nothing'. One is reminded of Christopher Robin going off 'to do nothing':

> What I like best is doing nothing . . . It's when people call out at you just as you're going off to do it, 'What are you going to do, Christopher Robin?' and you say, 'Oh, nothing.' and then you go and do it. (A. A. Milne, *Winnie the Pooh*)

12.7.2 Pragmatics and action theory

We can look at pragmatic acts from two points of view: the societal and the linguistic. From the point of view of society, we are dealing with constraints imposed on the individual in the form of necessary limitations on personal resources: life history, education, class, gender, age and so on. These are the factors identified by Fairclough under the caption of 'MR' ('member resources', namely: the resources that I dispose of as a member of the communication community, and that are 'often referred to as background knowledge'; 1989: 141).

The other point of view is that of language: What language can I use to perform a pragmatic act? Sometimes the question should be put in the passive, so to speak: What language is used to create the conditions for me to perform a pragmatic act? Here, the aspect of what Verschueren (1987) has called the adaptability of language enters the picture: this means that the individual members of society rely on language as their principal tool to adapt to the ever-changing conditions surrounding them. Clearly, what classically is called a 'speech act' belongs in this category: speech acts are among the tools that we have at our disposal to control our environment, and in turn to adapt to it. As Levinson aptly remarks, the function of a promise as a speech act is to put one context to work to change another: 'speech acts are functions from context to context' (1983: 276).

However, the focus on speech acts as the unique or even chief means of control and adaptation, as historically has characterized much of pragmatics, should be reconsidered in the light of the examples given above. As we have seen, in many cases of pragmatic acting it is impossible to point to one particular instance of any speech act. When, e.g., people practise 'indirect denial' or 'co-opting', the speech acts used are not 'commensurate' with the pragmatic acts performed (as when I try to invite people into a community of consumers by asking a question: 'What kind of man reads *Playboy*?').

It is for this reason that pragmatic acts cannot be simply considered to be some particular sub-type of what is usually termed 'indirect speech act' (see chapter 7). For example, in a dinner-table situation, there is a difference between an indirect request such as

Can you pass me the salt?
(compare the direct request 'Pass the salt')

and 'hints' or 'prompts' such as

I'd like some salt

Isn't this soup rather bland?

Both the latter utterances can be seen as efforts to have somebody pass the salt, yet neither of them 'counts as' a request; rather, they are pre-sequences (see section 11.5.1) to requests, 'pre-requests' that somehow obtain the desired result most of the time, without having to be developed into full-blown requests: the salt is passed on.

Hence, we can say that while speech acts, when uttered in contexts, are pragmatic acts, pragmatic acts need not be speech acts (not even indirect ones). What makes this come about is the 'underlying goal orientation' that participants in the discourse have (Jacobs and Jackson 1983b: 291). The interpretation of a particular utterance relies on the context of goals, not just the communicative ones, but in general, the goals of the interaction. The hinting and prompting statements in the example above are not interesting as informative utterances (A: 'I'd like some salt'; B: 'Thank you for sharing this with me'), but as pre-requests to a request which is usually not formulated, and maybe not even needed, for the interaction to be successful.

Interestingly, when we look at the developmental aspects of pragmatic acts, it seems to be the case that children learn to deal with such uses of language long before they discover the existence of 'real' speech acts. The framing of a sequence is often sufficient to obtain the right result, as every educator knows. Learning how to manage speech acts, including their 'correct' verbal uptake, occurs later in the child's life than learning to respond to them in the form of an appropriate action. Speech acts, in the form of literal responses, e.g. to requests, are acquired later in life than are appropriate reactions to pragmatic acts: 'children have to learn that a literal response is possible', as Jacobs and Jackson remark (1983b: 295).

12.7.3 Pragmatic acts as social empowerment

From what has been said, we see again how important the concept of context is in all discussions on pragmatics. Pragmatic acting is contextualized adaptive human behaviour: it can be described as adapting oneself to a context and, on the basis of past situations and with a view to future situations, adapting the context to oneself. All this is done through the intermediate use of language as the tool helping us to select the relevant features of any situation in the total context. In a sense, language can be called the generalized frame or script for all human context(s), both as a repository of earlier experience and as an tool-box for future changes.[103]

In their study of this adaptive behaviour, Jacobs and Jackson have concentrated on 'conversational influencing' (1983b), meaning: the ways in which speakers try to influence each other through the use of language in order to realize their goals. What these authors correctly emphasize is the importance of contextual information in establishing the expectations that will allow the various influencing patterns to yield the desired result. What they don't emphasize sufficiently, though, is the extent to which this context already is pre-figured, pre-cast, so to speak, in the mould of society. It is actually society itself that 'speaks' through the interactants when they try to influence each other: call it convention, culture, social structure, felicity conditions or what have you. The classical approach, which bases itself upon the rational action performed by the single individual, fails inasmuch as it does not take into account the degree to which this rationality itself is societal, hence supra-individual.

In another set of terms, people often speak of rules and principles (cf. above, section 4.2). We see now that neither of these notions does justice to the concept of pragmatic act. The rule that says: 'Such and such is a speech act of X' (where X can be an act of requesting, promising, etc.) cannot collect all the forms of speaking we encounter when people actually are performing requests, promises, etc. Similarly, the principles, taken as such, cannot ever explain why an action that 'flouts' a principle may be highly successful in a wider perspective. Thus, the principle of cooperation cannot tell me why it may be more 'cooperative' for me not to cooperate by complying with a certain request, if for example that request is not relevant to what I perceive as the real intention of the requester (cf. the example in section 12.4.3, as when I say, in reply to the query: 'What is Lars' phone number?' 'He's in his office').

Elsewhere (Mey 1991a), I have proposed to supplement the notions of rule and principle with that of 'constraint'. That is, rather than having rules for telling us what is a correct speech act, and principles to tell us how we should execute a speech act, we prefer to have a *constraint* that, given the actual situation in a conversation, can identify the possible ways to proceed towards the goals we want to obtain. Rules that prescribe the correct sequence in conversation (such as the so-called 'adjacency rules') are able to tell us what can happen, conversationally, but not what the outcome of the conversation is going to be, pragmatically. The constraints I'm talking about are not those that are imposed by conversational structure or conversational context as such. Rather, they represent the wider structure of society, reaffirming the relationships of dependency and hegemony that are existent in any actual situation (on 'constraints' as a metapragmatic notion, see chapter 13, especially section 13.6).

Pragmatic acts are called pragmatic because they are essentially based on the actual users' language, not on a use defined only by syntactic rules or by semantic selections and conceptual restrictions. All pragmatic acts are heavily marked by their context: they are both context-derived, and context-restrained. That means, they are determined by the broader social context in which they happen, and they realize their goals in the conditions placed upon human action by that context.

A pragmatic act of 'co-opting' (as in, e.g., 'What kind of man reads *Playboy*?') is only effective because it presupposes a context where certain men are thought of as prototypical *Playboy* readers, and the visual display going along with this ad reinforces the type: racing cars, expensive clothes, good-looking women and so on. Only in that context, and given those conditions, is the act effective as a means of selecting a particular audience as consumers of particular products.

Similarly, when I say something like: 'Real programmers do it on the console,' I evoke a context in which a computer programmer spurns the use of a computer language to facilitate contact with the machine, and goes the rugged way of talking to the computer in 'machine language'. By this evocation, I invite in, and 'co-opt', all those who are supposed to feel the way I do: I establish a 'little circle of friends', one of the most powerful ways of discriminating socially against 'outsiders'. Again, no speech acts (direct or indirect) are being used that could be said to have exactly this kind of effect.

A pragmatic act can thus be defined as the exercise of a societal empowerment, rather than of 'power' in the usual sense of the word. 'Empowerment' means that I have been *put into* a position of power: this position limits me in my exercise, because it is only a limited, since derived, power I may exercise; yet it enables me to do the things I want to do, precisely because of my placement in the context (concretely: because of my belonging to the institutions in which I operate and live). The pragmatic act, we could say, is the 'social default' in a given situation, by which a free agent operates within the constraints that society has imposed. To a certain extent, this is a paradox: it reminds us of the famous case of Herbert Simon's ant, who is said to display intelligent behaviour when he goes about finding his way back to the ant-hill. Yet, since the ant has nowhere else to go, his intelligence is an instance of a pragmatic act of 'ant default'. If our use of language can be likened to the firing of a 'loaded weapon' (to use Bolinger's colourful image; 1980), then we should also not forget to remind ourselves of who put the bullets in. Again, the question is: 'Whose language are we using?' (see Mey 1985).

EXERCISES AND REVIEW QUESTIONS

1. Consider the following text, a Notice from the US Department of Agriculture, that greets you upon going through Customs at O'Hare International Airport's International Arrivals Hall in Chicago:

AGRICULTURE'S BEAGLE PATROL
[*a colour cartoon of three nice beagles*]
Our dogs don't bite!

They sniff out illegal food or meat in passenger baggage, in order to
protect U.S. agriculture and livestock. Please collaborate! Report all
plant, food, and animal products to the Department of Agriculture
inspectors. You will be prosecuted for attempted smuggling.

U.S. Department of Agriculture

Questions:

What do you think of the coherence of this piece?

What sense does it make? (if it does)

What speech acts are involved?

Why does the Department of Agriculture talk about 'beagles', when the
dogs sniffing you actually are quite another breed (golden retrievers)?

2. Travelling through Japan, a tourist arrives in a city by the name of
Nikko, situated about fifty miles north of Tokyo. In Nikko, one finds a
great number of famous and beautiful shrines and temples, all gathered
in a big complex in the foothills of impressive, cedar-clad mountains.
Walking through this immense compound, a tourist sooner or later may
have to respond to nature's call. Looking around for any familiar words
or symbols (pictographic, architectural or otherwise), and not finding
any, the tourist then addresses himself to a young, kimono-clad temple
attendant, who seems to be in charge of visitor information. The following dialogue ensues:

Tourist: Is there a toilet around here?
Attendant: You want to use?
Tourist (somewhat astonished): Sure I do.
Attendant: Go down the steps.

Somewhat puzzled, the tourist then discovers the stairs, and lo and
behold, there is the men's room. Now what can we learn from this little
story? Here are some leading questions:

If you were to categorize the speech acts being used here, how would you vote?

What type(s) of speech acts are involved?

Can you elucidate the misunderstanding(s) involved?
What framework(s) would you invoke to characterize those misunderstanding(s)?

What does a 'normal' understanding of the tourist's request presuppose?

(For further particulars on this scene, including its 'pre-sequential' aspects, see below, section 14.5.)

3. You are in Pisa, Italy, and want to have a meal in one of the local restaurants, *La Stanzina*, which has been recommended to you by some of your friends. Unfortunately, neither the owner of the restaurant, Roberto, nor his genial and voluminous wife, Simonetta, speak a word of English. Also, the menu is in Italian only, and you understand very little of its culinary terminology. When you sit down to order your meal, you have certain expectations as to what is going to happen (based on your previous experiences from eating out). This general context will enable you to interpret certain pragmatic acts taking place in the restaurant, even if you may be at a loss as to how to interpret the actual Italian words used. Thus, e.g., when Roberto comes to your table, all smiles, and welcomes you in Italian, you need not understand the exact wording of his greeting. And when he hands you the menu, you will understand this as a pragmatic 'pre-sequence' to 'taking your order'.

Questions:

What further pragmatic acts are likely to take place in this context of 'La Stanzina'?

Is the menu itself (part of) a pragmatic act?

In particular, what is the pragmatic value of the spatial arrangement of the menu?

Let's say you are familiar with the term *pasta*. You also remember having eaten something with seafood in it, going by the name of *marinara*. How can you figure out an entry like *penne alle vongole*, supposing it is placed under the heading *Paste*, and before the item *linguine marinara*?

What pragmatic act(s) is (are) involved here?

How would the notion of 'script' (discussed in section 12.5) be useful in this context?

You could, of course, avoid all the above problems and whip around the corner to Borgo Stretto or Piazza Cavour, and get your every wish fulfilled at one of the American fast-food places. What would the difference mainly be, from the point of view of pragmatic acting (apart from the actual food that is involved)?

13

Metapragmatics

13.1 INTRODUCTION: WHY METAPRAGMATICS?

In accordance with an established use of language in philosophy and in the sciences, I use the prefix *meta-* to indicate a shift of 'level': from that of talking about an object to that of discussing the talk itself. The latter level is called the 'meta'-level. Thus, I will speak of a 'metalanguage' to indicate a language that is 'about' (a) language, one level 'up' from that language (also called (an) 'object language'; the terms were originally invented by the Polish logician Alfred Tarski in the thirties).

A 'metalanguage' thus is a language that comments on, examines, criticizes, etc., what happens on the level of language itself, the 'object language'. In everyday life, we use metalanguage when we put things in (verbal or literal) parentheses or in quotes. E.g., I can say:

This is strictly off the record, but . . .

Here, we have a 'verbal parenthesis', defined by overt metalanguage: I tell my listeners or readers that what follows should be regarded as unofficial; the extent of the 'verbal parenthesis' is not audibly or visibly marked off, but is usually understood as being bounded by the quote's internal cohesion, or by the topic that is being dealt with 'off the record'.

In the following, we have a literal quote, clearly marked off by quotation marks functioning as a metalanguage statement saying, 'This is a quote':

And she goes: 'Don't give me that shit'.
(from Tama Janowitz, *Slaves of New York*,
New York: Washington Square Press, 1987, p. 43)

Metalanguage is also used to discuss phenomena and problems that
occur in the daily, object language; thus, a statement of the form:

The word for 'red' is an adjective in English, but a participle
in Inuit

is technically a part of the metalanguages of the respective grammars of
English and Inuit.

In the same vein, we can say that the metapragmatic level is where we
discuss theoretical issues in pragmatics having to do with pragmatics
itself: a pragmatic discussion on pragmatics, if one wishes.

The question is now: Where does 'metapragmatics' come into the
picture for us? What can we use it for? In particular, what can we do with
it at this point in our study?

There are two basic considerations that come into play whenever
metapragmatics is mentioned. One is the fact that pragmatics, by itself,
cannot explain or motivate its principles and maxims. The reason that
pragmaticians operate with, e.g., a Coherence Principle, or a Cooperative
Principle (with its attending four maxims) cannot be found inside of
pragmatics; neither can such principles be deduced from the observation
of pragmatic phenomena.

To take but one example: in pragmatics, we not only specify principles
and rules (see chapter 4), but we also comment on those rules and
principles and interpret them from our personal points of view. We make
and break the rules: we can choose not to be polite, for example, and (as
it is called by Grice) 'flout' the principle of politeness, if our circumstances are such that we think our aims and goals are better realized by
not being polite. When I publicly announce my 'flouting' by saying, e.g.,

You did a great job, and I'm not being polite,

then the latter half of my utterance contains a metapragmatic statement.

The other consideration is more complex. It has to do with the fact
that our explanatory framework for the observed pragmatic facts, by
definition, cannot be restricted to a single context. The world in which

people live is one in which everything hangs together. None of the phenomena of our daily or scientific lives can be explained in isolation from the rest. We already had some inkling of this in preceding chapters, such as when we discussed 'pragmatic presuppositions' in section 10.4.3, or when we appealed to those presuppositions as important factors in establishing and explaining coherence (see section 12.6). But all that was only the tip of the iceberg.

The fact of the matter is that the whole of pragmatics, not only conversational analysis, is tightly bound up with what people do in their daily lives, and what they use language for. Nothing in our existence can be explained in isolation; neither can our language.

More specifically, and on an even deeper level, metapragmatics should worry about the circumstances and conditions that allow us to use our language or prevent us from using it (or from using it adequately, as the case may be). An investigation into these conditions is necessary and timely, yet it cannot be dealt with on the level of the observed phenomena alone; which is why we must refer to metapragmatics for a discussion of such problems.

The above thoughts were at the basis of our earlier reservations with respect to the conversation analysis (CA) approach and its results, inasmuch as it purports to keep to a strictly 'formal' method of dealing with conversation. Such a method, no matter how refined, will only be able to show what's happening on the surface of the language, where people exchange words in turns. What they do with these words, and what the result of those exchanges may prove to be, are not any of the concern of the conversation analyst.

However, restricting oneself to the problems of description that one encounters during the analysis of actual conversation puts a severe limitation on the explanatory potential of one's analysis. A satisfactory account of the realities of conversation relies heavily on the wider context of the conversational interaction, and will not limit itself to strictly linguistic, or strictly CA-relevant factors. A pragmatic analysis cannot remain on the object language level, describing 'the facts, all the facts, and nothing but the facts', as the conversational analysts (often implicitly) seem to advocate. A pragmatic explanation requires a meta-level, where the facts and factors of the analysis are placed in an overall explanatory framework, and where the analyst him-/herself is engaged beyond the immediate context. This higher level of analysis (often called 'critical') is where societal critique and social action have their places –

topics which, in the eyes of many scientists, including linguists, are as much anathema to their profession as the introduction of meaning into linguistic descriptions used to be for the strict structuralists of the thirties and forties.

As two European sociolinguists have expressed it recently,

> Ethnomethodological research results, inasmuch as they only re-produce the formal structures which interactants generate in their communication in order to solve a problem, cannot pretend to contain insights that would be more encompassing, more exact, more general, more 'scientific' than the interactants' themselves. Ethnomethodology, in rejecting social critique, at the same time renounces a scientific explanation. (Flader and Trotha 1986: 43; my translation)

13.2 RULES ON RULES?

The term 'metapragmatics' does not occur in any of the three major works on pragmatics which have appeared during the past ten to fifteen years: Gerald Gazdar's *Pragmatics* (1979), Stephen C. Levinson's *Pragmatics* and Geoffrey N. Leech's *Principles of Pragmatics* (the last two published in 1983; for a review, see Mey 1988).

Despite this absence of explicit involvement, however, one of the three at least, the book by Leech, offers an interesting discussion on the concept of rules in grammar and their motivation; in this connection, Leech mentions the term 'metagrammar'. While maintaining the arbitrariness of language (in accordance with Saussure's theory of the linguistic sign), Leech points out that the assumption of arbitrariness *in* the grammar does not necessarily entail the absence of a non-conventional motivation *of* the grammar: the rules are conventional (or arbitrary), but the reason why we have those rules may be motivated by what Leech calls 'extralinguistic considerations' (1983: 25).

For this reason, we must reckon with two levels of linguistic explanation:

> The rules of a grammar (that is, of the grammar of a particular language) are arbitrary [read: conventional]; but there is also a 'metagrammar': an explanation of the typological or universal characteristics of grammars in general. (Leech 1983: 25)

As an example, Leech quotes the imperative in English: since the 'subject'[104] of an imperative is always understood as 'you', there is no harm in not expressing this subject, since 'nothing [is] to be lost by its omission' (p. 25).

While the argument in itself does not carry too much weight, either from a grammatical or from a typological point of view (see note 104), the case of the 'imperative subject' aptly illustrates what I would call a typical 'metapragmatic' kind of reasoning about the grammar, in particular about grammatical rules. What Leech calls 'metagrammar' is in fact a reasoning about rules, an effort to 'rule' certain rules in order, that is to say, in accordance with the conventions of grammar, even though they may seem motivated non-conventionally: 'Rules on rules'.

There are, says Leech, two kinds of statements for such cases:

... the first states the rule as a matter of convention, and the second states that given that this rule exists, it is a reasonable [*assumption?*], on extralinguistic grounds, that it does so. (1983: 26)

Leech's 'metagrammar' becomes a metapragmatics (even though he does not use the term) the moment he discusses rules having to do with the grammatical rules and their users, and we must have recourse to the 'extralinguistic evidence' that Leech (somewhat reluctantly, it seems) appeals to. The conventionality of the grammatical rules that Leech states as his first case is limited to the grammar and has no life outside it; every time we discuss a point of grammatical order, we have to move out of that order and beyond it, entering a higher order, that of the 'metagrammar'.

However, the metagrammar, and by extension, metapragmatics (Leech's second case) rests on a base that is much more solid than would appear from the above quote. It is simply established by the fact that no rule can be used without the user – the use of the rules of grammar is by definition subject to a pragmatic meta-rule which incorporates all of the users' context. When we discuss such meta-rules, having to do with the use and the users of the rules of grammar, we are in metapragmatic territory.

What holds for grammatical rules is *a fortiori* true of the pragmatic principles and maxims themselves: they cannot be discussed within pragmatics (and they are, indeed, seldom discussed, whether within pragmatics or outside it). The following section will give a few examples-cum-discussion.

13.3   PRINCIPLES AND MAXIMS REVISITED

In chapter 4, I discussed some of the principles and maxims that are said to operate in pragmatics, in particular the principles according to which people cooperate in their use of language, are polite to each other or make economic use of scarce linguistic means: Grice's Cooperative Principle, the Politeness Principle (propounded mainly by Leech), the Economy Principle (invoked by many authors, but never defined in precise terms), and so on, as well as the maxims subsumed under the respective principles (see section 4.4 for details). Leech remarks, quite consistently with his approach (as outlined above), that

> [p]art of the essence of Grice's CP [Cooperative Principle] is its extralinguistic motivation in terms of social goals. (1983: 27)

In the next chapter, I will go into more detail as regards the social character of these goals, and how they can function as 'extralinguistic motivation' of the various principles. Here, I only want to point out the inconsistency of having a principle *within* the grammar (or within pragmatics) that is extralinguistically motivated and defined. If the essence of a pragmatic principle such as that of cooperation is in its 'extralinguistic motivation', then that principle belongs outside of pragmatics, on the metapragmatic level; the same can be said about the other principles that are viewed as being part of the grammar, or indeed of pragmatics itself.

I will take as the target of my discussion not the Cooperative Principle (which I have discussed extensively elsewhere; see Mey 1987), but the somehow less controversial, less often disputed, so-called 'Principle of Economy' in language use. I will not argue that such a principle (in principle!) could not be formulated; only that its possible rationale is not only outside linguistics, but strictly outside pragmatics as well. Pragmatically speaking, if we want to defend the workings of a 'principle of economy' in people's use of language, we have to ask ourselves under what conditions, in which contexts of language use, positing such a principle would be acceptable, or even plausible. In other words, we will have to invoke metapragmatics.

If the Principle of Economy were indeed among our 'first principles', then one would suspect it to be present not only on special occasions, whenever some pragmatician needs to invoke it in order to safeguard an hypothesis, but also under more general circumstances. A principle is precisely something by which we abide no matter what: a 'person of principles' is not easily swayed, a 'principled account' is one which holds up in the face of even serious objections and so on.

Along this line of reasoning, we should expect 'economical use of language' to be the norm, not the exception, in language use. However, such is not the case. Naturally enough, language economy is practised only where it is economically necessary or desirable, such as when we send a telegram, where every word costs money. When we use the services of companies such as Western Union in the US, or KDD in Japan, a 'principle of economy' imposes the well-known 'telegraphic style' on our communication, and for a reason: our (private) economy.

But how about our everyday use of language? It seems to make little sense to talk about 'economy', when we see competent language users in action. Good speakers or able stylists take pride in expressing themselves in well-wrought, ably crafted poetry or prose; their clever use of insightful similes and judiciously applied tropes, of ornate embellishments and effective repetitions are a far cry indeed from all sorts of economy, principled or not.

Contrariwise, the person expressing him-/herself 'economically', that is, in as few words as possible, may be obeying certain self-imposed or externally motivated restrictions, but is certainly not going to be complimented on his or her use of the language. The noble savage speaking in monosyllables or uttering his final 'Howgh' is by no means a role model for the modern, civilized language user, whose corresponding speech acts of 'solemnly confirming what has been said' (worded by expressions such as 'Amen', 'So help me God', etc.) are severely restricted as to their allowed usage, both contextually and content-wise. Which leads me to believe that the whole idea of an 'economy principle' is based on the same kind of misunderstanding that elevates simple language and restrained behaviour to the level of virtues, in force of some ill-understood notion of a frugal life-style as the ideal of good housekeeping, linguistic or otherwise.

In spite of its conceptual poverty, the economy principle carries an amazing weight in many contexts, and is often used as a kind of final, incontestable argument – whether it appears under the guise of the 'law of least effort', the 'efficiency principle' or a general 'principle of economy'. Here are two examples:

> I think there is operating in our language, as in most forms of human behavior, a principle of least effort, in this case, a principle of maximum illocutionary ends with minimum phonetic effort. . . . (Searle 1969: 60, discussing one of the preparatory conditions for the speech act of promising);

and (to quote an earlier source):

> . . . the linguist must keep in mind . . . the principle of least effort, which makes him restrict his output of energy, both mental and physical, to the minimum compatible with achieving his ends. (Martinet 1962: 139).[105]

Compare also the following

> PRINCIPLE OF EFFICIENCY: Given nothing to suggest the contrary, whenever a further utterance would be redundant one can infer that the speaker need not make the utterance but that he will operate as if he had made it and will expect the hearer to operate similarly. (Fraser 1975: 195)

In the third extract, the catch is in the words 'need not make'; the question is what kind of 'need' we are talking about here, and where it comes from. A need for 'economy', efficiency or other kinds of verbal penury does not exist unless it is imposed by outer circumstances that are not only extralinguistic, but outside of normal conditions of linguistic operation altogether.

Thus, a need for 'economy' in language use typically arises whenever the difference between life and death is a matter of seconds. Speed and efficiency in communicating are of course crucial in such a setting: one calls out 'Fire!', and not 'I hereby announce to you that a great fire has broken out in the dining-room.' Similarly, where other restrictive conditions, such as the state of one's postal expense account or one's balance in the bank, impose an 'economical handling of scarce resources', a 'principle of economy' in one's use of language may make sense; otherwise, it doesn't. (For a more detailed critique of the 'Principle of Economy', see Mey and Talbot 1989.)

13.4 'RIGHT OR WRONG, MY...'

Metapragmatics studies the conditions under which pragmatic, i.e. users', rules are supposed to hold. It cannot come as a surprise that such conditions may vary greatly from time to time and from place to place, and that there cannot be any truly 'universal principles' in the sense of principles that are valid for any linguistic practice anywhere at any given time. At most, we can say that there are, in any given culture or group of language users, certain principles that the members of the culture, the users of the language, agree on as working guidelines in their language practice.

Saying this does not void metapragmatics of its importance for the study of language use; on the contrary, it puts such studies in their proper perspective; that is to say, it provides a healthy antidote against all forms of ethnocentrism that so easily creep up on the linguist or pragmatician who is looking for correspondences across languages, and tends to establish such correspondences (almost unavoidably) with one of their terms deeply anchored in his or her own culture or language.

The much-quoted and widely accepted Cooperative Principle is a good example of this tendency. In particular, some of its maxims, such as that of 'quantity', can be questioned for its ethnocentric bias towards what is sometimes called 'Standard Average Western European/North American'. In many other cultures, the virtues of linguistic parsimony are not extolled to the same degree as is allegedly the case in our society. As examples, compare the research (referred to in section 4.4.5) that has been carried out on Malagasy language and culture regarding the alleged universality of conversational implicature (Keenan 1976), or the studies done on many of the peoples of the Caribbean (see, among others, Allwood 1976, 1993; Reisman 1989), who respect and value verbal proficiency, rather than efficiency.

13.5 PRAGMATIC CONSTRAINTS

The world of pragmatics is not predictable in the same way that morphological or syntactic worlds are. That is to say: No strict rules and conditions can be set up for such a pragmatic 'universe'; neither can any stringent hypotheses be formulated and tested that would create the illusion of a well-formed world, as is done in 'regular' grammar.

A pragmatic approach to language cannot, therefore, be captured by the 'exact' methods of sciences such as mathematics or physics. As Nunberg has observed in a thoughtful (but unfortunately little-known) article, the criticism that pragmatic explanations on the whole lack the rigour of explanations in syntax and phonology is 'inappropriate, as it arises out of a native [naïve?] conception of what a pragmatic explanation should look like, based on the assumption that semantics and syntax ought to have the same methodology' (1981: 199). As the main reason for this, Nunberg gives the impossibility of using the well-known testing procedures of linguistics on a phenomenon such as conversational implicature: the allegation that we are dealing with a pragmatic phenomenon, rather than with a 'genuinely' linguistic one 'is not subject to empirical confirmation in the sense of the natural sciences' (p. 220). The ultimate reason for this need of 'Verstehen', rather than 'scientific explanation' in the traditional sense, is that the pragmatician 'has to be able to put at least part of his foot into his subject's shoes' (p. 220). To quote Caffi's elegant aphorism,

> The program of metapragmatics (its manifesto) might be the sentence that Socrates would have added to his motto 'I know [that] I don't know', had he not been forced by the tyrants to drink the hemlock: 'I don't know enough that I do know'. (1994b: 2465)

Pragmatics views the world as a world of users ('subjects', as they are called in the above quote) and tries to capture the general conditions under which the users of a language have to work. Rather than speculating on what the user possibly could (or could want to) say, pragmatics investigates what the user actually can, and normally will, be expected to say. Instead of speculating on the 'possible worlds' of abstract semantics, we focus our attention on a 'feasible-world' pragmatics. In other words, we constrain the world of use in accordance with our (explicit or implicit) knowledge of the users, and with the expectations that follow from that knowledge.

Efforts at computer modelling of human language behaviour have made us aware of the importance of user goals, embodied in devices such as *scripts* (cf., e.g., Schank and Abelson 1977). Scripts have very little to do with rules in the traditional sense; rather, they are realizations of certain general constraints which guide us as we strive to realize our goals. If we want to deviate from the 'normal' case, we have to qualify these constraining conditions, while staying within the general set of expectations; alternatively, we must create a wholly new set of constraints, another script. The goals and expectations that are embodied in such constraints are essential to a pragmatic understanding of human activity, much more so than are correctness of sentence construction and observance of the rules of grammar.[106]

As Carberry observes,

... [this] strategy utilizes pragmatic knowledge, such as a model of the information-seeker's inferred task-related plan and expected discourse goals. The power of this approach is its reliance on knowledge gleaned from the dialog, including discourse content and conversational goals, rather than on precise representations of the preceding utterances alone. (1989: 76)

Thus, what we are looking for in metapragmatics are, in Caffi's words, those 'units of action which are constitutive of a given interaction' (1984b: 464). However, it is not necessarily and always given that those actions can be captured by rules for the use of certain distinguished, 'canonical speech acts' – on the contrary: in order to state something, I usually avoid using the 'speech act verb' *to state*, as Caffi perceptively remarks (p. 456). And indeed, linguistic actors rely on what is implicit in the scenario (the 'script'), as well as on what is explicitly stated (in the dialogue); that is, the whole framework of 'discourse' is invoked, both on the general level (a story, an argument, a report, etc.) and on the individual level of this particular story, argument, report, etc., with the parameters indicated by the agreed-on conventions between, and limitations of, the interactants (see also Caffi 1984a).

The problem with available models of discourse, however (as pointed out by Borutti), is that they tend to be 'deterministic and idealistic' (1984: 445); when we're dealing with a script, the general cases are those that are least interesting from a pragmatic point of view. We are not actually and always interested in people following the normal route, just as, in Nietzsche's famous words, an elegant error can be much more interesting than a plain truth; it all depends on our goals.

This is not to say that a view of metapragmatics as subject to the constraints of (idiosyncratic) human discourse is uncomplicated and problem-free: 'in order to understand discourse', Borutti reminds us,

> the procedures of making meaning normal and constant are very important . . . '[t]o obtain a correct representation of the subject's discourse, we must consider the linguistic strategies of the speaker, the effects he or she is planning, the anticipation of the hearer'[s] mental reactions, his or her pre-existing context of speaking, etc. (1984: 445)

13.6   A CONSTRAINED WORLD?

We are thus looking for a concept which at the same time embodies the metapragmatic conditions that naturally and necessarily surround the human potential of language use, and the ideals of constancy and consistency that guarantee a consistent and well-functioning mechanism of discourse.

Here, it may be worth our while to consider what goes on in the environment of the world of art, more specifically that of the literary work. The essence of participating in a literary universe is, for 'consumers' and 'producers', for readers as well as for writers, the acceptance of a set of constraints governing the use of that world, in particular the particular constraints relating that universe to language, and vice versa.

Literary universes are introduced and established in vastly different ways, using widely divergent means, from period to period, from culture to culture. For instance, compare the detailed descriptions of time, space, actors, geography, characters, physiognomy, apparel, etc. that were customary in the Romantic period to the extremely frugal and indirect lighting of the literary scene by modern novelists such as Alain Robbe-Grillet or Jorge Luis Borges.

The problem of 'making up' a literary world – that is, among other things, of establishing the proper script for one's characters – is closely related to that of setting up conditions for the proper use of language; say, in a conversational environment. In both cases, the constraints cannot be universal, but have to respect the individual actors' idiosyncrasies; yet, as an author or conversationalist, I have to keep those constraints constant as well as consistent throughout my work (be it literary or conversational), on penalty of becoming unintelligible and losing my potential collaborators in the literary or conversational effort, my readers or interlocutors.

Thus, the literary constraints function as necessary and sufficient conditions on our reading; by extension, they can be interpreted as pragmatic constraints on our use of language.

It has been said that readers, on opening a book, deliver themselves wholesale into the hands of the author. Evidently, this is only partly true – the true part being the voluntary acceptance by the readers of the author's world and of the constraints that are imposed by the text. In Umberto Eco's words, 'Reading is born as a cooperative agreement between the reader and the text' (Lilli 1990).

Notice also that in order to be most effective, such constraints must not be explicitly stated: they are inferred from what we notice about the actors as they are described, by comparing their behaviour with our own familiar and expected ways of being, and by applying the inference schemas that we use in our own daily lives.

The main advantage of a 'constraint' approach, over a 'rule' or 'principle' one, as a metapragmatic explanatory device is borne out by the ease with which literary constraints are manipulated by, and in turn manipulate, the users (in this case the readers), as compared to the clumsy use of rules and the dubious influence of principles. The literary work balances on the line between everything else being the same, as a rule, yet nothing being the same, on principle. *Ceteris paribus, nullis paribus.*

Pragmatics being the science of the unsaid, however, just what *is* the same, and what different, is never explicitly stated, nor is one told how to handle these samenesses and differences; that is, how to interpret the constraints. Reading a novel by Sir Walter Scott in 1993 is quite a different cup of tea from reading the same book over 150 years ago, when his work first saw the light of day. Even in today's literature, no amount of elegant and skilful pastiching (as an example, take recent work by John Fowles, e.g., *A Maggot*) can obscure the fact that authors and readers must work with their texts. Hence the ways textual and dialogical constraints are manipulated depend entirely on the contemporary conditions against which these constraints are defined by authors and readers: conditions that will have to be re-defined by each new generation.

This point of view has consequences for our pragmatic dealings in our everyday lives and usual surroundings. Much of linguistic pragmatics has been characterized by a certain 'idealism' (both in its plain variety and in the strict, philosophical sense). The feeling that we 'accept' or 'reject' the constraints in a literary work, and in general, decide on our own goals and expectations by incorporating them in a script (possibly after first unearthing them from the dark chambers of our subconscious), reflects also on our dealings with language on a day-to-day basis. The playwright 'sets the stage' in the literal sense of the word; that is, words the plot on stage by manipulating the constraints of dialogue and stage directions; likewise, we feel that we are able to model and change the world of our lives, using the words that are at our disposal when dealing with that world: 'wording our world', as I have called it elsewhere (Mey 1985: 179ff.).

This 'wording' poses a double problem: first, that of matching and second, that of changing. As to the first, the extreme case, of course, is where the traditional linguist pretends to match the human speaker's native competence by means of abstract, grammatical rules. In a pragmatic surrounding, the ideal of matching comes up, for instance, when we start to realize that a certain use of language reflects the real-world situation rather poorly. This can be either because the words belong to another, earlier period (this, we normally can live with: nobody thinks of 'sailing' as an unorthodox activity, even when mentioned in connection with such definitely 'sail-less' contraptions as atomic submarines), or because they reflect an altered consciousness of the world. If we feel constrained by such a state of affairs, it usually means that the constraints aren't right. And this leads us directly to the other problem, that of changing, as the following example will show.

One of the constraints (or 'meta-rules', as some would call them) of English grammar concerns the so-called 'generic' use of the third-person masculine personal pronoun *he*. The (mis) 'match' here is that half the world's population is female; so how can we refer to them by the masculine?, people say. A solution ('change') is to introduce the hybrid form *s/he*; alternatively, one could declare the feminine to be the proper generic form, and exclusively use *she*.

In the latter case, the change concerns not the real state of the world (which remains more or less the same all the time), but the constraints we place on our use of language in describing that state. But notice that what we do here is to change the scenario, a limited discourse, more or less as we did with the literary universe that I referred to above. We don't change the world (at least not directly) by using the generic *she*; at best, we may change (or 'raise', as it used to be called) our consciousness about the problem. And of course there is nothing wrong with that, as I have argued elsewhere (e.g., Mey 1985: 365–8).

However, a naïve belief in the 'magic' of the meta-level in pragmatics could lead to such absurdities as the proposed use of the 'generic' feminine in 'societies' where the majority or even 100 per cent of the population is masculine (e.g. the military or the Catholic priesthood).[107] The function of a feminine form, under the constraints that operate in our actual world, is first of all to denote a female being: to change that, we would have to use other means than (however meaningful) pragmatic insights. The world in which more or less half of the inhabitants are female, half are male, exists; but likewise, we are dealing with a world in which social power is not fairly distributed, and not at all in accordance with the more or less equal division of the sexes.

The metapragmatic conditions of language use reflect, not the actual state of world affairs, but the societal state of human meanings, as expressed in the pragmatic constraints on language that tell us how to use, and how not to use, the words that go with that world. The following chapter will examine this societal aspect of pragmatics in more detail.

EXERCISES AND REVIEW QUESTIONS

1. In her 1992 article 'Indirectness: A gender study of flouting Grice's maxims', American linguist Suellen Rundquist brings statistical evidence for the fact that men, much more than women, tend to 'flout' the maxims laid down by Grice for conversation (on the notion of 'flouting', see above, section 4.4.5). Here is an example from Rundquist's (1992) work:

In a family mealtime conversation, participants talk about field hockey, and how 'Mum' has allegedly been active in this sport for a very long time. 'Dad' sees fit to offer some ironic comments on Mum's sportive achievements, and he does this by flouting a particular maxim, that of quality; in other words, he exaggerates to the point of ridiculing the whole business:

[Mum:] I used to spend a lot of time playing field hockey, good sport.

[Dad:] Yeah, Mummy was probably playing field hockey when
        Herbert Hoover took office.
[Mum:] Yeah
[Dad:] Woodrow Wilson and Teddy Roosevelt.
[Mum:] Mhm
[Dad:] George Washington
[Child:] Abraham Lincoln
[Dad:] Aristotle and . . .
[Child:] Thomas Jefferson
[Mum:] Yeah, . . . even when they bombed Pearl Harbor I was.
                                          (Rundquist 1992: 437)

As Rundquist remarks, Dad not only instigates the flouting, but manages
to engage everybody, including a child participant and finally 'Mum'
herself, in this technique of 'Mummy-bashing'. This corresponds to
Rundquist's findings that in general, 'men initiate flouting of maxims
much more than women do'. This implies, according to Rundquist, that
the classic theory of speech acts (as shaped by Grice and Searle) fails to
recognize one of its own preconditions, the limited access to social power
for women, as compared to men. In particular, as in this case, a principle
or maxim can be disregarded, or 'flouted', in different ways and under
different conditions, depending on whether the speaker is male or female.
The males, being the more socially powerful, are able to define the
conditions that prevail in a given social situation, including the right to
'flout' a maxim: to be polite or not, to be relevant or not, etc. Such a
breaking of maxims says less about their cognitive content or conversational importance in a given situation than about who is in control of
that situation. Rundquist's conclusion is that principles such as Politeness, Relevance, etc., cannot be discussed in terms of cognition only, and
that therefore, conversational inference cannot 'be based entirely on a
cognitive foundation' (p. 445).

Questions:

In what respect is Rundquist's last remark a metapragmatic one?

What is the impact of Rundquist's findings on a theory of cognition,
viewed in relation to societal parameters?

What particular societal factors come into play in this particular context? Discuss Rundquist's findings in terms of

(a) the Politeness Principle
(b) the Principle of Relevance.

2. I'm sure everybody knows this old joke:
Two psychiatrists, Drs Finkelstein and Birnbaum, pass each other in the hallway of the clinic. The following dialogue is reported to have occurred:

  Dr Finkelstein: You are fine, how am I?
  Dr Birnbaum: Thanks, you're OK too.

Questions:

What is needed for our understanding of the joke?

What metapragmatic assumptions are at play here?

In particular, do you think this joke is racist?

14

Societal Pragmatics

14.1 INTRODUCTION: LINGUISTICS AND SOCIETY

The question of a societally sensitive pragmatics is intimately connected with the relationship between linguistics as a 'pure science' and the practice of linguistics as applied to what people use their language for, to 'what they do with their words', to use a formula that may be on the verge of becoming trite. Traditionally, in linguistics this split reflects itself in the division of the discipline into two major branches that do not seem to speak to each other: theoretical linguistics and applied linguistics.

Traditionally, too, the former kind of linguistics has carried all the prestige of a 'real' (some would say: 'hard') science, whereas the latter was considered the soft underbelly of linguistics, prone to all sorts of outside and irrelevant, since 'extralinguistic', kinds of influences.

It has been one of the hallmarks of pragmatics, ever since its inception as an independent field of study within linguistics, to want to do away with this split. Pragmatics admonishes the linguistic 'scientists' that they should take the users of language more seriously, since they, after all, provide the bread and butter of linguistic theorizing; it tells the practical workers in the applied fields of linguistics, such as language teaching or remedial linguistics, that they need to integrate their practical endeavours towards a better use of language with a theory of language use. However, despite much good will, many efforts and a generally propitious climate for such endeavours, the 'unification of linguistics' is not something that is easily achieved. Pragmatics will probably, for a long time to come, be considered by many linguists not so much a 'science' in its own right as an aspect (albeit a valuable one) of, and a complement (albeit a necessary one) to, traditional linguistics.

The user aspect has from the very beginning been the mainstay of pragmatics. Already in the very first mentions of the term (such as by Charles Morris 1938, following earlier work by Charles S. Peirce), the term 'pragmatics' is closely tied to the user of language; pragmatics is thus clearly distinguished from, not to say opposed to, both syntax and semantics.[108]

But the users not only had to be discovered, they had to be positioned where they belonged: in their societal context. 'Context' is to be taken here not only as the developmental basis for language user activity, but as the main conditioning factor making that activity possible. A question such as 'How do people acquire their language?' turned out to be more of a social issue than a strictly developmental problem that could only be discussed properly in a strictly psychological environment, as was maintained earlier by psychologists and educationalists alike. With the advent of pragmatics, a societal window on language acquisition and language use had been opened, and pretty soon pragmaticists found themselves joining hands with a number of psychologists, sociologists and educationalists who had been working in these areas for many years.

The question naturally arises what distinguishes pragmatics from those neighbouring disciplines (among which several others could have been mentioned, e.g. anthropology, or various branches of applied linguistics, such as the study of languages-for-special-purposes (LSP) or professional ('trade') languages, the study of problems of translation, of language pedagogy, language politics and maintenance, and so on).

The answer is that pragmatics places its focus on the language users and their conditions of language use. This implies that it is not sufficient to consider the language user as being in the possession of certain facilities (either innate, as some have postulated, or acquired, as others believe them to be, or a combination of both) which have to be developed through a process of individual growth and evolution, but that there are specific societal factors (such as the institutions of the family, the school, the peer group and so on) which influence the development and use of language, both in the acquisition stage and in usage itself.

Whereas earlier (according to mainstream, especially faculty psychology), the use of speech was said to develop only if it was stimulated during the so-called psychologically 'sensitive period', it has become somewhat of a pragmatic tenet that such stimulation is social more than it is psychological, in the strict sense of the term. The social conditions for language use are 'built in', so to say, in the very foundations of language acquisition and use; but because of that, those same conditions are difficult to detect and determine as to their exact effect: the results of linguistic development in very early life only become evident much later, when the young persons enter the first stages of their formal education by joining the school system.

It is therefore not surprising that some of the earliest research-interests of a truly pragmatic nature concentrated precisely on the problems of school vs. home environment. A positive correlation could be established between children's school performance and their social status; school achievement is in important respects dependent on the learner's earlier development in the home. On the whole, white middle-class children could be shown to be significantly better school performers than their peers from the lower strata of society (that is, from non-white, and in general, non-mainstream environments).

The young person's school achievement is a good illustration of what pragmatics is really about; it also very clearly demonstrates why the pragmatic pattern of thinking originally met with such resistance, and why many of the earliest impulses to pragmatic research had to come from the outside, so to speak, that is, not only from linguists such as William Labov, but also, and even mainly, from the ranks of education-alists and sociologists, among others. Here, first of all, names such as those of Basil Bernstein and Paolo Freire deserve to be mentioned.[109]

The core of the matter here is that the pragmatic determinants nearly always are totally hidden: they have to be postulated almost without any regard to their initial plausibility. Social theory, at least as it was prac-tised until the mid-sixties, had no explanation to offer for its own statistical results. It was not until the hidden conditions of societal structure and domination were brought into the open that certain prag-matic features could be identified as important for language use. One of the most crucial of these turned out to be the question of the 'ownership of cultural goods', and how this ownership was administered through various patterns of 'hegemony', in cultural as in other respects.[110]

In the following, I will deal with some of these hidden assumptions; I will do this by playing out some of their characteristic motifs, all orches-trated as variations on the main theme: 'Whose language are we speak-ing, when we use "our" language?'

14.2 LANGUAGE IN EDUCATION: A PRIVILEGED MATTER

'Morals are for the rich,' Bertolt Brecht used to say, echoing an earlier saying by another German playwright, Georg Büchner (*Woyzeck*, 1838). With a slight variation on this dictum, we could say that education is only for those who can afford it. Here, I am not only thinking of the prohibitively high costs of education in countries such as the US, when the best educational facilities often operate under a kind of so-called 'free enterprise' system,[111] but also of the 'affordances' having to do with coming from the right social background.[112] The same classes that have established the institutions of higher education have also been instrumental in structuring that education and organizing its curricula; we are faced with a co-opting, self-perpetuating system that favours those who are most similar to those already in it, *pares nobis*, as the expression used to be.

One of the requirements for those who aspire to participate in any college or university programme in the United States is to take the appropriate tests, such as the SAT ('Scholastic Aptitude Test') before entering college, and the GRE ('Graduate Record Examination') as a prerequisite to entering graduate school. These tests, although apparently devised as standard measures of intelligence and scholastic ability, are in reality disguised roadblocks on the way to higher education, designed to eliminate all those who (for whatever reason) have not been sufficiently exposed to American mainstream culture and thinking. Most serious educationalists agree that the tests are worthless as measures of aptitude for academic work;[113] still, the tests are maintained, because they allow weeding out of undesirable elements and promoting those who promise to cause least trouble for the establishment in their later professional lives.

Characteristically, the tests are geared to the values of the white, middle-class segments of society; minority students and foreigners typically do less well on these tests. It is not uncommon to observe an intelligent foreign student performing relatively well on the mathematical parts of the GRE, but almost failing the verbal part; this alone should induce a healthy scepticism towards the value of such testing as a whole, and draw our attention to the part that language plays in devising, administering and taking these tests.

At stake here is, among other things, what many educational researchers have dubbed the 'hidden curriculum'. Schools are not only supposed to mediate a professional subject matter through their teaching; equally important are the attitudes and beliefs that are fostered and reinforced through the educational institutions. If one asks what these attitudes are about, one has to go back once more to the question of societal power, raised above: the prevalent attitudes reflect the attitudes of the powerful segments of society, and are (implicitly or explicitly) geared towards perpetuating the possession of that power by the ruling classes.

This means, with respect to language, that the people who are able to decide what language can be deemed acceptable, which uses of language should be furthered and encouraged or demoted and discouraged, are the same people who, from their position of power, control the future of whole segments of the population by controlling their actual language behaviour.

The classic case of this linguistic oppression (as it is called) is that of 'low' vs. 'high' prestige dialects of one and the same language, or that of 'pidgin' vs. 'standard' languages, where pidgins are considered to be mere deteriorated variants of some high naughtiness called 'the' language.[114] Gross cases of oppressive linguistic behaviour-control include the total or partial criminalization of local or vernacular idioms, as in the case of the 'Basque stick' (a punitive device used in the schools in the Basque region, where pupils were forced to carry a stick on their outstretched arms as punishment for having used a Basque word or expression, to be relieved only by the next transgressor in line; see Mey 1985: 27).

In a more profound sense, we can ask 'whose language' is the controlling norm and guideline for people's linguistic behaviour. This question boils down to asking whose behaviour is to be the standard of our language use, and what aims should be set for such a use. We can answer these questions by referring back to Brecht, as quoted at the beginning of this section. If morals are indeed for the rich, then moral behaviour is something you should be able to afford (but as a rule, cannot). However, while appealing to some universally valid laws of justice and equity (which are strictly valid only under idealized circumstances in a so-called perfect, but nowhere existing society of the Utopian kind), we allow the rich to get away with corruption and embezzlement, but string up the petty thief and the poacher: 'One man can steal a horse and another cannot look over the fence.'

What we are dealing with here is no longer the blatant oppression that was described above. The term *linguistic repression* (as an alternative to oppression) has been suggested, to cover a subtler, but equally pernicious form of social control through language (see Mey 1985: 26; the distinction between 'oppression' and 'repression' is originally due to Pateman 1980). The concept of repression plays an important role in defining and describing some pragmatic paradoxes that arise in contemporary pedagogical thinking: either the student is considered to be a completely passive receptacle for the ideas and knowledge to be imparted by the teacher – the 'banking concept' as it has aptly been called (Freire and Macedo 1987: xvi) – or alternatively, the students are supposed to be in the possession of exactly those qualifications, as prerequisites to learning, that the teaching is supposed to imbue them with. In either case, the underprivileged students are doomed to lose out: either they enter the 'rat race' on the ruling classes' premises (and obtain the privilege of membership in the rat club), or they will never make it in the race because they got off to a stumbling start.

14.3 OTHER SOCIAL CONTEXTS

Even though the educational system is perhaps the most obvious instance of the unequal distribution of social privilege as it reflects itself in, and is perpetuated through, language, it is by no means the only one. Among the cases of linguistic repression that have attracted most attention are the language of the media and the medical interview. In both these cases, we are faced with hidden presuppositions of the same kind as the ones we characterized above; I will discuss them briefly below.

As to the language of the media (especially newspapers, but including other informative media, such as radio and TV), much has been said and written about the criteria for 'good' journalism, 'objective coverage' of the news, 'fairness' in public broadcasting and televised interviewing, and so on. There seems to be a certain consensus (as expressed also in a number of documents with legal or semi-legal status) that although the air waves in principle are free, there should be some control over what is put on those waves, and in particular, that one should not allow powerful interests to monopolize the media (e.g., by creating interlocking chains of radio and TV-stations with newspapers), for their own or others' profit. In the US, these rulings are issued and monitored by the FCC (Federal Communications Commission), and they should of course not be made light of, even though in practice, overt or hidden monopolization does occur far too often, resulting sometimes, and certainly not too often, in lawsuits and the breaking up of such chains, or at least in the denial of ulterior broadcasting and televising licenses to the media magnates.

In Europe, the situation is fundamentally different. Historically, this has a lot to do with the development of the media culture in the twenties, where a strong social-democratic movement obtained control of a large segment of the radio media. At first blush, European broadcasting policy, when compared to that in the US, seems to be a good deal more geared towards fulfilling the idealistic demands of free access to the air waves for all opinions, groups, creeds, and so on, not only in practice but also in the official lawmaking documents.

Thus, in Denmark and (what used to be West) Germany, the criteria for inclusion in the news are, at least in theory, tested against standards of objective reporting and 'balanced coverage'. The Danish legal language on this point mentions explicitly the 'political, religious and other similar groups' that should be accorded fair treatment in the distribution of broadcasting time, both with respect to quantity of time (number of hours), and to where those time-slots are to be placed in the daily programming (Mey 1985: 91ff.).

Also as to content, the newscasters should strive to represent all opinions in an equitable manner, and not use language that could be prejudicial against any 'group' in the above sense. The official news and other programmes should maintain a neutral stance towards all the opinions that are found in a democratic society, and the majority should not be allowed to impose its views against the minority's wishes. This philosophy of newscasting appears, of course, even more fair when one realizes that until 1988, the Danish media were a state monopoly, and that no private broadcasting (by so-called 'pirate' transmitters) was allowed.

On paper, all of this sounds fine. Yet, if one looks below the smooth surface, the picture becomes somewhat less glossy. When a major labour conflict disrupted the normal course of events in Danish society for a whole week in November of 1976, the newscasting in connection with strike events was far removed from the ideals of neutrality, from the 'objectivity' and 'well-balancedness' that were supposed to be the hallmark of the official, state-owned media.[115]

The reasons for this are manifold: for one thing, this particular strike (which had its origin in a wage dispute between an oil company and one of the oil truck drivers' local unions) ended up paralyzing the whole of the Danish economy, with effects in sensitive areas such as the supply of oil products to institutions and private homes; in the end, people even feared it might jeopardize the production of such traditional Christmas staples as turkeys and poinsettias. Thus, initial public support for the workers quickly turned sour, as the public realized that their own walls were on fire. But from a more principled vantage point, there is a fatal flaw in the otherwise well-intentioned formulation of the 'objectivity' criterion, inasmuch as it is based on a concept of 'neutrality' which in actual fact cannot be said to qualify as 'neutral' itself.

The word 'neutral', according to its etymology, means 'not belonging to either (of two opposites)'. If there are two choices (two opposed political views, two alternative solutions, two parties to a conflict and so on), then 'being neutral' implies not leaning to either of the sides. A basic presupposition for neutrality is the existence of a 'zero point' between the two extremes; even more importantly, we must be able to determine, and agree on, the location of such a 'zero point'. This assumption is clearly hypothetical; moreover, it is to a certain extent circular. Setting the zero point can only be done if we know what the values are; however, those values are precisely what should be determined on the basis of the distance from point zero. The reason for this circularity is that the opposite values themselves are determined in accordance with what the 'setter' of the zero point believes them to be. However, we have to determine the intersecting coordinates first, in order to be able to establish their intersection; we cannot pick the origin of a coordinate system without knowing the range of values represented by its coordinates.

To give but one example among many: in the terminology of political parties, one usually operates with 'left' and 'right', as metaphors for 'progressive' (or even 'revolutionary') vs. 'conservative' or (as it is now frequently called, with an interesting shift in focus, 'moderate'). However, a quick look at the history of politics shows that in many cases, what used to be 'left' in the past, now counts as 'centre', or even 'right': for instance, Denmark's traditional 'Left Party' (*Partiet Venstre*), originally formed around 1880 as a counterweight to the then reigning 'Right' or Conservative Party, and with the purpose of representing the small farmers' interest against what, somewhat anachronistically, could be called the big 'agribusiness' of the period, was one of the pillars of the right-wing coalition that led Denmark for more than ten years, from 1982 to 1992.[116]

With regard to the labour conflict mentioned above, the 'neutrality' that the media were trying to establish, being based on this imaginary 'zero' point, was just as chimerical as the objectivity itself that the existence of such a point is supposed to safeguard. The media coverage of the strike did not offer any objective information about the conflict, although it was served up as such; rather, the media reflected the interests of that particular segment of the population which was chiefly concerned about 'business being as usual', and wanted to bring the conflict to a conclusion, no matter what the costs, and no matter how the original problem (the inequality in wages that was at the root of the strike) was going to be resolved.[117]

As to medical language, the French sociolinguist Michèle Lacoste has, in a thoughtful study (Lacoste 1981), drawn attention to the fact that the doctor–patient interview, despite its obvious usefulness and even necessity, sins gravely by way of linguistic repression. What the physician allows the patient to tell him (or her), is not what the patient wants to tell, or is able to tell, but rather, what in the institutionalized discourse of the doctor–patient relationship is pragmatically possible. The pragmatic conditions that govern the use of language in this particular case are those that are defined by the social institution of the medical interview in which the interaction between doctor and patient takes place. In the extreme case, this form of discourse may be reduced to filling out forms with pre-set categories of questions and answers. For the patient, this has nothing to do with expressing oneself or manifesting one's problems; it is more like submitting oneself to a 'multiple choice' type of examination. Conversely, for the doctor this situation may result in an inability to obtain all necessary information, as we saw in the case of the failed medical interview, described by Treichler et al. (1984), which was cited in section 7.2.4.

In the case referred to by Lacoste, an elderly lady is complaining to her doctor about pains in her spleen. However, the doctor (who is a male) rejects this complaint, and instead, locates the pains in the lady's stomach. When the patient repeatedly and rather indignantly denies his suggestion on the grounds that it is *her* body, and that she, if anyone, must be familiar with her own pains, the doctor cuts her off abruptly by saying that she doesn't even know what a spleen is, far less where it is located in the body.

This example shows two things. For one, mere knowledge of vocabulary (here, of an expression from medical terminology, such as 'spleen'), and even the ability to use that knowledge correctly, are worth nothing, as long as the pragmatic conditions governing such knowledge and use are not met. In this doctor–patient conversation, the old lady's voice is not heard, because she does not possess the necessary professional standing and social clout to make herself understood. This observation is valid also in other connections, such as the academic tests mentioned in the previous section, where verbal and other abilities are gauged in situations of unequal social power; all such cases bear clear testimony to the importance of the hidden conditions that determine the use of language and steer its users (see also below, section 14.8).

The other point to be made in this connection is that the linguistic repression we are witnessing may even have certain unexpected, dangerous side-effects. The powerlessness of the repressed can easily turn into self-incrimination (by which the powerless attribute their lack of value in society to factors such as fate, God's will, their predestined position in society ('Knowing one's place'), their own lack of capability and potential and so on). Or it may result in resignation – as happened in the case of the old lady, who ended up saying: 'Whatever you say, doctor,' thereby possibly exposing herself to the risk of a faulty diagnosis, with all its concomitant dangers both to herself (as a patient) and to the physician (as the potential target of a malpractice suit). Clearly, what we need here is some form of technique or strategy aimed at providing appropriate aid to the societally and linguistically oppressed; I will come back to this in section 14.7.

Summing up, then, the case of the medical interview is an outstanding example of an institutionalized discourse in which the value of the individual's linguistic expression is measured strictly by the place he or she has in the institution. Only utterances which meet the criteria of the official discourse are allowed, and indeed registered; others are either rejected, or construed as symptoms of (physical or mental) illness, lack of knowledge or even intelligence, and in general dependent or inferior status. The 'good patient', who knows that survival is the name of the game, quickly learns how to place him-/herself in this official discourse. A 'good' patient has symptoms; does not question his or her being institutionalized; takes the medicine prescribed by the staff; follows all the rules, including the No. 1 Rule: 'Thou Art Sick'; and so on. By contrast, a 'bad patient' tries everything to get out, and as a result, is beaten back into submission by the institution. In the extreme case, 'bad' patients are physically reduced to silence and/or inaction (the straitjacket or 'the operation', a.k.a. lobotomy, come to mind).

A 'bad' patient may end up accepting the institutional discourse and become 'good', even to the point where the possibility of a release is resisted in the end; the patient has become one with the institution, and does not want to leave. In a touching story by Gabriel García Márquez, a woman accidentally enters a lunatic asylum 'just to make a phone call' (as the title of the story has it; Márquez 1992b). She is immediately 'recognized' as a patient and enrolled in the discipline of the institution. Her innumerable efforts to get in touch with her husband are without result. In the end, she begins to feel herself at home in the safety and the routine of the asylum, and when the husband finally tracks her down, she doesn't want to go home.

As Goffman remarks, much to the point (his observation has primarily to do with mental institutions, but applies to all sorts of institutional discourses):

Mental patients can find themselves in a special bind. To get out of the hospital, or to ease their life within it, they must show acceptance of the place accorded them, and the place accorded them is to support the occupational role of those who appear to force this bargain. (Goffman 1961: 386)

14.4 LANGUAGE AND MANIPULATION

The 'special bind' that Goffman talks about in the quote at the end of the previous section is a particularly clear case of what can be called manipulation, understood as: making people behave in a certain way without their knowing why, and perhaps even against their best interests and wishes. Most often, the instrument of manipulation is language; hence, we speak of manipulatory language and linguistic manipulation. The latter can be defined as the successful hiding of societal oppression by means of language (also called 'veiling'; Mey 1985: 209ff.).

A case in point is the medical interview, as we have seen in section 14.3. Another, closely related case is the professional manipulation of schizophrenic patients' speech and its classification as a 'non-language', that is, a symptom (so-called 'schizophasia'), rather than a means of communication. To see this, consider the following two, analogical cases. Suppose that a political prisoner complains to his legal counsel about his letters being opened. Such a complaint makes sense in the context; the prisoner may not be successful in stopping the guards' practice of letter-opening, but his utterance: 'They are opening my mail' is at least taken seriously.

Not so with the psychiatric patient. The same utterance, in a psychiatric institutional environment, is registered as a schizophrenic symptom, proving that the person who utters the sentence is duly and properly a resident of the mental hospital. The patient, by complaining about his or her letters being opened, has furnished conclusive proof of the fact that he or she is not normal, hence has no right to complain. So, ironically, and in accordance with Goffman's observation quoted above, the only correct way of complaining is not to complain; which of course is sheer madness, and proves the point of the patient's being committed.

But we don't have to visit psychiatric institutions to find examples of such linguistic manipulation. Consider the following. Suppose I'm looking for a job. I tell myself that I must make a good impression on my potential future employer; I put on my best suit and tie, and go to the interview in the hope that he will 'give me the job'. Now, I may not be so lucky: the employer may tell me that the job has been 'taken'; somebody else 'got it'. That means they 'have no work' for me, and so on and so forth. In this linguistic universe, employers give, and employees take: viz., jobs. Such is 'our' language.

But what happens in real life? There, we have a totally different picture: it's the employer who takes the employee's labour, and converts it to his own profit. The employee gives his or her labour-power to the employer, in exchange for a salary offered; but there is one big catch: the wages, although they are called 'fair' and are arrived at in 'free negotiation', represent a form of societal oppression: the employer knows that he must make the employee accept less than the value of his or her labour, or there wouldn't be any profits. The wages are not the equivalent of a certain amount of work: rather, they represent a period of time during which the employer is entitled to press all the labour out of the employee that he possibly can. Wages express the market relation between labour-power as a commodity, and whatever else is bought and sold in the market-place; hence the wages can be called 'fair' only in the sense that they obey the market laws, not as any equitable representation of a certain quantity of work.

Here, too, the language we use hides the real state of affairs; thus we can be manipulated into doing whatever the powerful in society (such as employers and doctors) tell us to do. In this sense, the medical/psychiatric consultation and the job interview have a lot in common.

With regard to the latter, somebody might object that the worker doesn't *have* to take the employment: a potential employee is a free agent, and can refuse the employer's offer; also, once employed, the employee may give notice at any time. However, the very way we formulate this kind of reasoning is yet another instance of manipulatory language use. We perceive a linguistic relation of symmetry between the two nouns, *employer* and *employee*; this relation is expressed by the suffixes *-er* and *-ee*, denoting respectively the 'agent' and the 'patient' of the action (cf. interviewer–interviewee). Hence we are led to believe that the 'real world' relation between the two 'bearers' of those names is equally symmetrical: the employer is at the active end of the employment relation, the employee at the passive; basically, it seems to be the same relationship, only with a different orientation: the employer employs the employee, the employee is employed by the employer. Even the language tells us that this is a fair, symmetrical deal!

However, what the language does not tell us (and this is the catch), is which of the two has the power in this relationship. It is the employer who has the sole right to employ or not to employ. Conversely, for the employee there is no right to be employed; which shows where the true power in this situation lies, despite the superficial linguistic symmetry of the employment relation and its manipulatory potential.

14.5   PRAGMATIC PRESUPPOSITIONS IN CULTURE

That cultural presuppositions can be major stumbling-blocks on the road to understanding may sound like a truism; yet, it is often overlooked what these 'pre-suppositions', in an actual setting, have to say as pre-conditions to understanding. We have already seen how the discussion on the number and kind of SAVs (speech act verbs) suffered a great deal from this oversight, the particular verbs and their plausibility of occurrence being modelled on whatever the Standard Average European (or North American) finds plausible in his or her culture. One can easily get people to applaud the idea that probably no language in the world would contain an SAV expressing the act of 'asking for some coins to make a phone call to your maternal grand-uncle' – yet there is no reason in principle why such a verb could not be found; in any case, the borderlines are not easily drawn.[118]

To shed some light on the pragmatic presuppositions that are hidden beneath the surface of our cultural varnish, one has to look for those places where the varnish cracks and the underlying substance becomes visible. In sections 8.3.2.4 and 8.4.2, we saw some examples of such inter-cultural misunderstandings due to the presence of a non-acknowledged, and hence not shared, pragmatic presupposition. Here, I will discuss some further cases from this angle.

Challenging the presuppositions of an offer or a request is not easily done in our culture (unless, of course, one wants to ascertain that the speaker is in his or her right mind – to promise a casual acquaintance the moon, or a rose garden, is usually not taken as a serious offer). Recall the given example earlier of an inter-cultural misunderstanding based on different, hence unfamiliar, pragmatic presuppositions and the need to question them: the dialogue between a Western tourist and a Japanese temple attendant given as exercise 2 in chapter 12:

Tourist: Is there a toilet around here?
Attendant: You want to use?
Tourist (*somewhat astonished*): Sure I do.
Attendant: Go down the steps.

Clearly, the tourist (who happens to be the author of these lines) did not ask his question because he was conducting a comparative study of toilets West and East, or some such thing. The 'back-channel question' 'You want to use?' is highly unexpected, under the given circumstances; in the tourist's own culture, it probably never would have occurred in this form.

However, the pragmatic presuppositions in Japanese culture are clearly different, which is why it made sense for the attendant to ask the question. One could capture this 'sense' as the need to ensure that the 'type' of the speech act involved was correctly perceived; the attendant made sure of this by asking a question that would be able to disambiguate the tourist's question as a 'pre-sequence' either to a question about toilets, or to a request to be directed or taken to the toilet.

Alternatively, and perhaps more plausibly, it could be the case that the attendant wanted to find out whether the tourist's question could have anything to do with the different kinds of toilets that are now available in Japan: 'Japanese' or 'Western' style. Under this assumption, if the tourist wanted to use the toilet himself, he would have to be directed to another place than if the desired information concerned, e.g., an accompanying Japanese friend.

Having resolved her dilemma by obtaining an answer to the appropriate back-channel question: 'You want to use?', the attendant then decided to direct the tourist to what she thought was the proper place for him, namely a 'Western-style' toilet facility.

Cases of this kind occur, of course, also among members of the same culture. The following example is due to Tsui (1991: 120).

(*Two secretaries meet in the hallway of their common office*)
A: Would you like a piece of apple cake?
B: Have you got some?

Normally, in cultures such as ours, enquiring whether a person would like a piece of cake would be equivalent to offering him or her one. Furthermore, this indirect offer of a piece of cake would imply that one has some – otherwise, one would be playing games.[119] Likewise, in certain cultures the fact of enquiring, in a sales context, whether a particular item can be had, amounts to ordering that item.[120]

Tsui's explanation of the presumed oddity, however, is quite regular, and consists simply in revealing the piece of real-world information that we need in order to understand why, one, the expected speech act of 'accepting' is preempted (see section 12.4.3), and two, how to deal with the corresponding pragmatic presuppositions:

[the] presupposition is challenged because [the sequence] takes place in an office corridor and [A] does not have an apple cake with her when she makes the offer. (1989: 121)

In this case, we see how the pragmatic presuppositions of the dialogue constitute the indispensable link between the spoken words and the world of their users.

14.6   WORDING THE WORLD

Wording is the process in which humans become aware of their environment, their world, and realize this awareness in the form of language.

Words are not just labels we stick on things. The wording process is based on interaction with our environment: 'We bespeak the world, and it speaks back at us' (Mey 1985: 166).

The world we word is, furthermore, a world of people: we can only become language users through and in the social use of language. But also, once language is created, once the world has been worded, it influences our ways of looking at our environment. The available wordings shape our perception of our environment: without words, the world remains an unread book, a black box. Wording the world is seeing it, not just looking at it to make sure it's there.

One of the most effective ways of seeing the world is through the use of analogies: understanding one thing by way of another. I remember how my physics teacher in high school used to tell us that electricity is like water: you can explain how electricity flows through wires like water through pipes; how resistance increases, the narrower the pipes are; how its 'potential' makes it flow from high to low, etc. Water is a metaphor for electricity; seeing electricity as 'water' is essentially a metaphorical understanding, a way of 'seeing the world', at least insofar as that part of the world having to do with electricity is concerned.[121]

Metaphors are primary ways of seeing, of wording the world. In a well-known study, Lakoff and Johnson (1980) have investigated the importance of metaphor as one way of realizing this 'wording'. Another study, by Judge (1988) even speaks of a 'metaphoric revolution'. The metaphoric view of wording is different from the classic, referential one, according to which words are thought of as 'labelling' things in the 'real' world, 'out there'. Metaphors express a way of conceptualizing, of seeing and understanding one's surroundings; in other words, metaphors contribute to our mental model of the world. Because the metaphors of a language community remain more or less stable across historical stages and differences in dialect, they are of prime importance in securing the continuity, and continued understanding, of language and culture among people.

Metaphors are essential for our understanding of how people communicate, despite differences in class, culture and religion, across geographical distances, and even across periods. The study of metaphors is thus a unique way of understanding the human cognitive capability, and an indispensable tool when it comes to solving problems in language understanding and acquisition.

Above, in section 4.3.2, I dealt in some detail with aspects of metaphor in language; let me here add a few thoughts on why I think that metaphors are not the last word in wording, and why they cannot be the ultimate solution to all problems of human cognition.

Briefly, the current view on metaphor, as defended by, among others, Lakoff and Johnson (1980) and Judge (1988) is both too limited and too restrictive. It is too limited, because it only takes certain aspects of the problems into account, namely, those that the metaphor can handle, i.e., we place limits on the *scope* of our understanding. If, for instance, following Judge, I say that a change of government from time to time is healthy for a nation because that's what we do in agriculture when we rotate crops, I limit myself to the actually occurring changes in agriculture that fit the metaphor. This weakens my explanation, because, among other things, I do not ask why changes are necessary, what the effects of the changes are outside the 'field' I'm focusing on, and so on. People clamouring for political change just for the sake of change, or because that's what one does in farming, may be in for big surprises (as, by the way, will be the farmer who practises crop rotation without carefully planning what to plant when, and why).

But such a view is also extremely restrictive, in the sense that it restrains the *depth* of our metaphoric understanding. True, metaphors are ways of wording the world. But this wording, in order to obtain the true pragmatic significance that it is usually assigned, should include and respect its own context: after all, it is the context of our lives which determines what metaphors are available and what our wordings are going to be. An uncritical understanding of metaphor, especially as manifested in a purely descriptive way of dealing with the issue ('Look and describe, but don't ask any questions') is not only wrong, but outright dangerous from a pragmatic point of view (Mey 1985: 223). And even if our metaphors can provide some of the answers, certain pragmatic questions still have to be asked.

As an illustration, consider the following. In the book quoted above, Lakoff and Johnson routinely assign the human female to the metaphorical 'low' position, whereas the corresponding 'high' is taken up by the male; this happens about ten times in the course of one and a half pages (1980: 15–16). If an explanation has to be found for this curious phenomenon, it seems reasonable to assume that the authors' particular wording has a lot to do with the way they see our society in terms of power: men on top, women at the bottom of the metaphorical 'power pyramid'.

However, the conceptual path from society and its power structures to language is not a direct one; we cannot go straight from one 'universe' (that of power) to another 'universe' (that of language). Rather, we should understand that the way we deal with the world is dependent on the way we metaphorically structure the world, and that, conversely, the way we see the world as a coherent, metaphorical structure helps us to deal with the world. Put another way, metaphors are not only ways of solving problems: they may be, in a deeper sense, ways of *setting* the problems. As Donald Schön remarks, in an important early study,

> When we examine the problem-setting stories told by the analysts and practitioners of social policy, it becomes apparent that the framing of problems often depends upon metaphors underlying the stories which generate problem setting and set the directions of problem solving. (1979: 255)

There is, in other words, a dialectical movement from word to world and from world to word. Neither movement is prior to the other, logically; as to their ontology, both arise at the same time in the history of the human development. In particular, as regards the ontogeny of the individual human, the child acquires its language, being exposed to 'worlding' at the same time as it begins its 'wording' process; the world is not prior to the word, either ontologically or epistemologically.

As Treichler and Frank point out,

> ... [it can be] argue[d] that language constructs as well as reflects culture. Language thus no longer serves as the transparent vehicle of content or as the simple reflection of reality but itself participates in how that content and reality are formed, apprehended, expressed, and transformed. (1989: 3)

In order to determine what a particular wording is worth, therefore, one has to investigate the use conditions that hold in the context of that wording. We must ask what kind of 'seeing' is represented by metaphor, and in what way this 'seeing' affects our thinking – or even, perhaps, determines a particular mind-set (for which it was developed in the first place, in all likelihood).

The social consequences of this view of wording are that one cannot understand one's partners in dialogue unless one has a good grasp of their word-and-world context (which includes, but is not limited to, making metaphors). That is, in order to understand another person's wording, I have to participate in his or her contexts, to word the world with him or her. The pragmatic view of language (and, in general, of all social activity; cf. the quote from Schön 1979 above) demands thus a 'sympathetic' understanding, a practice of 'co-wording in solidarity' with the context of its users.

To understand an utterance, I ideally would have to be able to say it myself, in my conversational partners' context – which, after all, is no more than we expect of our interlocutors in any good conversation. Language-in-use (and in particular, the use of metaphor) is therefore at the same time a necessary instrument of cognition and the expression of that cognition itself: it is a users' language, a users' pragmatic precondition to understanding their context, and to being understood in and through that context (which, in its turn, includes the other language users).[122]

A pragmatic view of 'metaphoring' can serve to point the way to a better understanding of our fellow humans, in particular of what other groups in society, other classes, other nations, attach weight to in their daily interaction with themselves, the others (including us) and the environment. (Think, as an example, of the different possible metaphors surrounding the 'rain forest' and its destruction, when seen from a Western intellectual's point of view, as contrasted to that of a poor industrial slave worker in the Amazonas.) But also in other respects the pragmatic view can help us better to understand our own privileged position in society. This is especially needed in cases where the privileges are, so to speak, self-perpetuating: in an educational context. The following section will go into some detail on this aspect of the social struggle.

14.7 Pragmatics and the Social Struggle

The growing interest in pragmatics as a user-oriented science of language naturally leads to the question: In what sense is pragmatics *useful* to the users? In particular, given the fact that a sizeable portion of the users of any language are 'underprivileged' in their relation to language, and are so, on a deeper level, because of their underprivileged position in society, it seems only reasonable to assume that an insight into the causes of social underprivilegedness could trigger a renewed insight into the role of language in social processes, and that conversely, a renewed consciousness of language as the expression of social inequality could lead us towards what is often called an 'emancipatory' language use.

The first efforts at establishing 'remedial programmes' of language training date back to the sixties, when the so-called 'Head Start' programmes endeavoured to give underprivileged children from the North American urban ghettos a chance to keep up with their white, suburban peers, by teaching them the extra skills (in particular, language capabilities) that they needed in order to follow the regular curriculum. The results of these programmes, if there were any, usually did not last, because the teaching concentrated on the pure transfer of skills, without any connection to the contexts in which these skills were going to be used, or to the real reasons for the lack of cultural and educational privilege of the children in question: their social condition.

The concept of 'underprivileged', applied to language and its use, reflects an awareness of the fact that first of all, language is a common human privilege, a human right, and second, that this privilege, just as all other human rights, is very unevenly distributed among the people living on our earth. Those without access to the full privileges of language are also those who miss out on other opportunities: education, better jobs, cultural goods, decent housing, health care, retirement and old age benefits and so on. As far as the children are concerned, the notion of 'underprivilegedness' translates into deprivation: children who are socially deprived are considered scholastic underachievers and potential school drop-outs, with shorter life expectancies and no social future except in terms of a life on the street corner.

The social concerns of the sixties that reflected themselves in the so-called 'remedial' programmes of language teaching mentioned above, were also the prime moving force in Basil Bernstein's work. In the late fifties, Bernstein, himself a school teacher by profession, started to speculate on the connections between poor school achievements and social background. Based on his experiences, Bernstein set up a rule of thumb predicting that children from lower social classes would do less well in school than their peers from the middle and upper classes.

According to Bernstein, lower-class children, by virtue of their social origin, do not have access to the 'elaborated linguistic code' that is used in school teaching. These children, being native speakers of a 'restricted code', cannot identify with the school language (which simply is not theirs); therefore, their school achievements stay significantly below those of the other children who are dealing with the school's 'elaborated' code as a matter of course, since they have been exposed to that code all their lives.

In Bernstein's early works (1971–5), 'restricted' and 'elaborated' codes were chiefly thought of as linguistically clearly identifiable ways of speaking. Thus, for instance, he points to such things as the use of pronouns instead of nouns for referring purposes (e.g., referring to one's parents as 'he' or 'she' rather than 'Dad' and 'Mom' is a clear instance of restricted code, in Bernstein's sense, and indeed was considered 'vulgar' in middle-class families such as my own); a greater reliance on listener feedback (use of expressions such as 'you know', and so-called 'tag questions': 'isn't it', 'does it'); a less varied use of verbs and adjectives; use of slang, fixed expressions and so on. Since this code only had restricted access to the riches of language, it was called by Bernstein a 'restricted code'.

By contrast, according to Bernstein, an 'elaborated code' would, in addition to avoiding the 'restrictions' mentioned, also often be the expression of a more independent way of looking at things – a use of the first person singular in describing and stating, an imaginative choice of expressions and in general, a higher level of abstraction all being part and parcel of the linguistic privileges of the middle and upper classes. Since the schools, almost by definition and certainly by tradition, emphasized the importance of such qualifications, the status of lower-class students was defined, and traditionally accepted, as 'underprivileged' and less suitable for the curriculum of the educating institution.

As his critics were quick to point out, and Bernstein himself was forced to admit in his subsequent writings, the term 'code' was from the very beginning an infelicitous choice: there were the connotations with other uses of 'code'; there was the confusion of 'code' with social and regional dialects; there was the fact that restricted ways of dealing with the world are typical for a great number of social and other contexts that have nothing to do with the concept of 'underprivileged', but a lot with that of 'specialization' (take the case of professional jargon, for instance). The development of Bernstein's theories (e.g. 1981) takes these criticisms into account by developing a more structured model of socially diverse language use; in this model, the importance of the social context is stressed, and 'code' is no longer thought of as synonymous with some particular kind of language. Thus, in his latest work so far, Bernstein (1990) ascribes the origins of codes not so much directly to class factors as to what he calls 'symbolic control', as found in religious and other systems of values (1990: 111).

Such control systems can be thought of as centred around the system's objective values, as embodied in the controller's position within the system, or around the more subjective realization of these values in the person of the controller. A preacher may appeal to the 'Eternal Truth', of which he is a legitimate representative and an ardent advocate, often endowed with punitive powers, or he may bare his breast and beat it in front of his audience in an effort to influence the faithful. The first approach is called the 'positional', the second the 'personal' one; they represent different attitudes to such social phenomena as respect for authority, obeying the laws, telling the truth to one's superiors, paying one's parking tickets or taxes and so on. With regard to the various ways in which these approaches are realized linguistically, we notice important differences, too; it is generally assumed that in education, the positional approach reflects the 'restricted' code, the personal the 'elaborated' – with whatever implications there are for the social distribution of approaches to education in general, and school education in particular.

As an example, compare the following conversation overheard in the Oak Street Market, a local 'alternative' grocery store in Evanston, Illinois, chiefly frequented by a white, middle-class, mostly academic clientele. The situation is as follows: a young woman drags a little boy around while she is doing her shopping. The kid is naturally bored out of his mind, because the mother's activities are completely centred around herself, and she has no time or energy to engage her son in what she's doing. Frustrated, the boy begins picking off items from the shelves. He is told not to; a reason is given, and the following 'dialogue' takes place:

Mother: I hate to use my money for stupid things, and if you are going to throw those jars on the floor they'll break and we'll have to pay for them and that means there will be no money to buy Christmas presents.

The child does not react at all to this homily, and continues his provocative actions. (All of this happened towards the end of August, I should perhaps add.)

Mother: I told you that we don't have much money, and if you want your Christmas presents, you'd better stop it.

When this, too, is without effect, the mother starts enumerating all the things the boy won't have for Christmas, and how there will be no money to travel to Grandpa and Grandma's, and a whole panoply of other real and imaginary threats. At this point, the boy breaks into a howl, clutches his mother's arm and begins to kick her.

Clearly, what we see in this little interchange is a case of mismatching codes and positions. The mother argues with the child in elaborated code: she talks to him out of an understanding of herself as a responsible adult, as a thinking and reasoning academic person, and will not use the power that is inherent in her position as a mother. As such, she probably would have used another code, spoken from another position: 'Stop that, d'you hear me!' – and the educational process would perhaps have been more effective and less traumatic.

The positions generated by systems such as those mentioned above (religious, social, professional, etc.) are less fixed and 'non-transposable' than those emanating from a traditional class analysis based on the realities of the production system. Bernstein prefers to talk of 'coding orientation' rather than of 'code' in his later works, and ties up orientation with the person's position in, and attitude towards, the societal framework. Codes can be more oriented towards the framework, and hence be 'positional', as in the case of traditional social roles: parent–child, teacher–student, doctor–patient, and so on, or they can be more 'personal', i.e., oriented towards the person, the individual expressing him- or herself in a particular use of language. Code is considered as the regulative instance, the producer of rules for 'good linguistic behaviour'. As Bernstein rightly remarks, any orientation requires an orienting institution; the legitimacy of the code used requires a legitimator. Therefore, '[c]ode presupposes a concept of *whose* relevance and *whose* legitimacy' (1990: 102; my emphasis).

The insights that resulted from Basil Bernstein's work with underprivileged children served as guidelines for much of Western (European) sociolinguistics and other, pragmatically inspired educational research in the seventies. The terminology that Bernstein developed (in particular, his distinction between an 'elaborated' and a 'restricted' code) was, for a decade or so, dominant in the discourse of emancipatory linguistics. Still, for all their good intentions, the Bernstein-inspired solutions to the problem of selectively deficient school instruction did not yield the desired results. For one thing, the early, rather exclusive focus on the formal, descriptive (morphological, syntactic, etc.) aspects of the 'codes', rather than on matters of content and how that content was transmitted, stayed with the theory, and most of its practitioners never took cognizance of the amendments that Bernstein offered to this theoretical apparatus during the seventies and eighties. This was also the time when people started to become aware of the social implications of the code theory and of the need for a thorough rethinking of Bernstein's codes and their societal background. Where earlier, the chief motivation for doing research in an 'emancipatory' framework had been to combat social injustice wherever it was found (such as here: in the classroom), the need for a better-founded theory of social relations made itself felt especially in the later years of the period. It turned out that the framework provided by Bernstein did not have the conceptual stringency that was needed to convince a majority of educationalists; conversely, wholesale appeals to social conscience and to the need of an emancipatory praxis were no longer of use by themselves, but served only as possible motivational support for doing more serious theory-based research (as Bernstein himself of course was well aware of, witness his later works.)[123] .

From a general, sociolinguistic standpoint, one can safely say that (despite all its weaknesses, and with all the restrictions alluded to above) Bernstein's notion of the societal conditions, especially as this concept is manifested in his theory of social stratification, was significantly more relevant than the class analyses undertaken by the majority of his contemporary North American and earlier European colleagues (such 'analyses' mainly consisted in setting up levels of social standing depending on how much money people made, or how often they went to the theatre or concert hall, and so on).

14.8 THE LIGHT AT THE END OF THE TUNNEL

In the wake of the 'student movement' of the sixties, there have been many attempts at making linguistics 'socially relevant', as the slogan went. Many of these efforts have not yielded the expected benefits, such as the earlier mentioned Bernstein-inspired reform movements in the school curricula. Other setbacks included the cuts in bilingual education programmes (not only in the US, but also in many European countries such as Sweden, Germany and Denmark), and the failure to achieve a consistent and internationally accepted policy towards minorities and their linguistic rights. Two of the flagrant examples that come to mind here are, one, the complete lack of respect that the Turkish government has shown for the language of the Kurdic minority group (the government even tried to deny the language its independent status by calling it

'Mountain Turkish', an appellation that flies in the face of all linguistic evidence); and two, the 'English as an official language' movement that has gained momentum in many states of the US, and which aims at more or less outlawing the use of minority languages (in this case, mostly Spanish) in official contexts.

On the other hand, some programmes have had a modicum of success, at least on matters of principle: consider the various efforts at improving communication between public offices and the people. Thus, in Sweden, the government has appointed an official commission to investigate the use of 'public language' whose recommendations for drastic changes have then been put into effect; in the US, various measures have been adopted that aim at reducing the amount of paperwork and simplifying the language of official documents (Paperwork Reduction Act of 1980); and so on.

On balance, the important question may be not what has been achieved, but whether there is a movement in the right direction: Is there a light at the end of the tunnel? Can there be any hope of practising pragmatics in the sense of what used to be hopefully called 'emancipatory linguistics'?

How we deal with this question depends, of course, to a great extent on what we understand by 'emancipation'. If that concept is understood as the elimination of social injustice, as a getting rid of the 'bonds' that are inherent in the very word 'emancipation' (from the Latin word *mancipium* 'slavery, bondage'), then language is not the only, or principal, tool to use. Whether we like it or not, the world is governed by politicians – as Chancellor Axel Oxenstierna told his King, Gustavus Adolphus of Sweden, three and a half centuries ago. Linguists have no political clout. So what does a linguist do, given the 'bondage' that is in effect in our society, and which is instrumental in creating and maintaining its divisions: between have's and have-not's, between rich and poor, between male and female, young and old? What are the opportunities for pragmatic linguists to step into the fray and contribute positively to the outcome of the struggle for a more equal distribution of society's goods, and for an abolition of those divisive patterns?

The answer to these questions is implicitly contained in the definition of pragmatics that I offered earlier (section 3.4). Indeed, if 'pragmatics is the study of the conditions of human language use in a societal context', then a pragmatic orientation towards the greater context of society and its problems will save linguists and linguistics from focusing exclusively on their own problems. A consciousness of the social problems will spur the linguist towards inventing and suggesting remedial treatment of socially-caused linguistic problems; metaphorically, one could speak of a concern for our common linguistic environment in the sense of a 'linguistic ecology' (a term first coined by Einar Haugen in the sixties).

Such an orientation towards the pragmatic aspects of linguistics implies, naturally, a focus on the users of language. A 'conscious linguistics' may contribute to making the language users, too, more conscious of their language; in particular, it can make underprivileged users consciously transcend the boundaries of their underprivileged ('restricted') use without having them buy into the myths and fantasies of the privileged classes. *Vice versa*, the privileged users' consciousness should be raised, too, so they no longer consider the privileges of their societal position as natural and non-controversial.

Questions of this kind touch upon some basic issues regarding the relationship that typically holds between language and society. Earlier (in section 5.1.4), I remarked that our language use, and in particular the system of language itself, both in its referential and its syntactic aspects, has a certain affinity with the prevailing social conditions (the example given was the change in gender-based reference and syntactic agreement rules for professional titles in Spanish). While these correspondences are of undoubted empirical value, the other side of the coin has to be examined as well. In fact, the problem is a variant of that other, age-old dilemma: Which is first, the chicken or the egg? Transposed to the current context, the question is: Does society influence and determine language or does language influence, and perhaps determine, society? (I will not go into a debate on their relative historical priority: the origins of language are probably just as cloudy as those of society.)

The British feminist linguist Dale Spender (1984: 195) has remarked that the relationship between language and reality can be summarized in two seemingly contradictory statements: on the one hand, language represents the world in a symbolic fashion, on the other hand, language is also an instrument that we use for organizing the world, and specifically, in Berger and Luckmann's (1966) phrase, for the 'social construction of reality'. (See also the Treichler and Frank quote in section 14.6.)

How can we reconcile these seemingly incompatible views on the relationships of language and reality? The solution is similar to the one we might come up with, in a Zen-inspired philosophy, for the chicken-and-egg problem: What does it matter? And why should it matter? Why worry?

This answer is based on the observation that there have always been chickens and eggs, as far as we are concerned; we don't have to start from scratch, like Adam (for whom the problem arguably did not even exist) or Noah (who, I'm sure, was careful enough to take along some eggs with his hen-and-rooster pair, just in case). But the dilemma points up a serious aspect of the discussion on language and the ways we think about changing society. That aspect can be said to revolve around the notion of consciousness, and what it takes to change it.

The world as an abstract *tohu-wa-bohu*, prior to creation, cannot have been of much interest to anybody, except the Creator. Rather, it is the world as it is populated by humans, and conceptualized by humans, that has our interest. Similarly, we are not interested in the drab lives of our fellow humans, except in so far as some inspired genius is able to present an exciting and personal account of the human condition, re-creating it (and ourselves) in the form of literature, painting, music or even science. It is only in re-creation that the creation truly comes to life; in this sense, all our lives are one long, uninterrupted re-creative activity. However, this process of re-creation is not a literal one: we don't 're-make' the world in its physical shape; instead, we use our instruments of consciousness, first and foremost our language.

Language, in the somewhat worn phrase first coined by Marx and Engels, is our 'practical consciousness' (1974: 51). But this consciousness is not an independent entity; as Dupré remarks, 'consciousness is deter-mined by language, and language arises out of social relations, which themselves depend upon the material production' (1966: 155).

This means that language is both the 'record-keeper' of our actions, in that it reflects them; and is the 'guide-line' of our actions, in that it (re-)creates reality through our actions. Thus, language is the practical consciousness of our actions: it tells us what we're doing; but language is also the instrument of our planning: it tells us what to do (Mey 1985: 218-20).

However, we should not forget that what has been said here does not apply only to our individual consciousness. If it is true that our con-sciousness, hence our language, is a practical one, then it is by the same token, a *social* consciousness: our practice cannot be anything but social, inasmuch as we are born into human society, even before we realize that we are individuals.

From this, we may conclude that any effort at making things better in society has to involve, at some level or other, a consciousness of the conditions we, along with all the other humans, live under. However, such a consciousness is not always present, or even if it is present, it may be dormant, not fully awake. In many instances, it must be 'raised': hence the familiar expression 'consciousness-raising' which gained currency during the seventies and eighties in the wake of the feminist movement.

Let us now go back to the question: To what extent can language help us in fighting social injustice, inequality and plain oppression? In other words, can we think of linguistics as an 'emancipatory' activity? If there is an answer to this question, the place to look for it is in the above. In order to focus our discussion, let's concentrate on a particular case that may illustrate the potential of such a pragmatic approach.

For thousands of years, the social relations under which most of our species has lived have been characterized by the dominance of the males over the females, a relationship which I have called an oppressive societal condition (Mey 1985: 25ff.): one in which the powerful dominate the powerless, not only in material respects, but also regarding other, less tangible matters. If linguists are to engage themselves actively on the side of the oppressed, in this case, the women, then the first thing to do is to become aware of the oppression, of the fact that 'man made language', to quote the title of another of Dale Spender's works (1980).

Awareness alone, of course, does not make the oppression go away. But forcing ourselves to bring out the problem in the open, that is to say, 'wording it', is one major, if not the only, way for us to deal with it in a practical perspective. This practice includes, as well as is included in, the use of language. Hence, using 'emancipatory' language, that is, language that does not subscribe to the commonly established prejudices about, and skewed images of, women, will change men's ways of thinking of women, while it makes women conscious of the fact that their language is their life, their life their language. Every time men, or women, force themselves to use a form like 'she or he', rather than the so-called generic 'he' (supposedly covering both sexes), a little step is taken towards the realization of the fact that 'man-made language' is an historical accident, and that things need not be like that forever. The presence of women in the language can be emphasized and protected through this seemingly insignificant small shift – and therefore, it is not useless or in vain.

The British philosopher and educationalist Trevor Pateman, asking himself how an outer change can affect an inner attitude, remarks that the practice we change is a 'restructuring of a . . . social relationship, and that experience in the new social relationship thereby created . . . can effect the inner change' (1980: 15). In turn, and just as naturally, the inner change will affect the outer world: language is a social activity, and a change in language is a way of telling the world that it has to change as well. The ideal of an emancipatory language must be the 'adequate expression of a true societal consciousness, one which is neither oppressed nor oppressing', as I have formulated it elsewhere (Mey 1985: 374).

For some decades now, we have had a 'linguistic war' against sexism; small, but significant victories have been won in this skirmish – witness the growing number of journals that subscribe to the guidelines for the 'nonsexist' use of language, adopted and promulgated by various scientific societies, such as the American Psychological Association, the American Anthropological Association, the Modern Language Association of America, the Linguistic Society of America, and their various journals: *American Anthropologist, Language, Journal of Pragmatics* and so on.

Of course, the mere substitution of a combined pronoun such as *s/he* for the supposedly 'generic'[124] *he* does not, in and of itself, change anything in the conditions of society that oppress and underprivilege its female members. But if it is true, as Sally McConnell-Ginet says, that

> ... earlier feminist research has established that *he*, no matter what its user intends, is not unproblematically interpreted as generic, and the consequent shift in the community's beliefs about how *he* is interpreted has influenced what one can intend the pronoun to convey (1989: 49)

then it also is permissible to use this example as one of the areas in which emancipatory linguistics actually has been successful, albeit to a modest degree; namely, by establishing a whole new code for the use of pronouns in English – pronouns that reflect the growing consciousness of women's presence in society, but that at the same time, and with apparent success, change the ways society's members (both female and male) speak, write and think about women, treat women and interact with women.

Concluding, and particularly with regard to language, let me once more quote McConnell-Ginet:

> [language] matters so much precisely because so little matter is attached to it; meanings are not given but must be produced and

reproduced, negotiated in situated contexts of communication (1989: 49);

that is, the *use* of language needs to be negotiated between the *users* of language themselves in their social and communicative relations and linguistic interactions.

Thus, the question I raised at the beginning of this book, 'why pragmatics?' is (at least partially) answered: Pragmatics is the societally necessary and consciously interactive dimension of the study of language. Cases like the above furnish a modest illustration of 'what pragmatics is all about', and thus extend our theoretical speculations into the realm of the practical, by showing us how pragmatics can assist people, as language users, in their endeavours to realize their personal goals in the societal setting in which they live.

EXERCISES AND REVIEW QUESTIONS

1. WBEZ, the Chicago Public Radio station, had an interview on 28 August, 1992 with the (male) director of advertising of a New York firm, which had placed an ad in the *New York Times* for tartan bras (complete with matching boxer shorts) for the astonishing price of $78. The topic of the discussion was: Why would women be willing to pay so much for underwear?

The (male) interviewer suggested that it might have something to do with the feeling that underwear was important to women, so important in fact that the girls thought it was normal, if one went out with a man, that he'd pay for the dinner, since they had already paid so much for the underwear! Next, he mentioned the curious fact that although this was a typically feminine subject of discussion, the two people who were discussing the matter were both male. The interviewer continued:

[Interviewer:] So here we were discussing this at the office with a group of women, and how come when I call, that I'm talking to a man?

[Director of advertising:] Well I'm the director of advertising, and since you enquired about an ad ...

[Int.:] Well, Mr O'Brien, I suppose that if it had been a woman

who'd called, the interview would have gone better.
[Dir.:] It went badly??
(*microphone cut off by interviewer*)

Questions:

What kind of assumption underlies the postulate of the high cost of underwear as an excuse for not paying one's share for dinner?

Does the journalist have the right to assume that the interview 'might have gone better' if the interviewer had been a woman?

What is the journalist trying to do here? How does he do it?

What does the director's reaction show?

Did this interview 'go badly'? In what respects, would you say?

In your answer, concentrate on the linguistic phenomena as they occur in the text of the interview, both as it is referred to above and as it is quoted.

2. 'Generic' vs. 'gender'-determined pronouns
Consider the following case:
   In July 1992, Judge Robert Zack of Broward County, Florida, found topless hot-dog vendor Terri Cortina not guilty of indecent exposure. In court Zack read aloud a law that stipulated that it is illegal

'for any person to expose or exhibit his sexual organs'.

Said Zack,

'I don't think this lady has male sexual organs. I [have] no choice but to release her.' (*Reader*, Chicago, 4 December, 1992)

Questions:

Was Judge Zack right? Why (not)?

How should the law be interpreted (a) under a 'generic' view; (b) under a 'gender-based' view?

Is the judge's decision pragmatically acceptable?

What would be needed to obtain such an interpretation?

3. Euphemism

In classical rhetoric, 'euphemism' is defined as: talking about something in terms that are deliberately chosen to preempt any negative reaction on the part of the receiver. Thus, euphemism is current in areas that are subject to heavy taboos: sex, death, sickness, money, religion, politics, bodily functions, etc.

Questions:

Can you give examples of euphemism in each of the areas referred to above?

Next, consider the following transcript:

US Army Speaker Peter Williams is interviewed on national public television about the role of the US military in the invasion of Panama:

> 'No, the military folks wouldn't do a thing like that ... I cannot recall having seen any evidence of military folks being engaged in operations like burning down houses.'
> (From the documentary film *The Panama Deception*, directed by Barbara Trent, written and edited by David Kasper; Empowerment Project, 1992)

(Notes: 'a thing like that' refers to previous accusations by journalists of willful killing of civilians and destruction of their property by the American invasion forces.

The context of the quote in *The Panama Deception* is that this excerpt of the public TV transmission was shown after a screening of actual movie and video clips of the US military going into a poor section of Panama City and methodically destroying street after street by throwing hand grenades and incendiary bombs into each house, as they went along.)

Questions:

Can you identify the euphemism(s) in the above passage?

What connotations does the expression 'military folks' carry for you?

What are the manipulative aspects of this official US Army spokesperson's comments?

How do the filmmakers exploit the contrast between the speaker's words and the actual footage of the invasion?

Would you call this exploitation a manipulatory manœuvre? Why (not)?

A full pragmatic analysis would also have to take into account other aspects of the message. Name some of these. (Hint: the key word here is 'credibility', used mainly in connection with a person's appearance on the visual media: facial expression, voice quality, body language, implied intimacy with the audience, etc. Former President Ronald Reagan was a prime example of these media virtues; in the case at hand, the lacking visual components must necessarily be left to the reader's imagination.)

4. A large part of the linguistic manœuvre of manipulation (cf. the previous question) is based on metaphor.

Consider, for instance, the press's use of metaphoric expressions to characterize the US military action against Iraq in January of 1993, as documented by the following expressions, found in the Chicago daily newspapers:

US warplanes punish Iraq

A slap on the wrist for Saddam Hussein

Saddam receives spanking

What do you make of these expressions?

What do they stand for, and how do they manipulate the reader?

In the case that all the readers would agree as to the use of these metaphors, would we still be able to speak of manipulation? Justify your answer.

5. Conditionals
The sentence pair 'if–then' is usually called a conditional; it consists of two elements, the first called *protasis*, the second *apodosis* (these names stem from classical Aristotelian rhetoric). Logic, as well as common sense, tells us that if the condition of the protasis is fulfilled, then the situation announced in the apodosis will become reality. (Examples of conditionals were given in section 5.2.2.)

However, in everyday language use, the role of the 'if–then' pair is not so straightforward. The 'then' may be omitted (as may sometimes the 'if') – but that doesn't make any difference, usually. What is worse is that in many cases, the condition seems to be no real condition at all, but something that happens on another level of conceptualizing, as in the following examples:

There's a natural affinity between Swedish *gravlaks* and Russian *blini* and caviar if one thinks about it, and chef Katsuo Nagasawa has . . . . (*Gourmet* magazine, 52(5), May 1992, p. 46)

The way times change, it's nice to know that quality like that hasn't changed one bit. Come to think of it, it's that kind of quality that made Uncle Ben's converted Brand Rice more than just a part of American cooking, but part of a legend, as well. (*Bon Appetit* magazine, 37(6), June 1992, p. 67)

In these examples, the notion of 'condition' is rather far gone; not to mention in the following:

If you think our waiters are rude, you should see the chef. (Bruce Fraser)

where, at least on one reading, the 'if–then' condition is close to being ludicrous.

Suzette Haden Elgin has, in a series of books, discussed the manipulatory potential of these 'if–then' sentences, and comes to the conclusion that they really aren't conditionals at all, but rather indirect verbal attacks. The basis for this postulate can be found in the classical theory of the 'irreal conditional': the conditional whose protasis is assumed to be false. Hence, in sentences of the type

If you really X, you would not Y,

the message is 'you don't X' – but the part that attracts attention is the 'Y'. For instance, in the following case:

If you really wanted the job, you wouldn't come to the interview in jeans the discussion is bound to turn on the question of whether or not jeans are appropriate attire for a job interview, while the underlying postulate: 'You are not interested in the job' is quietly and unobtrusively smuggled into its place.

Haden Elgin calls the 'if'-part the hook, the 'then'-part the bait: one swallows the bait (one starts discussing the 'then'-part: 'are jeans acceptable for a job interview?'), but forgets that in doing so, one has automatically and implicitly ingested the hook; that is, one has accepted the non-truth of the 'if'-part ('is the person interested in the job?'). (Suzette Haden Elgin 1989)

Question and task:

What is the manipulatory importance of Haden Elgin's construction?

Illustrate her point by construing five cases in which an 'if'-part functions as hook, a 'then'-part as bait.

Notes

1 What the oracle actually said was (Ennius, *Annales* 167; cf. Cicero, *De divinatione* 2: 116): 'Aio te Aiacida Romanos uincere posse', which is translated as either 'I'm telling you, offspring of Aiacus, that you can win over the Romans' or, on an alternative reading, 'I'm telling you, offspring of Aiacus, that the Romans can win over you.' The 'correct' reading of this construction, an *accusativus cum infinitivo*, where either accusative can be interpreted as the subject or the object of the sentence, depends on how we are 'set up' to understand it (and, albeit to a lesser degree, on what we perceive as the 'normal' order of constituents in a sentence: subject first, then object, then verb). On the importance of being 'set up' for a particular understanding, see section 12.7.1.

2 The allusion is to several well-known series of monographs and books published under the common name of *Pragmatics and Beyond* by John Benjamins, Amsterdam/Philadelphia, since 1978.

3 The notion of 'progress' in conversation is discussed extensively in Stalpers 1993.

4 The language reflects this conceptual dichotomy by its different referential pronominalization; and the moral is that we should pay attention to this in *indexing* our 'cases'. Not all swimming is alike; not all swimming in one language is called 'swimming' in some other (cf. that inanimate objects such as logs can 'swim' in German, but not in any other Germanic language that I know, the exception being, perhaps, Early Modern English: 'And the man of God said, Where fell it? And he shewed him the place. And he cut down a stick, and cast it in thither; and the iron [i.e. the ax head] did swim.' (II Kings 6: 6). Note also that some languages do indeed have different words for motion verbs where animals are concerned, as opposed to humans. (In West Greenlandic Inuit, a human *arpappuq*, an animal *pangalippuq*. Both mean 'he/she/it runs'.)

5 A favourite party game among linguists is to discuss whether or not a

particular expression is 'correct' or 'grammatical'. Such discussions (which as a rule take place in the immediate vicinity of the refrigerator, to secure a constant supply of cold drinks during the often heated debates) invariably end with one or several of the discussants invoking the authority invested in themselves as native speakers of some dialect of English (or whatever), in which precisely such and such a construction is 'grammatical' or 'ungrammatical', whichever the case may be. Robin Lakoff comments on this curious phenomenon as follows: 'So one linguist's intuitive judgment was equal to another's, and there was no way to discriminate. "That's not in my dialect", you could say to a colleague, but that didn't obligate him to change his mind. Hence Ross's version of the American Linguist's National Anthem: "Oh, see if you can say . . ." ' (1989: 960).

6   Incidentally, this example also shows that the logical so-called 'principle of compositionality' (the truth value of a compound sentence is the conjoined truth value of its components) is not valid in pragmatics (see also section 10.3). A lot has been written on presuppositions, not all of it relevant to pragmatics. The interested reader is referred to Levinson (1983: 175ff.) for a complete account. I will deal in more detail with pragmatic presuppositions in a later section (10.4.3; see also 12.6).

7   This seems to be Carnap's (1956) stance; cf. also Levinson (1983: 2–3): 'explicit reference is made to the speaker, or to put it in more general terms, to the user of the language.'

8   This example is due to Alvaro G. Meseguer (1988: 108).

9   Depending on whether one prefers to delimit the semantic field or the pragmatic field most closely, the result of the delimitation and its effect on the practitioners in each field will vary. Typically, one school wants to create a sharp line of demarcation setting semantics off from all the rest by a strict criterion such as the operation of truth conditions. Then, in pragmatics we can be working with as broad a sense of 'meaning' as possible, taking in aspects such as metaphor, irony, implicit communication and so on. Conversely, we could define a strictly linguistic pragmatics, in the sense discussed above, viz., one that will only recognize pragmatic phenomena to the extent that they are linguistically marked. Here, the pragmatic 'module' becomes a bit neater, and its boundaries with the other disciplines a bit clearer; however, the price we pay is to have to do away with all the interesting fringes.

10   It is worth noting also what Östman says in his next paragraph: 'Admittedly, that latter [unit] is to be seen as a process rather than as an "object", but it is doubtful in what sense any units of analysis for semantics are that much more object-like.'

11   Bühler remarks, somewhat facetiously, that he has chosen the term *Appell* because of a certain current fashion: '. . . today, as everybody knows, we have a sex appeal, and it seems to me that next to that, a *speech appeal* must be just as real a thing' (1934: 29).

12   According to Levinson, in the area of conversation analysis, 'at least, the would-be functionalist is offered the kind of rich and intricate structure

that may match the detailed organization of linguistic structure, and so can be claimed plausibly to stand in a causal relation to it' (1983: 47).

13 Cf. the title of Leech's book: *Principles of Pragmatics*. (On the metapragmatic status of principles, see section 13.4, below.)

14 These latter cases, even though as to their substance they cannot be separated from the pragmatic endeavour, will only be dealt with very superficially here; for a fuller treatment, see especially section 12.2.

15 For more details, see Leech (1983: 9), from whom the example is originally taken. (Cf. also the title of an early, seminal paper by Cutler (1974): 'On saying what you mean without meaning what you say'.)

16 Many linguists refer to this opposition as the distinction between 'linguistic' (or 'sentence') meaning' and 'speaker meaning'.

17 The obvious exceptions are words that imitate sounds, the so-called onomatopoietic terms, but even here one can be misled: for instance, animal sounds are rendered in vastly different ways across languages, as everybody knows.

18 See also Leech's 'Aunt Rose' example (1983: 30ff.), to be discussed in section 5.3.

19 In fact, precisely this criticism has been made of Ronald Wardhaugh's otherwise sensible approach to conversation analysis, *How Conversation Works* (1986).

20 The expressions 'positive' and 'negative politeness' are due to Brown and Levinson who, in a ground-breaking monograph (1978), have studied the phenomena of politeness in different circumstances and different cultures from the point of view of what they call 'face'. (For more on this notion, see section 4.4.4.)

21 The trouble with this example is, of course, that it is highly informative and relevant – to the right hearer: *Sapienti sat!*

22 'If you can't say anything nice, don't say anything at all.' (American folk maxim)

23 This kind of argumentation reminds one of the old, rhetorical term *argumentum ex baculo*, that is, the stick-behind-the-door argument. As an example, cf. the following text, often seen on the back of Norwegian trailer trucks: 'UTEN BILEN GÅR NORGE I STÅ' (i.e. 'Without cars (lit.: the car), Norway stops functioning'). Here, an implicit threat is formulated as a statement. However, the threat has only a limited effect and scope, since the statement itself is ambiguous: 'stop functioning' may either be read as 'normal functions no longer being performed' (such as: getting to the stops or to the doctor's office, carrying goods and mail across the country, and so on), or as 'stop functioning under the currently prevailing conditions', which would imply, among other things, an end to the unlimited proliferation of (especially private) automotive transportation, the uninhibited construction of new roads (often at the cost of massive destruction of the human habitat), and so on. Clearly, only in the former sense can the threat concealed in the statement above be said to affect all (the inhabitants of) 'Norway'; by contrast, the reading of the statement in the latter sense (that

of 'providing a check on the ideology of growth at all cost') has its scope in the limited class of true believers in the blessings of automotive transportation.

24 Hartmut Haberland (personal communication) has drawn my attention to the fact that 'face', in its original Chinese context, represents an acquired and ascribed status an individual has in society. In this sense, it cannot be 'lost'. When the Japanese borrowed the concept from the Chinese, it was 'nipponized' to a certain degree, that is, it received a typical Japanese orientation towards what Kasper (1990: 195) has called 'social relativism'. This means, among other things, that '. . . while negative politeness, addressing territorial concerns for autonomy and privacy, derives directly from the high value placed on individualism in Western culture[, f]or Japanese society, by contrast, the overarching principle of societal interaction . . . compris[es] concerns about belongingness, empathy, dependency, proper place occupancy and reciprocity . . .' (Kasper 1990: 195).

25 Cf. the case of Muhammad Ali, who caused a great international commotion by pronouncing that 'there are two bad men in the world. The Russian white man and the American white man. They are the two baddest men in the history of the world' (Smitherman 1984: 103). Smitherman comments: 'In the semantics of inversion used by the descendants of African slaves . . . "bad" can mean powerful, omnipotent, spiritually or physically tough, outstanding, wonderful, and with emphasis very good' (p. 104).

26 Levinson expresses this as follows: '. . . the reason for linguistic interest in the maxims is that they generate inferences beyond the semantic content of the sentences uttered. Such inferences are, by definition, conversational implicatures, where the term *implicature* is intended to contrast with terms like *logical implication, entailment*, and *logical consequence* which are generally used to refer to inferences that are derived solely from logical or semantic content. For implicatures are not semantic inferences, but rather inferences based on both the content of what has been said and some specific assumptions about the *co-operative nature of ordinary verbal interaction*' (1983: 103–4; last italics mine. On implicatures etc., see chapter 5).

27 Cf. the following joke (due to Leech 1983: 91):

Steven: Wilfrid is meeting a woman for dinner tonight.
Susan: Does his wife know about it?
Steven: Of COURSE she does. The woman he is meeting IS his wife.

28 'Bottom-to-top' (or 'bottom-up') and 'top-to-bottom' (or 'top-down') are metaphorical expressions from the area of automated sentence analysis: one can either start 'parsing' a sentence, beginning with the grammatical categories ('top-down'), or with the string of words ('bottom-up').

29 Compare Gazdar's warning: 'Informal explanations, not based on formal theory, particularly those that trade on words like "relevant", are always liable to the fallacy of equivocation' (1979: 54).

30 An interesting aside is that this implicature would not be possible unless both agents had the information necessary to determine the location of honey, given the usual facts about beehives. We assume this to be a simple inference, but that needn't be the case, as we see in the sad case of Joe Bear in another of his computer-generated mishaps: 'One day, Joe Bear was hungry. He asked his friend Irving Bird where some honey was. Irving told him there was a beehive in the oak tree. Joe walked to the oak tree. He ate the beehive' (Meehan 1981: 218).

31 'Deictic' is the adjective to 'deixis', from the Greek verb *deíknumi* 'show'. It is used to indicate the function that certain words, such as personal and demonstrative pronouns, place and time adverbs like 'here', 'now' and others have in the language. That function is always bound up with the time and place of the utterance, seen in relation to the speaker. Thus, we say 'Come here,' but 'Don't stand over there.' See further sections 5.1.3 and 5.1.4.

32 The word 'proper' has historically a somewhat different connotation – 'properly belonging; correct; real', etc. – than the one we usually associate with it today.

33 'A context will here be a set of *pragmatic indices, co-ordinates* or *reference points* (as they are variously called) for speakers, addressees, times of utterance, places of utterance, indicated objects, and whatever else is needed. Sentences can therefore express different propositions on different occasions of use' (Levinson 1983: 58).

34 The human 'pointer' *kat'exochèn* is the body part called 'index', from the Latin word *index*, 'pointer, forefinger'. The word is etymologically related to the Greek word for pointing, *deíxis*. (See also note 31.)

35 Honorific expressions (literally: 'honour makers') mark the social distance between the speaker and his/her interlocutor(s) by prescribing a particular linguistic expression to be used in particular circumstances.

36 It is a matter of taste and terminology whether one wants to term this kind of reference 'text-deictic' or 'discourse-deictic' (cf. the not-too-conclusive discussion in Levinson 1983: 86–7).

37 Just as the Latin *proconsul* used to be the representative of the highest state authority in his province: the *pro-consul* served precisely *pro consule*, in lieu of the *consul*.

38 Cf. also the more technical-philosophical terms 'to implicate' and 'to explicate', which are derived from the same original Latin root and have related meanings. Not all authors distinguish between 'implication' and 'implicature'; for instance, Leech and Thomas (1988: 19) call an 'implicature' simply a 'pragmatic implication'. Consider also the following quote from Bilmes:

> We come now to the subject of implication. In everyday talk, we often convey propositions that are not explicit in our utterances but are merely implied by them. Sometimes we are able to draw such inferences only by referring what has been explicitly said to some

conversational principle. In certain of these cases, we are dealing with 'conversational implicature'. (1986: 27)

I will return to this problem in section 5.2.2.

39   Some call this relationship 'material implication' (for a discussion, see van der Auwera (1985: 202); most logicians do not distinguish between 'logical' and 'material' implication).

40   A Biblical *à propos*: the owner of the vineyard in St Matthew 20: 1–16 thus acted correctly, when he gave the latecomers the same hire as he had promised those who had borne the 'burden and heat of the day'. What he had said was: 'If you go into my vineyard, I'll give you a penny each' – and so he did at the end of the day. There was no law against giving the penny also to those who hadn't worked, or not worked enough. The vineyard owner did what he thought he had to do ('whatsoever [was] right'), and acted, moreover, in strict conformity with the laws of logic (albeit not under any trade-union-backed interpretation of these).

41   One can make these logical equivalencies clear with the aid of so-called 'truth tables' indicating the conditions under which a proposition or a combination of propositions is true or false. Most handbooks of logic will tell you how to construct a truth table; however, this kind of logical workout is outside the scope of the present work.

42   I have borrowed this term from Sperber and Wilson, who call 'an explicitly communicated assumption an explicature' (1986: 182).

43   When Grice 'concocted' his famous 'notion of conversational implicature', he wasn't too careful about telling us how to derive this substantive: from the everyday verb 'to imply' or from its philosophical cousin 'to implicate'. For Grice, implicature is a kind of implication, hence he sometimes uses 'implies' as a non-technical synonym for 'conversationally implicates' (cf. Grice 1981: 184, 185).

44   The famous unsuccessful denial of Jesus by St Peter in the High Priest's courtyard is a case in point: 'Surely thou also art one of them; for thy speech betrayeth thee,' said the damsel (Matthew 26: 73); and no amount of denying could convince 'them that stood by' that the addressed was *not* a Galilean, hence potentially associated with the 'King of the Jews'.

45   The word 'received' has acquired a certain fame as a euphemism for 'higher class' pronunciation, as in 'RP' (received pronunciation) – the 'public [sic!] school' variety of spoken English propagated by vast numbers of English-as-a-foreign-language teachers all over the world.

46   Such an automatic conclusion is often called 'entailment': the first sentence 'entails' the second; however, the converse is not true (see Horn 1984: 15).

47   The notion of 'exploitation' by 'flouting' a maxim (e.g. of politeness; Grice 1975) has been employed in precisely this way. Thus, I can flout the politeness maxim in order to obtain a special effect, as when I say to a good friend, when meeting him on the streets of Bologna: 'Come va, vecchio stronzo?' (literally, 'How's it going, old fart?') (Umberto Eco, personal communication).

48 One is sometimes in doubt whether to speak of 'linguistic philosophy' or 'philosophy of language'; the two are often used indiscriminately. If a distinction is to be made, it should probably follow the lines suggested by John R. Searle: 'Linguistic philosophy is the attempt to solve particular philosophical problems by attending to the ordinary use of particular words or other elements in a particular language. The philosophy of language is the attempt to give philosophically illuminating descriptions of certain general features of language, such as reference, truth, meaning and necessity; and it is concerned only incidentally with particular elements in a particular language' . . . (1969: 4).

49 Often, the difference is termed one of 'constative' or 'descriptive' utterances vs. 'performative' ones (Leech 1983: 176).

50 This use of 'performative' should be kept apart from what in early, non-aligned transformational grammar started to be called the 'performative hypothesis'. (For more on this, see note 55, and sections 7.4 and 9.4.)

51 As we will see later, this 'naked' force is not the only one that an utterance can have. See section 7.2, on so-called 'indirect speech acts'.

52 Here is Austin's own formulation of the 'felicity conditions' (quoted after Levinson 1983: 229):

A. (i) There must be a conventional procedure having a conventional effect. (ii) The circumstances and persons must be appropriate, as specified in the procedure.
B. The procedure must be executed (i) correctly and (ii) completely.
C. Often, (i) the persons must have the requisite thoughts, feelings and intentions, as specified in the procedure, and (ii) if consequent conduct is specified, then the relevant parties must so do.

53 Similarly in the Bible; here, we are admonished by the Apostle St James to abstain from oaths and suchlike forceful speech acts: 'Let thy speech be Aye, Aye and No, No, lest thou shalt fall under judgment' (5: 12).

54 The five classes are: representatives, directives, commissives, expressives and declaratives. They will be discussed in more detail in chapter 8.

55 The 'performative hypothesis' assumes that there in all utterances can be found a hidden, 'performative' verb of 'declaring'. Thus, when I say

It's cold in here,

what I'm supposed to be really saying is

I'm stating the fact that it's cold in here.

Obviously, there is no end to this 'stating': so why not:

I state the fact that I state the fact that . . .

and so on, *ad infinitum*? (see also note 50, above, and section 7.4. For a history, and excellent critique of the 'performative hypothesis', see Leech 1980: 59ff.).

56 Needless to say (as already mentioned earlier), the term 'speech act' should not be understood as relating exclusively to 'speech'. One could insist on calling these acts 'language acts'; however, the tradition would probably overrule any such attempt, at least in the English-speaking (and -reading) communities. The French expression *acte langagier* is a more successful replacement of *acte de parole*, 'speech act'.

57 It goes without saying that not all linguists are overly happy with characterizations like this (not to mention literary critics).

58 The question can be raised here whether an insincere promise, that is, a promise without the intention to fulfil the act, is a promise. Searle seems to think so, but it is not quite clear what this kind of promise is worth, pragmatically speaking, especially with regard to the next condition.

59 Actually, condition 2 is not specific for promising either, contrary to what Searle implies: with varying content, one obtains varying speech acts.

60 The technical term 'encoded' may, in this context, be replaced by a vaguer but more commonly understandable word such as 'abstract' (as opposed to 'concrete' or, in this context, 'interactive').

61 As Levinson remarks, it would be more appropriate to speak of 'sentence types' 'instead of the misleading term *mood*' (1983: 243), mood being a strictly verbal inflectional category, only indirectly characterizing a type of sentence (see also Lyons 1977: 747).

62 Cf. the following sanguine reverie, found elsewhere in Verschueren's works: 'Language is certainly not less complicated than physical or biological reality. Biologists recognize about 30,000 different species of spiders and 250,000 species of beetles. I am convinced that if we kept making distinctions with as much patience as biologists have traditionally done, we would come up with a set of SAs [speech acts] approaching the astronomical number of species in the whole animal kingdom' (1980: 4).

63 The asterisk denotes a form that is not found in the language.

64 Compare the case of the schoolboy who, when asked how much is 3 × 9, is told that his answer 'I believe it's 27' is incorrect, because (as the teacher tells him): 'Believing is something you do in church – here, you have to know it!'

65 Verschueren (1979: 6–7) offers a lengthy list of some 180 such verbs.

66 The latter verb, 'to know', may indeed occur as a performative, as, e.g., in 'Know all ye men, women and children by these presents . . .' but only in this, and similar kinds of use. The performative use occurs implicitly in official, 'posted' signs: 'No hunting' (meaning: 'Know that hunting here is not allowed'), '55' ('Know that the speed limit here is 55 mph'), or the all-purpose 'Posted' ('Know that something is not allowed here'); or even explicitly, as in the suggested reading of the following road sign

TEXAS
SPUR
2

as: 'Know that it is 2 miles to Spur, Texas' – actually one of the more spurious multiple choices for an answer to a Texas driver's test question in 1966.

67 The original source is given as *90 Minutes at Entebbe* by William Stevenson (New York: Bantam Books, 1976), pp. 215–16.

68 Notice, however, that Searle himself admits that 'in normal conversation, of course, no one would consciously go through the steps involved in this reasoning' (1975: 63).

69 Some of my readers may think that this kind of detailed reasoning is going too far. Let them be assured that, in Searle's own opinion, this treatment has not been detailed enough; in his own words: 'I have not, for example, discussed the role of the assumption of sincerity, or the ceteris paribus conditions that attach to various of the steps'! (1975: 63).

70 Cf. Levinson: '. . . there are no isolable necessary and sufficient conditions on, for example, questionhood, but rather . . . the nature of the use to which interrogatives are put can vary subtly with the nature of the *language-games* or contexts in which they are used' (1983: 275).

71 English is a case in point: here, one has also 'to request', which is not different from 'to ask' except in its degree of formality (connoting greater 'force', as Searle would have it; see section 8.2.2).

72 I will exclude here the playful use of the paradox, as in children's games: 'I love you, but it's a lie'; 'You can have my bike, but it's a lie' (understood as: 'I promise something but I don't promise . . .' – perhaps more than just a childish game?).

73 Searle, in later work, calls these speech acts 'assertives' (see Leech 1983: 128).

74 Incidentally, these 'properties' need not be limited to inner states: in certain cultures, one can congratulate people on the acquisition of material objects such as new cars, snappy clothes, etc. In America, it is usual to congratulate people on getting a new job, or achieving a task, or winning in the lottery ('Congratulations! You may already have won!'). In Denmark, it is quite acceptable to congratulate people on their new car.

75 An interdict is a legal measure, inflicted by the Holy See on a certain part of its jurisdiction or on a certain (category of) person(s), and severing the connections between it (them) and the Church. It amounts thus to a 'territorial excommunication', an ecclesiastical state of siege.

76 For a more detailed treatment, see my book *Whose Language? A Study in Linguistic Pragmatics* (Mey 1985).

77 As is done, i.a., in the journal of that name, also founded by van Dijk (1981).

78 In the following, I will use this broader concept of 'context' as the unmarked term (the 'default'), and only talk about 'co-text' whenever I want to restrict its content.

79 Cf. Flader and Trotha (1986), quoted in section 13.1.

80 Swale is the name of a famous racehorse whose sudden and unexpected death has served as a classic example in much of the current literature on

computerized explanation of discourse (Schank 1986: 232; Riesbeck and Schank 1987: 30).

81 Some linguists call these 'imperatives-in-the-form-of-a-question' ('Why don't you get lost?') *whimperatives*. The term is originally due to Jerry Sadock (1974).

82 From the novel *Bright Lights, Bright City*, by Ian McInerney (New York: Doubleday, 1984), p. 71.

83 'Cohesion' is defined by Halliday and Hasan (1976: 29–30) as '. . . the linguistic means by which a text is enabled to function as a single meaningful unit'. Note that there is no mention of 'coherence' in these authors' work: however, one may consider it to be implicitly presupposed as that which makes the text different from a non-text, in the same way that we separate sense from non-sense.

84 As an instance, compare the many contributions on 'exotic' (especially Australian indigenous) languages that have been framed in one or the other of the Chomsky-descendant 'government and binding' ('GB') approaches. (For instances, see especially the journal *Natural Language and Linguistic Theory* (Dordrecht: Reidel).)

85 Agreed, all the time, that we indeed can talk about 'truth' here, in the sense defined by the logical-philosophical approach to sentence semantics.

86 Reportedly, the Smithsonian Institution in Washington, DC, is replete with all sorts of artifacts and tools that earlier anthropologists have brought back from field trips, but have forgotten to provide with explanatory labels. Today, these items sit on shelves in dusty cellars as silent witnesses to the users' mandatory presence in use.

87 Cf.: '[deixis is] the single most obvious way in which the relationship between language and context is reflected in the structures of languages themselves . . .' (Levinson 1983: 54).

88 Rabbi Levensohn is on his way to Cracow, when he meets his colleague Rabbi Meir. When asked where he is headed, Rabbi Levensohn answers, truthfully, that he is bound for Cracow. Whereupon his interlocutor starts accusing him of bad faith and cheating: 'You liar! You want me to believe you're going to Cracow? If you really were going to Cracow, you'd have said you were on your way to Lemberg!'

89 In philosophical terms, this can be expressed as the subordination of the logical systems (both formal, 'minor' logic, and the 'major' logic of epistemology) under the essential structure of ontology, which assigns these systems their referential and intensional meanings. The essential structures themselves are further subsumed under the transcendentality of existence, which provides the ultimate metaphysical structuring into what makes ('common') sense (Kant's 'practical reason'). This translates in linguistic terms as: the systems (rules) of morphology and syntax are informed by semantics, whereas the (syntactico-)semantic structures themselves are subsumed under the pragmatics of discourse, the latter being their transcendental condition of making sense in a human context.

90 As Coetzee himself remarks elsewhere, 'Blindness to the colour black is

built into the South African pastoral' (1988: 5).

91   The term *aizuchi* is said to refer to the striking of the iron by the blacksmith and his helper, operating in tandem: the strikes are timed exactly right so as to avoid clashes and let the work continue without interruption. (For an example of Japanese 'sucked-in breath' and its role in conversation, see section 11.6.)

92   A good example is provided by Allwood (1976), drawing on work on 'anarchic' conversation types in the West Indies (e.g., as described for Antigua by Reisman 1989 [1974]).

93   The term 'phatic' goes back to the Polish anthropologist and linguist Bronistaw Malinowski. Jakobson (1960), who is usually quoted as the source of this term, uses Malinowski's terminology ('phatic communion'), interpreted as: a communicative exchange which happens mostly for the purposes of contact (e.g. greetings). See Jakobson (1960: 357); Lyons (1968: 417).

94   To understand to what extent such phenomena are directly dependent on the language used (considered as an expression of the culture), cf. the case of the American student who tried to compliment a Japanese student at Boston University on her dress, and was rudely turned away. The problem was that he spoke Japanese, and in Japanese, such compliments from a male to a female are infelicitous. A fellow student, who spoke to the girl in English, congratulating her on her good taste in clothes, got the obligatory demure smile as his reward (Bruce Fraser, personal communication).

95   For complete details on repairs, see Levinson (1983: 339–42).

96   Example due to Bruce Fraser (personal communication).

97   Remember that earlier (section 10.2) we have discussed 'cohesion' as a strictly local organizing principle of text, as especially studied in text grammar (and, e.g., realized by morphological and syntactic devices).

98   ELIZA is the brain child of Joseph Weizenbaum, a well-known (now retired) computer scientist at MIT. Though not initially planned as a serious effort at simulating human cognitive activity, the program (which simulates a therapist–patient interaction) has become extremely popular among the general public. In the Artificial Intelligence (AI) community, by contrast, it is often gleefully quoted as an example of 'How *not* to do it'. As any introductory AI text with respect for itself mentions ELIZA, no specific references are given here except to Weizenbaum's original paper (1966).

99   One can summarize this view of coherence as the 'Principle of Conditional Relevance' (Levinson 1983: 306).

100   I will disregard the fact that one may get upset for other reasons, e.g. when we think we have a right to ask the question, and the answer we get is one like (iv).

101   On the notion of 'script', the standard references are Minsky 1975, Schank and Abelson 1977, Schank 1981.

102   Even if the addressee refuses to answer, his or her silence may be a relevant answer, because we're inside a 'pair', and hence interpret the silence as the second half of that pair (see section 12.4.2).

103   The notion of 'frame' has its origin in studies of modelling human behaviour on the computer (cf. Schank and Abelson 1979, the classic reference). An instantiation of the theory of adaptability (as contrasted to adaptivity) in the domain of the interaction between humans and computers is found in Mey (1992a, 1993a).

104   Leech means the grammatical, not the semantic or pragmatic subject. The reasoning here is somewhat dubious, since many languages suppress the grammatical as well as the semantic subject in contexts where such a subject would be expected in English; Japanese is a prime example. Yet, there is no ambiguity involved in such cases. Cf. the following Japanese dialogue:

> (*A young man comes hurriedly to the scene where his date is waiting for him*)
>
> Male: *Sumimasen – machimashita-ka.*
> Female: *E, sanjuppun mo machimashita.*
>
> ('I'm sorry – did you have to wait?'
> 'Yes, I have been waiting for half an hour.')

In the above, *machimashita* means: 'have waited'; the particle *-ka* expresses the question. No subject is expressed in either of the utterances, and the verb forms (apart from the particles attached to them) are completely identical. This use of the Japanese verb forms is perfectly normal.

105   Larry Horn, to whom I owe this quotation, establishes an even more original source for the introduction of this principle in linguistics: George K. Zipf, in the forties (Horn 1984: 11). Elsewhere in his article, Horn remarks, much to the point, that such general 'least effort' principles simply are too powerful (p. 28).

106   On the notion of 'pragmatic constraint' (as opposed to 'rule'), cf. Mey 1991b, and above, section 12.7.3.

107   It certainly is no valid argument for such a 'solution' that the masculine has been used in a pseudo-generic fashion for centuries in many languages.

108   Many linguists (and especially, many pragmaticians) do not feel the need to maintain such a strict, tripartite division of the linguistic disciplines. In fact, much of classical syntax and semantics leads us directly to pragmatic issues and problems, as we have seen in sections 2.1.5 and 2.1.6. For a review of the syntactic evidence for pragmatics, see Green (1989: 128ff.).

109   Bernstein's name is the one that most Europeans associate with this important research, even though later workers have come to have a more critical view of his theories. I will have more to say on this issue in section 14.7.

110   The term 'hegemony' is originally due to the Italian Marxist theoretician and linguist Antonio Gramsci.

111   Current yearly tuition costs for US private universities range from $14,000 to well over $20,000 a year (*Daily Northwesterner*, 10 January, 1991).

112   The term 'affordance' is due to the psychologist of vision James J. Gibson (1979), who created it to capture the way in which the human mind is 'preconditioned' to deal with a certain perceptual input.

113 What these tests measure is mainly test-taking skills, not verbal compre-hension and retention, as a recent report in *Science News* (137 (1990): 199) has shown.

114 For this, see Keesing (1989).

115 For a complete documentation and a critical discussion of what went on in the media during this week, see Mey (1985: ch. 2); Qvortrup (1979).

116 The party now prefers to call itself, in another interesting semantic devel-opment, 'liberal'.

117 Full details on the 1976 labour conflict, one of the biggest in Danish history, can be found in my 1985 book, where also a number of examples supporting the above assertions can be found. For reasons of space, I cannot, unfortunately, provide this supplementary information here.

118 The reader is referred to the discussion of 'special encodings' (called *ahads*) that is offered in the novel *Native Tongue* by the linguist Suzette Haden Elgin (1984). See also the review of this book by Mey (1989b).

119 Like those Hungarian kids that ask every tourist 'Sprechen Sie Deutsch?' – whereupon they vanish into thin air as soon as the tourist starts to answer in German!

120 Cf. the case of the Coquilles St Jacques, quoted above.

121 Gabriel García Márquez, in one of his bittersweet short stories ('La luz es cómo el agua'; 1992a), tells us about two boys who demand that their parents give them the boat they had promised them in return for straight As and making the honour list in their school. The parents point to the fact that the only available body of water for miles around is the shower in their fifth-floor Madrid apartment. However, the boys insist, and one night, when their parents are away at the movies, they get out the boat and flood the apartment with light. When the parents come home, they find the sleepy sailors floating around in the living-room on a sea of light: their father had once told them how light is like water, you turn it off and on like you turn the water tap off and on, and they had not only believed, but lived the metaphor.

122 This concept of 'wording' is different from that introduced by Halliday (e.g. 1978: 200, 208). For him, 'wording' represent the coding of meaning at the lexico-syntactic level (where the 'words' are). To me, this concept of 'wording' is too narrow, in that it considers the level of the 'words' as semi-independent of the rest of the language, with the contact mediated only through coding and decoding processes ('meaning' is coded into 'wording', 'wording' into 'sounding' or 'writing', respectively).

123 The classic references to Bernstein are to be found in his two-volume work *Class, Codes and Control* (1971–73), later expanded to include two addi-tional volumes (1975 and 1990). Bernstein (1981) attempts to frame the theory more explicitly in terms of social classes. In his latest work to date (1990), Bernstein answers the criticisms that have been raised, among other things by de-emphasizing the code as a particular form of language use (but even so, he cannot escape the ghosts of the past, as when he speaks of 'classroom talk' as being 'restricted': 1990: 107 *et passim*).

124 Understood as the assertion of '[t]raditional grammars . . . that the word *man* functions . . . to encompass human beings of both sexes: "Man stood upright, and a new day dawned" ' (Frank et al. 1989: 3).

References

Allwood, Jens 1976: *Linguistic Communication as Action and Cooperation*. Gothenburg: Gothenburg University (Ph. D. dissertation; Gothenburg Monographs in Linguistics, 2).

Ariel, Mira 1991: *Accessing Noun Phrase Antecedents*. London and New York: Routledge.

Austin, John L. 1962: *How to Do Things with Words*. Oxford: Oxford University Press.

Bar-Hillel, Yehoshua 1971: Out of the pragmatic waste-basket. *Linguistic Inquiry*, 2: 401–7.

Barton, Ellen L. 1990: *Nonsentential Constituents: A Theory of Grammatical Structure and Pragmatic Interpretation*. Amsterdam/Philadelphia: John Benjamins (Pragmatics and Beyond, New Series, 2).

Berger, Peter L. and Thomas Luckmann 1966: *The Social Construction of Reality*. New York: Doubleday.

Bernstein, Basil 1971–5: *Class, Codes and Control*. 3 vols. London: Routledge and Kegan Paul.

—— 1981: Codes, modalities, and the process of cultural reproduction: A model. *Language in Society*, 10: 327–63.

—— 1990: *The Structuring of Pedagogic Discourse*. Vol. 4 of *Class, Codes and Control*. London and New York: Routledge.

Bernstein, Carl and Bob Woodward 1974: *All the President's Men*. New York: Simon and Schuster.

Bickhard, Mark and Robert Campbell 1992: Some foundational questions concerning language studies: With a focus on categorial grammars and model theoretical possible worlds grammars. *Journal of Pragmatics*, 17(5/6): 401–33 (Special issue on 'Foundational questions concerning language studies').

Bilmes, Jack 1986: *Discourse and Behavior*. New York/London: Plenum.

Blakemore, Diana 1990: *Understanding Utterances: The Pragmatics of Natural Language*. Oxford: Blackwell.

Bolinger, Dwight D. 1980: *Language, the Loaded Weapon: The Use and Abuse of Language.* London: Longman.

Borutti, Silvana 1984: Pragmatics and its discontents. *Journal of Pragmatics,* 8(4): 437–47 (Special issue on 'Metapragmatics', ed. Claudia Caffi).

Brown, Penelope and Stephen C. Levinson 1978: Universals in language usage: politeness phenomena. In Esther Goody (ed.), *Questions and Politeness: Strategies in Social Interaction,* Cambridge: Cambridge University Press, pp. 56–311 (Cambridge Papers in Social Anthropology, Vol. 8).

Bühler, Karl 1934: *Sprachtheorie.* Jena: Fischer.

Caffi, Claudia 1984a: Introduction. *Journal of Pragmatics,* 8(4): 433–5 (Special issue on 'Metapragmatics', ed. Claudia Caffi).

—— 1984b: Some remarks on illocution and metacommunication. *Journal of Pragmatics,* 8(4): 449–67 (Special issue on 'Metapragmatics', ed. Claudia Caffi).

—— 1994a: Pragmatic presupposition. In *Encyclopedia of Language and Linguistics,* Oxford: Pergamon, Vol. 6: 3320–3327.

—— 1994b: Metapragmatics. In *Encyclopedia of Language and Linguistics,* Oxford: Pergamon, Vol. 4: 2461–2465.

Carberry, Sandra 1989: A pragmatics-based approach to ellipsis resolution. *Computational Linguistics,* 15(2): 75–98.

Carnap, Rudolf 1956: *Meaning and Necessity.* Chicago: University of Chicago Press.

Casares, Julio 1947: Femenismo mal entendido. In *Divertimentos filológicos,* Madrid: Calpe, pp. 302–6.

Chomsky, Noam 1957: *Syntactic Structures.* The Hague: Mouton (Janua Linguarum, Series Minor, Vol. 4).

—— 1965: *Aspects of the Theory of Syntax.* Cambridge, Mass.: MIT Press.

Coetzee, J. M. 1984: *The Life and Times of Michael K.* New York: Viking Press.

—— 1988: *White Writing: On the Culture of Letters in South Africa.* Johannesburg: Radix.

Cortázar, Julio 1985: 'Historia con migalas'; 'Clone' [1981]. In *Queremos Tanto a Glenda y Otros Relatos.* Madrid: Ediciones Alfaguara, pp. 29–44; 56–75.

Cutler, Anne 1974: On saying what you mean without meaning what you say. In *Papers from the 10th Regional Meeting, Chicago Linguistic Society,* Chicago: Chicago Linguistic Society, pp. 117–27.

Dupré, Louis 1966: *The Philosophical Foundations of Marxism.* New York: Harcourt, Brace and World.

Dürrenmatt, Friedrich 1956: 'Die Panne' [The Breakdown]. Zurich: Arche (Engl. trans. Richard and Clara Winston, *A Dangerous Game* (London: Jonathan Cape, 1960)).

Egner, Thorbjørn 1960: Folk og Røvere i Kardemomme By. Oslo: Aschehoug.

Elgin, Suzette Haden 1984: *Native Tongue.* New York: DAW Books.

—— 1989: *The Gentle Art of Verbal Self-defense.* Englewood Cliffs, NJ: Erlbaum.

Fairclough, Norman 1989: *Language and Power.* London: Longman.

Fasold, Ralph 1990: *The Sociolinguistics of Language.* Oxford: Blackwell.

Fillmore, Charles J. 1981: Pragmatics and the description of discourse. In Peter Cole (ed.), *Radical Pragmatics*, New York: Academic Press, pp. 143–66.

Flader, Dieter and T. Trotha 1990: *Über den geheimen 'Positivismus' und andere Eigentümlichkeiten der ethnomethodologischen Konversationsanalyse* [1986] (MS., Vienna University, mimeographed).

Foucault, Michel 1972: *The Archeology of Knowledge* [1969]. Trans. A. M. Sheridan. New York: Harper.

Frank, Francine Wattman and Paula A. Treichler (eds) 1989: *Language, Gender, and Professional Writing: Theoretical Approaches and Guidelines for Nonsexist Usage*. New York: The Modern Language Association of America, Commission on the Status of Women in the Profession.

Fraser, Bruce 1975: Hedged performatives. In Peter Cole and Jerry Morgan (eds), *Syntax and Semantics*, vol. 3: *Speech Acts*, New York: Academic Press, pp. 187–210.

—— 1980: Conversational mitigation. *Journal of Pragmatics*, 4(4): 341–50.

—— 1990: Perspectives on politeness. *Journal of Pragmatics*, 14(2): 219–36.

Freire, Paolo and Donaldo Macedo 1987: *Literacy: Reading the Word and the World*. South Hadley, Mass.: Bergin and Garvey.

Gazdar, Gerald 1979: *Pragmatics: Implicature, Presupposition and Logical Form*. New York: Academic Press.

—— 1980: Pragmatic constraints and linguistic production. In Brian Butterworth (ed.), *Language Production*, vol. 2, New York: Academic Press, pp. 49–68.

Gibson, J. J. 1979: *The Ecological Approach to Visual Perception*. Boston, Mass.: Houghton Mifflin.

Giddens, Anthony 1979: *Central Problems in Social Theory: Action, Structure and Contradiction in Social Analysis*. Berkeley: University of California Press.

Goffman, Erving 1961: *Asylums*. New York: Doubleday.

—— 1967: *Interaction Ritual*, New York: Doubleday Anchor.

—— 1976: Replies and responses. *Language in Society*, 5: 257–313.

—— 1983: Felicity's condition. *American Journal of Sociology*, 1: 1–53.

Green, Georgia M. 1989: *Pragmatics and Natural Language Understanding*. Hillsdale, NJ: Erlbaum.

Grice, H. Paul 1971: Meaning [1958]. In Danny Steinberg and Leon Jakobovits (eds), *Semantics: An Interdisciplinary Reader in Philosophy, Linguistics, and Psychology*, Cambridge: Cambridge University Press, pp. 53–9.

—— 1975: Logic and conversation. In Peter Cole and Jerry Morgan (eds), *Syntax and Semantics*, vol. 3: *Speech Acts*, New York: Academic Press, pp. 41–58.

—— 1978: Further notes on logic and conversation. In Peter Cole and Jerry Morgan (eds), *Syntax and Semantics*, vol. 9: *Pragmatics*, New York: Academic Press, pp. 41–58.

—— 1981: Presupposition and conversational implicature. In Peter Cole (ed.), *Radical Pragmatics*, New York: Academic Press, pp. 183–98.

Gundel, Jeanette, Nancy Hedberg and Ron Zacharski 1993: Cognitive status and the form of referring expressions in discourse. *Language*, 69(2): 274–307.

Haberland, Hartmut and Jacob L. Mey 1977: Editorial: pragmatics and linguistics. *Journal of Pragmatics*, 1(1): 1–16.

Halliday, M. A. K. 1978: *Language as Social Semiotic: The Social Interpretation of Language and Meaning*. London: Edward Arnold.

Halliday, M. A. K. and Ruqaiya Hasan 1976: *Cohesion in English*. London: Longman.

Haugen, Einar 1972: The ecology of language [1971]. In A. S. Dil (ed.), *The Ecology of Language. Essays by Einar Haugen*, Stanford, Calif.: Stanford University Press.

Hinkelman, Elizabeth 1987: Relevance: computation and coherence. *Behavioral and Brain Sciences*, 10(4): 720–1.

Hjelmslev, Louis 1929: *Principes de grammaire générale*. Copenhagen: Munksgaard.

—— 1943: *Omkring sprogteoriens grundlæggelse*. Copenhagen: Munksgaard. Trans. Francis Whitfield, *Prolegomena to a Theory of Language*, Madison: University of Wisconsin Press, 1953.

Holberg, Ludvig 1914: *Comedies* [1722]. Trans. Oscar J. Campbell and Frederic Schenk. New York: The American-Scandinavian Foundation.

Horn, Laurence R. 1984: Toward a new taxonomy for pragmatic inference: Q-based and R-based implicature. In Deborah Schiffrin (ed.), *Georgetown Round Table on Languages and Linguistics 1984*, Washington, DC: Georgetown University Press, pp. 11–42.

Jacobs, Scott and Sally Jackson 1983a: Speech act structure in conversation: rational aspects of pragmatic coherence. In Robert T. Craig and Karen Tracy (eds), *Conversational Coherence*, Beverly Hills and London: Sage, pp. 47–66.

—— 1983b: Strategy and structure in conversational influence attempts. *Communication Monographs*, 50: 285–304.

Jakobson, Roman 1960: Closing statement: linguistics and poetics. In Thomas A. Sebeok (ed.), *Style in Language*, Cambridge, Mass.: MIT Press, pp. 350–77.

Judge, A. J. N. 1988: Recording of networks of incommensurable concepts in phased cycles – and their comprehension through metaphor. Paper presented at a Round Table Discussion on 'Metaphor', International Symposium on Models of Meaning, Varna, Bulgaria, September 1988

Karttunen, Lauri 1969: Pronouns and variables. In Robert Binnick et al. (eds), *Papers from the Fifth Regional Meeting, Chicago Linguistic Society*, Chicago: Chicago Linguistic Society, pp. 108–16.

—— 1971: Implicative verbs. *Language*, 47: 340–58.

Kasher, Asa 1982: Gricean inference reconsidered. *Philosophia*, 29: 25–44.

Kasper, Gabriele 1990: Linguistic politeness: current research issues. *Journal of Pragmatics*, 14: 193–218.

Katz, Jerry J. 1977: *Propositional Structure and Illocutionary Force*. New York: Crowell.

Katz, Jerry J. and Jerry A. Fodor 1963: The structure of a semantic theory. *Language*, 39(2): 170–210.

Keenan, Elinor [Ochs]. 1976: On the universality of conversational implicatures. *Language in Society*, 5: 67–80.

Keesing, Roger 1989: Solomons pijin: colonial ideologies. In Richard Baldauf and Allan Luke (eds), *Language Planning and Education in Australasia and the*

South Pacific, Clevedon: Multilingual Matters, pp. 149–65.

Kiparsky, Paul and Carol Kiparsky 1971: Fact. In Danny Steinberg and Leon Jakobovits (eds), *Semantics: An Interdisciplinary Reader in Philosophy, Linguistics, and Psychology*, Cambridge: Cambridge University Press, pp. 345–69.

Kramarae, Cheris, Muriel Schulz and William M. O'Barr (eds) 1984: *Language and Power*, Beverly Hills and London: Sage.

Kuhn, Thomas S. 1964: *The Structure of Scientific Revolutions*. Chicago: The University of Chicago Press.

Kunst-Gnamuš, Olga 1991: Politeness as an effect of the interaction between the form and content of a request and the context of utterance. In Igor Z. Žagar (ed.), *Speech Acts: Fiction or Reality?* Proceedings of the International Conference, Ljubljana, Yugoslavia, 15 November, 1990; Ljubljana & Antwerp: IPrA Distribution Centre for Yugoslavia, Institute for Social Sciences, pp. 49–62.

Labov, William 1966: *The Social Stratification of English in New York City*. Washington, DC: Center for Applied Linguistics.

—— 1972: *Language in the Inner City*. Philadelphia: University of Pennsylvania Press.

Lacoste, Michèle 1981: The old lady and the doctor. *Journal of Pragmatics*, 5(2): 169–80.

Lakoff, George 1971a: On generative semantics. In Danny Steinberg and Leon Jakobovits (eds), *Semantics: An Interdisciplinary Reader in Philosophy, Linguistics, and Psychology*, Cambridge: Cambridge University Press, pp. 232–96.

—— 1971b: Presupposition and relative well-formedness [1968]. In Danny Steinberg and Leon Jakobovits (eds), *Semantics: An Interdisciplinary Reader in Philosophy, Linguistics, and Psychology*, Cambridge: Cambridge University Press, pp. 329–40.

Lakoff, George and Mark Johnson 1980: *Metaphors we Live By*. Chicago: The University of Chicago Press.

Lakoff, Robin 1989: The way we were; or, The real truth about generative semantics: A memoir. *Journal of Pragmatics*, 13(6): 939–88.

Leech, Geoffrey N. 1980: *Explorations in Semantics and Pragmatics*. Amsterdam/Philadelphia: John Benjamins (Pragmatics and Beyond, 5).

—— 1983: *Principles of Pragmatics*. London: Longman.

Leech, Geoffrey N. and Jennifer Thomas 1988: *Pragmatics: The State of the Art*. Lancaster University: Lancaster Papers in Linguistics, 48.

Levinson, Stephen C. 1981: The essential inadequacies of speech act models of dialogue. In Herman Parret, Marina Sbisà and Jef Verschueren (eds), *Possibilities and Limitations of Pragmatics*, Amsterdam/Philadelphia: John Benjamins (Studies in Language Companion Series, 7), pp. 473–92.

—— 1983: *Pragmatics*. Cambridge: Cambridge University Press.

Lewis, David 1969: *Convention*. Cambridge, Mass.: Harvard University Press.

Lilli, Laura 1990: Caccia al cammello. [Interview with Umberto Eco] *La Repubblica*, 7 December, 1990.

Lodge, David 1992: *Paradise News*. Harmondsworth: Penguin.

Lyons, John 1968: *Introduction to Theoretical Linguistics*. Cambridge: Cam-

bridge University Press.
—— 1977: *Semantics*. 2 vols. Cambridge: Cambridge University Press.
Márquez, Gabriel García 1992a: 'La luz es cómo el agua'. In *Doce Cuentos Peregrinos*, Buenos Aires: Edición Sudamericana, pp. 207–13.
—— 1992b: 'Sólo vine a hablar por teléfono'. In *Doce Cuentos Peregrinos*. Buenos Aires: Edición Sudamericana, pp. 103–26.
Martinet, André 1962: *A Functional View of Language*. Oxford: Oxford University Press.
Marx, Karl and Friedrich Engels 1974: *The German Ideology* [1845–6]. Ed. C. J. Arthur. New York: International Publishers.
McConnell-Ginet, Sally 1989: The sexual (re)production of meaning: a discourse-based theory. In Frank and Treichler 1989: 35–50.
Meehan, James 1981: Tale spin. In Roger C. Schank and Christopher K. Riesbeck (eds), *Inside Computer Understanding*, Hillsdale, NJ: Erlbaum, pp. 197–226.
Meseguer, Alvaro G. 1988: *Lenguaje y Discriminación Sexual*. 3rd ed. Barcelona: Montesinos.
Mey, Jacob L. 1985: *Whose Language? A Study in Linguistic Pragmatics*. Amsterdam/Philadelphia: John Benjamins (Pragmatics and Beyond, Companion Series, 3).
—— 1987a: The dark horse of linguistics: two recent books on pragmatics. *Acta Linguistica Hafniensia*, 20: 157–72.
—— 1987b: Poet and peasant: a pragmatic comedy in five acts, dedicated to Jens Allwood. *Journal of Pragmatics*, 11(3): 281–95.
—— 1989a: The end of the copper age, or: pragmatics 12 1/2 years after. *Journal of Pragmatics*, 13(6): 825–32.
—— 1989b: Not by the word only. Review of Suzette Haden Elgin, *Native Tongue, Journal of Pragmatics*, 13(6): 1035–45.
—— 1991a: Between rules and principles: some thoughts on the notion of 'metapragmatic constraint'. Paper presented at Symposium on Metapragmatic Terms, Budapest, 2–4 July, 1990. *Acta Linguistica Academiae Scientiarum Hungaricae*, 39: 1–6.
—— 1991b: Metaphors and solutions: towards an ecology of metaphor. Paper presented at a Round Table Discussion on 'Metaphor', International Symposium on Models of Meaning, Varna, Bulgaria, September 1988 (forthcoming).
—— 1992a: A note on adaptability. *AI and Society*, 6(1): 1–23.
—— 1992b: Pragmatic gardens and their magic. *Poetics*, 20(2): 233–45.
—— 1994a: Adaptability. In *Encyclopedia of Language and Linguistics*, Oxford: Pergamon, vol. 6: 25–7.
—— 1994b: Educating Archie, on fooling the reader. In Herman Parret (ed.), *Pretending to Communicate*, Berlin: Walter-De Gruyter, pp. 154–72.
—— 1994c: Pragmatics. In *Encyclopedia of Language and Linguistics*, Oxford: Pergamon, vol. 7: 3260–78.
—— 1995 (forthcoming) Problems and solutions: towards an ecology of metaphor. *RASK* 4: 53–67.
Mey, Jacob L. and Mary Talbot 1989: Computation and the soul. *Semiotica*, 72: 291–339.
Mininni, Giuseppe 1990: 'Common speech' as a pragmatic form of social repro-

340   References

duction. *Journal of Pragmatics*, 14(1): 125–35.

Minsky, Marvin 1975: A framework for representing knowledge. In Patrick H. Winston (ed.), *The Psychology of Computer Vision*, New York: McGraw-Hill, pp. 211–77.

Mizutani, Osamu and Nobuko Mizutani 1986: *An Introduction to Modern Japanese* [1976]. Tokyo: The Japan Times. (Includes audiotapes of Japanese texts.)

Morris, Charles H. 1938: *Foundations of the Theory of Signs*. In *International Encyclopedia of Unified Science*, 2:1, ed. Rudolf Carnap et al., Chicago: The University of Chicago Press.

Mumby, Dennis K. and Cynthia Stohl 1991: Power and discourse in organization studies: absence and the dialectic of control. *Discourse and Society*, 2(3): 313–32.

Navarro, Vicente 1991: Class and race: life and death situations. *Monthly Review*, 43(4): 1–13.

Nissen, Uwe Kjær 1990: A review of language and sex in the Spanish language. *Women and Language*, 13(2): 11–29.

Nunberg, Geoffrey 1981: Validating pragmatic explanations. In Peter Cole (ed.), *Radical Pragmatics*, New York: Academic Press, pp. 198–222.

O'Barr, William M. 1984: Asking the right questions about language and power. In Cheris Kramarae, Muriel Schulz and William M. O'Barr (eds), *Language and Power*, Beverly Hills and London: Sage, pp. 260–80.

Östman, Jan-Ola 1988a: Adaptation, variability and effect: comments on IPrA Working Documents 1 & 2. In *Working Document #3*, Antwerp: International Pragmatics Association, pp. 5–39.

—— 1988b: Implicit involvement in interactive writing. In Jef Verschueren and Marcella Bertucelli-Papa (eds), *The Pragmatic Perspective: Selected Papers from the 1985 International Pragmatics Conference*, Amsterdam/Philadelphia: John Benjamins, pp. 155–78.

Partee, Barbara H. 1972: Opacity, coreference, and pronouns. In Donald Davidson and Gilbert Harman (eds), *Semantics of Natural Language*, Dordrecht: Reidel, pp. 415–41.

Pateman, Trevor 1980: *Language, Truth and Politics* [1975]. Lewes, East Sussex: Stroud.

Paul, Hermann 1891: *Prinzipien der Sprachgeschichte*. Halle/Saale: Niemeyer (5th ed. trans. H. A. Strong, *Introduction to the Study of the History of Language*, London, 1920).

Petöfi, János S. 1976: Formal pragmatics and a partial theory of texts. In Siegfried J. Schmidt (ed.), *Pragmatik/Pragmatics 2*, München: Fink, pp. 105–21.

Phillipson, Robert 1991: *Linguistic Imperialism*. Cambridge: Cambridge University Press.

Phillipson, Robert and Tove Skutnabb-Kangas 1993: Linguicide. In *Encyclopedia of Languages and Linguistics*, Oxford: Pergamon.

Qvortrup, Lars 1979: *Danmarks Radio og Arbejdskampen*. [Radio Denmark and the labour struggle]. Odense: Odense University Press (Bidrags Skriftserie, 2).

Reisman, Karl 1989: Contrapuntal conversations in an Antiguan village [1974].

In Richard Bauman and Joel Sherzer (eds), *Explorations in the Ethnography of Speaking*, Cambridge: Cambridge University Press, pp. 110–24.

Reuland, Eric 1979: *Principles of Subordination and Construal in the Grammar of Dutch*. Groningen: Dijkstra Niemeyer (Groningen University Ph. D. dissertation).

Riesbeck, Christopher K. and Roger C. Schank 1987: *Inside Case-based Reasoning*. Hillsdale, NJ: Erlbaum.

Rosenbaum, Bent and Harly Sonne 1986: *The Language of Psychosis*. New York and London: New York University Press (Originally published in Danish: Der er et bånd der taler, Copenhagen: Gyldendal, 1979).

Ruiz Mayo, Jaime 1990: Rumor's delict (delight?) or: The pragmatics of a civil liberty. *Journal of Pragmatics*, 13(6): 1009–12, 1034.

Rundquist, Suellen 1992: Indirections: A gender study of flouting Grice's maxims. *Journal of Pragmatics*, 18(5): 431–49.

Sacks, Harvey 1992: *Lectures on Conversation* (ed. Gail Jefferson). 2 vols. Oxford: Blackwell.

Sacks, Harvey, Emanuel Schegloff and Gail Jefferson 1974: A simplest systematics for the organization of turn-taking in conversation. *Language*, 50(4): 696–735.

Sadock, Jerry M. 1974: *Towards a Linguistic Theory of Speech Acts*. New York: Academic Press.

Schank, Roger C. 1981: *Dynamic Memory*. Hillsdale, NJ: Erlbaum.

—— 1984: *The Cognitive Computer*. Hillsdale, NJ: Erlbaum.

—— 1986: *Explanation Patterns*. Hillsdale, NJ: Erlbaum.

Schank, Roger C. and Robert P. Abelson 1977: *Scripts, Plans, Goals and Understanding*. Hillsdale, NJ: Erlbaum.

Schank, Roger C. and Danny Edelson 1990: A role for AI in education: using technology to reshape education. *The Journal of Artificial Intelligence in Education*, 1(2): 3–20.

Schegloff, Emanuel A. 1972: Sequencing in conversational openings. In John Gumperz and Dell Hymes (eds), *Directions in Sociolinguistics*, New York: Holt, Rinehart and Winston, pp. 346–80.

Schegloff, Emanuel A. and Harvey Sacks 1973: Opening up closings. *Semiotica*, 7: 289–327.

Schön, Donald 1979: Generative metaphor: a perspective on problem-setting in social policy. In Andrew Ortony (ed.), *Metaphor and Thought*, Cambridge: Cambridge University Press, pp. 254–83.

Searle, John R. 1969: *Speech Acts: An Essay in the Philosophy of Language*. Cambridge: Cambridge University Press.

—— 1975: Indirect speech acts. In Peter Cole and Jerry Morgan (eds), *Syntax and Semantics*, vol. 3: *Speech Acts*, New York: Academic Press, pp. 59–82.

—— 1977: A classification of illocutionary acts. In Andy Rogers, Bob Wall and John P. Murphy (eds), *Proceedings of the Texas Conference on Performatives, Presuppositions, and Implicatures*, Washington, DC: Center for Applied Linguistics, pp. 27–45.

—— 1979: The classification of illocutionary acts. *Language in Society*, 8: 137–51.

Smitherman, Geneva 1984: Black language and power. In Cheris Kramarae, Muriel Schulz and William M. O'Barr (eds), *Language and Power*, Beverly Hills and London: Sage, pp. 101–15.

Spender, Dale 1980: *Man Made Language*. London: Routledge and Kegan Paul.

—— 1984: Defining reality: a powerful tool. In Cheris Kramarae, Muriel Schulz and William M. O'Barr (eds), *Language and Power*, Beverly Hills and London: Sage, pp. 194–205.

Sperber, Dan and Deirdre Wilson 1986: *Relevance: Communication and Cognition*. Cambridge, Mass.: Harvard University Press.

Stalnaker, R. C. 1977: Pragmatic presuppositions [1974]. In Andy Rogers, Bob Wall and John P. Murphy (eds), *Proceedings of the Texas Conference on Performatives, Presuppositions, and Implicatures*, Washington, DC: Center for Applied Linguistics, pp. 135–47.

Stalpers, Judith 1993: *Progress in Discourse: The Impact of Foreign Language Use on Business Talk* (Tilburg University Ph. D. thesis, Tilburg, The Netherlands).

Stubbs, Michael 1983: *Discourse Analysis*. Oxford: Blackwell.

Talbot, Mary M. 1987: The pragmatic analysis of presuppositional phenomena in Levinson's *Pragmatics*. *Acta Linguistica Hafniensia*, 20: 173–87.

—— 1994: Relevance. In *Encyclopedia of Language and Linguistics*, Oxford: Pergamon, vol. 6: 3524–7.

Treichler, Paula A. 1989: From discourse to dictionary: how sexist meanings are authorized. In Frank and Treichler 1989: 51–79.

Treichler, Paula A., Richard M. Frankel, Cheris Kramarae, Kathleen Zoppi and Howard B. Beckman 1984: Problems and problems: power relationships in a medical encounter. In Cheris Kramarae, Muriel Schulz and William M. O'Barr (eds), *Language and Power*, Beverly Hills and London: Sage, pp. 62–88.

Treichler, Paula A. and Francine Wattman Frank 1989: Introduction: scholarship, feminism, and language change. In Frank and Treichler 1989: 1–34.

Tsui, Amy B. 1991: Sequencing rules and coherence in discourse. *Journal of Pragmatics*, 15(2): 111–29.

Van der Auwera, Johan 1985: *Language and Logic*. Amsterdam/Philadelphia: John Benjamins (Pragmatics and Beyond, Companion Series, 4).

van Dijk, Teun A. 1977: *Text and Context*. London: Longman.

—— 1981: *Text*. Berlin and New York: Mouton de Gruyter.

Verschueren, Jef 1979: *What People Say They Do with Words*. Berkeley: University of California (Ph. D.) dissertation.

—— 1980: *On Speech Act Verbs*. Amsterdam/Philadelphia: John Benjamins (Pragmatics and Beyond, 4).

—— 1987: Pragmatics as a theory of linguistic adaptation. In *Working Document #1*, Antwerp: International Pragmatics Association.

Wardhaugh, Ronald 1986: *How Conversation Works*. Oxford: Blackwell.

Weizenbaum, Joseph 1966: ELIZA: a computer program for the study of natural language communication between man and machine. *Communications of the ACM*, 9: 36–45.

Whorf, Benjamin L. 1969: *Language, Thought and Reality* [1956]. Ed. John B.

Carroll. Cambridge, Mass.: MIT Press.

Wodak-Engel, Ruth 1984: Determination of guilt: discourse in the courtroom. In Cheris Kramarae, Muriel Schulz and William M. O'Barr (eds), *Language and Power*, Beverly Hills and London: Sage, pp. 89–100.

Wodak, Ruth, Peter Nowak, Johanna Pelikan, Helmut Gruber, Rudolf de Cillia and Richard Mitten 1990: '*Wir sind alle unschuldige Täter*'. *Diskurshistorische Studien zum Nachkriegsantisemitismus*. Frankfurt am Main: Suhrkamp (STW 881).

Index

229, 283–4
and pragmatics 22, 24
and presuppositions 200

Haberland, Hartmut 324 n.24
Haden Elgin, Suzette 319–20, 333
  n.117
Halliday, M. A. K. 31, 224, 330
  n.83, 333 n.121
Hasan, Ruqaiya 330 n.83
Haugen, Einar 311
hearer 163, 201, 217–18
hegemony 264, 288
Heidegger, Martin 261
Hinkelman, Elizabeth 82
Hjelmslev, Louis 12, 53, 139, 182
Holberg, Ludvig 257–8
Horn, Laurence R. 77, 78–9, 332
  n.105
Husserl, Edmund 91
Hymes, Dell 31

imperatives
  'bald' 68, 73
  polite 48, 68
  and requests 143–4, 192
  subject of 273
  see also directives
implication, material/logical
  99–100, 101, 326 n.39
implicature 99–106, 108
  and context 40, 55–8, 102–3, 105
  conventional 25, 28, 84, 103–6,
    203
  conversational 51–2, 55–8,
    75–6, 83–4, 100–3, 203,
    204–6, 277, 278
  and cooperation 75–6, 83–4, 324
    n.26
  definition 99
  and implication 99–100, 325, n.38
  and scalarity 56–7, 83, 84
imposition, and thanking 141
index field 92
indexicals
  'floating-point' 96–7

pragmatic functions 91–5
  and reference 75, 90–1
inequality, social 49, 283, 284,
  289–91, 295–8, 302–3,
  309–10, 313
influencing, conversational 256–7,
  263
insertion sequences 223–7
institutions, social, and speech acts
  157, 159–61, 168, 171, 188
intention
  and adjacency pairs 243, 246
  informative 80, 111
  and macropragmatics 181–2, 238
  and pragmatics 18
  primary/secondary 144–5
  and speech acts 114–15, 251–2
  see also force, illocutionary
interaction, and language use 30,
  147–8
interchange, two-person 185
interest, and speech act criteria 157
interlocutors 26
interruption, and turn-taking 218;
  see also insertion sequences
interview, medical 147–8, 294–6,
  297–8
intonation, as signal 69, 218–19
irony
  and context 60
  Irony Principle 70

Jackson, Sally 247, 256, 259, 263
Jacobs, Scott 247, 256, 259, 263
Jakobson, Roman 47, 90, 220
Jefferson, Gail 243
job interview 297–8
Johnson, Mark 62, 301–2
Judge, A. J. N. 62–5, 301–2

Kafka, Franz 161
Karttunen, Lauri 28, 98
Kasher, Asa 188
Kasper, Gabriele 324 n.24
Katz, Jerry J. 36, 183
Kiparsky, Carol 29